Economic Security and Intergenerational Justice

THEODORE R. MARMOR
TIMOTHY M. SMEEDING
VERNON L. GREENE
Editors

Economic Security and Intergenerational Justice

A Look at North America

THE URBAN INSTITUTE PRESS
Washington, D.C.

THE URBAN INSTITUTE PRESS
2100 M Street, N.W.
Washington, D.C. 20037

Library of Congress Cataloging in Publication Data

Economic Security and Intergenerational Justice: A Look at North America / editors, Theodore R. Marmor, Timothy M. Smeeding, Vernon L. Greene

1. Social security—United States. 2. Economic security—United States. 3. Social security—Canada. 4. Economic security—Canada. I. Marmor, Theodore R. II. Smeeding, Timothy M. III. Greene, Vernon L.

HD7125.E267   1994   94-7382
368.4'3'00973—dc20   CIP

ISBN 0-87766-620-2 (paper, alk. paper)
ISBN 0-87766-619-9 (cloth, alk. paper)

Printed in the United States of America

Distributed by University Press of America
4720 Boston Way   3 Henrietta Street
Lanham, MD 20706   London WC2E 8LU ENGLAND

THE URBAN INSTITUTE is a nonprofit policy research and educational organization established in Washington, D.C., in 1968. Its staff investigates the social and economic problems confronting the nation and public and private means to alleviate them. The Institute disseminates significant findings of its research through the publications program of its Press. The goals of the Institute are to sharpen thinking about societal problems and efforts to solve them, improve government decisions and performance, and increase citizen awareness of important policy choices.

Through work that ranges from broad conceptual studies to administrative and technical assistance, Institute researchers contribute to the stock of knowledge available to guide decision making in the public interest.

Conclusions or opinions expressed in Institute publications are those of the authors and do not necessarily reflect the views of staff members, officers or trustees of the Institute, advisory groups, or any organizations that provide financial support to the Institute.

For Robert M. Ball
and
Daniel Patrick Moynihan

ACKNOWLEDGMENTS

The editors of this volume have a number of debts to acknowledge. The American Donner Foundation made fiancially possible the 1991 Yale conference on Aging in North America at which initial drafts of the comparative chapters in this book were presented. We are particularly grateful to William Alpert, the Foundation's program officer, for supporting the research for these chapters, sponsoring the conference, and encouraging book publication. We also want to acknowledge the intellectual contribution of Professors Keith Banting of Queen's University and Martha Ozawa, scholars who reviewed the comparative work to our benefit.

This volume represents the fusion of papers prepared for the Yale conference and a comparable one at Syracuse University. We wish to thank the Prudential Foundation and William B. Tremayne, Senior Vice President for Public Affairs of the Prudential Insurance Company of America, for sponsoring the 1991 Donald S. MacNaughton Symposium on Social Policy for an America Growing Older at Syracuse University.

At Yale, Elizabeth Auld marvelously managed the logistical burdens that conferences and manuscript preparation impose and deserves our warmest expression of thanks. Lynn Murinson completed the job with cheerful competence. Nancy Marquardt, Director of Special Events at Syracuse University, coordinated hotel and banquet facilities for the Syracuse conference. Martha W. Bonney and the graduate assistants of the All-University Gerontology Center provided administrative and manuscript support for the presenters and participants. We are grateful to them all.

CONTENTS

Foreword   xvii

1 The North American Context and Volume Overview
*Theodore R. Marmor, Timothy M. Smeeding, Vernon L.
Greene, and Deborah A. Chassman*   1
     Comparative Policy Studies within North America   1
     Economic Status of the Elderly in North America
         versus Western Europe   6
     The Comparative Politics of Economic Security for
         the Elderly   10
     Resolving Conflicting Claims among Generations   11
     Policy Dimensions   12

PART ONE   **THE COMPARATIVE POLITICS OF ECONOMIC
SECURITY FOR THE ELDERLY**

**2 Shifting Fortunes of the Elderly: The Comparative
Politics of Retrenchment** *Paul Pierson and
Miriam Smith*   21
     The Politics of Retrenchment and Programs for
         the Elderly   23
     The United States: Social Security and Medicare
         in a Period of Austerity   25
     The Politics of Retrenchment in Canada   32
     Summing Up   39
     Policy Divergence: Generational Politics in the
         United States   43
     From Intergenerational to Intragenerational
         Transfers: The Medicare Catastrophic
         Coverage Act   47
     Distributing Burdens between Generations: The
         Social Security Trust Fund Debates   50
     Conclusion   51

**3 The Politics of Income Security for the Elderly in
North America: Founding Cleavages and Unresolved
Conflicts** *John Myles and Jill Quadagno*   61
   The Origins of Old Age Security in Canada and the
     United States   62
   Explaining the Difference   66
   The Politics of Old Age Security since the 1970s   69
     The Balance of Class Power   70
     The Structure of Old Age Support   72
   Conclusion   80
   Appendix 3.A: The Economic Status of the Elderly in
     Canada and the United States, 1975   86

**4 The Salience of Intergenerational Equity in Canada
and the United States** *Fay Lomax Cook, Victor W.
Marshall, Joanne Gard Marshall, and Julie E. Kaufman*   91
   Emergence of the Intergenerational Equity Issue   92
     The Policy Community   92
     The Academic Community   94
   Relative Salience of the Intergenerational Equity
     Issue in Canada and the United States   96
     Media Attention   96
     Academic Attention   99
     Political Attention   101
     Public Opinion   104
   Explaining the Differences   108
     Value Differences   109
     Differences in Poverty Status   111
     Social Policies and Programs   115
     The Political Process   117
     Explaining Similarity in the Domain of Public
      Opinion   119
   Conclusion   120
   Appendix 4.A   124

PART TWO   **RESOLVING THE ECONOMIC CONFLICT AMONG
GENERATIONS**

**5 A Truce in the Age Wars? Intergenerational Justice
and the Prudential Lifespan Solution in Health Care**
Margaret Pabst Battin   133
   Policies and Conflict in the Age Wars   133

A Coherent Resolution? The Prudential Lifespan
    Approach to Issues of Intergenerational Justice   136
Disadvantages of the Lifespan Approach   140
Advantages of the Lifespan Approach   144
What the Lifespan Approach Reveals   148

6 **Transcending Intergenerational Equity**   *Robert H.*
Binstock   155
    Compassionate Ageism and the "Old Age Welfare
        State"   156
    The Emergence of the Aged as Scapegoat   157
    The Aged and America's Problems   158
    Equity as an "Intergenerational" Construct   160
    Transcending Intergenerational Equity   162
        The Political Power of the Aged   163
        Increasing Dependency Ratios   166
        Perspectives on Rationing the Health Care of
            Older People   168

PART THREE **POLICY DIMENSIONS OF ECONOMIC SECURITY**
FOR THE ELDERLY

7 **Balancing Interests and Controlling Risks across**
Workers and Retirees   *Carolyn L. Weaver*   189
    Social Security and Advance Funding   192
    Private Pensions and Government Regulation   196

8 **The Needy or the Greedy? Assessing the Income**
Support Needs of an Aging Population   *Marilyn Moon*
and Patricia Ruggles   207
    The Economic Status of Older Americans   208
    Growth in Well-Being and Prospects for the Future   211
    Future Policy Issues   218

9 **Kinder and Gentler: A Comparative Analysis of**
Incomes of the Elderly in Canada and the United
States   *Michael C. Wolfson and Brian B. Murphy*   227
    Data and Methods   227
    Are U.S. Families Richer?   229
    Elderly Singles and Couples   234
        Average Incomes of the Elderly   234
        Sources of Income for the Elderly   236

Income Sources by Income Range   238
Private Pensions and Saving   243
The Future   247
Conclusions   249
Appendix 9.A: Further Detail on Income Distribution
    Differences between Canada and the
    United States   252

**10 On Being Old and Sick: The Burden of Health Care
for the Elderly in Canada and the United States**
*Morris L. Barer, Clyde Hertzman, Robert Miller, and
Marina V. Pascali*   263
Health Care Entitlement in Canada   264
Health Care Entitlement in the United States   265
The 'Costs' of Universality   265
Taking Care of the Elderly   266
Coverage and Costs for the Elderly in Canada   267
Coverage and Costs for the Elderly in the
    United States   269
Uncle Sam Retires in Victoria: An Elderly American
    in Canada   273
Patterns of Service Use   274
Longer and Healthier, or Grimmer and Poorer?   278
Data Needed for Better North American Comparisons   280

**11 Long-Term Care in the United States: Problems and
Promise** *Robert L. Kane*   287
What Is Long-Term Care?   287
The Historical Context of Long-Term Care in the
    United States   290
New Developments in LTC Delivery   294
Evolving Quality Assessment and New Modes of
    Accountability   296
Information Technology Can Help   299

12 Financing Long-Term Care: Lessons from Canada
Robert L. Kane and Rosalie A. Kane   303
Two Approaches to Financial Coverage   303
    Case Examples   304
Internal Variation   308
Floors versus Ceilings   311

Fragmentation and Coordination 314
Canada 314
United States 316
Regulation 318
Conclusions 319

13 Housing the Elderly: The Demographic Imperative
Langley C. Keyes 325
The Elderly and Their Housing: A Profile in
Parallelism 326
Elderly Housing History: The Policy Domain 330
Elderly Housing: A Desired Good 330
Housing Policy History: A Singular Tale of Two
Countries 331
The Current Policy Paradigm 333
The Convergent Policy Challenge 333
The Emerging Elderly Housing Paradigm 334
Conceptualizing Elderly Shelter: Categories or
Continuum 335
Implementing the Continuum 337
Housing Assistance and Long-Term Care: The
Missing Link 342
Program Design: The Challenge of Targeting 343
Public Attitudes: Fair Play or Beat the System 344

About the Editors 349

About the Contributors 351

Tables

1.1 Estimated Percentages of Population Age 65 and
Over Age 80 7
1.2 Income, Poverty, and Benefit Adequacy among the
U.S. Elderly in a Cross-National Context 8
1.3 Differences in Low-Income Rates among Nonaged
Households, Elderly (Head 65 +), Single
Women Living Alone, and Elderly Couple
Units: Poverty Rates for Households at U.S.
(40% Median) Poverty Line 9
2.1 Generational Benefits and Burdens in Canada and
the United States, 1990 46

3.A.1 The Relative Economic Status of the Retired
        Elderly in Canada and the United States   86
4.1   Media Attention to the Issue of Intergenerational
        Equity in Canada and the United States,
        1980–1992   97
4.2   Academic Attention to the Issue of
        Intergenerational Equity in Canada and the
        United States, 1980–1992   100
4.3   Percentage of Canadian Citizens Who Prefer
        Various Levels of Government Activity in
        Assistance to Different Groups   107
6.1   Federal Outlays, by Category, Fiscal Year 1992   161
6.2   Nationwide Vote Distribution, by Age Groups and
        Gender, in Elections for U.S. President, 1980,
        1984, 1988, 1992   164
9.1   Proportions and Average Family Size by Adjusted
        Income Ranges, Canadian and U.S. Families,
        1988   231
9.2   After-Tax Incomes by Age and Family Type,
        Canadian and U.S. Families, 1988   235
9.3   Average Incomes of Elderly Cohorts as
        Percentages of the Average Incomes of the
        Pre-Retirement Cohort (Age 55 to 64),
        Canadian and U.S. Families, 1988   236
9.4   Numbers and Average Incomes by Source, Family
        Type, and Age, Canadian and U.S. Elderly
        and Near-Elderly Families, 1988   237
9.5   Numbers, Average Incomes, and Labor Force
        Status by Age, Family Type, and Adjusted
        Income, Canadian and U.S. Elderly and Near-
        Elderly Families, 1988   239
9.6   Average Incomes by Age Group, Family Type,
        and Adjusted Income, Canadian and U.S.
        Elderly and Near-Elderly Families, 1988   240
9.A.1 Selected Statistics by Percentile Rankings for U.S.
        and Canadian Families, 1988 Rankings Based
        on Unadjusted Before- and After-Tax Incomes   254
9.A.2 Selected Statistics by Percentile Rankings for U.S.
        and Canadian Families, 1988 Rankings Based
        on Before- and After-Tax Incomes Adjusted
        for EAU   256

9.A.3 Selected Statistics by Percentile Rankings for U.S. and Canadian Families, 1988. Ordering Based on Before- and After-Tax Incomes Adjusted for EAU and Weights Adjusted for Family Size   258

10.1 Percent of the Public Who Reported They Were "Very Saisfied" with Services, by Type of Service   264

10.2 Charges to Senior Citizens Enrolled in Provincial Drug Plans in 1991   268

10.3 Charges to Senior Citizens Enrolled in Selected State Pharmaceutical Plans in 1988   271

13.1 Advantages and Disadvantages of Selected Alternative Housing Arrangements   338

13.2 Housing Alternatives and Housing Levels   340

Figures

3.1 Old Age Security and Maximum Guaranteed Income Supplement, as Percentage of Average Wage, 1967-1985   76

4.1 Percentage of Persons below the Poverty Line by Age Group in the United States, 1966-1991   112

4.2a Percentage of Persons in Low Income Families by Age in Canada, 1981-1991   114

4.2b Percentage of Persons with Low Income for Selected Family Unit Types in Canada, 1981-1991   114

4.2c Percentage of Persons with Low Income by Age in Canada, 1981-1991   114

8.1 Sources of Income for the Aged   213

8.2 Health Care Spending as Share of Income, Persons 65 +   216

9.1 Average After-Tax Income Distribution, Canadian and U.S. Families, 1988   230

9.2 The Three Nations of North America?   233

10.1 U.S. Physician Visits per Person, 1985 versus 1975   275

10.2 Deflated Physician Billings per Capita, by Patient Age, British Columbia   276

10.3 U.S. Hospitalizations per 1000 by Age Group, 1987 versus 1965   277

10.4 Hospital Age-Use Curves in British Columbia,
        1971 and 1982/83. (A) Male Separations per
        Thousand Population (B) Female Separations
        per Thousand Population   279
13.1 Continuum of Types of Living Arrangements   337

FOREWORD

Our society is aging at the same time as it is seeking ways to control public spending and reduce the federal deficit. This combination puts into sharp relief the rising proportion of the federal budget now allocated to social security and other benefits for elderly Americans. Other western industrial societies are in the same position. As our most similar neighbor, Canada provides a unique opportunity to put U.S. policy toward the elderly into comparative perspective.

Economic Security and Intergenerational Justice: A Look at North America examines a variety of dimensions of U.S. policy towards its elderly, and compares U.S. and Canadian approaches with respect to income security, health care, long-term care, and housing. It also traces the history of policy development in the two countries, looking for the historical reasons for the similarities and differences in policy and attitudes towards the elderly. Two authors address the issue of intergenerational justice and discuss more fruitful ways to frame the debate than the simple elderly versus young formulation.

This book continues the Institute's commitment to the comparative study of the well-being of the nation's dependent populations. In particular, it is a follow-on to *The Vulnerable*, published by the Urban Institute Press in 1988, which compared the public resources going to the elderly and children in the United States with the situation in western Europe, Australia, Canada, and Japan.

The contributions that follow shed new light on the issues that confront both Canada and the United States as our populations continue to age. I hope these insights will contribute to the public debate on how best to address the needs of the growing elderly population as we move into the 21st century.

William Gorham
President

Chapter One

THE NORTH AMERICAN CONTEXT AND VOLUME OVERVIEW

Theodore R. Marmor, Timothy M. Smeeding,
Vernon L. Greene, and Deborah A. Chassman

In a world of increasingly constrained resources, debate about population aging and its effects on the proportion of national resources going to support the elderly has taken on a new urgency. In the United States this urgency has been accompanied by renewed concern about the long-run solvency of the Social Security system and a sometimes shrill debate about what is a just and equitable sharing of the social pie between old and young. In Canada a similar aging trend does not seem to have been accompanied by the same sense of rivalry, or the same sense that the elderly are living high off the hog at the expense of the next generation.

The purpose of this book is to take a detailed look at the intergenerational issue and why it is treated differently in the two countries, to discuss ways of resolving the apparently competing claims of the old and the young, to examine the situation of the elderly in the United States, and to compare it with the situation of the elderly in Canada. Because this book stems from papers presented at two conferences with different but related objectives, some chapters focus on the U.S.-Canadian comparison and others on the U.S. context alone.

This chapter begins the volume by explaining the particular value of U.S.-Canadian comparisons and giving a brief overview of similarities and differences between the two countries. It then discusses briefly some descriptive statistics that put U.S.-Canadian differences and similarities within the context of Western European countries. The chapter ends with an overview of the major messages of the chapters that follow.

COMPARATIVE POLICY STUDIES WITHIN NORTH AMERICA

Before the stagflation of the 1970s, it was hard to find people in the United States who were seriously interested in learning from the public policy experience of other industrial democracies. As the richest and apparently the most self-sufficient country on earth, the U.S. seemed to stand in little need of lessons from others.

Now that we face economic woes that threaten our future standard of living, we have greater interest in cross-national research.[1] In the 1990s, we appear more willing to look abroad, to investigate, even to listen.[2] It is surely right that we look beyond U.S. borders for potentially promising responses to our major domestic policy problems. But to whom should we listen?

Where many quite different countries have similar experiences, the cross-national implications are exceedingly important. The very emergence of common results from seemingly different settings suggests powerful converging forces at work. But such generalizations— while powerful—are relatively rare. They include, for example, links between democratization and the development of welfare state programs, and include monetary and fiscal regularities that overcome institutional differences among countries (Flora and Heidenheimer 1981).

When nations closely resemble each other, different lessons are possible. One nation can function as a natural experiment for the other. What happened here, it can be reasonably asserted, will in all likelihood happen there—whether the focus is social change, identification of a policy problem, or estimation of the likely effects of a particular policy remedy tried in one or another similar site. Precisely because of similarities, nuances noticed in comparison—in the formulation of problems or the framing of policy options—can improve national policy discussion. Indeed, for specific policy and program learning, the more similar, the better. "If the [comparative] focus . . . is the transplantability of ideas or models," clearly "the two environments should not be too different"[3] (Marmor and Klein 1986, p. 21).

All western democracies, we are often reminded, have adopted broadly similar welfare states despite significant political and cultural differences. Their programs commonly protect against income loss from unemployment, retirement, disability, and illness; they also redistribute access to medical care, education, and housing in ways the market would not guarantee. In this sense, the western pattern of provision for the economic security of the elderly is a fit subject for broad comparative study. But we believe that detailed North American comparisons are particularly useful because of more precise similarities.

Our common language and our comparable ethnic and demographic mix make North America an obvious instance of similar (though far from identical) societies. In addition, as discussed in detail in chapter 3 of this volume, both Canada and the United States have, in the 20th century, adopted comparable forms of a modern welfare state. Developed later than in Europe, the two North American welfare states now have practically the whole galaxy of social insurance and poverty programs that one finds in the developed world (Flora and Heidenheimer 1981; Wilensky 1975).[4] Comparably rich, Canada and the United States have over the past two decades experienced similar economic unrest and related questioning of the affordability, desirability, and governability of their welfare state programs. Likewise, both countries have, despite the fiscal strains, continued to protect their elderly inhabitants from most of the predictable pains of retirement and old age.

In every society there are skeptics concerning the importation of 'foreign' models, whatever the claimed advantages. This argument has less bearing on North American phenomena, where the flow of professionals, firms, and ideas is continuous. The results of polls reported by Robert Blendon and others provide an illustration. In the health area, 60 percent of Americans questioned said they would prefer the Canadian to American health care arrangements. This preference presumed that what has worked reasonably well in Canada would do so in the United States as well (Blendon and Donelan 1990; Blendon et al. 1990).

It is hard to imagine North Americans regarding the Swedish national health system in the same way. The corporatist, social democratic society of Sweden and its medical practice standards would appear unfamiliar to North Americans. Language is especially important—even differences seem less alien if conveyed in a common parlance. This will be especially clear to those who have been taken ill while traveling and have had to communicate their needs in a strange setting and in another language.

The political institutions and ideology of Canada and the United States are similar in that they reflect a common heritage in British political thought. Programs are simultaneously centralized and decentralized in both countries. Our federal regimes draw financial resources together through national governments but leave much of both the policymaking and the management of programs to decentralized provinces/states. A common core of program requirements is nationally required, but there is substantial provincial/state variation in the interpretation of federal policy, the way the programs are administered, and whether the provision of minimum federal benefits is supplemented by other jurisdictions.

Canadian health insurance and American Medicaid are cases in point. Canadian Medicare provides universal, comprehensive benefits that are portable across the country. The scheme is publicly administered in each province, which decides how to raise the local share of the financing, how to administer the program, and whether to offer additional benefits. Nova Scotia's and British Columbia's versions of national health insurance in Canada are, as a result, somewhat different (Marmor 1991).[5] In the United States, Medicaid is financed jointly by the federal government and the states. The states are governed in their administration of the program partly by federal statute and regulations and partly by state authorized statutes, regulations, and policies. States can adopt or decline to adopt federal options and can supplement federally authorized expenditures with additional state financed benefits. New York's and Mississippi's versions of Medicaid, as a result, are very different (Marmor 1991).[6]

In the medical world, up to the consolidation of Canadian national health insurance in 1971, the patterns and styles of care in the two nations were nearly identical. They are not far apart now. Contributions to medical journals easily cross Canadian/U.S. boundaries and medical meetings regularly include practitioners from both countries (Evans 1989; Marmor 1993; Marmor, Mashaw, and Harvey 1992, p. 204): all illustrating the comparable arrangements for medical care and physician training in the post-war world.

Until the collapse of Meech Lake, the fractiousness of Canadian constitutional federalism was perhaps less apparent than in the United States. Disputes in the United States have been somewhat more open, but the similarities are now even more obvious. Nevertheless, one cannot dismiss the importance of the historical difference between the Canadian and U.S. responses to the possibility of fracturing the nation—a Canadian civil war hardly seems possible.

Finally, since the second World War, the surge of immigration from Asia, the Caribbean, and both southern and eastern Europe to Canada has exposed it to a cultural mix in many ways comparable to the United States' melting pot. In fact, Canadian-American similarities are often taken for granted. Many cross-national studies of social welfare policies don't even deal with the North American welfare states as separate entities. Instead, they assume the Canadian and American systems are similar or they group Canada and the United States together.[7]

This is, of course, misleading and obscures the very differences from which we can learn. As Seymour Martin Lipset (1990, p. 225) recently noted, "Canada and the United States resemble each other more than either resembles any other nation." But when studied as "closely-linked neighbors" rather than subjects of "cross-cultural variation on a broad international scale," important North American differences come into focus. Just as wider cross-national comparison "brings out [North American] similarities, the narrower focus highlights dissimilarities."

Canadians are understandably more sensitive to the differences than their usually less informed and less concerned neighbors on their southern border. Less insulated than the United States from global forces because less self-sufficient economically, Canada has, perhaps by necessity, been more cosmopolitan intellectually, exhibiting greater willingness to learn about issues and to learn from others. Ties to Britain on the one hand and to France on the other have, no doubt, also affected Canada's permeability to European ideas.

In addition, there is a major asymmetry in the influences of one nation on the other, one that is partly media-related. Because so much of the Canadian population is concentrated on the northern border of the United States, Canadians are barraged by American radio and watch American television. A much smaller segment of the United States population directly encounters Canada's media.

But the influence of the media is only part of the explanation. Whatever the North American cultural and institutional similarities and differences, the United States *affects* Canada more than the other way around. Canada's business cycle closely follows that of the United States; the value of its currency, the level of its interest rates, and— since free trade—the fate of many of its firms depends substantially on the fiscal, monetary, and trade policies of the United States. Geographical and demographic differences between Canada and the United States accentuate this asymmetry. Canada's population is not only concentrated on the U.S. border but is only about 1/10th of the U.S. population. That part of the Canadian populace not living in close proximity to the United States is spread out in a huge, thinly populated land mass of 3.8 million square miles, stretching nearly to the Arctic Circle and slightly larger than the U.S. land mass of 3.6 million square miles.

Canada's federal structure reflects the combination of a huge land mass and a sparse population by placing its population in 10 geographically large provinces. The much larger U.S. population is divided into 50 states. However, these differences are tempered by the fact that in both countries there can be found jurisdictions with similar mixes of population density and land mass. U.S. states can be found with geographical orientations, political ideologies, and economic concerns remarkably similar to those of Canadian provinces. The innovative populist policies of Saskatchewan and Wisconsin have both had disproportional influences on the policies of their respective countries; the boom and bust oil economies of Alberta and Texas have produced extremes in libertarianism; and the Maritime Provinces and Maine, both poor and dependent on federal transfers, still exhibit a similar economic and social structure.[8]

Yet geographical and demographic variations do influence the institutions, structure, and workings of government. The difference between having 10 or 50 governmental entities involves more than pure scale. Both negotiating and managerial complexities are introduced with the 50 components that make up the United States. Ten people at a round table can have a meaningful interaction; a round table discussion of 50 people seems considerably less instructive.

The difference in scale has contributed to institutional arrangements in Canada that make it relatively easier for a party majority to translate to a programmatic majority. In contrast, the impressive number of veto/blocking points in the United States—including the actions of powerful committees or individuals in Congress, or the President— leads to policymaking by the "lowest common denominator." In fact, only an overwhelming crisis permits coherent national policymaking in the United States. The fragmented enactments that result from this system have made the fractiousness even worse, with Americans showing both a greater lack of faith in government and an increasing hostility to government failure (Marmor et al. 1990).[9]

It does not require a deep social psychology to realize that Canadians emphasize their cultural distinctiveness partly to distance themselves from a powerful, often neglectful neighbor. But these understandable motives—and the undeniable national differences that do exist—reinforce rather than repudiate the substantial North American similarities in values, institutions, and practices. These similarities provide the basis for comparative investigations that support a particularly valuable kind of policy learning.

ECONOMIC STATUS OF THE ELDERLY IN NORTH AMERICA VERSUS WESTERN EUROPE

With respect to population aging (table 1.1), the United States and Canada will go into the 20th century with younger populations than those of Western Europe. Until 2020, although the trends converge

Table 1.1 ESTIMATED PERCENTAGES OF POPULATION AGE 65
           AND OVER AGE 80

Country	1980		1990		2000		2020		2040	
	65+	80+	65+	80+	65+	80+	65+	80+	65+	80+
Canada	9.5	1.8	11.4	2.2	12.8	2.8	18.6	4.2	22.5	7.0
United States	11.3	2.3	12.2	2.5	12.1	2.9	16.2	3.1	19.8	5.7
France	14.0	2.9	13.8	3.7	15.3	3.3	19.5	5.0	22.7	6.9
Germany	15.5	2.6	15.5	3.8	17.1	3.7	21.7	5.4	27.6	7.3
Great Britain	14.9	2.7	15.1	3.2	14.5	3.2	16.3	3.3	20.4	5.1

Source: OECD, Aging Populations: The Social Policy Implications, 1988, page 22.
The table reports the baseline mortality calculations; and Tables A.1, A.2, and A.3,
pages 78–83.

somewhat, the U.S.-Canadian populations will still be younger. By
2040, however, Canada will have reached European levels, if current
projections hold, while the United States will still be younger than
Canada, France, or Germany.

With respect to economic well-being of the elderly, Canada looks
more like Western Europe than like the United States. To provide a
context for the political, philosophical, and policy discussions that
follow, it is useful to review the U.S. and Canadian trends in population aging and economic well-being of the elderly in the context of
trends in Western Europe. This highlights the extent to which Canada
can be seen as a bridge between the U.S. and European experience.

First, the United States does have a low poverty rate measured by
the U.S. absolute poverty threshold. But it stands out dramatically in
its higher rate of the near-poor elderly (defined as the percentage
below 40 percent of median income)—a rate much higher than any
other country reported here, and nearly five times that of Canada (table
1.2, column 1). At the same time, the United States provides a relatively low public guarantee against poverty among elderly persons.
Even counting such noncash benefits as income disregards and food
stamps, the guarantee is not commensurate with the levels of income
security found in other nations of comparable wealth (table 1.2, col-
umns 2 and 3).

Second, U.S. historical patterns of wages and employment—and
their close link to the pension system which reinforces these differences—have led to a system in which older, widowed, and otherwise
single women are particularly prone to be poor or near poor.

Table 1.3 illustrates the point. Low-income rates for the United
States are uniformly higher—for the nonelderly, elderly couples, and
elderly single women—than for other countries. Within the United

Table 1.2 INCOME, POVERTY, AND BENEFIT ADEQUACY AMONG THE
U.S. ELDERLY IN A CROSS-NATIONAL CONTEXT

Country/Year	Low-Income Rates among Elderly Persons[a] 40% Median/LIS	Minimum Old Age Benefit as Percent of Adjusted Median Income[c]	
		Single Elderly Person	Elderly Couple
Canada (1987)	2.2	54	59
United States (1986)	10.9	34	37
Australia (1985–86)	4.0	52	62
Netherlands (1987)	.1	72	69
Sweden (1987)	.7	66	72
France (1984)	.7	48	68
Germany (1984)	3.8	56	58
United Kingdom (1986)	1.0	45	49
Overall Average[b]	2.8	52	59

Sources and Notes: Luxembourg Income Study and Smeeding (1992).

a. Poverty rates are percent of persons age 65 and over whose disposable after tax incomes fall below the specified percentage of adjusted median income. Adjusted income is derived using the U.S. poverty line equivalence scales which are such that a single elderly person needs 64 percent of the income of a three-person family, while an aged couple needs 82 percent as much to reach the same standard of living. The U.S. poverty line was 40.7 percent of adjusted income in 1986. (Source: LIS data base.)
b. Simple column average.
c. Minimum benefits as published by the OECD were compared to adjusted median income after adjusting for national price changes. For the U.S. the figures include the SSI benefit, plus the OASI disregard, plus food stamps as indicated in the House Ways and Means Committee Greenbook. For other nations the combination of benefits was determined by OECD. In Netherlands and Sweden benefits are adjusted for income taxation. (Source: LIS. OECD, Reforming Public Pensions, 1988.)

States the low-income rate for elderly couples is lower than for the nonelderly population but dramatically higher for elderly single women.

Median income for the elderly group as a percentage of median income for the total population (both adjusted for differences in family size) shows the same stark fact in a different way. Elderly couples in the United States have higher median incomes than the U.S. population as a whole (109 versus 100 percent). Yet, elderly single women have median incomes that are only 62 percent as high as for the population as a whole. In the international context the contrast is even more dramatic. Relative to the population median, U.S. elderly women are worse off than elderly women in all the other countries listed (with the exception of Australia). But U.S. elderly couples are better off than elderly couples in all the other countries listed.

Table 1.3 DIFFERENCES IN LOW-INCOME RATES AMONG NONAGED
HOUSEHOLDS, ELDERLY (HEAD 65 +), SINGLE WOMEN LIVING ALONE,
AND ELDERLY COUPLE UNITS: POVERTY RATES FOR HOUSEHOLDS AT
U.S. (40% MEDIAN) POVERTY LINE[a]

| Country | Year | Low-Income Rates | | | Ratio of Adjusted Median Income Group to National[b] | | |
		All Non-aged Units[c]	Elderly Couples	Single Elderly Women	All 65 +	Couples	Single Women
United States	1986	13.5	6.0	17.6	85	109	62
Canada	1987	8.9	.6	3.2	80	88	70
Australia	1985	7.2	4.2	3.8	66	70	56
Germany	1984	3.1	2.7	2.4	91	103	83
Sweden	1987	7.7	.2	1.7	82	97	73
United Kingdom	1986	3.1	.9	.4	77	83	68
Netherlands	1987	5.8	0.0	0.0	88	97	82
France	1984	6.2	.7	.8	93	99	86
Overall Average[d]					83	93	73

Source: Luxembourg Income Study and Smeeding (1992).

a. Poverty rates given as percent of each type of unit poor with poverty measured at
40 percent of adjusted median income using the LIS equivalence scale. (See below.)
b. Income is adjusted using the simple LIS equivalence scale which counts the first
person as 1.0 and all other persons as .5 regardless of age. Hence, a single aged person
needs 50% of the income of a three-person family while an aged couple needs 75
percent as much to reach the same standard of living. Ratio of group adjusted household median to overall adjusted household median income are presented. (Source:
LIS database.)
c. All units with head under age 65.
d. Simple column average.

The implication is inescapable. The income distribution among the
elderly in the United States is far more unequal than in any of the
other countries in the comparison except Australia. When discussing
the economic situation of the U.S. elderly, averages, whether means
or medians, are particularly misleading (see Quinn 1987; Smeeding
1992; chapter 8 of this volume).

In spite of the greater inequality among the U.S. than the Canadian
elderly, the U.S. political debate typically treats the elderly as a homogeneous well-off group and, in the last decade or so, has tended to
portray them as getting more than their fair share at the expense of
the younger generation. The rest of the book examines the reasons
behind the U.S.-Canadian differences in both politics and policy toward the elderly.

THE COMPARATIVE POLITICS OF ECONOMIC SECURITY
FOR THE ELDERLY

Part One of the book examines political explanations for the differences in social provision for the elderly between Canada and the United States, and the role intergenerational conflict plays in the politics of the two countries. How the new atmosphere of austerity has affected political struggles over social policy for the elderly is the question that chapter 2 addresses. Despite differences in the political rhetoric surrounding benefit policy toward the elderly, Pierson and Smith identify a common politics of retrenchment, in which efforts to cut back—with their inevitable identification of losers—tend to be less successful the more entrenched the constituency they serve. This comparative look at Canada and the United States indicates that the elderly have survived relatively well in both countries, at least so far, but that differences among programs add up to important differences between the two countries.

The authors find that the most comprehensive programs in the two countries (Social Security in the United States, health care in Canada) have been the most successful. That the benefits of the former are age-based and the latter are universal is a major reason, in their judgment, for the emergence of the politics of intergenerational conflict in the United States and not in Canada. More generally, as they see it, failure of the United States to develop a range of programs that provide clear benefits to all generations is emerging as a major weakness of public social provision—and is retarding extension of public benefits to the nonelderly in the United States.

Looking at the politics of social provision through the lens of history is the goal of Myles and Quadagno (chapter 3). They identify major similarities in the two welfare states of North America in comparison to those in Europe, but they also find major differences that have importantly influenced the degree of generational conflict apparent in the political debate. But these authors eschew the traditional cultural explanation of the differences, finding founding cleavages and unresolved conflicts more persuasive explanatory factors.

In the United States, the effects of region and race are pivotal in their judgment. In Canada, region and language play the major role. The north-south and black-white cleavages in the United States retarded development of a social safety net but permitted development of a strong wage-based benefit system. Canada, in sharp contrast— using the welfare state to bind the nation together—developed a strong safety net. The United States has singled out the elderly for universal benefit programs, financed by contributions from the current working population. Canada has favored non-age-related social insurance, paid for largely from general revenues. The Canadian approach makes it harder to raise the age issue on either the benefit or financing side.

Differences in the salience of intergenerational conflict, as reflected in citations in academic, media, policy, and public opinion sources, are the focus of Cook and her coauthors (chapter 4). Although the mention of such conflict is not as frequent even on the U.S. side as might be expected, the authors find many more U.S. mentions in every arena except public opinion poll data. The elderly are the beneficiaries of strong public opinion support on both sides of the border. The authors attribute the substantial U.S.-Canadian differences in academic, media, and political discourse to the greater predominance of universal programs in Canada (which provides better balance for old and young) and to differences in political structure (which focuses Canadian politics more on specific divisions among provinces than is true in the United States). As the authors look ahead to the 1990s, they see no rise in intergenerational political strife in Canada and possible decline in the United States.

RESOLVING CONFLICTING CLAIMS AMONG GENERATIONS

Part Two of the book searches for ways to diffuse the potentially explosive potential of age-based politics.

The relative obligations of younger and older cohorts to each other will always be a potential source of conflict unless a comprehensive solution can be found that enables the obligations to be balanced in a way that is manifestly just. Battin (chapter 5) searches for such a solution in the health care arena through the prudential lifespan approach—following Norman Daniel's use of Rawls's theory of justice— to consider the principles prudent persons might apply to life choices in the absence of knowledge about their personal characteristics (in this case health). When she applies these principles to the U.S. health care system, she finds that it is not unjust. It treats all persons equally by providing care in their old age. But it is inefficient. To the extent that some forms of health care are not efficient when applied to the elderly, rational self-interest maximizers (in the absence of any knowledge about their individual health prospects) would disagree with the current allocation of resources. But they would not disagree on equity grounds—everyone is getting the same. They would disagree on efficiency grounds—everyone is getting less than their money's worth. If the government is to provide any of its citizens, young or old, with health care, on this argument, it must do so as part of a comprehensive, rationally defensive, efficient program for all age groups—because it owes them not only equity but also efficiency.

The lifespan approach does not solve the problem, even theoretically, for Binstock (chapter 6). He attributes the intergenerational conflict that has characterized the political debate over the past decade to ageism, "the attribution of the same characteristics, status, and just deserts to a heterogeneous group that has been artificially homogenized, packaged, labeled, and marketed as 'the aged'."

Compassionate stereotypes dominated the debate until the late 1970s, which helped create what Binstock calls the "old age welfare state." The benefits thereby accruing to older Americans led to a dramatic reversal of the stereotype—to the more current but equally oversimplified picture of a prosperous, hedonistic, and powerful elderly generation. The change—and Binstock implicates the prudential lifespan theorists in this turn of events—has led to calls for rationing health care for the aged on cost-benefit grounds, a proposal Binstock argues against with great force. He quotes evidence that the elderly can benefit greatly from a variety of medical interventions. He points out that only a small fraction of the funds spent on health care for the elderly go to dramatic technological interventions. And he quotes studies for both Canada and the United States indicating that aggressive medical interventions in the last year of life are comparable across adult age groups.

Binstock makes the point that "justice between rich and poor" may be a better metaphor for the dilemmas of equity the U.S. confronts in rationing health care than "justice between age groups." He ends by stressing the fundamental importance of making our principles of equity explicit in the policy choices we make—rather than allowing issues of intergenerational equity to divert our attention from other ways of viewing tradeoffs and options, which may be not only more morally defensible but also more cost-beneficial.

POLICY DIMENSIONS

Part Three of the book focuses on the policies that govern economic security for the elderly: income security, health care, long-term care, and housing.

The pressures of a rapidly aging population on both public and private provision for retirement are the focus of Weaver (chapter 7) using the United States as her example. She addresses the need both to institute advance funding of Social Security in a way that guarantees the security of public retirement benefits and to reform federal regulation of private pensions to guarantee the security of private retirement benefits.

She sees the problem with the Social Security system as twofold. Currently, there is no guarantee that the surplus will be invested in a way that guarantees a competitive rate of return, and there is no guarantee that future retirees will get the benefits. Her preferred policy approach to both problems is to rebate the surplus revenues to workers for direct deposit into individualized retirement accounts or permit workers to contract out of the public system to the extent that they are covered by a comparable employer-sponsored plan. This would make the market return on their investment available to them and earmark it at the same time.

Weaver's concern with the private pension system is that government tax and regulatory policy may be shrinking the proportion of employers who offer and employees who participate in private pension plans. She does not think mandating private pension coverage is the answer, but rather that tax and regulatory policy governing pensions should be designed to permit private pensions to evolve more easily to meet the diverse and changing interests of employees and employers. A particular policy recommendation she offers is to make the tax advantages now available to people saving through company pensions available to other people saving for retirement. This would create healthy competition for company plans and reduce the need for public regulation of employer plan participants.

The income security needs of the U.S. elderly are addressed by Moon and Ruggles (chapter 8). They demonstrate that, despite average increases in economic well-being of major proportions, there is considerable income disparity among the elderly in the United States, many of whom are only just above the poverty line, and their future improvements are likely to come at a slower pace than in the recent past. The authors are particularly concerned lest policy change further disadvantage the neediest elderly, who are virtually ignored in much of the current debate. They suggest that ability to continue working and health status are better predictors of economic status than age and are, therefore, better measures of need.

They also take issue with proposals, including Weaver's in chapter 7, to privatize Social Security. Their point is that, although some people could undoubtedly obtain higher returns in the private sector, Social Security was never equivalent to private pensions, but represents a combination of retirement investment (the pension portion), disability coverage, and protection against low earning years, job loss, and other uncertainties across a lifetime of work.

Income security in comparative perspective is addressed by Wolfson and Murphy (chapter 9). They provide evidence supporting the Moon and Ruggles picture of widely varying economic well-being among the U.S. elderly. They also show that public pension provision in Canada does a more effective job of smoothing out income inequalities among elderly Canadians than does the U.S. system. Although average family income is higher in the United States than in Canada, median family income is higher in Canada for all age groups. And both lower and middle income elderly Canadians have higher incomes than their U.S. counterparts.

Health care presents perhaps the best study in contrasts between the two countries, as described by Barer and coauthors (chapter 10). Canada provides universal coverage to its entire population under a single system. Canadians are not responsible for any direct payments for medical or hospital care, and most provinces have out-of-pocket ceilings on pharmaceuticals (which in any case apply only to out-of-hospital drugs). Even though the United States has universal health insurance (Medicare) for the elderly, it has premiums for all but hospital care, deductibles and coinsurance that can reach high levels, and no coverage of prescription drugs. Thus, the financial risk run by the elderly under the two systems differs dramatically.

The authors estimate that the average out-of-pocket costs of the elderly in the United States are at least double those of the Canadian elderly. When risk of catastrophic health payments is included, the difference is much more dramatic because no Canadians are in fact exposed to such risk. "The maximum imaginable out-of-pocket costs in Canada," according to the authors, "are in all likelihood less than half the mean equivalent costs in the United States." Interestingly, trends in age-related patterns of utilization have been very similar in the two countries, and the two elderly populations have similar disability and mortality rates.

Canada also has province-based chronic or long-term care, paid for by a combination of public budgets and private out-of-pocket payments tied to a de facto minimum retirement benefit. Kane (chapter 11) documents the lack of a comprehensive long-term care system in the United States and Kane and Kane (chapter 12) compare the two countries. They point, in particular, to the patchwork of funding sources in the United States, which not only lets those in need fall through the cracks but is artificially fragmented by "type of care." Since long-term care needs constitute essentially a continuum—with the same services deliverable in a wide variety of settings—this fragmentation erects essentially artificial barriers that distort the choices available to the elderly and their families, and potentially drives up costs.

Canada avoids these perverse incentives. Canada is increasingly concerned about inappropriate use, however, and shows eagerness to learn from the United States about market incentives to curb it. The United States is also more actively involved than Canada in promoting quality assurance in long-term care delivery and emphasizing accountability on the basis of health and functioning outcomes.

Housing for the elderly, closely connected with the issue of long-term care, ends the book, with a discussion by Keyes (chapter 13). Keyes emphasizes that housing is an area where the two countries are very alike. They have similarly huge proportions of the population in fully paid up owner-occupied housing, in sharp contrast to Europe. Their policies are similarly missing the mark in failing to take sufficient account of this fact in developing housing policy for the elderly.

Keyes notes the need in both countries to develop a range of services and incentives for the elderly that represent a cost-effective combination of physical and social services.

The one important difference between the two countries that Keyes observes is that Canadians may be in a better position to merge the housing needs of the elderly with their long-term care needs. This is because the Canadian sense of "civic behavior," helped by more flexible funding rules, may be more conducive to cooperation between housing and nursing home authorities than appears likely in the current U.S. context. But national culture explanations, as emphasized in Part I of the volume, may need to be accompanied by more concrete policy factors to be persuasive.

Notes

1. See, for example, Doran (1991), Lipset (1991), and Marmor (1991). Also see the Rockefeller Foundation Cross-National Exchange Meeting on Poverty, Washington, D.C., April 11–12, 1988. For additional illustration, note the special issue on "Comparative Health Policy," 1992.

2. Although a Canadian model single-payer health care system was not seriously considered by the Clinton health care task force, the Canadian health care experience has not been ignored by American health care planners. A close examination of the President's plan shows we have learned a great deal from Canada. In fact, the working principles for health care reform announced by the Administration include the key elements of the Canadian experience: universality, global budget limits, state involvement, comprehensive benefits, and recently, a choice of physician option. Moreover, the President's selection of the untried American "managed competition" model appeared to result less from rejection of the Canadian single payer alternative than from fear that the powerful insurance lobby will succeed in blocking a single-payer design. For more discussion of this, see Hamburger and Marmor (1993); and Marmor (1993).

3. For extensive discussion of the logic of comparative policy studies, see, among many others, Ashford (1978), Flora (ed) (1988), and Wilsford (1991).

4. Although the United States eventually adopted many welfare state programs, it remains the only industrialized western democracy without national health insurance and without family allowances. It is also the only one of these nations which offers means-tested benefits specifically for food purchased.

5. Blendon et al. (1990) credit the overwhelming dissatisfaction with the U.S. health care system (89 percent of Americans reported they desired a fundamental change in the U.S. health care system), rather than an understanding of the Canadian system for the preference shown for the Canadian system. But without the basic trust of Canadians that exists, a favorable response to a system not well understood could not have occurred.

6. New York provides categorical Medicaid coverage to a higher percentage of its population than Mississippi because it extends AFDC eligibility to New York families with higher incomes than Mississippi. New York has also adopted a larger number of Medicaid optional programs than has Mississippi.

7. In Flora and Heidenheimer (1981) the experience of Canada and the United States are handled by one chapter (Kuderle and Marmor, chapter 3) where it is noted that Canada has received little attention in the comparative welfare state literature. That chapter also discusses the distinctive North American flavor to political debate about the welfare state. The United States and Canada are also clustered in Esping-Anderson (1990). See also Wilensky (1975).

8. See chapter 8, "Regionalism and Income Security," in Banting (1981) and Porter (1965) for Canadian regional differences.

9. The vicious cycle in the United States also causes overselling of policy options (e.g., a $1 billion work program as the "welfare reform" which will solve the poverty problem among the nonelderly), and so the resulting policies always under-perform. This in turn affects the ability to effectuate future changes, because of the disillusionment.

References

Ashford, Douglas E., ed. 1978. *Comparing Public Policies: New Concepts and Methods.* Beverly Hills, CA: Sage Publications.

Banting, Keith. 1987. "Regionalism and Income Security." Chap. 8 in *The Welfare State and Canadian Federalism.* Kingston and Montreal: McGill-Queen's University Press.

Blendon, R., and K. Donelan. 1990. "The Public and the Emerging Debate over National Health Insurance." *New England Journal of Medicine* (July 19).

Blendon, R., et al. 1990. "Satisfaction with Health Systems in Ten Nations." *Health Affairs* (Summer).

Bouvier, Leon R. 1991. *Peaceful Invasions: Immigration and Changing America.* Center for Immigration Studies. Pine Hill, CA: Pine Hill Press, Inc.

Doran, C. R. 1991. "Canada's Role in North America." *Current History* (December).

Esping-Anderson, Gösta. 1990. *The Three Worlds of Welfare Capitalism.* Princeton, NJ: Princeton University Press.

Evans, Robert, et al. 1989. "Controlling Health Expenditures: The Canadian Reality." *New England Journal of Medicine* 320 (9, 2 March).

Flora, Peter, ed. 1988. *Growth to Limits: The Western European Welfare States since World War II.* New York: de Gruyter.

Flora, Peter, and Arnold J. Heidenheimer, eds. 1981. *The Development of Welfare States in Europe and America.* New Brunswick: Transaction Books.

Hamburger, Tom, and Theodore Marmor. 1993. "Dead on Arrival." *Washington Monthly* (September).

Kalbach, Warren E. 1990. "A Demographic Overview of Racial and Ethnic Groups in Canada." In *Race and Ethnic Relations in Canada*, edited by Peter S. Li. New York: Oxford University Press.

Kudrle, Robert, and Theodore Marmor. 1981. "The Development of Welfare States in North America." In *The Development of Welfare States in Europe and America*, edited by Peter Flora and Arnold J. Heidenheimer. New Brunswick: Transaction Books.

Lipset, Seymour M. 1990. *Continental Divide: The Values and Institutions of the United States and Canada.* New York: Routledge.

————. 1991. "Canada and the United States: The Great Divide." *Current History* (December).

Marmor, Theodore. 1991. "Canada's Health Care System: A Model for the United States." *Current History* (December).

————. 1991. "Testimony Prepared for the Committee on Ways and Means, U.S. House of Representatives." Hearing on Health Care Coverage and Cost Issues, Special Panel: International Perspectives, April 16.

————. 1993. "Health Care Reform in the United States: Patterns of Fact and Fiction in the Use of Canadian Experience." *The American Journal of Canadian Studies* (Spring).

Marmor, Theodore, and Rudolf Klein. 1986. "Cost vs. Care: America's Health Care Dilemma Wrongly Considered." *Health Matrix: The Quarterly Journal of Health Services Management* 4 (1, Spring).

Marmor, Theodore, Jerry L. Mashaw, and Philip Harvey. 1990. *America's Misunderstood Welfare State*. New York: Basic Books, paperback edition.

Organization of Economic Cooperation and Development. 1987. "Summary and Policy Implications." In *Social Policy Studies No. 5: Reforming Public Pensions*, Part IV. Paris: OECD.

Porter, John A. 1965. *The Vertical Mosaic: An Analysis of Social Class and Power in Canada*. Toronto: University of Toronto Press.

Quinn, Joseph. 1987. "The Economic Status of the Elderly: Beware of the Mean." *Review of Income and Wealth* 33: 63–82.

Samuelson, Robert. 1990. "Pampering the Elderly." *Washington Post* (October 24).

Smeeding, Timothy. 1988. "The Children of Poverty: The Evidence on Poverty and Comparative Income Support Policies in Eight Countries." Oral statement given to House Select Committee on Children, Youth, and Families, U.S. House of Representatives, February 25.

——————. 1992. "Cross National Comparisons of Poverty, Inequality and Income Security Among the Elderly in Eight Modern Nations." Paper presented at the Executive Seminar on Poverty and Income Security, National Academy on Aging, Washington, D.C., June.

Tobin, James. 1988. "The Future of Social Security." In *Social Security: Beyond the Rhetoric of Crisis*, edited by Theodore Marmor and Jerry L. Mashaw. Princeton, N.J.: Princeton University Press.

U.S. Department of Commerce. Bureau of the Census. 1990. *Statistical Abstract of the United States, 1990*.

Warsh, David. 1990. "Trying to See through the Murk in the Social Security Debate." *Washington Post* (January 31).

Wilensky, Harold L. 1975. *The Welfare State and Equality: Structural and Ideological Roots of Public Expenditures*. Berkeley: University of California Press.

Wilsford, David. 1991. *Doctors and the State: The Politics of Health Care in France and the United States*. Durham, N.C.: Duke University Press.

Part One

THE COMPARATIVE POLITICS OF
ECONOMIC SECURITY FOR THE ELDERLY

SHIFTING FORTUNES OF THE ELDERLY: THE COMPARATIVE POLITICS OF RETRENCHMENT

Paul Pierson and Miriam Smith

Welfare states in all the advanced industrial democracies face difficult challenges. The lengthy post-war period of widely supported expansion has given way to an atmosphere of austerity. Poor economic performance has generated severe fiscal pressures. In addition, the electoral resurgence of political forces generally hostile to extensive public provision has changed the parameters of policy debate. Finally and less dramatically, the new cognizance of limits partly reflects the maturation of social programs. As these programs came to account for a sizable share of GNP, it was inevitable that the rapid expenditure growth rates of the 1950s and 1960s would prove difficult to sustain.[1]

This chapter examines how the new atmosphere of austerity has affected political struggles over social policy for the elderly in Canada and the United States. How vulnerable has public social provision for the elderly been? Why have some programs proven to be more resilient than others? How similar are the experiences of the two countries, and what might explain important differences? We suggest that programs for the elderly have so far weathered the storm fairly well, though there are important differences among the experiences of individual programs, and increasingly important differences between the experiences of the two countries.

We first consider why some programs for the elderly have been more vulnerable than others. In both countries, one can describe a *politics of retrenchment*, in which advocates of cutbacks are hard pressed to overcome the political supports for well-entrenched social programs. Retrenchment politics are distinctive.[2] Advocates of cutbacks face a difficult task, since retrenchment imposes visible pain on specific groups, usually in return for diffuse, long-term, and uncertain benefits. In addition, voters exhibit a "negativity bias"—remembering losses more than gains. Overcoming opposition has required either successful efforts to "divide and conquer" potential opponents or,

more often, careful identification of openings for low-visibility reforms that do not produce a public outcry. Successful retrenchment
has occurred under some circumstances, but not often.

Like a number of recent studies of social policy development, our
analysis of the politics of retrenchment emphasizes the role of what
are sometimes called "policy feedbacks" or "policy legacies."[3] Once
adopted, social programs help to structure the development of interest
groups, provide cues to voters, and establish a range of rules governing
procedures for reform. Opportunities for retrenchment depend very
much on whether pre-existing program structures facilitate the exe-
cution of "divide and conquer" strategies or low-visibility reforms.
While other factors, such as the nature of political institutions, have
also been important in retrenchment politics, their impact is also
conditioned by programmatic structures. Canadian federalism, for example, exerts quite different influences on reform politics depending
on the specific characteristics of particular social programs.

The second part of our chapter addresses the major difference in
the character of struggles over social provision that has emerged between the two countries. In the United States what we call (with some
trepidation) a *politics of generational conflict* has developed in recent
years. Since the mid-1980s, debates about the social distribution of
burdens and benefits have often been framed explicitly or implicitly
in terms of age. The "generational" issues presented are ambiguous
and frequently inconsistent. In some cases, it is the current generation
of elderly that is seen as overprivileged; in others, the concern seems
to be the unwillingness or inability of current "baby-boom" workers
to adequately prepare for the high carrying costs associated with their
own retirement in the first half of the 21st century. Despite this am-
biguity, what distinguishes the new politics is the way in which broad
debates about economic and social policy are linked to generational
concerns, and then, in turn, linked to the status of programs for the
elderly.

Nothing similar has occurred in Canada. Although the fundamental
problems confronting Canadian social programs are in many respects
similar to those in the United States, discussions are almost never
cast in generational terms. It is not that Canadian programs for the
elderly do not face close scrutiny. On the contrary, the politics of
retrenchment remains very much in force. Yet the ways in which
"problems" are defined and "winners" and "losers" identified are
now quite different in the two countries. Ultimately this matters, because mass and elite conceptions of distributive justice are likely to
have an impact on political struggles over social provision. Indeed,

there are already clear signs that the emerging debate over generational burdens is influencing policy development in the United States.

Why has this new dimension of political conflict over programs for the elderly developed in the United States but not in Canada? Just as we believe that program structures have had a critical influence on retrenchment politics, we suggest that the explanation for this divergence can be found in the peculiar shape of the American welfare state. Often described as a "laggard," the welfare state in the United States could more accurately be described as Janus-faced. For the elderly, the United States has developed a system of social insurance, covering both health and income needs, that can be compared with Canada and indeed much of Western Europe. For the nonelderly, however, the contrast between Canadian social provision and U.S. policies is striking. Whereas Canada offers universal health benefits and extensive child allowances, the United States has provided only meager means-tested assistance; even these programs are generally restricted to subcategories of the poor. Characteristically, the one U.S. social insurance program of greatest immediate relevance to the working-aged population, Unemployment Insurance, has become increasingly threadbare in the past decade.

Broad economic and social issues are submitted to age-based scrutiny in the United States because the American welfare state, to a unique extent, is structured on the basis of age. This has become increasingly clear as Social Security and Medicare have matured in the past two decades. A very high proportion of social expenditure is explicitly targeted on the elderly, and the financial burdens on the working-aged population, levied as payroll taxes, are equally explicit. These trends have fueled a debate on distributional issues defined more by age than by other possible cleavages. Because of the distinctive shape of American social policy, general pressures of austerity will be complicated in the forseeable future by the new dimension of generational conflict.

THE POLITICS OF RETRENCHMENT AND PROGRAMS FOR THE ELDERLY

Poor economic performance, the electoral resurgence of conservative parties, and the maturation of social programs have all contributed to the recent atmosphere of austerity. Programs of public social provision have faced an intense challenge, as governments have sought to reduce expenditures and restructure programs along more market-oriented lines. Yet social programs for the elderly retain widespread public support. Successful retrenchment, which appears to require the effective demobilization of program supporters, has been the exception rather than the rule.

A range of research in political psychology and voting behavior suggests that retrenchment initiatives are likely to be politically hazardous. Retrenchment generally requires the imposition of concentrated and often substantial losses, while the benefits to voters are for the most part diffuse, long-term, and uncertain. Furthermore, voters possess a "negativity bias" that makes them far more cognizant of losses than commensurate gains.[4]

At the same time, advocates of retrenchment may possess some tactical options that diminish the dangers. In particular, those seeking cutbacks are likely to pursue "divide and conquer" strategies and strive to minimize the visibility of their reforms. While the potential for organized opposition in a particular policy area may be large, it is sometimes possible to isolate subgroups within that opposition. That "divide and conquer" is an obvious political ploy need not render it any less effective. The constituencies of all public programs are to some extent heterogeneous. The targeting of cutbacks on particular subgroups minimizes the size of the potential opposition to proposed reforms. In a context where cutback initiatives are widely anticipated, program beneficiaries who are spared the axe may feel quietly grateful that the burden has fallen on someone else (although of course, next time it may be their group that finds itself singled out for attention). In any event, they are unlikely to mobilize effectively against retrenchment efforts.

The role of "visibility" in politics is often mentioned casually but little understood. All political actors possess imperfect information about issues relevant to their interests. Furthermore, the distribution of information is usually highly unequal. In this context, it may be possible for policymakers to lower the political costs of retrenchment actions by raising the costs to possible opponents of obtaining relevant information—that is to say, by lowering the visibility of their actions. As Douglas Arnold (1990) has argued, two different kinds of visibility should be distinguished. First, retrenchment advocates can try to lower the visibility of the *effects* of policy change. Not all consequences of policy changes are equally apparent. Some reforms will have consequences that attract massive attention; others will not. Visibility can be reduced by making the effects of reforms indirect, as when policy changes are imposed on health care producers who pass on cost increases to consumers. The visibility of effects can also be diminished by increasing the complexity of reforms. The consequences of simple cuts are easy to identify, but even though elaborate rule changes may ultimately have the same or even greater impact, that impact is often harder to detect.

As an alternative or supplement to efforts to lower the visibility of policy effects, policymakers can try to diminish the visibility of their own *responsibility* for those effects. Since it is the fear of being held accountable for unpopular actions that constrains policymakers, they are likely to seek means of covering their tracks. One option is to shift responsibility for imposing cutbacks to local officials, who may then attract some of the blame. An alternative is to make cutbacks "automatic." Changes in indexation, for example, can lead to annual reductions without requiring repeated, visible actions on the part of policymakers.[5]

"Never be seen to do harm." Often cited as the first maxim of electoral politics, this folk wisdom has not been well-integrated into theories of policy development. By obscuring the impact of policy changes—or one's responsibility for them—politicians can dramatically lower the costs of pursuing a retrenchment agenda. Information is a crucial resource, and one that is distributed in a highly unequal way. Its importance in political struggles has been vastly underrated. As the following discussion of retrenchment politics in the United States and Canada makes clear, efforts to lower visibility, combined with steps to "divide and conquer" opponents, have on occasion opened up opportunities for significant retrenchment.

The United States: Social Security and Medicare in a Period of Austerity

Neither Social Security nor Medicare has undergone radical change in the past fifteen years. Social Security has emerged with an undiminished reputation for resilience. Retrenchment advocates have paid a heavy political price for assaults on the popular pension scheme— so much so that Republican members of Congress have become wary of even "bipartisan" proposals to cut benefits. Medicare has not fared so well. Inextricably connected to the broader crisis of the American health care system and more vulnerable to low-visibility retrenchment strategies, Medicare's protection of the elderly from the risks of health care costs has been eroded although not fundamentally challenged.

SOCIAL SECURITY

Social Security has always enjoyed tremendous political support, and this has continued to be the case despite a worsening budgetary climate.[6] In part, Social Security's political strength stems from qualities common to many old-age pension systems: the elderly are widely seen as "deserving," universalism generates widespread support, and reliance on payroll tax "contributions" solidifies a perception that benefits have been earned and hence constitute an inviolable entitlement. Furthermore, a comparative perspective suggests that Social Security's specific design has been remarkably well-suited to maintaining political support. The early adoption of a unified, earnings-related, pay-as-you-go pension system helped generate strong common interests within the elderly population and great popular enthusiasm for Social Security. Countries that adopted more fragmented plans, were slow to adopt earnings-related benefits, or chose to rely on "funded" schemes were more likely to have trouble establishing politically untouchable programs.

The existence of a single dominant plan simplifies the process of mobilizing public support for old-age pensions. By enhancing the stake of the middle class in public pensions, provisions for earnings-related benefits serve the same role. Pay-as-you-go financing, where current payroll taxes are used to pay current benefits, has two important consequences. First, it provided major political advantages during the crucial start-up phase of public pension systems. Because a huge workforce is available to fund benefits for an initially very small group of eligible pensioners, very low payroll taxes can fund very generous benefits.[7] Thus, pay-as-you-go systems enjoy a popularity premium during the long period when they move towards maturity. Once pay-as-you-go systems reach maturity, where a working generation is paying the taxes that finance the entire previous generation's retirement, a second, equally important consequence emerges. The development of a chain of commitments linking generations makes it extremely difficult to alter pension policies dramatically, especially in the direction of privatization. Since private plans must pay benefits from earnings rather than taxes, privatization means introducing a "funded" system. This presents a "double-payment" problem: current taxpayers must continue to finance current retirees while saving for their own retirement. This "double-payment" problem is likely to create insurmountable political difficulties for privatization advocates.

Indeed, the experience of Social Security during the recent period of budgetary austerity suggests that it maintains a remarkably strong political base. Advocates of cutbacks have repeatedly argued that overall deficit reduction required savings from what is after all by far the largest domestic spending program. Without exception, attempts to enlist Social Security in efforts to reduce the deficit have failed, often with painful political repercussions for those advocating cuts. David Stockman's debacle in 1981, in which proposed sharp cuts in early retirement benefits led to a stunning defeat for Ronald Reagan after a string of legislative victories, was the most dramatic example. However, serious proposals were also floated in 1980, 1985, and 1987 with the same result. Even bipartisan budget summits, built on the principle of "shared sacrifice" and presumably offering the best opportunity to minimize outcry against Social Security cuts, have either floundered on the Social Security issue or stressed that the popular program was "off the table." In 1990, for instance, participants in the budget summit proposed that Medicare shoulder 50 percent of the total reduction in domestic spending, while Social Security remained untouched.

Despite the presence of strong advocates of welfare state retrenchment and on-going budget difficulties, only one circumstance has permitted serious action on Social Security: the threat of trust-fund imbalances within the program itself. By 1982, Democrats and Republicans had to acknowledge that poor economic performance was raising the prospect of major trust fund shortfalls. The problem was particularly delicate for Ronald Reagan. Reagan was reluctant to tamper with Social Security. After the 1981 conflict, the Democrats had quite effectively portrayed the administration as a threat to the elderly. As the trust funds dwindled, the Reagan administration feared that a new initiative would give the Democrats another opportunity to raise the "fairness" issue. Seeking a way out, Reagan announced the creation of a commission to develop a plan for eliminating the projected trust fund deficits. Conveniently, the commission would not report until after the November 1982 mid-term elections.

"Blue-ribbon" commissions can serve an array of purposes, but they very rarely produce policies. However, while the administration may have seen the commission as a useful delaying tactic, House Speaker Tip O'Neill and Senate Majority Leader Howard Baker each appointed members whose support would be essential to any successful bargain. To the surprise of many, key commission members eventually worked out a satisfactory compromise with Reagan's aides.[8] Unlike every other confrontation over Social Security in the 1980s, this struggle actually produced significant program cuts.

Once again, the program's design dictated the prospects for retrenchment. The role of Social Security's financial structure in producing this outcome was evident. As conservatives had long maintained, the existence of a separate "trust fund" which could not be allowed to go "bankrupt" structured the political debate. Faced with the specter of imminent insolvency—probably the only outcome that was more politically dangerous than benefit cuts—a wide range of political actors were forced to embrace a compromise solution.

Given the commission's diverse composition, it was not surprising that the proposals did not call for a radical restructuring of Social Security. The approved changes did, however, include an array of significant revenue and benefit reforms: accelerated payroll tax increases, an increase in payroll taxes for the self-employed, partial taxation of benefits for high-income pensioners, a 6-month COLA delay, and a gradual increase in the retirement age. Although the 1983 Social Security Amendments were widely seen as a compromise based largely on the administration's capitulation, the result was a considerable reduction in long-term benefits. In short, the 1983 Act revealed that American political institutions did not prohibit significant retrenchment. A recent analysis indicated the magnitude of the reductions involved. Between 1985 and 2030, replacement rates for a 65-year-old retiree are projected to fall from 63.8 percent to 51 percent for low earners and 40.9 percent to 35.8 percent for average earners (Aaron et al. 1989).

Yet the reform did not alter the fundamental structure of the American pension system, and suggested that the Reagan administration had given up any radical plans for Social Security. And events since the 1984 election have confirmed the difficulty of imposing Social Security cuts in the absence of a trust fund crisis. Continued concerns about the deficit and recognition that large reductions were unlikely without a contribution from Social Security led politicians to return repeatedly to the topic of pension cutbacks. In 1985 and 1987, Senate Republicans seriously explored possibilities for including Social Security cuts in a larger deficit reduction package, only to retreat after meeting stiff opposition. Each case strengthened Social Security's reputation as the "third rail" of American politics.

MEDICARE

Alone among major industrial nations, the United States has failed to develop a system of national health insurance. The impasse between liberals seeking a larger role for public provision and conservatives (backed by health care providers) seeking to maintain a market-oriented approach has yielded a hybrid system. A predominantly private health care system coexists with two major public programs: Medicare, which provides support to the elderly and disabled who are eligible under Social Security, and Medicaid, a means-tested program restricted largely to those eligible for AFDC and SSI.[9] By the time Reagan entered office, this hybrid system faced a cost explosion.

Demographic and technological pressures increased health care costs, but there is little question that the specific design of the American system greatly exacerbated those pressures. Public health programs inject significant spending into the health care system, but without the controls that might restrain costs. The reliance on a diffuse group of "third parties" to pay medical bills after the fact provides powerful incentives for cost escalation.[10] By the early 1980s, the situation was clearly out of control. Total health expenditures had increased from 6.1 percent of GNP in 1965 to 9.4 percent in 1980 and continued to rise. Public expenditure for Medicare increased even more rapidly.

At first, the Reagan administration sensed little tension between its concern with expenditure constraint and its desire to expand the private sector's role in health care. Conservatives attributed the cost explosion to a too-intrusive public sector; health care inflation reflected the invisibility of costs to consumers. The administration began to design a set of "procompetitive" reforms to foster competition among providers and a heightened awareness of the costs of health care among consumers.[11] Regulatory impediments to a fully functioning health care market were to be stripped away, while the role of third-party payment was to be diminished. Vouchers for Medicare would lead to a new cost-consciousness, as would a cap on tax subsidies to employer-provided health care.

These proposals, however, generated both technical and political difficulties. Few in Congress shared the administration's confidence that a reduced federal role would solve the cost-containment problem. The strategy's reliance on increasing the financial burdens of health care consumers was a major political weakness. "Making the market work" required that consumers pay more of the cost of their care, but this entailed precisely the kind of clearly imposed, visible costs on a large constituency that Congress avoided whenever possible.

Yet the pressure to do something was intensifying. Health care costs continued to rise far faster than inflation in the early 1980s. In 1982 alone, health care costs rose 11 percent while the overall inflation rate was under 4 percent.[12] Like Social Security, the Medicare system faced an impending trust fund crisis. As budget pressures forced Congress to cut popular programs, escalating health care costs became intolerable. In this context, Congress acted. In less than a year, it managed to introduce the most radical reform of Medicare since the program's enactment in 1965: a new system of prospective payments (Russell 1989).

Prospective payment instituted centralized price controls on particular medical activities eligible for Medicare reimbursement. The establishment of elaborate price scales for diagnosis-related groups (DRGs) was designed to impose greater pressures for cost containment. It also represented the kind of governmental regulation of the health care industry that conservatives and medical interests have traditionally fought to avoid. That DRGs nonetheless became law provides a striking indication of the difficult choices the health care cost explosion has created.

Requirements for tougher cost controls were first floated in the deficit-reducing TEFRA legislation of 1982. TEFRA called for strict controls to be introduced if a system of prospective payment was not implemented within a short period. The imposition of this deadline led the Reagan administration and the hospitals (though not the health insurance industry) to back DRGs as the lesser evil. As a result, the legislation flew through Congress, aided by its attachment to the essential Social Security legislation of 1983.

In addition to this important piece of cost-containment legislation, public health programs have been repeated sources of expenditure constraint since 1981. While the trend towards cutbacks has slowed or even been reversed in some areas of social policy, in health care the pressure for austerity has remained high. Medicare has faced sustained retrenchment. Virtually every budget round since 1981 has involved some significant effort to reduce Medicare expenditures. Medicare contributed heavily to the spending cuts agreed to in the "budget summit" of November 1987, and fully one-third of the outlay cuts made in 1988 also came from Medicare (McCarthy 1988, House Ways and Means Committee 1988). The 1990 budget negotiations tested the limits of political tolerance for Medicare retrenchment. The initial bipartisan agreement called for $60 billion in Medicare cuts over five years—almost half of the total projected domestic spending cutbacks. This proposal was widely regarded as so extreme (and so weighted towards direct cuts on beneficiaries) that Congress rejected the entire package, eventually agreeing to $43 billion in cuts falling primarily on providers.[13] Yet the 1990 budget agreement indicated Medicare's precarious position. After a strong public outcry major cuts were still introduced, although they were redesigned to reduce the visible impact on voters. Social Security, by contrast, remained "off the table" throughout the negotiations.

It is extremely difficult to estimate the total size of cutbacks in health care programs. Projections of costs in the absence of reform are inexact, and it is hard to distinguish among "gimmick" cuts that meet budgetary spending targets but do not actually reduce spending, cuts that produce efficiency gains without reducing services, and cuts that reduce services or shift costs to consumers (Shick 1987). Some of the savings represent efficiency gains and much of the burden for real cuts has fallen on providers (Russell 1989).[14] Nonetheless, Medicare's protection of the elderly from the financial risks associated with health care has clearly deteriorated. Between 1980 and 1988, out-of-pocket health care expenses for the elderly rose from 12.8 percent of total income to more than 18.2 percent of total income. Put another way, where in 1980 it took the equivalent of 2.8 Social Security checks to cover health care expenses, in 1988 the average recipient needed to spend 4.5 Social Security checks.[15]

Two major factors account for the health care sector's relative vulnerability. First, the existence of a clear financial crisis within the sector encouraged drastic action. Second, the fragmentation and complexity of the health care sector offered opportunities to shield consumers from the direct impact of cutbacks. The health care crisis was both within and outside public programs (Marmor 1988). General medical cost inflation pushed up prices, while threatening the Medicare trust fund with insolvency. Both aspects of the problem fueled retrenchment. Cutbacks were easier to justify when something was so clearly wrong, and when it could be noted that real spending was actually increasing in spite of retrenchment. The need to balance the trust fund provided a sense of urgency which, as with Social Security, facilitated a rapid response.[16] That the trust fund crisis played a major role is indicated by the initial focus of cutbacks on the "Part A" hospital insurance part of the Medicare program, where trust fund imbalances loomed, rather than "Part B" physician reimbursement, which faced no such crisis.

The structure of health care programs, which allowed politicians to impose retrenchment on health care providers rather than directly on the massive constituency of Medicare and Medicaid consumers, has also facilitated cutbacks. Congress has repeatedly moderated proposed sharp increases in consumers' contributions to health care costs in favor of reductions in reimbursements to hospitals and physicians. While many of these cutbacks may have been passed on to consumers in one form or another, their impact has clearly been less visible and therefore less politically damaging.

As the 1990 budget negotiations made clear, the general atmosphere of austerity has had quite different implications for the two major

programs for the elderly. Social Security, protected by a range of programmatic characteristics that allow supporters to present a united
front, has caused so many problems for retrenchent advocates that
they studiously ignore it despite the huge outlays involved. Medicare,
by contrast, is implicated in the general health care cost explosion;
furthermore, it is far more difficult for program supporters to act in
unison. As a result, budget cutters have repeatedly found it to be a
relatively attractive target.

The Politics of Retrenchment in Canada

As in the United States, it has been the more fully developed public
program that has proven to be most resistant to retrenchment initiatives. Canada, however, has a universal national health insurance
system but an underdeveloped system of public pension provision. In
pensions policy, the debates of the late 1970s and early 1980s concerned expansion of the social insurance component of the Canadian
pensions system—Canada and Quebec Pension Plans (C/QPP). The
demogrant portion of Canadian pensions—Old Age Security (OAS)—
came under fire following the election of the Conservative government
in 1984, while the means-tested income supplement for the elderly,
Guaranteed Income Supplement (GIS) has been untouched by both
Liberal and Conservative governments. While the expansion of public
provision has been stymied, both governments subsidized the growth
of market-based pension provision. Since the 1970s, concern about
rising health care costs has prompted the federal government to search
for ways to curtail its share of the health care burden. Although the
Mulroney government has succeeded in shifting costs to the provinces, the health care system retains strong defenses against fundamental reform.

Pensions

The Canadian pension system is more complex and fragmented than
the system operating in the United States. Earnings-related provision
constituted a late and inadequate addition to the structure of public
provision (Banting 1987, National Council of Welfare 1989). This fragmentation opened the door to Conservative retrenchment efforts.
While not dramatic in their effect, these efforts have certainly reinforced the double-tiering of the system, with high-income seniors
using market-based pension provision while low-income seniors rely
on state provision (Prince 1987, Canada-Finance 1984).

Canadian public retirement provision is composed of several different programs. The first tier of the pension system is federal income transfers such as Old Age Security and the Guaranteed Income Supplement. GIS is an inflation-indexed, means-tested income supplement for the elderly. This program has been untouched in the retrenchment battles of recent years. The OAS was for many years a demogrant program which paid flat rate pensions to all elderly Canadians. As we will discuss below, the OAS has been transformed since the election of a Conservative government in 1984.

In addition, the contributory Canada/Quebec Pension Plan provides earnings-related pensions. The C/QPP was established much later than Social Security and both its contribution and benefit levels are much lower. The C/QPP was not intended to provide anything like full income replacement for retiring workers; rather, in tandem with the OAS, it was to provide a basic minimum income for the elderly. Thus, CPP benefits are limited to a minimum of 25 percent of earnings up to the average industrial wage and contributions are regressively financed above the pensionable limit (Banting 1987).

The relative underdevelopment of the C/QPP compared to Social Security is further complicated by the impact of Canadian federalism on the program. Changes in the C/QPP must be approved by two-thirds of the provinces with two-thirds of the population. Both Ontario and Quebec have de facto vetoes over changes to the Plan—Ontario by virtue of population, Quebec by virtue of the desire to keep the QPP in line with the CPP (Banting 1985). In addition, the nine anglophone provinces (covered by the CPP) have little incentive to favor the expansion of benefit levels because they have used the CPP surplus as a source of inexpensive loans (Baldwin 1987, Kennedy 1989).

The final component of public pension policy in Canada is federal tax assistance to private retirement savings through a number of vehicles such as Registered Retirement Savings Plans (RRSPs). This tax expenditure disproportionately benefits high income earners and constitutes one of the largest tax expenditures in the personal income tax system (Deaton 1989).

The overall result of the Canadian public pension system is that the low-income elderly are fairly well-protected through the GIS but that the mid- and upper-income elderly cannot rely on the public pension system for substantial income replacement. From the late seventies to the mid-eighties, there was an ongoing debate about the balance between public and private provision in Canadian pensions policy. Led by labor, women's groups, welfare organizations, and church groups, the proreform forces argued for the expansion of the Canada Pension Plan, an increase in contributions and benefits as well as a series of reforms to the rules such as mandatory credit splitting upon divorce. The private sector opposed CPP expansion but was divided on the alternative of extending the regulation of private pension plans (Myles 1988a).

The eventual defeat of the proexpansion forces resulted in a set of modest reforms to the CPP which were passed by the Conservatives in 1986. Contribution rates were increased by 0.2 percent for five years, followed by increases of .15 percent per year for the next twenty years. In addition, survivors and disability benefits as well as credit-splitting provisions were strengthened. In 1991, contribution rates were increased again from .15 percent to .2 percent. Nonetheless, increases to the CPP benefit level were not carried out. Moreover, the provincial role in borrowing from the CPP "surplus" remains. Under the 1986 reforms, the CPP fund will continue to be used to finance provincial governments to the extent of an estimated $1.2 billion per year. (Kennedy 1989, Baldwin 1987, Prince 1991).

In contrast to the failure to expand the CPP, tax expenditures on market alternatives in pension provisions have increased. Federal subsidies to private pension savings have resulted in a very high level of RRSP savings. In 1981, RRSPs contributed almost as much to total pension savings as did the C/QPP. The estimated size of the tax expenditure for RRSPs in 1982 was $4.9 billion, making it one of the largest tax expenditures in the personal income tax system (Deaton 1989, Doern 1989). Recent Conservative reforms have phased in increased contribution limits to RRSPs (up to $15,500 in 1995). While the 1986 income tax reform converted many deductions to tax credits, the government's failure to convert RRSP contributions suggests that the Conservatives are well aware of the distributional impact of RRSP expenditure. The effect is to reinforce the division between those with occupational plans and RRSPs and those who depend on the public pension system. Politically, the exacerbation of such divisions may undermine support for CPP expansion. As Myles has commented, "The more the middle classes become dependent on these programs the more ready they will be to support the expansion of the welfare state for the rich and to abandon traditional alliances with the less fortunate."[17]

The most successful of Conservative retrenchment efforts, the clawback of OAS, has exacerbated this cleavage. In 1991, OAS constituted 36 percent of federal transfers to persons and a sizable portion of the average pensioner's income.[18] Thus, recent changes in the program are very important to the welfare of the elderly and to the overall shape of the Canadian pension system. In the 1985 budget, the Conservatives proposed to partially deindex the OAS and Family Allowances as part of its overall deficit reduction strategy. The reaction from Canada's disparate seniors' groups was vociferous and immediate. In a rare Canadian outbreak of demonstrations, petitions, and letters, seniors descended on the government, accusing the Finance Minister and the Prime Minister of betrayal. After two months of intense pressure from seniors, the government backed down on OAS deindexing.[19]

In contrast, the government's 1989 clawback of OAS benefits to high-income seniors attracted very little attention. Prior to the clawback, the highest income earners were left after taxes with about 55 percent of their OAS benefits. The clawback undermines the universality of the OAS program by requiring recipients to pay back their benefits at a rate of 15 percent of individual net income above $50,000. High-income pensioners will pay back all their OAS. The most important effects of the clawback will only develop over time. The income threshold is indexed only to inflation over 3 percent. Thus, more and more seniors will be hit by the clawback as their incomes grow faster than the income threshold. Antipoverty organizations and seniors groups rightly fear that the clawback will erode support for social programs among middle-income earners who will eventually lose their benefits if the clawback is not rescinded (Canada, National Council of Welfare 1989).

The clawback scheme combined low visibility cutbacks, phased in over a lengthy period, with a classic "divide and conquer" strategy that exploited the already weak attachment of the affluent elderly to public sector provision. In contrast to the furor over the 1985 deindexing proposal, the clawback attracted almost no public outcry. Although the leaders of seniors groups, labor, and antipoverty organizations opposed the cut, they were unable to mobilize public support against the measure.[20] While the 1985 deindexing plan had imposed an immediate loss on all seniors, the clawback's immediate effect was restricted to high-income seniors, about 5 percent of the elderly. Furthermore, the clawback divided the losers and obscured the extent of their losses by spreading the cut over a large number of income brackets as well as over time. Thus, the clawback was a much less visible loss to seniors than deindexing. In addition, unlike changes to the CPP, the federal government did not need provincial agreement to proceed with changes to the OAS. The executive was free to proceed with a retrenchment agenda, unconstrained by either public mobilization or provincial interests.

The evolution of Canadian pension policy provides a clear indication that substantial conservative-initiated reform of the welfare state is possible under favorable conditions. The combination of continued inaction on the CPP, the increase in tax expenditure on private pension savings, and the gradual contraction of the OAS have helped solidify a two-tiered pension system. As a result, upper- and low-income seniors may be less likely to discern a common set of interests in state pensions provision.

HEALTH CARE

If the struggle over pensions in Canada has been a classic left-right debate over targeting vs. universalism, federal-provincial relations have fundamentally shaped public debates over Canadian health policy. While provincial involvement in program changes has been a constraining element in the expansion of the CPP, the effect of federalism on Medicare is more complicated. Federal and provincial governments jointly fund Medicare. However, the federal government does not need provincial consent to alter program financing, and because the provinces are responsible for service provision, the burden of federal retrenchment falls on provincial budgets. Since health insurance is popular, both levels of government try to claim political credit for the program. Yet because it has become increasingly expensive, they have also tried to impose the rising costs of the program on each other. Struggles over retrenchment in health care have been couched in terms of a debate over which level of government is responsible for funding health care (Badgley and Badgley 1987, Taylor 1987).

Prior to 1977, provinces had to meet certain conditions to qualify for federal funding. These conditions were: public administration, comprehensive services, access to insured services, universal coverage, and portability of benefits. In return, the federal government provided 50 percent of the national per capita costs of insured services. The important point here is that the federal government was committed to paying 50 percent of actual health care costs and that the federal government could "steer" provincial health programs in line with national objectives. The conditionality of federal funding ensured the provision of roughly similar services in all parts of the country.

As health care costs increased, the federal government attempted to scale back its fiscal contribution. Federal concerns over costs led to negotiation of a new formula—Established Programs Financing (EPF)—governing health care transfers to the provinces in 1977.[21] The EPF established a per capita block grant linked to a three-year moving average of increases in per capita GNP. The federal government also offered the provinces tax points equivalent to one-half of the existing federal contribution to Medicare. Equalization payments were made to poorer provinces to increase the yield of the tax points to the national average and a revenue guarantee was added to the federal transfer. Thus, transfers to the provinces after 1977 included two components: cash transfers and tax points. It is important to note that eligibility for tax point transfers was unconditional; the conditions under the original Medicare legislature applied only to the per capita grant. In addition, the new formula loosened the link between federal funding and the actual cost of Medicare (Badgley and Badgley 1987).

Contrary to the federal government's hopes, the EPF formula did not lead to a decrease in federal funding. Because of the effect of inflation on the financing formula, total EPF spending (including postsecondary education) resulted in an estimated $1.5–1.8 billion more in transfers than the provinces would have received under the previous rules.[22] In reaction to this, when EPF was renewed for 1982–1987, the federal government eliminated the revenue guarantee at a loss of an estimated $5 billion to the provinces for the 1982–1987 period (Taylor 1989). As Medicare costs increased, financial pressures on provincial governments opened the door to creeping privatization (increased extra billing by doctors and user fees in some provinces). Furthermore, neither the original legislation nor the EPF provided a formula for the federal government to enforce conditionality via the withholding of the cash grant except by "overkill" (withholding all federal transfers to punish provinces that permitted extra billing or user fees).

While creeping privatization measures did not affect large numbers of health care consumers, they were highly visible and unpopular symbols in a system of universal, comprehensive public health care. Pressure mounted on the federal government, which was seen as the guarantor of universal and accessible health care, to enforce its own conditions for federal financing. This suited the Liberal government of the day. Intervention in defense of the popular universal program embodied the Trudeau Liberals' vision of the federal government as the instrument for creating national identity. By 1984, the Liberal government had retreated from its centralizing and nationalizing thrust in economic and energy policy; intervention in health care gave the government a popular means to reassert its nationalizing role while passing on the political and financial costs to the provinces.

The Liberal intervention in health care—the Canada Health Act (1984)—strengthened and clarified the federal conditions for health

care financing. The Act established clear criteria governing conditionality and provided sanctions proportional to the extent of provincial
utilization of user fees and extra billing. These conditions only applied to the cash portion of the federal transfer. The federal government could not impose conditions on tax points that had already been
surrendered to the provinces. The Act was resoundingly popular but
failed to secure partisan advantage for the Liberal government as the
Mulroney Tories, in opposition, supported the Act. In Mulroney's
words (Taylor 1989, p. 443), "As far as the Conservative party is
concerned, Medicare is a sacred trust which we will preserve."

While Liberal attempts to curtail federal responsibility for health
care costs were only partly successful, the Conservatives quickly
showed that the federal government's unilateral capacity to alter the
complicated and obscure EPF formula could be used to facilitate retrenchment. In 1986, the Minister of Finance restricted federal transfers under EPF to GNP increases less 2 percentage points. The 1989
budget accentuated this trend by changing the indexing formula to
GNP increases less 3 percentage points (Canada, National Council of
Welfare 1989). The 1990 budget went even further by freezing the cash
component of EPF expenditure at 1989–90 levels, a freeze which was
continued in the 1991–92 budget. These changes will save the federal
government an estimated $2.3 billion over the five-year period begin-
ning in 1991.[23]

The effect of these cuts has been to erode the federal government's
ability to enforce the conditions of the Canada Health Act. The (conditional) cash portion of the federal transfer has decreased relative to
the (unconditional) tax portion. In 1991–92, cash transfers will account for only 41.8 percent of total federal spending on health care,
down from 57.5 percent in 1985.[24] Moreover, if this decremental cut
continues, the cash portion of the federal transfer will be eliminated
by 2008.

In the face of declining federal funding and rising medicare costs,
provincial governments have several options. First, they could attempt
to eliminate the federal cash contribution to medicare (while it still
exists) in exchange for more tax points. This strategy is favored by
Quebec and some Western provinces. If this were to succeed, the
portability, universality, and comprehensiveness of coverage across
the country could be jeopardized in the long run as the federal government would no longer set national standards. Second, the provinces could attempt to cut costs or raise taxes in the face of the fiscal
crunch. NDP governments, in power in British Columbia, Ontario,

and Saskatchewan, pursued this option. And, finally, the provinces can permit extra-billing and user fees.

If the experience of the Canada Health Act is any guide, the creeping privatization of the system will focus the political blame for the erosion of medicare squarely back on the shoulders of the federal government. The Conservative government was willing to cut medicare as long as the complexity of the funding arrangement shielded these cuts from public scrutiny. If user fees and extra-billing begin to appear once again in the system, however, the federal government will be held responsible. While such privatization affects only a very small proportion of health care consumers, the symbolic effect of the erosion of "national standards" is potent indeed.

Thus, conflicting dynamics are at work in this policy area. On the one hand, the complexity of funding and the executive's unimpeded ability to impose relatively invisible funding cuts opens the door to retrenchment. Eventually, however, when fiscal strain in the medicare system opens the door to privatization, the federal strategy is forced out into the open. Because of the popularity of universal and accessible health insurance, no federal government can afford to pay the political price of dismantling it.

Summing Up

Cutting social programs is a difficult political task. Retrenchment generally offers diffuse, uncertain, and long-term benefits, and it frequently imposes immediate and concentrated losses. Voters tend to be more cognizant of losses in any case. Not surprisingly, we find that social programs for the elderly have generally proven to be fairly resilient despite a lengthy period of austerity and conservative governance. There are, however, important exceptions. Caught between escalating health care costs and repeated cutback initiatives by the Reagan and Bush administrations, Medicare in the United States has faced significant pressure. Even more dramatically, the Canadian pension system has been substantially revamped. The Mulroney government introduced reforms that will further institutionalize a two-tiered pension system, based largely on flat-rate benefits for those on modest incomes and state-subsidized private pensions for the affluent.

What accounts for these outcomes? Political struggles over retrenchment in the past fifteen years suggest that governmental success depends heavily on the identification of strategies to prevent the mobilization of program supporters. Where strong opposition to reform has emerged, retrenchment advocates in both countries have generally retreated. Mobilization of opposition can be limited if policy changes are hard to identify or attribute to particular decision-makers, or if the negative repercussions of change are hard to communicate to those affected. Alternatively, mobilization can be reduced if new initiatives divide important interests by affecting some clienteles much more than others.

Under what circumstances, then, are governments likely to be able to prevent the mobilization of program supporters? The comparison of retrenchment efforts demonstrates that different program structures create different opportunities for conservative reformers. For each country's most comprehensive social program (pensions in the United States, health care in Canada), retrenchment has not been a political possibility. These programs enjoy broad popular support. Each possesses features that make cutbacks a risky proposition.

Social Security is the most politically successful program in the history of American social policy. The political benefits of the long phase-in of an extensive pay-as-you-go system have been evident. Unlike Canada's fragmented pension system, which has facilitated efforts to divide potential opponents of cutbacks, Social Security's undisputed central role in retirement provision has made any retrenchment initiatives extremely hazardous. Program structure has also dictated the circumstances where modest retrenchment is possible. Reductions in benefits have only been achieved in the context of efforts to eliminate looming deficits in the program's finances. In the case of Canada's equally popular health care system, retrenchment has been on the agenda because of rising costs. However, neither the federal nor provincial governments want to take the political blame for cuts and both levels of government want to reap the political benefits of preserving the "sacred trust."

The less comprehensive programs discussed here—pensions in Canada, health care in the United States—have proven far more vulnerable. Because these programs are more fragmented, they have provided a number of opportunities for retrenchment advocates to prevent the mobilization of program supporters. The fact that both programs are tightly integrated with extensive private sector arrangements has allowed each government to pursue strategies that incrementally shift the balance between public and private provision. Cutbacks have been designed to affect some beneficiaries and not others. Most effective of all has been the technique adopted with OAS. Retrenchment is being phased in gradually, which both lowers the visibility of the cutbacks and means that at any given time only a small group of the elderly will experience a significant change in their benefits.

If program structure is important, there is also evidence that political institutions play an important if complex role in the retrenchment process.[25] Many have argued that because the concentration of political authority lowers the number of effective veto points, parliamentary systems will have a much greater capacity to pursue radical policy change.[26] By the same logic, programs where central governments have exclusive authority should be more vulnerable than those where different jurisdictions share power. As a basic account of institutional effects, this is persuasive. However, in the case of retrenchment—which often involves the pursuit of unpopular initiatives—this argument must be qualified.

Because governmental power is more centralized in parliamentary systems, accountability is more centralized as well. Governments can act to prevent groups from suffering losses, and the public knows that they can do so. Furthermore, parliamentary arrangements reduce the accountability of the opposition: the opposition is certain to publicize unpopular initiatives, because it can only hope to influence policy by toppling the government. Because of the government's greater accountability in a parliamentary system, it may choose to forgo opportunities that concentrated power would have allowed it to undertake.

Thus, the theoretical case for believing that one institutional arrangement generally favors retrenchment is weak. We are left with the empirical question of whether concentration-of-power effects outweigh accountability effects. The evidence here suggests that in fact they do, but only if the government can identify strategies that successfully demobilize retrenchment opponents. The institutional advantage possessed by a government operating in a parliamentary system is that such strategies, once identified, can be implemented without facing the obstacle course of the American system of checks and balances.

Mulroney's most successful retrenchment effort—the expansion of RRSPs and contraction of OAS—is illustrative. With both deindexing and the clawback, the executive was able to put through legislation without facing the multiple vetoes of the U.S. system of divided authority and weak party discipline. Concentrated authority within the parliamentary system focused political blame on the party in power for highly visible retrenchment efforts (deindexing) but also facilitated low-visibility retrenchment efforts (the clawback). The clawback/deindexing comparison confirms that the concentration of authority characteristic of parliamentary systems is a two-edged sword. Deindexing, a poorly designed retrenchment initiative, resulted in heavy political costs for the Mulroney government.[27] However, centralization also made possible the much more successful clawback strategy.

Federalism is also an important aspect of political institutions. While scholars have examined the role of federalism in the development of the welfare state, the effect of federalism on retrenchment has received less scrutiny (Banting 1987, Cameron 1978). Our comparison suggests that the impact of federalism on retrenchment is not constant, because federalism's shape varies dramatically depending on how program structures allocate authority among different jurisdictions. Federalism clearly constrains reform of the Canada Pension Plan; on the other hand, the federal government can act without provincial consent in the fields of tax expenditures, health care, and federal demogrant programs (OAS). Nonetheless, the impact of federalism in these areas is mixed.

In the case of health care, the federal government's upper hand on financing is tempered by the political risks associated with retrenchment in a popular program. In the short run, the complexity of fiscal transfers to the provinces and the federal government's ability to unilaterally impose spending freezes on the cash portion of the health care transfer gives the federal government leeway for retrenchment by stealth, but federal cuts impose increasing costs on provinces. Financial pressures open the door to cost-saving initiatives at the provincial level that are overwhelmingly unpopular, even if they affect only a small percentage of health care consumers. Implementation of user fees or permission of extra billing are highly symbolic acts that attract immediate public attention. Antiprivatization backlashes from the provinces keep the system in balance by concentrating the political blame on the federal government for failing to "maintain national standards." Thus, while divided authority affects the decision rules governing health care policy, its impact is to eventually and circuitously swing the political blame back to the federal government. All this suggests that the role of federalism is conditional on how particular programs allocate authority among different actors. The relationship between federalism and retrenchment is as complicated as the relationship between federalism and welfare state expansion.

The concise conclusion is that retrenchment is a daunting task, but programs for the elderly may sometimes be politically vulnerable. A majority party in a parliamentary system, unconstrained by federalism, faces the fewest obstacles in pursuing a retrenchment agenda. However, retrenchment policies may nonetheless exact a heavy political cost unless advocates can find a way to demobilize program supporters, either by lowering the visibility of policy changes or by pursuing a "divide and conquer" strategy. Prospects for pursuing these strategies depend crucially on the characteristics of existing programs.

POLICY DIVERGENCE: GENERATIONAL POLITICS IN THE UNITED STATES

Austerity did not end in the late 1980s. Budgetary pressures in both countries have remained acute. However, in the United States the interaction between budgetary politics and the status of public programs for the elderly has begun to undergo a significant change. The late 1970s and early 1980s, we have argued, was marked by a politics of retrenchment in both countries. Programs for the elderly were seen, like other public expenditures, as possible targets for marginal cuts (and not as particularly attractive targets at that). In the past several years, however, the tone of policy debate has shifted in the United States. Fundamental issues of program design have been raised, often in the context of explicit or implicit consideration of intergenerational questions.

Given the very strong political supports that continue to exist for Social Security and the significant if weaker protections of Medicare, it is unlikely that the sudden prominence of intergenerational issues will sharply increase the near-term vulnerability of programs for the elderly. Nonetheless, this emerging generational focus is likely to have a substantial impact on social policy. Across the political spectrum, policy advocates have been led to an age-focused orientation in designing proposals. Conservatives have attempted to utilize the language of generational conflict to encourage retrenchment.[28] Liberals have found that the combination of extensive provision for the elderly, regressive taxes with few immediate benefits for the working population, and continuing deficits provides a poor environment for expansive social policy initiatives. In a moment, we will show how this new generational politics has affected two dramatic social policy struggles of the past few years, over catastrophic health care and the Social Security trust funds. Partly by influencing the definitions of "problems" and partly by influencing how social actors decide who "we" are and who "they" are, age now plays a central role in shaping welfare state politics in the United States. Nothing similar has occurred in Canada, where the politics of social policy revolves around debates defined by issues of class or federalism. Age is simply not a crucial organizing principle, either analytically or politically.

This difference is largely traceable to the differing development paths of the Canadian and U.S. welfare states. Again, the nature of existing social policies has structured politics. When compared with most of Europe, the scope of Canadian social policy is rightly seen as constricted. However, in key areas, Canada succeeded in moving significantly beyond the level of public social provision established in the United States, enacting universal health care, family allowances, and a far more extensive system of unemployment insurance. By contrast, advocates of an expanded social welfare state in the United States were defeated or forced to compromise at crucial junctures. The end result of these failures has been creation of a uniquely age-based structure of social provision with long-term implications that are only now beginning to emerge.

This is not the place to review the historical development of the United States' distinctive welfare state, a task that has recently been executed with great skill (Weir, Orloff, and Skocpol 1988). Neither of the two great waves of Democratic-party-led social reform succeeded in establishing a system which offered extensive public provision for the range of social risks confronting participants in a market economy. Instead, the United States developed a two-tiered welfare state. The first tier, offering social insurance to the elderly, has been extremely popular and has gradually expanded to become a central component of American social life. The second tier, providing means-tested assistance to some categories of the economically and politically marginalized, has been hotly contested, stingy in its provision, and divisive in its effects.

The political consequences of the extensive U.S. reliance on this second tier are now well-understood.[29] By targeting efforts on the have-nots while offering little or nothing to the have-littles, the programs associated with the War on Poverty heightened tensions within the broad coalition of wage-earners that has supported extensive social provision in Europe (and, to a lesser extent, in Canada). That the patterns of government activity often accentuated racial cleavages exacerbated the political problem. Vast elements of the white working class, facing intense economic pressure and increasingly open to the argument that "government is not the solution but the problem" deserted the Democrats beginning in 1968. The new Republican majority in Presidential elections was founded upon a new, antitax alliance between much of the white working class and the Republicans' traditional base.

The scholarly focus on the political consequences of the welfare state's second tier has been understandable. The first tier, after all, was popular, and "universal" in the sense that most Americans could hope to receive benefits under its provisions at some point in their lives. Yet what is distinctive about social provision in the United States is not only the gap between the "second tier" for the poor and the rest of the working-aged population. There is also a gap between the working-aged population and the "first tier" of extensive provision for the elderly. Both of these gaps are lines of potential political cleavage, in which a sense of unequal treatment may galvanize political demands for redress. The gap between the working-aged population and the poor is based on class and race; from the mid-1960s on, it activated a politics of "white backlash" that shattered the New Deal coalition. The gap between the working-aged population and the elderly is, by contrast, based on age. This gap is beginning to generate significant tensions, although the long-term political consequences remain unclear.

The age-based structure of the first social insurance tier has important, so far underappreciated consequences, that have contributed to the growing anxiety about the future of the American welfare state. For reasons to be explained, until recently these consequences have been masked. Even now, it seems highly unlikely that this new "generational politics" will be translated into any direct threat to social provision for the elderly. Yet for some time the United States is likely to be dealing with age-based political dynamics that have no parallel in Canada.

It is worth repeating at this point the two important senses in which we mean that the United States has developed an age-based system of social provision. As table 2.1 suggests, this is true in two important senses. First, a very high proportion of social spending, especially at the national level, is targeted explicitly on the elderly. Second, and less appreciated, the contribution of essentially age-based revenues (payroll taxes) to social provision is much higher than in Canada, which has relied more on general revenues.

In the prolonged period of austerity since the mid-1970s, three factors have made these facts about American social provision more salient. First, the burdens associated with public provision for the elderly have grown considerably. By the mid-1980s, social insurance programs in the United States were rapidly approaching maturity. The days of "popularity on the cheap," when the relatively small size of the eligible population and the large pool of payroll taxpayers delivered the magic combination of low contributions and high benefits,

Table 2.1 GENERATIONAL BENEFITS AND BURDENS IN CANADA AND THE
UNITED STATES, 1990

	Canada	United States
Program for the Elderly		
Share of Federal Social Spending (%)	27.4	55.8[a]
Share of GNP (%)	4.9	6.2[a]
Payroll Taxes		
Share of Federal Revenues (%)	18.1	36.9
Share of GNP (%)	3.4	7.0

Sources: Author's calculations from Congressional Research Service Report #90-EPW,
1991 Budget Perspectives: Federal Spending for the Human Resource Programs, April,
1990, Tables 3.3 and 3.4; House Committee on Ways and Means, *1991 Green Book*
(Washington, D.C.: Government Printing Office), p 1518; Ken Battle and Sherri Torjman,
Opening the Books on Social Spending (Ottawa: Caledon Institute of Social Policy),
1993, pp. 7, 14; Canada, Finance, *Public Accounts of Canada*, 1991, Vol. I, pp. 3.4, 7.5;
Regie des rentes du Quebec, *Le Regime du Rentes du Quebec: Statistiques 1992* (Quebec:
1993), p. 19.
a. 1989

were over. From here on, the programs would have to be truly "pay as
you go" in the sense that the working population needed to pay program costs for the entire retired population. If one includes the employer's share, which most economists agree falls ultimately on the
employee, three-fourths of U.S. taxpayers pay more in FICA taxes than
they do in income taxes. In a context where working-class wages have
been falling, the rising burden of payroll taxes required by the maturing of Social Security and Medicare began to be a political problem.

Second, as the 1980s wore on and the rounds of bitter budget disputes accumulated, it became increasingly clear that not all programs
had experienced the same fate. As two careful analysts (Peterson and
Rom 1988, p. 224) concluded, "The clearest domestic winners during
the Reagan era, as in earlier decades, were the elderly. In fact, the
growth in pensions and medical insurance since 1965 has been so
great that one cannot understand the forces shaping federal fiscal
policy without first coming to terms with this basic fact."[30] This divergence stemmed partly from the maturation of the major social
insurance programs (expanded numbers of beneficiaries, many entitled to larger benefits), partly from the surge in Medicare outlays
generated by mounting health care costs, and partly from the greater
success of programs for the elderly in holding off cutbacks.

Finally, both these aspects of program maturation—increased
spending and increased tax burdens—have coincided with mounting
frustration among policymakers over the political logjam created by

continuing deficits. Reagan aides David Stockman and Richard Darman had accurately predicted in 1981 that the flurry of tax and spending breaks for the wealthy and the military enacted during Reagan's first year in office had put politicians "out of business for a decade" (Stockman 1986, p. 283). The deficit indeed created an enduring political impasse. With control of policy divided between a firmly Democratic Congress and a Republican White House, deficit reduction efforts repeatedly floundered on the unwillingness of either side to accept the other side's proposals. The deficit became everyone's "second best" solution: Democrats preferred it to spending cuts, and Republicans preferred it to tax increases. With policy entrepreneurs nonetheless eager to mount new initiatives, efforts to find ways out of the stalemate have continued. A focus on intergenerational issues has been identified as one such mechanism. Conservatives have hoped that the "generational equity" card could be used to undermine public support for social insurance.[31] Liberals, more warily, are using generational burden issues as a way of drawing attention to the unmet needs of the young and the regressive consequences of tax changes during the 1980s.[32]

The place of generational issues in the politics of U.S. social policy remains ambiguous. The meaning of "generational equity" is itself unclear. Nothing reveals the unsettled form of this developing debate more than the sharp divisions *within* the ranks of both conservatives and liberals about whether to base policy arguments on generational concerns. Nonetheless, an examination of two recent struggles related to programs for the elderly indicates that the framing of issues in age-based terms already has had important political consequences.

From Intergenerational to Intragenerational Transfers: The Medicare Catastrophic Coverage Act

As other contributors to this volume have noted, Medicare's coverage of the health care costs of the elderly is far from comprehensive. Prolonged or acute health problems can be financially devastating for elderly Americans. As health costs continued to climb in the 1980s, advocates for the elderly began pushing vigorously for an expansion of social insurance to address these unmet risks. They received an unexpected boost when the Reagan administration, hoping to offset its tarnished reputation on Social Security, proposed the enactment of insurance against catastrophic health care costs. Democrats in Congress took the opening, and after adding some significant benefits were eventually able to gain the support of key groups such as the AARP.

The result, the Medicare Catastrophic Coverage Act, was passed with substantial bipartisan backing in 1988. It was the most significant programmatic expansion of Medicare since 1965.

Rarely has a bill been so aptly named. The legislation turned out to be a political catastrophe, as relatively affluent senior citizens, many of whom felt that they received little benefit from the new program, were asked to shoulder much of the cost. Facing vocal opposition (most dramatically in a highly publicized street-side confrontation between Ways and Means Chair Dan Rostenkowski and a group of elderly constituents), legislators initially retreated to a set of proposals for scaling back the new program. Finally, only a year after enacting the legislation, Congress capitulated entirely, voting to repeal all the Medicare provisions of the Act.

There is insufficient space to outline here all the twists and turns that produced first enactment and then repeal. The point we wish to emphasize is that the evolution of the catastrophic health care issue reveals how the politics of programs for the elderly has shifted since the early 1980s, with a new focus on intergenerational issues. Repeal of a major middle-class entitlement program was unprecedented, and the history of programs for the elderly would have provided little basis for anticipating such an outcome. What happened was that intergenerational concerns led to a crucial alteration in the design of this entitlement—an alteration that proved politically fatal.

There is widespread agreement that the political problems with the catastrophic act revolved around its financing provisions (Haas 1990). In the past, popular social insurance programs had been financed through payroll taxes. This strategy obscured the distributional consequences of programs by establishing links between generations. The rhetoric of insurance was powerful. Individuals asked to "contribute" could see this as at least implicitly a provision for their own future needs. By contrast, the catastrophic legislation required the relatively well-to-do among the elderly to pay for their own benefits and openly subsidize benefits for their less well-off brethren. The program's designers substituted a politically untenable interclass, intragenerational redistribution for the traditionally acceptable strategy of intergenerational transfers.

Committed to the proposition that the elderly should finance their own benefits, program designers settled on a formula in which a small premium ($48 per year) on beneficiaries would be supplemented by a much larger, income-tested premium. This "surtax" could be as high as $800, but relatively few would pay the highest rate, and the majority of beneficiaries would pay no surtax at all. However, the surtax quickly became a focus of vigorous opposition. General opposition to inter-class transfers was heightened by two factors. First, many of the afflu-ent elderly already had employer-provided insurance or private "medi-gap" policies that made them devalue the new Catastrophic benefits. Second, in part because of rather dubious mass mailings from the National Committee to Preserve Social Security, a far larger percent-age of the elderly expected to pay the full surtax than would actually be required to do so. Despite the continued support of the AARP and compelling evidence that the program represented an excellent value for most recipients, the outcry from the elderly eventually led Con-gress to repeal the new legislation.[33]

The growing concern over intergenerational equity is the key to understanding the fateful decision to scrap a uniquely successful fi-nancing mechanism in favor of a traditionally unsuccessful one. In blunt terms, the elderly were told that if they wanted additional ben-efits they would have to pay for them. President Reagan made this shift inevitable when he promised to veto any expansion of benefits for the elderly financed by payroll taxes or general revenues. However, Reagan's position was widely supported. The issue of who should bear the burden for Catastrophic was discussed in detail in the debate over the initial legislation, and those who had pushed the matter pointed to the financing provisions as a sign of their impact. Senator David Durenberger, a key legislative actor on the Catastrophic Act as well as the principal figure in Americans for Generational Equity, put the issue clearly:

> [Passage of the Catastrophic Act] is a signal this place is ready to do things differently than it has in the past. For the first time we have added a benefit for a large number of Americans without passing the cost of that benefit on to Americans in general in the form of increased general taxation or expanded payroll taxes.[34]

During the long rearguard action against repeal waged by program supporters, the salience of generational issues remained evident. A number of proposals were advanced that would have shifted the pro-gram's financing (either to payroll taxes or general revenues). None could garner widespread support, indicating a fairly broad consensus that the elderly should pay for their own benefits. The Catastrophic story is a remarkable development in United States social policy. Leg-islation rarely gets overturned so rapidly; expansions of entitlements never do. The rise and fall of the Catastrophic Act provides clear evidence that the gap between the American welfare state's first tier and (non)provision for the working-aged population is becoming increasingly relevant.

Distributing Burdens between Generations: The Social Security Trust Fund Debates

To the dismay of many politicians, Social Security was back in the news at the end of 1989. As in the early 1980s, the circumstances revealed the extent to which the program's trust-fund structure shapes Social Security politics. Yet the debates of the past few years have had a different character from those that led eventually to the 1983 Social Security Amendments. In 1983 the issue was straightforward: How do we "save" Social Security? The political problems were solved by isolating discussions of Social Security from all other policy issues. By 1989, Social Security was no longer treated in isolation. Instead, it was seen as a central piece in the complex distributional and political puzzle produced by the interacting trends of increasingly burdensome payroll taxes, unequal spending trends across programs, and the continuing stalemate over persistent deficits.[35] Furthermore, the particular framing of the new Social Security issue was suggestive: What should be done about the payroll tax burdens that current Social Security law imposes on the working-aged population?

One important but little noted consequence of the 1983 Amendments was a very dramatic rise in trust fund reserves. As the baby-boom generation reached its peak earning years, Social Security was scheduled to shift to a partly funded system, accumulating contributions to prepare for the increase in outlays when these large cohorts retire. Trust fund reserves are then scheduled to be drawn down gradually between 2020 and 2045. The fund's projected size is staggering. At its peak in 2020, the OASI fund is scheduled to reach 30 percent of GNP, the equivalent of over $1 trillion in 1984 dollars (Munnell and Blais 1984).

The surplus rapidly became a major issue.[36] Many economists and fiscally conservative politicians worried that the surpluses were simply being used to mask the overall federal budget deficit. The agreement in 1990 to remove Social Security from the unified budget at least partly addressed this concern. However, Senator Moynihan and many liberal Democrats were equally concerned that regressive payroll taxes were funding general federal programs. Moynihan's proposal to return Social Security to a pay-as-you-go basis by cutting payroll taxes received wide-

spread attention and was the subject of sustained controversy both between the two parties and within the Democratic party.

Moynihan's objection was not couched in directly generational
terms. Instead, he criticized the fact that the trust fund surplus was
not really being used to create a partially funded system (i.e., increased savings) but was instead offsetting spending (and borrowing)
elsewhere in the budget. Given the regressive nature of payroll taxes,
he argued, this arrangement was unacceptable. If the budget could not
be balanced, allowing existing payroll taxes to produce a real surplus,
the system should be returned to a pay-as-you-go basis.

There are, however, two important generational aspects of this controversy. First, the payroll tax is levied on the working-aged population, and the heightened focus on FICA burdens raises clear generational issues.[37] Second, the Moynihan initiative reflects the problems
generated by the gap between the U.S. welfare state's first tier and its
nonprovision for most of the working-aged population. It is striking
that liberal Democrats, usually advocates of expanded public provision, settled on a massive tax cut as a central element of their social
policy proposals.[38] Caught in a straight jacket not only by the deficit
but by skepticism among the working-aged population about new
social programs, advocacy of a progressive tax cut seemed the most
promising way of attracting working-class "Reagan Democrats" back
to the Democratic coalition.

How this issue will be resolved is unclear. So far, the Moynihan
proposal has lost two major votes in the Senate.[39] For the foreseeable
future the deficit is likely to remain a major barrier to such a massive
tax cut. However, the surplus will continue to mount, and the issue is
therefore unlikely to go away. It is very doubtful that this represents a
major challenge to Social Security. The purpose of the proposal, after
all, is simply to return the system to its traditional pay-as-you-go
basis.[40] As with Catastrophic, what the emergence of this issue demonstrates is the growing concern that social policy in the United States
is unbalanced. We can expect continued efforts by both parties to
appeal to the large segment of the increasingly strapped working-aged
population that perceives itself as the government's paymaster but has
little sense of receiving benefits in return.

CONCLUSION

The welfare state in both Canada and the United States has faced
serious challenges in the past 15 years. Protracted economic difficul-

ties and conservative governance have tested the limits of political support for public social provision. In general, programs for the elderly have proven to be durable. These programs are popular, and while conservative governments have managed to restrain spending growth, they have not been willing to pay the political costs that a more radical strategy would exact. There are important exceptions, however. The record is a complex one, even when limited to the four programs studied here. Nonetheless, we would suggest that the evidence supports a straightforward conclusion. The more comprehensive programs in the two countries (Social Security in the United States, health care in Canada) have been the most politically successful. Public social provision is most secure when it has a broad but cohesive political base and where the benefits provided are clear and immediate. Advocates of retrenchment found their opportunities largely shaped by the programmatic choices of their predecessors. Only when preexisting program structures made it possible to divide opponents and obscure what policymakers were doing did opportunities for cutbacks emerge.

The narrow scope of social policy also helps to explain why age-based instabilities are now emerging in the United States but not in Canada. The failure of the United States to develop a range of programs that provide clear benefits to all generations is beginning to emerge as a major weakness in public social provision. The impact of this development is unclear, although the repeal of catastrophic care legislation suggests that a widespread sense that the elderly have "more than their share" is likely to impede any expansion of public provision for the elderly. Yet as this volume indicates, the gaps in American provision for the elderly are far less extensive than for other age cohorts. Ironically, the indirect effect of imbalances in American social provision may well be to retard extensions of public provision to the nonelderly. Skepticism about the public sector among the electorate is widespread. The push among liberals to roll back payroll taxes on the working class is only the most striking reflection of a common and understandable sense among working-aged Americans that taxes they pay always go to benefit someone else.

Notes

We would like to thank Peter B. Rutledge for research assistance and helpful suggestions and Ted Marmor, Robert Binstock, Jon Oberlander, and Michael Wolfson for comments on an earlier draft of this paper.

1. On all these points, but especially the last, see Klein and O'Higgins (1988).

2. For detailed discussions of the distinctiveness of retrenchment politics, see Weaver (1986) and Pierson (forthcoming).

3. See, for example, Heclo (1985), Esping-Andersen (1985), and Weir, Orloff, and Skocpol (1988).

4. On the first point see Arnold (1990). On the second point, see Tversky and Kahneman (1981) and Kahneman and Tversky (1984).

5. On indexation as a mechanism of "blame avoidance," see Weaver (1988).

6. For a more detailed discussion, see Pierson (1992).

7. Social Security's first pensioner, Ida May Fuller, received 25 years of benefits following her retirement in 1940, having paid a total of $24.50 in payroll taxes.

8. For a detailed account of the negotiations, see Light (1985).

9. On the development of the health care system in the United States, see Starr (1982) and Marmor (1973).

10. As scholars have noted, the weak arsenal of cost controls was the price paid for the passage of Medicare and Medicaid. See Starr (1982). For a comparative analysis which lucidly outlines the flaws in America's hybrid system, see Evans (1986).

11. See *National Journal*, September 12, 1981, pp. 1616–20; *Congressional Quarterly Almanac 1981*, p. 474; *National Journal*, January 22, 1983, pp. 170–73.

12. See *Congressional Quarterly Almanac 1983*, p. 392.

13. See *Congressional Quarterly Weekly Report*, October 6, 1990, pp. 3217–22; *Congressional Quarterly Weekly Report*, October 13, 1990, pp. 3416–418; *Congressional Quarterly Weekly Report*, November 3, 1990, p. 3700.

14. Russell's research suggests that the DRG reform has moderated health care cost increases without spurring significant cost-shifting to patients.

15. Report prepared by Ed Roybal, Chair, House Select Committee on Aging. See U.S. Congress (1988).

16. This pressure is certain to continue and will likely generate further retrenchment in the future. See Holahan and Palmer (1988).

17. See Myles (1988b). Also on the low visibility of tax expenditures in the Canadian system, see Doern (1989).

18. Calculated from *Canada, 1990–91 Estimates: Part I The Government Expenditure Plan*, pp. 71, 74.

19. On the government's proposals see Canada, Finance (1985); see also, Canada, Health and Welfare (1985). For some fine examples of "stab in the back" and "granny bashing" rhetoric, see *Toronto Star*, June 4, 1985, pp. A1, A14 and June 22, 1985, p. A1.

20. That the clawback posed important problems of visibility for interest groups is clear from the testimony of the groups appearing before the Commons committee considering the plan. See House of Commons, *Minutes of Proceedings and Evidence of the Legislative Committee on Bill C-28*, pp. 1–43ff. On elderly lobbies, see Gifford (1990); Riddell-Dixon and Riddell-Dixon (1987).

21. EPF also governs transfers to the provinces for postsecondary education.

22. See Canada, Parliamentary Task Force on Federal-Provincial Relations (1981). For a sophisticated evaluation of the effects of EPF on federal contribution levels, see Brown (1986).

23. See Canada, *1991–92 Estimates: Part I The Government Expenditure Plan*, pp. 11, 41; Canada, *1990–91 Estimates: Part I The Government Expenditure Plan*, p. 72–73.

24. Calculated from Canada, Health and Welfare, *1986–87 Estimates: Part III Expenditure Plan*, p. 2–23; *1987–88 Estimates: Part III Expenditure Plan*, 2–21; *1988–89 Estimates: Part III Expenditure Plan*, 2–21; *1989–90 Estimates: Part III Expenditure Plan*, 2–21; *1990–91 Estimates: Part III Expenditure Plan*, 2–52; *1991–92 Estimates: Part III Expenditure Plan*, 2–53.

25. We draw here on the argument developed in Pierson and Weaver (1993).

26. See, for example, Lloyd Cutler (1980).

27. The deindexing debacle also suggests that the importance sometimes given to interest group organization needs to be qualified. Canada's elderly lobby is relatively weak; not only does it lack the channels to legislative influence enjoyed by U.S. elderly lobbies, but it has little access to the crucial bureaucratic networks enjoyed by other interest groups in the Canadian system. Yet in the deindexing case, the elderly lobby was able to mobilize intense opposition. Despite their lack of an institutional foothold in the legislature and limited access to the bureaucracy, the elderly lobbies were successful in defeating an unpopular measure. This suggests that even a weak set of interest groups can achieve success in the face of a poorly designed retrenchment strategy that imposes widespread and immediate losses.

28. The development of Americans for Generational Equity, a group financed largely by elements of the "private welfare state," is illustrative of the possibilities for using generational equity arguments to promote a strategy of dismantling public social provision. On this point see Quadagno (1989). AGE is a symptom of the generational politics, but it is hardly the cause. Politically, AGE has been a marginal actor. Even before recent scandals weakened its credibility, its annual budget of about $400,000 was modest by Washington standards. AGE's initiatives were significantly shaped by the political needs of its driving force, Senator David Durenberger. The willingness of private corporations to fund it probably reflected their desire to curry favor with the ranking Republican on the Senate's health subcommittee rather than any belief that AGE would spearhead a transformation of the welfare state. On AGE's peculiar structure and recent difficulties, see Black (1990).

29. The extensive literature includes Rieder (1985); Kuttner (1987); Wilson (1987); Weir, Orloff, and Skocpol (1988); Skocpol (1991).

30. Indeed, the "second tier" of means-tested programs also fared better in the Reagan years than is generally recognized. It was the "everything else" category of domestic spending that fell drastically in the 1980s (Peterson 1992).

31. The work of Peter Peterson is representative; see Peterson (1987) and Peterson and Howe (1988). For a critique, see Marmor, Mashaw, and Harvey (1990).

32. A recent, well-publicized Ford Foundation report on social policy was framed explicitly in generational terms, calling for greater funding of programs for children and the working aged, to be financed by a tax on social security benefits. See Ford Foundation (1989).

33. The role of the AARP helps to explain how Congress could make such a remarkable reversal in such a short period, despite the many institutional barriers to policy change in the United States. AARP initially had doubts about the legislation, but was brought on board when a significant prescription drug benefit was added to the package. AARP's support was taken as clear evidence that "the elderly" favored the program. However, this assumption was based on AARP's record with previous initiatives which relied on traditional, intergenerational financing. What became clear in the Catastrophic case was the inability of the AARP to "deliver" the elderly in the context of intragenerational financing, especially when forced to contend with interest groups eager to issue competing appeals to the elderly.

34. See *Congressional Quarterly Weekly Report*, October 31, 1987, p. 2678.

35. Here, again, the Canadian contrast is revealing. Although the CPP has been in surplus while the federal budget is in acute deficit, few draw any connection between the two facts. The rules governing CPP funds ensure that the fund is not counted as part of general government revenue. Indeed, part of the deal that secured provincial agreement to the CPP was that provinces could borrow the surplus in the CPP fund. This surplus is not entangled with the deficit, nor is it available as an object of political contestation.

36. Senator Daniel Moynihan's skillful press campaign is often credited with this development. However, the growing magnitude of the imbalances between payroll tax receipts and program outlays was bound to create a reaction at some point. Competing proposals emerged well before Moynihan's was announced. See Haas (1989).

37. It is worth noting that Moynihan has been active in promoting efforts to respond to increasing child poverty rates and the problems of the working poor. Despite recent increases in the Earned Income Tax Credit, high payroll taxes are particularly burdensome for low-income workers.

38. This helps to explain the peculiar coalitions generated by Moynihan's proposal. Mainstream Republications, including former President Bush, remained adamantly opposed. However, the more "Reaganite" right was fairly supportive, arguing that a tax cut was a tax cut. The fact that the Democratic party was both the opposition and part of the government helps define its internal divisions. Those responsible for budgetary propriety (especially Bentsen and Rostenkowski, but also Foley) opposed Moynihan's proposal. Those eager to act as an opposition and dedicated to efforts to reconstruct a Democratic electoral coalition were supportive (e.g., Gephardt, DNC Chairman Ron Brown, Mario Cuomo).

39. In April 1991, following intense lobbying by the White House, Bentsen, and others, two dozen Democrats voted against the plan, which was defeated 60–38.

40. Indeed, this might be a safer status for Social Security, since it would reimpose the "double payment" problem which constitutes a major barrier to privatization initiatives. In the long run a large surplus could open up avenues for privatization strategies. A number of Republicans have suggested that taxpayers be allowed to contribute their "surplus" contributions to alternative private plans in return for reduced Social Security entitlements.

References

Aaron, Henry J., Barry P. Bosworth, and Gary Burtless. 1989. *Can Americans Afford to Grow Old?* Washington, D.C.: Brookings.

Arnold, R. Douglas. 1990. *The Logic of Congressional Action.* New Haven: Yale University Press.

Badgley, C. Charles, and Robin F. Badgley. 1987. "Health and Inequality: Unresolved Policy Issues." In *Canadian Social Policy,* rev. ed., edited by Shankar A. Yelaja. Waterloo: Wilfred Laurier University Press. 50–51.

56   *Economic Security and Intergenerational Justice*

Baldwin, Bob. 1987. "Pension Reform." *Canadian Labour* 32 (3, March): 12–15.
Baldwin, Peter. 1990. *The Politics of Social Solidarity.* Cambridge: Cambridge University Press.
Banting, Keith. 1985. "Institutional Conservatism: Federalism and Pension Reform." In *Canadian Social Welfare Policy: Federal and Provincial Dimensions,* edited by Jacqueline S. Ismael. Kingston and Montreal: McGill-Queen's University Press. 48–74.
————. 1987. *The Welfare State and Canadian Federalism.* 2nd ed. Kingston and Montreal: McGill-Queen's University Press.
Black, Edwin. 1990. "The Tragedy of Senator Dave Durenberger." *Podiatry Today* (January): 26–39.
Brown, Malcolm C. 1986. "Health Care Financing and the Canada Health Act." *Journal of Canadian Studies* 21(2): 111–132.
Cameron, David R. 1978. "The Expansion of the Public Economy: A Comparative Analysis." *American Political Science Review* 72: 1243–61.
Canada, Finance. 1984. *A New Direction for Canada: An Agenda for Economic Renewal.* 70–75.
————, Finance. 1985. *The Fiscal Plan* (May): 2–5.
————, Health and Welfare. 1985. *Child and Elderly Benefits Consultation Paper* (January).
————, National Council of Welfare. 1989. *The 1989 Budget and Social Policy* (September).
————, Parliamentary Task Force on Federal-Provincial Relations. 1981. *Fiscal Federalism in Canada.*
Cutler, Lloyd. 1980. "To Form a Government." *Foreign Affairs* 59, (1, Fall): 126–43.
Deaton, Richard Lee. 1989. *The Political Economy of Pensions: Power, Politics and Social Change in Canada, Britain and the United States.* Vancouver: University of British Columbia.
Doern, G. Bruce. 1989. "Tax Expenditure and Tory Times: More or Less Policy Discretion?" In *How Ottawa Spends 1989–90,* edited by Katherine A. Graham. Ottawa: Carleton University Press. 75–106.
Doern, G. Bruce, et al. 1988. *Public Budgeting in Canada: Politics, Economics, and Management.* Ottawa: Carleton University Press.
Esping-Andersen, Gösta. 1985. *Politics Against Markets: The Social Democratic Road to Power.* Princeton: Princeton University Press.
Evans, Robert G. 1986. "Finding the Levers, Finding the Courage: Lessons from Cost Containment in North America." *Journal of Health Politics, Policy and Law* 11 (4): 585–615.
Ford Foundation Project on Social Welfare and the American Future. 1989. *The Common Good: Social Welfare and the American Future.* New York: Ford Foundation. (May).
Gifford, C.G. 1990. *Canada's Fighting Seniors.* Toronto: Lorimer.
Haas, Lawrence. 1989. "Security Blanket." *National Journal* (December 9): 2999–3002.

————. 1990. *Running on Empty: Bush, Congress and the Politics of a Bankrupt Government.* Homewood, Ill.: Business One Irwin.

Heclo, Hugh. 1974. *Modern Social Politics in Britain and Sweden.* New Haven: Yale University Press.

Holahan, John, and John L. Palmer. 1988. "Medicare's Fiscal Problems: An Imperative for Reform." *Journal of Health Politics, Policy and Law* 13 (1, Spring): 53–81.

Kahneman, Daniel, and Amos Tversky. 1984. "Choices, Values and Frames." *American Psychologist* 39 (April): 341–50.

Kennedy, Bruce. 1989. "Refinancing the CPP: The Cost of Acquiescence." *Canadian Public Policy* 15 (1):34–42.

Klein, Rudolf, and Michael O'Higgins. 1988. "Defusing the Crisis of the Welfare State: A New Interpretation." In *Social Security: Beyond the Rhetoric of Crisis*, edited by Theodore R. Marmor and Jerry L. Mashaw. Princeton: Princeton University Press. 203–26.

Kuttner, Robert. 1987. *The Life of the Party: Democratic Prospects in 1988 and Beyond.* New York: Viking Penguin.

Light, Paul. 1985. *Artful Work: The Politics of Social Security Reform.* New York: Random House. 163–228.

Marmor, Theodore R. 1973. *The Politics of Medicare.* Chicago: Aldine.

————. 1988. "Coping with a Creeping Crisis." In *Social Security: Beyond the Rhetoric of Crisis*, edited by Theodore R. Marmor and Jerry L. Mashaw. 177–79.

Marmor, Theodore R., Jerry L. Mashaw, and Philip L. Harvey. 1990. *America's Misunderstood Welfare State: Persistent Myths, Enduring Realities.* New York: Basic. 136–74.

McCarthy, Carol M. 1988. "DRGs—Five Years Later." *New England Journal of Medicine* 318 (23 June): 1683.

Munnell, Alicia H., and Lynn E. Blais. 1984. "Do We Want Large Social Security Surpluses?" *New England Economic Review* (September–October) 5–21.

Myles, John. 1988a. "Social Policy in Canada." In *North American Elders: United States and Canadian Perspectives*, edited by Eloise Rathbone-McCuan and Betty Havens. New York: Greenwood Press. 37–53.

————. 1988b. "Postwar Capitalism and the Extension of Social Security into a Retirement Wage." In *The Politics of Social Policy in the United States*, edited by Margaret Weir, Ann Shola Orloff, and Theda Skocpol. Princeton: Princeton University Press, 265–84.

National Council of Welfare. 1989. *A Pension Primer.* Ottawa: National Council of Welfare.

O'Higgins, Michael. 1986. "Public/Private Interaction and Pension Provision." In *Public/Private Interplay in Social Protection*, edited by Martin Rein and Lee Rainwater. Armonk, N.Y.: M.E. Sharpe. 99–148.

Peterson, Paul E. 1992. "The Rise and Fall of Special Interest Politics." *The Politics of Interests: Interest Groups Transformed*, edited by Mark P. Petracca. Boulder: Westview. 326–42.

Peterson, Paul E., and Mark Rom. 1988. "Lower Taxes, More Spending, and Budget Deficits," *The Reagan Legacy*, edited by Charles O. Jones. Chatham, N.J.: Chatham House Press, 213–240.

Peterson, Peter G. 1987. "The Morning After." *The Atlantic Monthly* (October): 43–69.

Peterson, Peter G., and Neil Howe. 1988. *On Borrowed Time: How the Growth of Entitlement Spending Threatens America's Future*. San Francisco: ICS Press.

Pierson, Paul. 1992. " 'Policy Feedbacks' and Political Change: Contrasting Reagan and Thatcher's Pension Reform Initiatives." *Studies in American Political Development* 6 (2): 361–392.

Pierson, Paul. Forthcoming. *Dismantling the Welfare State? Reagan, Thatcher and the Politics of Retrenchment*. Cambridge: Cambridge University Press.

Pierson, Paul, and R. Kent Weaver. 1993. "Political Institutions and Loss Imposition: Pension Cutbacks in Britain, Canada and the United States." In *Do Institutions Matter?*, edited by R. Kent Weaver and Burt Rockman. Washington, D.C.: Brookings Institution, 110–150.

Prince, Michael J. 1987. "How Ottawa Decides Social Policy." *The Canadian Welfare State: Evolution and Transition*, edited by Jacqueline S. Ismael. Edmonton: University of Alberta Press. 247–273.

———. 1991. "From Meech Lake to Golden Pond: The Elderly, Pension Reform and Federalism in the 1990s." In *How Ottawa Spends: The Politics of Fragmentation (1991–92)*, edited by Frances Abele. Ottawa: Carleton University Press. 307–356.

Quadagno, Jill. 1989. "Generational Equity and the Politics of the Welfare State." *Politics and Society* 17 (3): 353–76.

Riddell-Dixon, Elizabeth, and Gretta Riddell-Dixon. 1987. "Seniors Advance, The Mulroney Government Retreats: Grey Power and the Reinstatement of Fully Indexed Pensions." In *Contemporary Canadian Politics*, edited by Robert J. Jackson, et al. Scarborough: Prentice Hall.

Rieder, Jonathan. 1985. *Canarsie: The Jews and Italians of Brooklyn against Liberalism*. Cambridge: Harvard University Press.

Russell, Louise B. 1989. *Medicare's New Hospital Payment System: Is It Working?* Washington, D.C.: Brookings Institution.

Shick, Allen. 1987. "Controlling the 'Uncontrollables': Budgeting for Health Care in an Age of Mega-Deficits." In *Charting the Future of Health Care*, edited by Jack A. Meyer and Marion Ein Lewin. Washington, D.C.: The American Enterprise Institute. 13–34.

Simeon, Rochard, and Ian Robinson. 1990. *State, Society, and the Development of Canadian Federalism*. Toronto and Ottawa: University of Toronto Press and Supply and Services Canada.

Skocpol, Theda. 1991. "Targeting Within Universalism: Politically Viable Policies to Combat Poverty in the United States." In *The Urban Underclass*, edited by Christopher Jencks and Paul E. Peterson. Washington, D.C.: Brookings Institution, 411–436.
Starr, Paul. 1982. *The Social Transformation of American Medicine.* New York: Basic Books.
Stockman, David. 1986. *The Triumph of Politics.* New York: Harper and Row.
Taylor, Malcolm G. 1987. *Health Insurance and Canadian Public Policy*, 2nd edition. Kingston and Montreal: McGill-Queen's University Press.
————. 1989. "Health Insurance: The Roller Coaster in Federal-Provincial Relations." In *Federalism and Political Community*, edited by David P. Shugarman and Reg Whitaker. Peterborough: Broadview Press. 73–92.
Tversky, Amos, and Daniel Kahneman. 1981. "The Framing of Decisions and the Psychology of Choice," *Science* 211 (30 Jan.): 453–58.
U.S. Congress. House. Ways and Means Committee. 1988. *Background Material and Data on Programs Within the Jurisdiction of the Committee on Ways and Means.* Washington, D.C.: Government Printing Office.
————. House. Select Committee on Aging. "An Assault on Medicare and Medicaid in the 1980s: The Legacy of an Administration." October 1988.
Weaver, R. Kent. 1988. *Automatic Government.* Washington, D.C.: Brookings Institution.
————. 1986. "The Politics of Blame Avoidance." *Journal of Public Policy* 6: 371–398.
Weir, Margaret, Ann Shola Orloff, and Theda Skocpol, eds. 1988. *The Politics of Social Policy in the United States.* Princeton: Princeton University Press.
White, Joseph, and Aaron Wildavsky. 1990. *The Deficit and the Public Interest.* New York: Russell Sage.
Wilson, William Julius. 1987. *The Truly Disadvantaged: The Inner City, the Underclass, and Public Policy.* Chicago: University of Chicago Press.

Chapter Three

THE POLITICS OF INCOME SECURITY FOR THE ELDERLY IN NORTH AMERICA: FOUNDING CLEAVAGES AND UNRESOLVED CONFLICTS

John Myles and Jill Quadagno

In the comparative literature on the welfare state, political theorists emphasize the similarity between Canada and the United States because of their similar mix of fiscal, labor market, and social policies. An important part of the similarity is the relative failure of organized labor ("the working class") to acquire a determining role in shaping these institutions. The apparent likeness of their political, economic, and policy structures makes Canada and the United States ideal-typical "liberal" welfare states.

Even within otherwise similar nations, however, there are important differences. Nowhere is this more evident than in the content of recent debates over the "welfare-state for the elderly." During the late 1970s and 1980s, the American public was caught up with the "crisis of social security." American Social Security, it was argued, was facing a trillion-dollar deficit. Early in his first term, President Ronald Reagan announced that it would be necessary to slash Social Security in order to save it. During this same period Canadians were engaged in the Great Pension Debate over how to *enlarge* Canada's income security system for the elderly.

In the middle of the 1980s, American old age politics entered a new phase. If Armageddon would not come as a result of a trillion dollar deficit, it would come as a result of an intergenerational class war. Sometime in the future America would blow up in a clash between cane-wielding "greedy grannies" and their over-taxed offspring.

Despite geographical proximity and the penetration of America's mass media in Canada, the apocalyptic scenarios that were so successful in capturing the American imagination had little success north of the border. While acknowledging that government expenditures on the elderly will rise in the future, until recently Canadian elites have accepted this development with relative equanimity.[1] In

1985, the new Conservative government of Brian Mulroney proposed a partial deindexation of universal Old Age Security benefits on the grounds that they were providing benefits to retired bank presidents, i.e., to the "rich." The rhetoric, however, was not that of intergenerational equity, but rather a traditional populist critique of social transfers to the rich. But even this modest version of the "greedy grannies" scenario was rejected.

How can we explain these differences? Do they merely reflect the more measured and restrained tones said to characterize Canadian political culture?[2] Possibly. But we think there is more to it than this. Old age politics in the two countries differ not only in the tones in which debates are conducted but also in the groups mobilized, the cleavages invoked, and the alliances created in the course of these debates. The reasons for this, we argue, is that national differences in debates *about* the welfare state are a function of the cleavages and interest groups created *by* the welfare state.

This argument may seem to transpose the traditional relationship between economic and political factors and social policy. More commonly, social cleavages and interest groups created by divisions of class, sex, race, and region are called upon to explain the *development* of social policy. But as Esping-Andersen (1990) has pointed out, once established, welfare states also *create* new political constituencies and social divisions.

In some respects, Canada and the United States moved along similar trajectories. However, they differed considerably in the timing of their development, the constituencies who were protected, the method of financing, and, most importantly, in the degree to which their respective welfare states incorporated and protected the non-elderly. We contend that these differences result from the way historic cleavages rooted in language and region in Canada and race in the United States have shaped the evolution of social policy in the two countries. In Canada, the welfare state has been a tool of national elites in the struggle to create a pan-Canadian identity in a nation whose construction has always been problematic. In the United States, racial cleavages—the legacy of slavery—was, and continues to be, the dominant force shaping American social policy.

THE ORIGINS OF OLD AGE SECURITY IN CANADA AND THE UNITED STATES

Modern welfare states have two functions: a social assistance function to redistribute income from the "rich" to the "poor" and a social insurance function to redistribute risk and to even out income flows over the life cycle. The first of these functions is often captured with the imagery of the "safety net": the state creates an income floor to catch those who fall out of the market. After World War II, countries that followed in the Beveridge tradition attempted to make the social safety net "universal," to provide all citizens with minimum standards of subsistence. But virtually all post-war welfare states went beyond the Beveridge model to develop nationally legislated *retirement pensions*, earnings-based benefits intended to permit (or induce) elderly workers to exit from the labor market with benefits sufficient to maintain preretirement living standards (i.e., income security).

In both their safety nets and in their earnings-based programs, the United States and Canada share some striking similarities but also key differences. Both countries stand out among the industrialized, capitalist nations as welfare state laggards. Canada's first national pension legislation for the elderly, the Old Age Pensions Act (OAP), was not introduced until 1927. Eight years later, in 1935, the Social Security Act was passed in the United States.

The major reforms of the two decades following World War II, extended coverage to include groups excluded by the initial legislation. In Canada, this was accomplished in a single stroke with the Old Age Security Act (OAS) of 1951. The means-test of the OAP was removed and benefits were now extended to all citizens over the age of 70 and, by 1970, to everyone over 65. In the United States, Social Security Amendments in 1950, 1954, 1956, and 1965 extended coverage to farm workers and domestic workers, state and local government employees, most self-employed professionals, and members of the armed forces.

They were also similar in regard to the generosity of their welfare states. Until the 1970s, both countries spent remarkably little on the elderly and provided comparatively low (and similar) levels of income replacement. By the early 1970s the average expenditure per beneficiary calculated as a ratio of GDP per capita was .291 in Canada and .259 in the United States, compared to an OECD average of .360 (OECD 1976). The income replacement rate for an elderly couple with average earnings in 1969 was .41 in Canada and .44 in the United States (Aldrich 1982). In contrast, the average replacement rate for nine European countries in 1969 was .54.

Finally, both countries experienced a significant rise in pension expenditures during the 1970s, as a result of reforms implemented during the 1960s and 1970s.

These broad similarities in the welfare state trajectories of the two countries conceal important differences, however. The initial Canadian legislation of 1927 was a classical liberal (pro-cyclical) act, which was introduced during an economic boom and provided no more than very low means-tested benefits for the elderly "poor." The 1935 legislation in the United States, in contrast, was part of a proto-Keynesian (counter-cyclical) body of legislation introduced in the midst of the Great Depression and had two components rather than one. The first component was the Old Age Assistance program (OAA), which, like the Canadian OAP, was a traditional social assistance program targeted at those elderly who through chance and circumstance found themselves "poor" in their declining years. But, the Social Security Act also contained an earnings-based Old Age Insurance program (OAI), the component now most closely identified with Social Security in the United States. Though modest in benefit levels and coverage, OAI was a decidedly forward-looking piece of legislation for a welfare state "laggard." It was, in William Graebner's terms, a piece of "retirement legislation" designed to reduce the massive unemployment of the Great Depression by removing older people from the work force (Graebner 1980). Sweden did not introduce a comparable insurance program until 1958, Canada until 1965, and the United Kingdom until 1975!

A second important difference is the character of the means-tested social assistance programs for the elderly. The Canadian Old Age Pensions Act of 1927 authorized the federal government to enter an agreement with the provinces to reimburse half the cost of pensions that met the requirements of the federal act. These requirements included the benefit level set at $240 per year paid in monthly installments and subject to a means test.[5] It also provided for uniform standards of eligibility. In the United States, in contrast, the states were free to pay OAA pensions of any amount and had the right to set eligibility criteria more stringent than those stipulated in the federal bill (Quadagno 1988).

Early introduction of earnings-based income security in the United States (1935) and late introduction of a comparable one in Canada (1965) had a profound effect on the subsequent development of the two systems. By the 1960s—when organized labor in both countries was pressing for a national pension scheme—American pension experts had three decades of experience with national earnings-related pensions. In Canada they were a novelty. According to Derthick (1978), a "ratchet" approach to improving the value of Social Security benefits was a deliberate strategy of the program's chief executives almost from inception. Although the American reforms of the late 1960s and early 1970s were profound, program administrators were able to build on a system already in place.

By contrast, Canadian reforms of the 1960s required a major departure from the past and a major new piece of legislation (the Canada and Quebec Pension Plans or C/QPP).

It was soon apparent that the American reforms had been more dramatic and more successful than the Canadian. In the late 1960s, the income replacement rate for an aged couple differed little in the two countries (.41 in Canada and .44 in the United States). By 1980, the gap had widened. According to Aldrich's estimates the income replacement rate for an elderly couple was .66 in the United States and .49 in Canada. For a single worker, the gap was smaller but still substantial—.44 in the United States and .34 in Canada.[6] In Canada, public pension expenditure as a percentage of gross national product (GNP) rose from 3.2 to 5.4 percent between 1970 and 1985. In the United States, it rose from 5.1 to 8.2 percent (OECD 1988).

The evolution of income support for low-wage workers and those marginal to the labor force—the social safety net—followed a rather different trajectory, with the Canadian system doing considerably better. In Canada the 1927 legislation provided for means-tested but uniform benefits for all Canadians over age 70. The 1951 Old Age Security Act (OAS) legislation extended these benefits to all Canadians over age 70 and, by 1971, to all Canadians over age 65. These changes established a universal and standard floor for all Canadians irrespective of past earnings or other income. The initial benefit of $40 per month was approximately 20 percent of the average wage which, for a couple, meant a monthly benefit that was 40 percent of the average wage. In 1967, the Guaranteed Income Supplement (GIS) was added based on an income (not a means) test. By 1985 the combination of the OAS and GIS provided an income floor equal to 50 percent of the average wage for an elderly couple and 31 percent of the average wage for a single individual.

In contrast, as noted, the safety net adopted in the United States (OAA) provided variable benefits and criteria of eligibility. Not until the advent of SSI in 1972 did the program become truly national in scope. And unlike the Canadian GIS, which is based on an income test, SSI is means tested. Because assets as well as income are counted in establishing eligibility for SSI, it retains the stigma of welfare, access is more difficult, and take-up rates indicate that up to 40 percent of those who are eligible do not participate (Schultz 1984). In 1981 Canada's guaranteed minimum income (OAS + GIS) for an elderly individual was $5,091 and for a couple, $9,014. SSI equivalents (in Canadian dollars) were $3,616 for individuals and $5,424 for a couple.[7]

EXPLAINING THE DIFFERENCE

It is tempting to turn to political culture to explain these differences. Americans, it could be argued, are more at home reproducing the inequalities of the labor market in their old age security system, while a more egalitarian ethos in Canada has produced greater protection for the poor and low-wage workers. But when one examines the record such an account falls apart. Throughout the history of pension reform in Canada, the principal objective of Canadian labor, the anti-poverty lobbies, and the women's movement has not been a better social safety net but a retirement wage for elderly workers that would make such a safety net unnecessary. Labor's goal in the Great Pension Debate was expansion of the earnings-based C/QPP, not a struggle for higher GIS benefits. To the contrary, the fact that a majority of the Canadian elderly continue to be eligible for GIS benefits was and is considered politically scandalous. During the debates over introduction of the C/QPP in the 1960s, the main defenders of the existing flat-benefit OAS were the insurance companies and other sellers of private pensions who (correctly) perceived the C/QPP as a partial "nationalization" of their industry. The only criticism of OAS made by the conservative business press in Canada has been that OAS provides benefits to "the rich," a practice the Mulroney government corrected in 1989 when it finally was able to implement a "clawback" of OAS benefits from the high-income elderly through the tax system.

The clue to the different trajectories, we argue, can be traced back to the initial legislation and the forces that shaped it. In the United States, one major force shaping welfare state development was the coexistence of two radically different political economies—an industrializing economy with a wage labor force in the Northeast and Midwest and a southern plantation economy based on share-cropping by black labor in the South. Universal programs that created national standards, while acceptable in the one, would have undermined the economic structure of the other. Exclusion of agricultural workers from the initial OAI was a result of objections by Southern congressmen that old age insurance, even at the meager sum of $15 a month, would provide more cash than a cropper family might see in a year. Old age assistance provided according to uniform national standards posed the same threat. National standards for SSI became possible in the early 1970s because the problem of regulating a labor force of black sharecroppers had become anachronistic (Quadagno 1988, 1994).

Canadian welfare state politics have also been dominated by regional and ethnic divisions but the effects have been rather different. The possibility that the American nation might be dismembered was settled with the Civil War that ended in 1865. In contrast, the federation of provinces and language groups created by the British North American Act of 1867 has always been a fragile one (and at the time of this writing threatens to become undone). As in the United States, the major ethnic cleavage (French-English) began with a territorial base. But unlike the United States, this territorial division has been accentuated by history, not eroded. Regional cleavages between an industrialized core in central Canada, a Western economy based in agriculture and resource extraction where primary producers were compelled to purchase expensive inputs and consumer goods from the core, and an economically underdeveloped region in the East have been the axes along which political cleavages and identities have been formed. Creating a nation out of a country of "regions" and "two founding peoples" has always been the major challenge for Canadian political elites. And since the 1920s[8] the welfare state has been the "pot of glue" to which these elites have turned to hold the country together even when party ideology has dictated otherwise.[9]

The effects of regional and linguistic divisions organized within a federal state structure on the development of Canada's welfare state have been analyzed extensively elsewhere (Banting 1985), and here we only summarize the conclusions. Divided jurisdiction between federal and provincial governments has been the source of both a conservative and expansionist dynamic in Canadian social politics, "with the relative impact of each side varying from program to program and from decade to decade" (p. 76).

During the 1930s, the inability of poorer provinces and municipalities to meet the relief burden of the Great Depression set in motion a process of "massive centralization" of responsibility for income security in Canada. The alternative to national programs and a high level of inter-regional transfers was an expansion of provincial jurisdiction which would have reinforced regional differences. Poorer provinces faced the prospect of providing lower average benefits or higher average taxes for their citizens. Unlike the United States, where self-interest dictated a strategy of local control among Southern elites, "fiscal imbalance" (p. 64) dictated a strategy of centralized, national legislation among elites and representatives of Canada's poorer regions. Despite the prospect of inter-regional transfers, elites and representatives in the industrialized core also found reason to support a national strategy. More prosperous provinces were hesitant to take the lead lest local social programs serve as a magnet to the poor of other regions and drive capital to relocate in provinces where lower social services also meant lower taxes. As a result, Jenson (1990) observes, Canada emerged from the war with a centralized system for income security, but one constructed around a "politics of place" rather than a "politics of class."

Adoption of a universal, flat rate, formula for OAS in 1951 was more than an exercise in treating all Canadians equally, however. As Bryden (1974) documents, the preference of the federal government at the time was for an earnings-based system which linked benefits to contributions. Support for the flat-benefit principle came from a variety of sources. The political left, the CCF (Cooperative Commonwealth Federation), advocated the flat-rate principle (demanding a benefit of $50 per month), but so too did the life insurance industry and the Canadian Chamber of Commerce (who claimed that $30 per month was preferable but $40 a month acceptable). The Canadian Congress of Labor wanted both a flat-rate benefit and a second tier contributory program that would link benefits to earnings.

In the end, it was federalism and Quebec opposition to expansion of the federal power that determined the outcome. A contributory plan would have required a constitutional amendment with approval from the provinces. The die was cast when Quebec Premier Duplessis opposed expansion of the federal power. In effect, the central ethno-linguistic division in the Canadian federation, not a culture of equality, dictated the form of Canada's first postwar pension reform.

In 1965, the role of Quebec was reversed when it embarrassed the federal government into accepting earnings-based pensions (the C/QPP) more generous than those initially envisioned by Ottawa. But the C/QPP is also the major exemplar of the conservative dynamic in Canadian federalism. The underdevelopment of Canada's earnings-based system does not reflect Canadian reluctance to use the welfare state to reproduce inequality in old age. Rather, during the 1960s and 1970s, it has reflected the effective veto power of the province of Ontario over CPP reform, a power it exercised on behalf of the Canadian life insurance industry concentrated in that province (Banting 1985).

In short, in the United States the politics of region and race retarded development of national, uniform benefits for those at the bottom of the labor market or outside it altogether. In Canada, divisions of region and language have forestalled expansion of the income security side of Canada's welfare state for the elderly but simultaneously encouraged the construction of a uniform base at the bottom. Since the 1970s, the politics of federalism have reinforced this pattern in Canada. Because reforms to the C/QPP require the consent of the provinces, such reform is difficult. Because GIS is administered within the tax system and is under federal jurisdiction, improving the social safety net for the "poor elderly" is easy. As a result, maximum GIS benefits have continued to rise relative to average wages, making the social safety net more secure with the passage of time. In contrast, the relative value of SSI benefits in the United States has tended to erode.[10]

THE POLITICS OF OLD AGE SECURITY SINCE THE 1970s

The reforms of the 1960s and early 1970s took place under what, in retrospect, were unusual conditions. These were the last years of the long economic boom that extended from World War II until the mid-1970s. In both countries, the Keynesian consensus was still ascendant, the bargaining power of labor was strong, and "big business" temporarily in disrepute.[11] The result was a leftward drift in the social policy agenda of both countries. With the end of the long economic boom, symbolically marked by the first OPEC oil shock in 1973, welfare state expansion came to a stop. Both countries experienced the stagflation of the 1970s, Keynesian demand-management strategies fell into disrepute, and monetary policies designed to contain inflation-generating wage pressure were adopted, culminating in the Great Recession of the early 1980s.

In other respects, however, the politics of welfare differed considerably in the two countries. Canada did not experience the assault on the welfare state associated with Reagan in the United States or Thatcher in Britain. Neither the "crisis of the welfare state" polemic nor the debate over the "social security crisis" that shaped American social policy debates in the late 1970s gained much political leverage in Canada despite familiarity with the rhetoric. The thesis that the welfare state is the cause rather than the cure of poverty popularized by Charles Murray in the United States in the 1980s has not been heard in Canada; nor have the elderly and their entitlements been blamed for growing poverty among the young. Two major factors explain Canada's much more muted embrace of the neoconservative agenda.[12]

The Balance of Class Power

Until the early 1980s, at least part of the answer can be found in the changing balance of class forces in the two countries. Edsall (1984, p. 107) describes the United States:[13]

> During the 1970s, the political wing of the nation's corporate sector staged one of the most remarkable campaigns in the pursuit of political power in recent history. By the late 1970s and the early 1980s, business, and Washington's corporate lobbying community in particular, had gained a level of influence and leverage approaching that of the boom days of the 1920s.

Edsall dates the origins of this mobilization of corporate America to November 1972 when two business organizations whose main purpose was to restrict the influence and bargaining power of organized labor joined to form the Business Roundtable, a policy forum and lobbying agency for America's largest corporations. This was followed by the revitalization of the Chamber of Commerce in which "many of the principals in the formation of the Roundtable participated" (p. 123). What made all this remarkable was not the amount of corporate activity in the political arena but, rather, its content. In the 1950s and 1960s, as Derthick (1978, p. 132) points out, the dominant strategy of business and conservative critics was not to dismantle Social Security but merely to "hold the line, wherever that line might be at the moment."

In the 1970s, all this changed. In Edsall's words (1984, p. 198), business "refined its ability to act as a class, submerging competitive instincts in favour of joint, cooperative action in the legislative arena." Rather than using up their political capital in competition with one another for a larger share of the government pie, business leaders represented in organizations such as the Roundtable joined forces to advance their *shared* interests—the defeat of consumer protection and labor law reforms, the enactment of favorable tax legislation, and the rolling back of America's recently modernized welfare state for the elderly.

Canadian business leaders soon followed the American lead and in 1976 created the Business Council on National Issues (BCNI). Explicitly modeled after the Roundtable, its goal was to move beyond the ineffective special pleading characteristic of traditional organizations such as the Canadian Manufacturer's Association and propose "constructive courses of action" on issues of national importance (Langille 1987, p. 48). The BCNI differs from the Roundtable, however, by avoiding direct confrontations with labor and attempting to engage in dialogue with labor leaders in joint ventures such as the Canadian Labor

Market and Productivity Centre. While critical of social programs for the middle class (such as universal old age benefits), the BCNI has advocated tax reductions for the poor as well as the rich.[14]

If the BCNI has adopted a more civil tone towards labor than its American counterparts, this is partly through necessity. While union density in the United States has declined dramatically since the 1960s, union membership in Canada has continued to grow, reaching approximately 40 percent of the nonagricultural labor force by 1986. The differing role of labor in shaping the political agenda of the two countries in the 1970s was not merely a matter of numbers, however. In the United States, labor more or less abandoned the social policy arena. In contrast, the late 1970s was a high point of participation for Canadian labor in national and regional politics.

During Social Security's formative years, according to Derthick (1978, p. 110), American labor had been "by far the most important ally of the Social Security Administration. It supported the SSA inside the advisory councils and lobbied and testified for the agency's legislative proposals." Much of the staff work supporting Medicare in the early 1960s was done at AFL-CIO headquarters. The AFL-CIO also founded and helped finance the National Council of Senior Citizens (NCSC), a nationwide organization of retired unionists that lobbied for Medicare and improved social security benefits (Derthick 1978, Quadagno 1988).

Beginning in the late 1960s, however, U.S. labor's willingness and capacity to act on behalf of national social policy reform began to erode. Internecine warfare within the union movement fractured labor's social policy agenda, and issues like the welfare explosion and urban unrest of the late 1960s further alienated trade unionists from a sense of broader class solidarity (Davis 1986).[15] The 1968 elections, in which the "new liberals" of the antiwar movement captured the Democratic party, estranged organized labor even more, and in 1969 AFL-CIO President George Meany even explored the possibility of links with the Republican party. The 1972 elections confirmed the breach between the Democratic party and the AFL-CIO, when organized labor deserted the Democratic party and its 1972 presidential candidate, fragmenting the coalition that had supported Social Security expansion (Barnard 1983). During the debates leading up to the 1983 amendments, the main source of opposition to neoliberal critiques of Social Security appears to have come from within the SSA itself.[16]

In contrast, Canadian labor came out of the political closet in the mid-1970s.[17] Politicized as a result of federal wage and price controls in 1975, the Canadian Labor Congress (CLC) embraced a Canadian variant of social corporatism in 1976 and actively began to seek an institutional role for labor in national economic, labor market, and social planning. As Miriam Smith writes (1990, p. 151), after 1975 ". . .it is clear that a confederation that had been largely content to accept the rules of the game had been fundamentally transformed. The Congress was no longer content to be a lobby. It wanted power." When tripartism failed, the CLC turned to electoral politics and, for the first time, openly threw its resources into the "parallel campaign" in support of the NDP during the federal election of 1979. In Quebec, organized labor formed a militant partnership with the social democratic wing of the Parti Quebecois.

In 1978, the CLC launched the Great Pension Debate and remained the dominant partner within the coalition of reform groups that sustained the movement until the debate's demise in the early 1980s. Labor's main proposal was to double C/QPP benefit levels so that together with OAS, the public pension system would replace 75 percent of preretirement earnings for workers earning the average industrial wage.

The Structure of Old Age Support

National differences in the balance of power between business and labor is only part of the story. Equally important to the content of the debates were real differences in the policy structures so recently put in place. By the mid-1970s, the effects and implications of the U.S. Social Security reforms of the early 1970s were already apparent. The large benefit increases of the 1960s and 1970s were implemented immediately, causing rising real incomes among the elderly and generating genuine short-term pressures on Social Security financing. In contrast, Canada's C/QPP was only a decade old, there were few beneficiaries, and the funds were generating enormous surpluses. The income replacement rates that the C/QPP had established in 1965 had been allowed to erode and the promised expansion in private sector coverage was not forthcoming. The maximum hypothetical C/QPP benefit, set at 25 percent of average wages and salaries in 1965, had fallen to 15.7 percent by 1976 (Task Force on Retirement Income Policy 1980). In 1975 the relative economic status of retired American workers and their families was far superior to that of their Canadian counterparts (see appendix 3.A). In sum, the fact that Canadians were locked in a debate over welfare state expansion while Americans were contemplating welfare state cuts had a material, not a cultural, basis.

Existing policy structures also account for the groups that were mobilized, the positions they adopted, and the challenge they faced in achieving their objectives. In the United States, business elites and conservative critics were faced with the challenge of dismantling a program that enjoyed wide popularity among middle-income Americans. In contrast, Canadian business leaders faced the more modest task of defending the status quo. Business resistance to C/QPP expansion was associated more with issues of capital formation and control over capital than with the "welfare state" as such. The problem was articulated by Geoffrey Calvert (1977), in a study commissioned by a coalition of Canada's leading financial and industrial firms (The Canadian Pension Conference) and published by Canada's leading financial newspaper, the *Financial Post*. The money provided by private pension funds had become the single largest source of new investment capital in the Canadian economy and was bound to expand in importance in the future.[18] If the C/QPP were to begin crowding out private pensions, this important source of investment capital could dry up. And, more important, because the C/QPP is a partially funded pension system, it could actually result in a major transfer of control over capital from the private sector to the state. In the past, business opposition to pension reform had been concentrated in the financial sector whose business is eroded by public plans. Now, the threat of more state control over capital flows brought industrial capital into the fray as well.[19] The result was a coalition and degree of class solidarity among Canadian capitalists unlike any previous confrontation over pension reform (Murphy 1982).

The task of the business coalition was made easier by the fact that the provinces, who could veto reform, had a vested interest in resisting liberalization (Banting 1985). In its original design, the CPP (like the vast majority of public pension systems) was to have been funded on a pay-as-you-go basis with no build-up of a capital pool. It was put on a funded basis at the insistence of the Quebec government who wanted the capital to finance Quebec's "Quiet Revolution." And this is precisely what happened. The Caisse de Depôt et Placement du Quebec was put in charge of managing the funds and became the engine used by the Quebec government to direct capital flows in the province and create an indigenous business class. By 1986, the Caisse controlled $25.2 billion in assets, was the eighth largest financial institution in the country and the single largest player in Canadian financial markets (Finlayson 1988). Over the same period, the other provincial governments had used the funds from the CPP to finance provincial debt at preferred rates. Indeed, guaranteed access to this

capital pool appears to have been a major motivator for their participation in the first place.[20] Any enhancement of CPP benefits, however,
would have the effect of speeding up the repayment schedule to the
fund by the provinces, a concern enhanced by the fact that the funds
would dry up as the plan matured.

In the end, the opponents to reform prevailed. With the onset of the
Great Recession at the end of 1981, Canadian labor turned its attention
to the battleground of jobs and unemployment insurance. Whether the
outcome could have been otherwise in the absence of recession is a
question about which we can only speculate. Several features of the
debate are cause for skepticism, however. First, the debate was conducted largely among policy elites in government, business, labor, the
women's movement, and the anti-poverty lobbies. Unlike the "Social
Security crisis" in the United States, concern over pensions did not
become a mass issue to which government was compelled to respond
for electoral reasons. Old age lobbies were not involved, nor were the
elderly likely to be mobilized in support of reforms that would benefit
future generations of retirees but not those currently alive. Unlike the
1972 Social Security increases that became effective immediately, the
object of the C/QPP reformers was simply to permit the current generation of workers to build up larger entitlements for their eventual
retirement.

Nor was pension reform a major issue among the rank-and-file of
the labor movement. Most union members were covered by employer
plans negotiated in the workplace. Public sector workers, the newest
recruits to the labor movement, had virtually 100 percent coverage
and high quality benefits by industry standards.

For the Liberal Party in the early 1980s, electoral success hung more
on responding to recession and pacifying a business community already outraged by initiatives such as the National Energy Policy and
a budget introduced in 1981 designed to eliminate a whole range of
tax benefits for corporations and high-income individuals. Moreover,
with the GIS at its disposal, it already had a readily available instrument for responding to popular concern over the "elderly poor" and
playing electoral politics. GIS increases become effective immediately
and—with GIS's high take-up rate (over 50 percent of the elderly
receive GIS payments)—cannot but help when elderly voters go to the
polls. The GIS has the added benefit that it is opposed by virtually no
one. Indeed, since the 1970s, a Guaranteed Income (GI) model of the
welfare state has become the model of choice among Canadian business elites as well as among liberally minded policy reformers.[21]
Among the former, it is seen as an "efficient" social program, since

scarce tax-transfer dollars are not wasted on the middle classes who are expected to purchase income security in the market like any other commodity. As shown in figure 3.1, successive Canadian governments have made liberal use of this policy tool. While the CPP and OAS have been left to stagnate, GIS benefits have risen continuously in relation to average earnings.

Except for the interlude surrounding the universality debate in 1984–85 (to which we return shortly), Canadian old age politics were remarkably tranquil during the 1980s. Both Liberal and Conservative governments focused on legislation to improve the quality of private pensions (which benefit most union members) and timely increases in GIS benefits. In contrast, efforts to cut back on already existing benefits in the United States set in motion a whole new political dynamic. When the Reagan administration proposed massive benefit cuts in 1981, the subsequent outcry made clear that the vacuum left by labor had been filled by the lobbying organizations representing America's seniors.

Through most of the postwar years, senior citizen organizations played only a modest role in shaping the public agenda in the United States. The American Association of Retired Persons (AARP), the largest voluntary organization in the United States, was founded in 1958 mainly to provide insurance to retirees. More politicized seniors groups were offshoots of the labor movement. The National Council of Senior Citizens, for example, was founded by the AFL-CIO in 1962 to lobby for Medicare. The threat of budget cuts, however, was a signal for change.

The elderly lobby first flexed its political muscle in 1979 when President Jimmy Carter suggested some minor cuts in Social Security. Save Our Security (SOS), a coalition of senior groups, protested vehemently but then became dormant. It was revived as a result of the much more massive cuts proposed by the Reagan administration in 1981. By the end of the year its membership grew from less than two dozen elderly groups to over 100. By 1982 SOS could claim approximately 125 labor and elderly advocacy organizations with 35 to 40 million members.

In 1982 the National Committee to Preserve Social Security and Medicare was formed. It has more than five million members, a budget of $40 million, and a well-funded political action committee. Although the AARP, with 98 million members, maintains a nonpartisan stance in terms of politics, it too began to flex its political muscle. It has a paid staff of 1,300, an annual budget of approximately a quarter of a billion dollars, and its magazine, *Modern Maturity*, has the high-

Figure 3.1 OLD AGE SECURITY AND MAXIMUM GUARANTEED INCOME
SUPPLEMENT, AS PERCENTAGE OF AVERAGE WAGE, 1967–1985

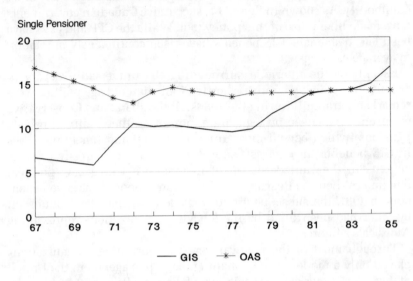

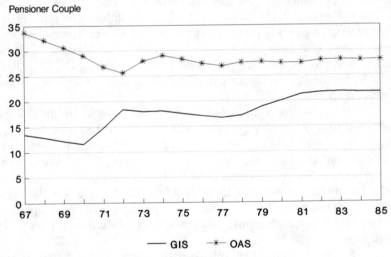

Source: National Council of Welfare

est circulation of any magazine in the United States (Day 1990). Modern *Maturity* publishes voter's guides on candidates' positions on relevant issues for older people, runs a wire service that provides newspapers with reports on elderly issues, and sponsors a weekly television series. During the 1988 presidential election, in New Hampshire alone, AARP mailed out 250,000 pieces of literature detailing the candidates' positions on Social Security, long-term health care, and other issues of relevance to older people.

The growth of "interest group" politics and a distinctive old age lobby is unique to the United States. What has spurred the growth of this lobby is that the two age-based entitlement programs—Social Security and Medicare—provide direct and tangible benefits to the middle class.[22] These programs have helped create a political constituency for the welfare state that is willing to take political action when these programs are threatened. However, the role of the old age lobby has been relatively passive. Because its membership is so diverse, it has had little influence in creating a policy agenda. Rather it has been most effective in mobilizing against threatened cuts to Social Security. And even this degree of influence is not absolute. In 1993 increased taxes on Social Security and cuts in Medicare imposed by the Clinton administration generated little sustained reaction.

It is also important to recognize that this constituency consists primarily of retired wage earners, not the poor. And unlike poverty programs, the politics of race and region are not a constraint on Social Security. If anything, Social Security transfers income from blacks to whites, a result of continuing disparities in black–white life expectancies.

Differences in policy structure also explain why the intergenerational equity debate took hold in the United States but not in Canada. In the 1980s political debates surrounding Social Security became dominated by the curious logic that Social Security benefits for the old were the *cause* of growing poverty among the young. Initially, generational equity arguments suggested that the generosity of entitlements to the old created poverty among children. "The old," Philip Longman wrote in the *Washington Monthly* (1982, p. 24), "have come to insist that the young not only hold them harmless for their past profligacy, but sacrifice their own prosperity to pay for it." Because of entitlements, older people, only 7 percent of whom were in poverty in 1982 according to Longman's calculations, were taking resources from the young, squandering the nation's limited wealth rather than investing in future economic growth. In contrast, 23 percent of children were in poverty, and funding for programs that support children had been subject to budget cuts as expenditures for the aged increased.

As the decade wore on, the message became more sophisticated. The month prior to the 1987 stock market crash, Peter G. Peterson warned in the *Atlantic Monthly* that as a result of feeble productivity growth, we have "witnessed a widening split between the elderly, among whom poverty is still declining, and children and young families, among whom poverty rates have exploded—a development with dire implications for our *future* productivity" (p. 44). Although Americans, according to Peterson, endorsed smaller and leaner government, federal spending increased significantly between 1979 and 1986 with most of the growth concentrated in middle-class entitlements, which had grown from 5.4 percent in 1965 to 11.5 percent of GNP. By contrast, federal spending for America's public infrastructure, for research and development in industry (R & D), education, job skills, and remedial social services have been cut.

The idea of the elderly as a privileged class was made possible by a reorientation of federal policy that occurred in the 1980s. The combination of a shifting of the income tax burden downward and rising income inequality seemingly placed Social Security in competition with other domestic programs.

Between 1977 and 1988 America's richest one percent experienced a 7.8 percent decline in the effective income tax rate, whereas the poorest 10 percent experienced a 2.5 percent increase. As the tax burden on both earned and unearned income dropped, Social Security tax rates climbed upward, from 6.05 percent in 1978 to 7.51 percent in 1988. Between 1980 and 1988 the portion of total annual federal tax receipts from Social Security rose from 31 percent to 36 percent, while income tax contributions dropped from 47 percent to less than 45 percent. During this period total tax receipts remained relatively stable—19.4 percent of GNP in 1980; 19 percent of GNP in 1988 (Phillips 1990). Thus, a tax increase that disproportionately benefited higher income households was made up through a tax cut that disproportionately burdened low-income households.

The 1981 tax cuts occurred along with rising military outlays and cuts in domestic programs. Between 1980 and 1987 federal revenues for social programs declined from 28 percent to 22 percent, while defense spending increased from 23 to 28 percent. As lower income Americans absorbed a higher share of the tax burden and suffered further losses through cuts in social programs, the elderly remained protected from erosion of living standards by automatic cost-of-living increases. Small wonder that they should appear to be a protected generation. As James Dale Davidson, head of the National Taxpayers Union, declared (1987, p. 15), "It's time we told the widow in the East Side luxury condominium that she's getting what amounts to welfare at the expense of the low-wage worker in the South Bronx."

As generational equity became the accepted framework for discussion about federal spending, it capitalized on the fractured class interests that had split the Democratic party and turned working class Democrats to the Republicans. By focusing on middle-class discontent over the growing tax burden, the generational equity theme had appeal for young, educated Republicans. At the same time the emphasis on the penalty poor children were paying aroused the resentment of low-income groups in traditional Democratic strongholds over cuts in welfare benefits. For example, congressman Jim Moody (D-WI), who hailed from a working-class district, told the Allied Council of Senior Citizens in Milwaukee that "Many people receiving Social Security benefits are better off than those taxed to pay them. The federal deficit is out of control, and the young are too heavily taxed; everyone must sacrifice; Social Security must be curbed."

By Canadian standards, the American working-age population is indeed heavily, and regressively, taxed to support the elderly. The combined payroll tax for the C/QPP was set at 3.6 percent of contributory earnings when it began in 1966—1.8 percent from workers and 1.8 percent from employers. Small increases have been made since 1987. In 1989 the combined rate was 4.2 percent and is projected to rise to 5.8 percent in 1999. Such figures pale in comparison to American rates, which had risen to 15.3 percent by 1990. Both C/QPP and Social Security taxes are regressive and rose in the 1980s but, starting from a higher base, these increases clearly have had a much more impressive impact on American than on Canadian pay packets. The real tax rate on Canadian workers is, of course, much higher than indicated by C/QPP contribution rates. OAS and GIS are also paid for by taxes, but these benefits come out of general revenue and are largely invisible to most contributors. Since they rely on the income tax, the costs are more progressively distributed as well.

The visibility of old age support is further reinforced in the United States by the fact that the Medicare tax that supports the elderly is embedded in the regressive Social Security payroll tax. In contrast, the cost of health care for Canada's elderly is for the most part paid for out of general revenue, and health care for the elderly is embedded in a universal health care program that includes the middle-aged and the young. One cannot attack "free" health care for the elderly without also attacking free health care for everyone. In sum, the American welfare state singles out the elderly both on the benefit and financing side. Both income security and health care for the elderly are financed from a high and rising regressive tax on the nonelderly. While the theme of intergenerational equity no doubt required a push from organizations such as AGE to become part of the common-sense world of policy-makers and publics (see chapter 4 for detailed discussion), it is the structure of the American welfare state that makes it possible for the division between age groups to be constructed as a social cleavage. In contrast, Canadian social programs for the elderly provide thin soil in which to plant seeds of intergenerational conflict. The visible, and regressive, part of the tax base used to finance old age programs—the C/QPP contribution—is low by American standards. Health insurance is universal. OAS benefits for the "rich" have been eliminated. And the GIS is not unlike other tax-based credits and benefits that go to low-income families with children.

CONCLUSION

The fact that Canadians were fighting over expansion to the old age security system while Americans were fighting over potential cuts in the late 1970s is largely a function of the pre-existing pension structures that were consolidated during the late 1960s and early 1970s. Middle-income Americans had gained comparatively high levels of income replacement from the Social Security reforms of the early 1970s and fought to maintain them. Canada's earnings-related pensions were only a decade old by 1975 and it was clear that they were insufficient to provide retired workers with an adequate retirement income. American business elites and neo-liberal critics faced the challenge of dismantling a widely popular program, while their Canadian counterparts faced the less daunting task of defending the status quo. In Canada, organized labor mobilized to win increases in the benefits they would receive in the future. In the United States, senior citizen organizations mobilized the elderly to protect benefits they were receiving today.

Old age politics in Canada and the United States have been different because their welfare states are different. But how to explain these differences. The classic position, recently revived by Lipset but also embraced by Canadian notables of the 1960s such as Porter, Horowitz, and Clark, is that these differences reflect the long hand of history, the cultural ethos that unified the founding generations of the two countries. In this view, America and its institutions are the product of Lockean individualism and revolution against the old order. Canada, in contrast, was the child of counter-revolution and a Tory fragment consolidated the old order.

Our own account also looks to the long hand of history but emphasizes instead the founding cleavages and unresolved conflicts that divide the two societies. Historically, American society is the product of the intersection of two political economies, the industrializing North and a slave-based plantation economy in the South. The dominance of the former over the latter was established by civil war in the 1860s. But the continuing impact of region and race in shaping American social politics is still its most striking feature (Quadagno 1988 and 1994). The welfare state is but one of the terrains on which the struggles created by these divisions have been and continue to be played out.

In Canada, regionalism and language have played the same pivotal role. For English-speaking Canadians, "real" Canadian history begins with the British North America Act of 1867. For French-speaking Quebecois, it begins with the conquest that took place a hundred years earlier. Provincial rights and regional interests accentuated by the politics of Canada's "two nations" have been the major factors shaping both the growth and limits of the Canadian welfare state.

From the vantage point of the 1990s, the end result of all this policymaking was more fortuitous for Canadian than American seniors. During the 1970s while Canada's old age security system was still maturing, it was preferable to grow old in the United States rather than in Canada (see appendix 3.A). By the mid-1980s, however, the situation was reversed (Smeeding, Torrey, and Rainwater 1993; Wolfson, this volume). Both lower- and middle-income seniors now fare better in Canada than in the United States. And the Canadian elderly benefit from a far more comprehensive health care system than Medicare provides to the American elderly. As Keith Banting (forthcoming) has documented, these differences are symptomatic of a more general pattern of divergence in the social policy regimes of the two countries that can be traced to the 1960s and were accentuated in the 1980s.

By Canadian (and international) standards, the major flaw in the U.S. old age security system is its weak social safety net. Using a standardized international poverty level (50 percent of adjusted median income), Smeeding, Torrey, and Rainwater (1993) estimate that 22 percent of the American elderly were poor in 1986 compared to 6.8 percent in Canada and an international average of 6.4 percent. The main victims of this difference are elderly (mainly widowed) women.

The measured poverty gap (using U.S. poverty lines) between single elderly women and elderly couples in the United States in 1986 was 11.6 percent compared to 2.6 percent in Canada (Smeeding et al. 1993: table 6).

The reason for this Canada-U.S. difference is to be found in very different methods of provision for the low-income elderly—the *income-tested* Guaranteed Income Supplement in Canada and the *means*-tested Supplemental Security Income program in the United States. Income testing is relatively unknown in the United States and is still poorly understood by the American social policy establishment. In Canada, in contrast, income testing emerged in the 1970s as the model of choice for selective social transfers among both liberals and conservatives (Myles 1988).

But what of the future? Under the Clinton administration there is at least some hint of upward convergence in the social policy regimes of the two countries. The exception to the means-testing rule in the United States is the Earned Income Tax Credit (EITC) which provides income-tested benefits to working-poor families. For most of its history, the EITC has had limited reach and low benefit levels. However, the 1993 Clinton budget raised EITC benefits by 27 percent with further increases and automatic indexing being phased in through 1996. As the principles of income testing become better understood and more entrenched, it is conceivable they will be extended to include other social programs such as SSI.

Similarly, the Clinton administration's proposal to make health care insurance available to all U.S. citizens suggests that perhaps history is not destiny. At long last, the American welfare state would incorporate the middle class and the middle-aged, as well as the poor and the elderly, and provide a model of "welfare" that does not evoke racial cleavages.

There are other signs of "convergence," however, whose consequences will be less benign. During the 1980s, governments in both countries took steps to reduce their long-term social insurance obligations to middle-income earners. When phased in, the 1983 Social Security amendments in the United States will reduce income replacement rates for average earners and raise the age of eligibility to 67 (Aaron, Bosworth, and Burtless 1989).[23] In Canada, the 1989 OAS "clawback" will eventually eliminate this "first tier" of income security for middle-income Canadians.[24] And as contribution rates for the Canada and Quebec Pension Plans begin to rise to American levels, as they must, Canadian political debates on income security for the elderly will no doubt take on tones not unlike the American debates of the 1980s.

The upshot of a reduced role for public sector social insurance for middle-income workers is growing dependency on private sector pensions and retirement savings programs. In both countries, however, private sector coverage is declining as a result of disproportionate employment growth in sectors where pension coverage is low—employees of small firms, nonunionized employees, and workers in personal services and retail trade (Economic Council of Canada 1989)—all of which employ a predominantly female labor force.

Left unchecked, the shift from public to private old age insurance will accentuate the already polarized distribution of income within the elderly population (Smeeding et al. 1993). Quite simply, the phenomenon of the "declining middle"—the polarization of wages, salaries, and pension entitlements—observed among the non-elderly since the 1970s is now making its way through the age pyramid. And in both countries, prolonged recession and rising government debt now impose hard limits on the range of policy initiatives available to governments.

It is always tempting to see common forces as generating pressures for convergence. All modern welfare states face common challenges associated with population aging, globalization, economic stagnation, and rising government debt. But just as an electrical charge produces different outcomes depending on whether it enters a refrigerator or a stove, the historical record of welfare states indicates that there are rarely unique outcomes that follow from otherwise similar historical forces. During the postwar years, Canada and the United States developed different versions of the modern welfare state reflecting the founding cleavages and unresolved conflicts that divide the two societies. As political and social events of the 1990s have made clear, these same cleavages and unresolved conflicts continue to be driving forces in national politics. It is highly unlikely that future developments in old age security will be immune to these forces.

Notes

1. See, for example, Canada's chief statistician, Fellegi (1988).

2. For such a view see Malcom (1985).

3. Our point is not that social classes do not matter in shaping welfare states or differences between them. Rather, the specific differences between Canada and the United States are not to be found in differences in the relative bargaining power, influence, or strategies of organized labor in the two countries.

4. For a comparison of Canada and the United States with the European experience, see Kudrle and Marmor (1981).

5. For a description of the Act and its implementation, see Bryden (1974).

6. For similar results for the late seventies, see Clark (1980).

7. Figures reported in the text are based on official exchange rates. Using 1981 "purchasing power parities" to convert U.S. to Canadian dollars produces somewhat lower estimates for the U.S.: $3552 for individuals and $5329 for couples.

8. Until the twenties, as Smith observes, patronage rather than the welfare state was the main instrument used by prime ministers "to create and hold constituency loyalties." See Smith (1989). For the role of patronage in shaping the American welfare state, see Orloff (1988).

9. This paradox was most evident during the Conservative regime of John Diefenbaker during the late 1950s and early 1960s. Diefenbaker's pan-Canadianism led to the national development policy, the extension of hospital insurance, and the Royal Commission on Health Services which resulted in the adoption of National Health Insurance when the Liberals returned to power. See Smith (1989).

10. Although SSI benefit levels are adjusted annually by changes in the Consumer Price Index, both the income and asset disregards are generally not, making eligibility criteria more stringent. See Schulz (1984).

11. For the United States, see Edsall (1984); Bowles, Gordon, and Weisskopf (1983). For Canada, see Wolfe (1985) and Wolfe (1984).

12. For a good description of the growth of neoconservatism in Canada see Banting (1990).

13. See also Michael Useem (1984).

14. For a complete discussion of the formation of the BCNI and its political agenda see Langille (1987).

15. See also Quadagno (1994).

16. The role of Robert Ball both in formulating the amendments of 1983 and defusing the criticisms of Social Security leading up to the amendments was especially notable. On the technical side it was Dean Leimer, an SSA researcher, who undermined the claim that Social Security was "deindustrializing" America by showing that Martin Feldstein's estimates of the effects of Social Security on the savings rate were the result of a programming error. See Feldstein (1974) and Leimer and Lesnoy (1982).

17. The shifting strategy and role of labor during this period is exhaustively analyzed in Smith (1990). See also Mahon (1983).

18. By 1986, private pension funds were supplying 55 percent of the funds raised in Canada's capital markets and accounted for seven out of every ten trades on the Toronto Stock Exchange. See "Pension funds dominate stock markets," the *Ottawa Citizen*, Jan. 6, 1989, D12.

19. Calvert (1977) lists the following as the most important corporations involved in financing his study: Alcan, Bank of Montreal, Canada Packers, Canadian Industries Limited, Canadian National Railways, Domtar, Dupont, Elliot and Page, Inco, Morguard Trust, Noranda Mines, Royal Trust, Saskatchewan Wheat Pool, Shell, Steel Company of Canada, Sun Life, Tomeson-Alexander, and Woody Gundy.

20. As one provincial official remarked: "The main reason for us was the creation of a large fund. It would provide money for development here and give us more liberty in the money markets. The fund was certainly the main reason for me; it was the reason."

21. On this see Myles (1988).

22. Welfare for the non-elderly middle classes and the rich is provided largely through the "hidden welfare state" embedded in the tax system. Mortgage interest deductions, for example, constitute a massive public housing program but are rarely counted as such in American welfare state debates.

23. The age of eligibility for full benefits is scheduled to rise to 67 in 1998 and replacement rates will fall substantially by the time the baby boom reaches retirement. See Aaron, Bosworth, and Burtless (1989).

24. The "clawback" was introduced so that at the outset benefits are taxed back from a small minority of high income families. However, the indexing provisions of the legislation were designed so that in the long run OAS payments will go only to the low income elderly.

APPENDIX 3.A THE ECONOMIC STATUS OF THE ELDERLY IN CANADA AND THE UNITED STATES, 1975

Table 3.A.1 compares the economic status of the retired elderly in Canada and the United States in 1975. The following notes identify the procedures used to derive these estimates.

1. *Income as a measure of economic welfare*

In order to standardize for family size, reported income was first divided by the square root of family size.

2. *Relative income status of the elderly*

To determine the relative economic status of each elderly family within the larger society, the standardized family income of each

Table 3.A.1 THE RELATIVE ECONOMIC STATUS OF THE RETIRED ELDERLY IN CANADA AND THE UNITED STATES

	Canada			United States		
	BT	AT	ATT	BT	AT	ATT
A. Total						
1. Very Poor	74.5	14.8	11.7	67.0	10.3	08.2
2. Poor	14.2	57.9	52.9	13.0	42.2	37.1
3. Near Poor	05.6	16.0	21.3	07.1	21.0	24.6
4. Comfortable	02.8	05.8	06.4	04.2	10.6	11.9
5. Quite Comfortable	02.9	05.4	07.7	08.7	15.9	18.3
	100%	100%	100%	100%	100%	100%
B. Marital Status: Married						
1. Very Poor	67.8	09.7	06.2	63.7	13.9	11.0
2. Poor	18.8	51.4	42.6	16.7	37.1	33.4
3. Near Poor	07.8	24.6	32.8	08.0	24.3	27.1
4. Comfortable	02.1	07.9	08.9	04.2	11.1	12.2
5. Quite Comfortable	03.5	06.4	09.5	07.4	13.7	16.3
	100%	100%	100%	100%	100%	100%
C. Marital Status: Unmarried						
1. Very Poor	78.4	17.8	14.9	69.1	08.0	06.4
2. Poor	11.5	61.7	58.9	10.6	45.6	39.5
3. Near Poor	04.2	11.0	14.6	06.5	19.0	22.8
4. Comfortable	03.2	04.6	05.0	04.2	10.3	11.7
5. Quite Comfortable	02.6	04.8	06.6	09.5	17.2	19.6
	100%	100%	100%	100%	100%	100%

NOTE:
BT = Income before tax and transfers
AT = Income after transfers but before tax
ATT = Income after transfers and tax

elderly family unit was recomputed as a ratio by dividing by the median family income (standardized for family size) for all families where the head of the household was aged 25–54. Other criteria were used including average industrial wages and per capita GNP. The results using these alternative criteria did not substantially alter the results reported here. From this computation, the following categories were established.

INCOME RATIO	CATEGORY
0.00–0.25	very poor
0.26–0.50	poor
0.51–0.75	near poor
0.76–1.00	comfortable
1.00 +	quite comfortable

3. *Sample*

Data were estimated from the following sample sources:

a) Canada: Survey of Consumer Finances, 1976.

b) U.S.: March Supplement, Current Population Survey, 1976.

In both cases reported income is for the year 1975.

4. *Retirement*

Retirement was operationalized by excluding all elderly family units with reported earnings from employment greater than $100 or equivalent.

5. *Income by source*

Since taxes paid were not reported in the U.S. data set, they were estimated using the TAXSIM computer program. Hence, the after-tax income of the elderly American families should be treated as an estimate.

Transfers include all income benefits derived from Government sources. Although the Canada Pension Plan was passed in 1965, it did not come to maturity until 1976. Thus the Canadian data may be considered indicative of the operation of a Beveridge-type flat benefit system.

References

Aaron, Henry, Barry Bosworth, and Gary Burtless. 1989. *Can Americans Afford to Grow Old?* Washington, D.C.: Brookings.

Aldrich, Jonathan. 1982. "Earnings Replacement Rates of Old-Age Benefits in 12 Countries, 1969–80." *Social Security Bulletin* 45 (11): 3–11.

Banting, Keith. 1985. "Institutional Conservatism: Federalism and Pension Reform." In *Canadian Social Welfare Policy: Federal and Provincial Dimensions,* edited by J. Ismael. Kingston and Montreal: McGill-Queen's University Press.

_____. 1990. "Social Policy in an Open Economy: Neoconservatism and the Canadian State." Paper presented to the annual meeting of the American Political Science Association, San Francisco, August.

_____. Forthcoming. "The Social Policy Divide: the Liberal Welfare State in Canada and the United States." In *Canada and the United States in a Changing Global Economy,* edited by Keith Banting, Richard Simeon, and George Hoberg.

Barnard, John. 1983. *Walter Reuther and the Rise of the Auto Workers.* Boston: Little Brown.

Bowles, Samuel, David Gordon, and Thomas Weisskopf. 1983. *Beyond the Wasteland: A Democratic Alternative to Economic Decline.* Garden City, N.Y.: Doubleday.

Bryden, Kenneth. 1974. *Old Age Pensions and Policy-Making in Canada,* Ch. 4. Montreal: McGill-Queen's University Press.

Calvert, Geoffrey. 1977. *Pensions and Survival: The Coming Crisis of Money and Retirement.* Toronto: MacLean Hunter.

Clark, Hart D. 1980. "A Comparison of the Retirement Income Systems of Canada and Other Countries." In *Task Force on Retirement Income Policy, The Retirement Income System in Canada: Problems and Alternative Policies for Reform,* vol. II, pp. 2.1–2.26. Ottawa: Minister of Supply and Services.

Davidson, James Dale. 1987. "Social Security Rip-off." *The New Republic* (April).

Davis, Mike. 1986. *Prisoners of the American Dream.* London: New Left Books.

Day, Christine L. 1990. *What Older Americans Think, Interest Groups and Aging Policy.* Princeton, N.J.: Princeton University Press.

Derthick, Martha. 1978. *Public Policy for Social Security.* Washington, D.C.: Brookings Institute.

Economic Council of Canada. 1989. *Legacies: 26th Annual Review.* Ottawa: Economic Council of Canada.

Edsall, Thomas. 1984. *The New Politics of Inequality.* New York: W.W. Norton.

Esping-Andersen, Gösta. 1990. *The Three Worlds of Welfare Capitalism.* Princeton, N.J.: Princeton University Press.

Feldstein, Martin. 1974. "Social Security, Induced Retirement and Aggregate Capital Formation." *Journal of Political Economy* 82 (Sept.-Oct.): 905–26.

Fellegi, Ivan. 1988. "Can We Afford an Aging Society?" In *Canadian Economic Observer* (October): 4.1–4.34.

Finlayson, Ann. 1988. *Whose Money Is It Anyway: The Showdown on Pensions*. Markham, Ont.: Penguin.

Graebner, William. 1980. *A History of Retirement*. New Haven, Conn.: Yale University Press.

Grey, Gratton. 1990. "Social Policy by Stealth." *Policy Options* 11 (March): 17–29.

Jenson, Jane. 1990. "Representations in Crisis: The Roots of Canada's Permeable Fordism." *Canadian Journal of Political Science* 23 (4): 653–83.

Kudrle, Robert, and Theodore Marmor. 1981. "The Development of Welfare States in North America." In *The Development of Welfare States in Europe and America*, edited by P. Flora and A. Heidenheimer. London: Transaction Books.

Langille, David. 1987. "The Business Council on National Issues and the Canadian State." *Studies in Political Economy* 24: 41–85.

Leimer, Dean, and Selig Lesnoy. 1982. "Social Security and Private Saving: New Time-Series Evidence." *Journal of Political Economy* 90 (June): 606–42.

Longman, Philip. 1982. "Taking America to the Cleaners." *Washington Monthly* (November): 24.

Mahon, Rianne. 1983. "Canadian Labour in the Battle of the Eighties." *Studies in Political Economy* (Summer): 149–75.

Malcom, Andrew. 1985. *The Canadians*. Toronto: Fitshenry and Whiteside.

Murphy, Barbara. 1982. *Corporate Capital and the Welfare State: Canadian Business and Public Pension Policy in Canada since World War II*. Unpublished master's thesis. Carleton University, Ottawa.

Myles, John. 1988. "Decline or Impasse? The Current State of the Welfare State." *Studies in Political Economy* 26 (Summer): 73–107.

Organization for Economic Cooperation and Development. 1976. *Public Expenditures on Income Maintenance Programmes*. Paris: OECD.

————. 1988. *Reforming Public Pensions*. Paris: OECD.

Orloff, Ann. 1988. "The Political Origins of America's Belated Welfare State." In *The Politics of Social Policy in the United States*, edited by Margaret Weir, Ann Orloff, and Theda Skocpol. Princeton, N.J.: Princeton University Press.

Peterson, Peter G. 1987. "The Morning After." *Atlantic Monthly* (October): 44.

Phillips, Kevin. 1990. *The Politics of Rich and Poor, Wealth and the American Electorate in the Reagan Aftermath*. New York: Random House.

Quadagno, Jill. 1988. *The Transformation of Old Age Security: Class and Politics in the American Welfare State*. Chicago: University of Chicago Press.

————. 1994. *Unfinished Democracy: Rights, Race and the War on Poverty*. New York: Oxford University Press.

Rainwater, Lee, Martin Rein, and Joseph Schwartz. 1985. *Income Packaging and the Welfare State: A Comparative Study of Family Income*. New York: Oxford University Press.

"Sacred Cow," 1987. *Time* (9 November): 24.

Schulz, James. 1984. "SSI: Origins, Experience, and Unresolved Issues." In *The Supplemental Security Income Program: A 10-Year Review*, Special Committee on Aging, United States Senate. Washington, D.C.: U.S. Government Printing Office.

Schwed, Paula. 1986. "A Dirty Little Secret." *Campus Voice* (August/September).

Simeon, Richard. 1972. *Federal-Provincial Diplomacy: The Making of Recent Policy in Canada*. Toronto: University of Toronto Press.

Smeeding, Timothy, Barbara Torrey, and Lee Rainwater. 1993. "Going to Extremes: An International Perspective on the Economic Status of the U.S. Aged." Luxembourg Income Study, Working Paper #87.

Smith, David. 1989. "Canadian Political Parties and National Integration." In *Canadian Parties in Transition: Discourse, Organization and Representation*, edited by Alain Gagnon and Brian Tanguay. Scarborough, Ont.: Nelson.

Smith, Miriam. 1990. *Labour without Allies: The Canadian Labour Congress in Politics*. Unpublished Ph.D. diss. Yale University.

Task Force on Retirement Income Policy. 1980. *The Retirement Income System in Canada: Problems and Alternative Policies for Reform*, vol I. Ottawa: Minister of Supply and Services.

Useem, Michael. 1981. *The Inner Circle*. New York and Oxford: Oxford University Press.

Wolfe, David. 1984. "The Rise and Demise of the Keynesian Era in Canada." In *Modern Canada: Readings in Canadian Social History Series*, vol. 5, edited by Michael Cross and Gregory Kealey. Toronto: McClelland and Stewart.

_____. 1985. "The Wolf, The Politics of the Deficit." In *The Politics of Economic Policy*, edited by B. Doern. Toronto: University of Toronto Press.

Wright, Erik. 1978. *Class, Crisis, and the State*. London: New Left Books.

Chapter Four

THE SALIENCE OF INTERGENERATIONAL EQUITY IN CANADA AND THE UNITED STATES

Fay Lomax Cook, Victor W. Marshall, Joanne Gard Marshall, and
Julie E. Kaufman

Citizens in both the United States and Canada found themselves in the midst of debates over the future of national social policies in the 1980s. Beginning the decade before, both countries, like most other advanced industrial democracies, endured fiscal crises. Some commentators traced fiscal difficulties to the oil crisis of the early 1970s, others to worker productivity, which began to grow at a much slower rate in the 1970s than in earlier years, and yet others to the growth of welfare state programs (Weir, Orloff, and Skocpol 1988). What often flows from such periods of perceived fiscal constraint is debate about how a more limited pie of resources must be divided between various policy domains. This chapter examines one aspect of this debate that took on a very different character in the United States than in Canada. In particular, it examines the issue of intergenerational equity that rose on the agenda of policymakers and scholars in the United States but not in Canada.

Intergenerational equity refers to the concept that different generations should be treated in similar ways and should have similar opportunities. The key aspect that differentiates it from general concerns about the economic costs of an aging population (e.g., Walker 1990) and from conflict among familial generations (e.g., Bengston et al. 1985) is that the economic costs of the aged are linked to those of the young with the argument that the young are being deprived of opportunities for well-being *because of* excessive allocation of resources to the old.

Chapters 2 and 3 of this volume both note the sharp contrast between the United States and Canada in regard to intergenerational equity as a political issue. The first part of this chapter documents that a substantial difference exists between the United States and Canada in the salience of the issue within media, academic, and policymaker circles, but shows that among the general public, opinion appears to be similar in the two countries. Why has intergenerational equity emerged in three arenas in the United States but not in Canada? The second part of the chapter addresses this question as well as the question of why public opinion is similar in the two countries, despite the differences we find in other domains.

EMERGENCE OF THE INTERGENERATIONAL EQUITY ISSUE

In 1984 in the United States, two independent events caused ripple effects that catapulted the issue of intergenerational equity to visibility in both the policy and academic communities. In the policy community, Senator Dave Durenberger (R-MN) founded Americans for Generational Equity (AGE). In the academic community, Professor Samuel H. Preston gave the Presidential Address to the Annual Meeting of the Population Association of America entitled "Children and the Elderly: Divergent Paths for America's Dependents." The address was later reprinted in the journal *Demography* and published in revised form in *Scientific American*. No similar events occurred in Canada.

The Policy Community

According to Durenberger, AGE's goal was "to promote the concept of generational equity among America's political, intellectual, and financial leaders" (quoted in Quadagno 1989, p. 360). His management intern, Paul Hewitt, became president and executive director of AGE. As research director, Durenberger and Hewitt chose Phillip Longman, the author of an article in a 1982 issue of the *Washington Monthly* entitled "Taking America to the Cleaners." It is the old, Longman argued, who are taking America to the cleaners because "The old have come to insist that the young not only hold them harmless for their past profligacy, but sacrifice their own prosperity to pay for it" (Longman 1982, p. 24).

Within three years, AGE grew from an organization with a budget of $88,000 and 600 members to an organization with a budget that had quadrupled in size due to funding from 85 organizations and businesses which included banks, insurance companies, defense contractors, and health care corporations (Quadagno 1989). Even at its largest, AGE was quite modest as an American organization. Its aims were not. According to its 1990 Annual Report, AGE called "into question the prudence, sustainability, and fairness to future generations of federal old age benefit programs" (AGE 1990, p. 2). The major vehicles for AGE's message included conferences; books, articles, and op-ed pieces in newspapers; and speeches and comments in the U.S. Congress by such AGE leaders as Durenberger in the Senate and Tim Penny (R-MN), Rod Chandler (R-WA), John Porter (R-IL), Bill Richardson (D-NM), and Jim Saxton (R-NJ) in the House. (These five Representatives are listed in AGE's 1990 Annual Report as constituting the Board of Congressional Advisors.)

What has been the impact of AGE within the policy community? AGE's 1990 Annual Report makes this claim:

> AGE was among the first voices to point out that the elderly were, on average, better off than the downwardly mobile young, whose taxes were increasingly being diverted to senior programs. This argument led policy makers to review the progressivity of aging policies, not only across generations but among the elderly themselves (AGE 1990, p. 2).

Further, the Annual Report credits the AGE argument with moving Congress to adopt a financing mechanism for the Catastrophic Care Act under which the cost of the new benefits would be borne totally by persons eligible for Medicare. The more well-to-do retirees would, in effect, subsidize poor retirees without depending on younger workers for tax contributions. As ranking minority member of the Health Subcommittee of the Senate Finance Committee, Durenberger played an important role in passage of this legislation. He sounded the AGE theme in his excitement about the bill's success:

> For the first time, we are income testing part of the social insurance program. . . . In other words, this law will not penalize one generation for the sake of another (Durenberger as quoted in AGE 1988).

Durenberger's excitement lasted less than a year. As the financing of the Catastrophic Care Act came to be understood by senior citizens' organizations, elderly people protested the large tax that some of them would have to pay, including some who already were covered privately for such risks. Under pressure from senior citizens and some of their organizations, Congress repealed the legislation in late 1989. Former Senator Thomas Eagleton (D-MO) described the debate in Congress in a column entitled "21st Century War: Young vs. Old":

> For now, the senior citizens have most effectively flexed their considerable political muscle. In so doing, they may have unwittingly triggered a political war for the nation's social conscience. How do we share the

pie in America? Where do we draw the line between the past and the future? (Eagleton, *St. Louis Post-Dispatch*, December 3, 1989)

Quadagno (1989) argues that over the long term the more important effect of AGE than this one piece of legislation "may be its influence in reshaping the parameters of the debate so that all future policy choices will have to take generational equity into account" (p. 364). As evidence, she cites the fact that other members of Congress picked up and repeated the AGE theme in public speeches and that a number of prominent newspaper articles have transmitted the AGE message to a broad audience. AGE is now defunct as an organization for reasons we describe later. Nonetheless, its influence was important both in the emergence of the issue of intergenerational equity and, as Quadagno correctly pointed out, in its reshaping of the political discourse.

The Academic Community

Professor Samuel H. Preston never mentioned the term intergenerational equity in "Children and the Elderly: Divergent Paths for America's Dependents," his Presidential Address before the Population Association of America, or in the articles in *Demography* (1984a) and *Scientific American* (1984b) that printed versions of his talk. Yet, it was clearly his theme.

Preston amassed and integrated large bodies of data on changes in three domains—well-being, the family, and politics. His data made a strong case that conditions have deteriorated for children and improved dramatically for the elderly and that "in the public sphere at least, gains for one group come partly at the expense of another" (Preston 1984a, p. 450). He argued that U.S. policymakers have made a set of choices that have dramatically altered the age profile of well-being:

> Let's be clear that the transfers from the working-age population to the elderly are also transfers away from children . . . and let's also recognize that the sums involved are huge. (pp. 451–2)

Many scholarly presidential addresses are delivered, then published and never referred to again. But Preston's work struck a chord among academics in at least three areas—poverty, child welfare, and gerontology—and among a number of foundations and agencies with these specializations. Between 1985 and 1992, according to the *Social Science Citation Index*, Preston's articles in *Demography* and *Scientific*

American were cited in 158 articles. This amount of attention classi-
fies the Preston work as what some scholars call a "research front."
Only 3 percent of scholarly papers are cited more than 24 times, and
only 1 percent are cited 50 times or more (Garfield 1984).

Preston's argument piqued the interest of scholars to analyze the
situation in more detail. In August, 1985, the National Academy of
Sciences brought together about 20 social scientists for a three-day
workshop in Woods Hole, Massachusetts. Entitled "Demographic
Change and the Well-Being of Children and the Elderly," the workshop
had three objectives: to develop a multifaceted picture of levels and
trends in well-being among children and the elderly in the United
States; to explore the relative importance of demographic change, the
performance of the economy, and public policies for the well-being of
these two groups over time; and to grapple with the policy implications of what was learned (Palmer, Smeeding, and Torrey 1988, p. xxi).

Over the next two years, the Alfred P. Sloan Foundation, the Ford
Foundation, and the John D. and Catherine T. MacArthur Foundation
funded two more workshops held in the United States and an international conference held in Luxembourg. The aggregate data presented in the volume resulting from the Luxembourg conference
(Palmer, et al. 1988) repeatedly bear out one of Preston's major conclusions: the economic experiences of the elderly and children in the
United States have diverged widely over the past 20 years. In addition,
the internationally comparative data showed that children in the
United States have much higher poverty rates than their counterparts
in most other countries with similar standards of living. However, the
scholars who wrote the chapter summarizing and interpreting the
findings of the volume were quick to say that although it is clear that
the elderly benefit more than do children from our federal social policies, "it is not at all clear that children's doing worse has enabled the
elderly to do better; our poverty rates for the elderly remain on the
high side among industrial nations" (Gould and Palmer 1988, p. 422).
The authors criticize the intergenerational equity framework as encouraging "us-vs.-them" thinking; yet, they also say that "the policy
making process will be fraught with much more intergenerational
tension than was true in the past" (p. 422).

Although, as noted, Preston did not use the term intergenerational
equity, scholars whose work he appears to have influenced use the
term frequently, and their research, along with Preston's, may have
helped to legitimize the general concept of intergenerational equity
in the United States by providing empirical data to underpin the

debate in the policy community. But exactly how salient is the intergenerational equity issue within the United States, and is it at all
important in Canada?

RELATIVE SALIENCE OF THE INTERGENERATIONAL EQUITY ISSUE IN CANADA AND THE UNITED STATES

The salience of an issue may be examined in at least four ways: (1)
attention to the issue as measured by reports in public media; (2)
academic discourse as reflected in published scholarly papers and
books; (3) political and government policy attention as measured by
legislative discussions and hearings; and (4) public opinion as gauged
through survey data. To assess the level of salience of intergenerational
equity in the United States and Canada, we employed each approach.

Media Attention

To examine the attention given to intergenerational equity in the media, we searched several publicly available online databases. Com-
puterized databases provide a unique source of empirical data about
knowledge and opinion recorded in newsprint. We selected several of
the most informative databases that provide access to newspapers and
popular magazines in either Canada, the United States, or both. For
Canada, we used *Canadian Business and Current Affairs* (CBCA),
which covers 500 magazines as well as 10 newspapers from 1980 to
1993 including *The Toronto Star*, Canada's largest circulation newspaper and *The Globe & Mail*, which purports to be Canada's national
newspaper. For the United States, we selected *Newspaper Abstracts*,
which covers 1984 through 1988 and *Newspaper and Periodical Abstracts*, which covers 1988 to the present; together, they index about
25 national and regional newspapers and over 300 magazines and
periodicals. A final database, the *Magazine Index*, provides access to
435 North American popular magazines and selected major scholarly
journals, most of which are U.S. publications, but at least 11 of which
are Canadian. Together, these databases provide a comprehensive view
of media coverage from 1980 to 1992. (The details of our search strategy are provided in appendix 4.A.)

We kept our retrieval broad and searched for any articles that dealt
with the social relationships between the young and the old, using
such key words that appeared in the content description assigned by

indexers as "children," "youth," "young," "old," "aged," "seniors," "elderly," and "aging." In addition, we searched for specific phrases such as "generation gap," "(inter)generational conflict," as well as the obvious "(inter)generational equity."

The four databases that we searched for media attention contained approximately 10 million records of newspaper or magazine articles. Of these, 109,812 articles referred to children or youth in some way, and 22,697 referred to elderly persons. The search uncovered only 517 articles that made reference to both the old and young within the same article, only 40 of which dealt with intergenerational equity or conflict. Table 4.1 shows the number of articles coded as dealing with generational equity or conflict by year in both Canada and the United States.

For Canada, the CBCA retrieved 18 citations to articles that dealt with the young and old together but only one that dealt with intergenerational equity. For the most part, cooperation and positive communication are the dominant message with titles such as: "Young and Young at Heart Give Education a New Twist: Children, Seniors, Learning from Each Other" (*Montreal Gazette*, June 7, 1990), "Bridging the Generation Gap: Students Get a Sense of Doing Something for Someone Else" (*Montreal Gazette*, March 11, 1990), and "Age Barriers

Table 4.1 MEDIA ATTENTION TO THE ISSUE OF INTERGENERATIONAL EQUITY IN CANADA AND THE UNITED STATES 1980–1992

	Number of Articles[a]	
	Canada	United States
1992	1	2
1991	0	5
1990	0	8
1989	0	4
1988	0	13
1987	0	4
1986	0	2
1985	0	0
1984	0	1
1983	0	0
1982	0	0
1981	0	0
1980	0	0
Total	1	39

[a]Database sources for media attention: For Canada, CBCA (Canadian Business and Current Affairs) and Magazine Index, the latter being North American in scope. For the U.S., Magazine Index, Newspaper Abstracts, and Newspaper and Periodical Abstracts.

Knocked Down as Youngsters Mix with Elderly" (*Winnipeg Free Press*, August 20, 1986).

The one exception appears in July, 1992, in the *Globe & Mail* which carried the dramatic headline "Seniors Gain at the Expense of the Young, Report Says: Growing Child Poverty May Fuel Debate Over Who Deserves Social Aid." As we shall see in the next section on academic attention, the author of the report being reviewed in the news article did *not* say that Canadian seniors have gained *at the expense of* the young and, furthermore, when describing the intergenerational equity debate in the United States, the author went to great pains to say that although some Americans argue that such a zero-sum relationship exists, it is by no means clear that it in fact does (Ng 1992: 15). However, the Canadian media account played up the drama of pitting young against old and noted that an "intergenerational war" has "raged for much of the past decade in the United States and Europe" (Mitchell 1992: A5). This is the type of dramatic media account that often prompts further media coverage. However, our database searches show that there were no further articles on the equity issue in the *Globe & Mail* (there was one letter to the editor) or in other newspapers in the second half of 1992 and in 1993.

For the United States, 39 articles on intergenerational equity or conflict appear during that time segment. The number of articles published in the mid-1980s increased from 1 in 1984 to 13 in 1988, decreasing somewhat after 1988 but not disappearing. Although not large in number, the titles contrasted dramatically with the majority of their Canadian counterparts: "Older Voters Drive Budget" (*Washington Post*, October 15, 1990); "U.S. Coddles Elderly but Ignores Plight of Children" (*Atlanta Constitution*, 1990); "America is at War with Its Children" (*San Francisco Chronicle*, October 12, 1989); "Robbing Baby Peter to Pay Aging Paul," (*Boston Globe*, February 10, 1991); "The Tyranny of America's Old" (*Fortune*, January 13, 1992).

Although the majority of the 39 articles on intergenerational equity in the U.S. pointed to conflict, some attempted to dissipate tension and reconcile differences: "The Old and Young Aren't Foes" (*New York Times*, April 8, 1987), for example, and "Time to Call in Bridge Builders for the Warring Generations" (*Chicago Tribune*, May 22, 1988).

In summary, the lack of discussion of intergenerational conflict in Canada is notable. Although the number of articles on intergenerational conflict in the United States is very small in relation to the large content of the databases, the majority of them have been dramatic in their portrayal of conflict and appeared in widely read newspapers.

Academic Attention

To measure the attention given to the issue in the academic arena, we used social science databases to locate articles, chapters, and books that dealt with the issue. After examining 17 social science databases, we chose to use one called AGELINE because it had the largest list of citations with the phrase (inter)generational equity or (inter) generational conflict.

Using the terms (inter)generational conflict (defined as "stresses and disagreements between generations in the family and in society"), (inter)generational transfers, and the word "(inter)generational" with conflict or equity anywhere in the subject fields of the record, our search produced a total of 258 citations. We reviewed the results of these three searches and eliminated citations dealing with family (as opposed to the social) aspects of intergenerational conflict and any popular (as opposed to academic) publications. As table 4.2 shows, this left 126 U.S. citations over a 13-year period covering 1980 through 1992, with a peak of 20 in 1989.

These 126 U.S. academic articles and books are often quite different from the media portrayals of intergenerational equity. Whereas many of the U.S. media portrayals make it appear as if "age wars" over scarce resources are taking place now or will do so soon, the academic publications often challenge the notion of a zero-sum distribution of resources between the young and the old and of impending conflict between the young and the old. Some provide analyses of data that show the story is not so simple as AGE and media commentators sometimes portray, while others provide philosophical, historical, or policy analyses of intergenerational equity concerns. Nonetheless, the academic discussion and presentation of both sides of the intergenerational equity debate and even the academic critiques of the issue serve to legitimize the importance of the issue and may help to perpetuate it on the policy and media agendas.

In comparison to the United States, academics in Canada paid little attention to the broad issue of generational conflict or its more narrow formulation as intergenerational equity. AGELINE contained references to only three articles dealing with intergenerational equity or conflict in Canadian academic sources over the 1980–1992 period. We scrutinized The Canadian Journal on Aging, Canada's leading ger-

Table 4.2 ACADEMIC ATTENTION TO THE ISSUE OF INTERGENERATIONAL
EQUITY IN CANADA AND THE UNITED STATES, 1980–1992

	Number of Articles, Books and Chapters[a]	
	Canada	United States
1992	1	17
1991	0	18
1990	0	10
1989	0	20
1988	1	17
1987	0	13
1986	0	9
1985	0	9
1984	0	7
1983	1	3
1982	0	0
1981	0	2
1980	0	1
Total	3	126

[a]Database source for academic attention: AgeLine, excluding articles considered to be about family intergenerational conflict or appearing in popular, as opposed to academic, sources. All searches were performed on the Dialog Online Information Retrieval Service, in Palo Alto, CA, January 1994. For details of database scope and coverage, consult that Dialog Database Catalog.

ontology journal, and two major policy journals, *Canadian Public Policy* and *Policy Options*, thinking AGELINE might have missed something. Not a single reference to generational equity issues or a generational equity debate appeared in those journals between 1980 and 1992. They carry articles about the financial costs of an aging population but not in intergenerational equity terms (e.g., Seward 1986; McDaniel 1987).

The major article of the three we found was the 1992 article in *Canadian Social Trends* by Ng. It reports on the changing incidence of low income among children and the elderly, and presents figures using data from Statistics Canada to show that the incidence of low income among those aged 65 and over has declined steadily since the 1970s but has changed very little for children, thus causing a disparity between the two groups. Further, it attributes the changes in the relative economic position of children and the elderly to the division of public resources. As far as we can tell from our research, this is the first time that such an argument has been made in Canadian academic publications. However, it is quite different from the first U.S. presentation of similar types of data by Preston (1984a, b). That is, Ng does not argue that fewer public resources go to children because so many go to the elderly; rather, he says that "the success of improving the lot of elderly people *demonstrates that effective change can be made in improving the lives of children*" (Ng 1992: 15; italics ours). Ng portrays the intergenerational equity debate in the United States as an issue of "growing concern" but he tries to differentiate the Canadian situation: "The Canadian situation is, however, very different from that in the United States. The United States does not have income support and medicare programs for all children the way family allowance and health care in Canada have been traditionally available for all children" (p. 15).

Although the intergenerational equity label did not emerge on academic agendas until the 1980s, some scholars warned earlier of the possibility of conflict between the generations. One of the first in the United States was Neugarten (1973) who wrote that "anger toward the old may also be on the rise. In some instances, because a growing proportion of power positions in the judiciary, legislative, business, and professional arenas are occupied by older people, and because of seniority privileges among workers, the young and middle-aged become resentful. In other instances, as the number of retired increases, the economic burden is perceived as falling more and more upon the middle-aged taxpayer" (p. 578). In Canada, Marshall (1979, 1981; Tindale and Marshall 1980) raised the issue of possible or actual conflict between age groups and specifically suggested that the high dependency of the aged on the state might lead to increased age-identification among the old, while the growth in the size of the old "has the potential to make it a target for the resentment of younger groups who are 'paying the bills'" (Marshall 1981: 94). However, neither Neugarten nor Marshall framed the issue as one in which the young would be deprived because of inappropriately generous provisions for the old.

Political Attention

To gauge political attention, we looked at activity within the U.S. Congress from 1980 to 1992. We used the *Congressional Record Index* (an index to all addresses and discussions on the floor of Congress) and the *Congressional Information Service Index* (CIS) (an index to congressional hearings and committee reports) to learn how much attention Congress has paid to intergenerational equity.

Looking under generational equity and intergenerational equity in these indices we found not a single entry. We found no references to "generations" in the Congressional Record Index, but we found four references to the Generations United organization and one reference to generations in the CIS. Generations United aims to promote greater consciousness about the ways generations are linked and to foster the development of social programs that integrate the concerns of young and old. Composed of representatives from both children's organizations and organizations for the elderly, Generations United is devoted to speaking out for the interdependence of the young and the old. The CIS references are to four congressional hearings in which representatives from Generations United testified as to the importance of programs which benefit both young and old (H341–74.3 in 1989; H141–21.2, H141–33.3, and H141–9.2 in 1987).

In 1986, the Select Committee on Aging in the House of Representatives held a hearing that was an explicit reaction to the emerging political issue of intergenerational equity. Entitled "Investing in America's Families: The Common Bond of Generations," the hearing brought together representatives from the Gerontological Society of America, children's interest groups (e.g., Children's Defense Fund), elderly interest groups (e.g., American Association for Retired Persons), and Americans for Generational Equity, as well a public opinion expert from Louis Harris and Associates. In his opening statement Congressman Edward R. Roybal, chairman of the Select Committee on Aging, made specific reference to intergenerational equity:

> Ladies and gentlemen, the purpose of today's hearing is to highlight the emotional and financial interdependence of families across generations and their common stake in programs for both young and old. It is also to take a critical look at what some see as an emerging conflict between old and young due to financial pressures on families (p. 1).

As far as we can tell, there was no recorded follow-up to the hearing in terms of reports, future hearings, or legislation. However, the terms of the debate may have shifted a bit. According to Nancy Smith, a staff member in the Select Committee on Aging, "the term 'intergenerational' is now in the vernacular" (Kuehne 1987). Smith said that after the hearing she noticed that lobbyists, researchers, and people interested in particular age groups began talking about strategy:

> The view was that we need to be talking about taking care of all the generations. . . . Right now, our strategy is to look for ways to benefit all the age groups. For example, we are supporting a National Health Program similar to Canada's where there would be health care for all ages. We're also supporting a change to the Social Security tax that would

reduce or give a break to those at lower incomes. And we're looking at the budget and those uninsured for health care. When we called witnesses, we called those representing the elderly AND children who need extended long term care.

We were not able to conduct an analysis for Canada that was comparable to our use of the *Congressional Information Service Index* or the *Congressional Record Index* because the quality and nature of indexing of *Hansard*, the official record of the Canadian Parliament, does not allow it. We therefore interviewed Frank Fedyk, a highly placed policy advisor in the Department of National Health and Welfare, and Marjery Boyce, the Departmental Policy Advisor to the Office of the Minister of State for Seniors (the cabinet minister with responsibility for the aged). Both Fedyk and Boyce said that intergenerational equity issues had not been discussed in the House of Commons or in the Senate, but they indicated an awareness of the U.S. intergenerational equity debate at the senior bureaucratic level of the federal government.

Boyce noted that she occasionally hears that "seniors have more than their share," but observed that, so far, "no one has rocked the boat" by introducing the issue into Canadian policy discourse. She suggested that it may be important to "educate" junior bureaucrats and politicians about the dangers of this formulation (M. Boyce, personal communication, February 15, 1991).

Fedyk suggested that federal policy initiatives for income security are turning increasingly towards children and youth because poverty among the aged has been reduced (see documentation in a later section) (F. Fedyk, personal communication, February 15, 1991). Recent policy changes have dealt with redistribution within the population of the aged, taxing back Old Age Security pension benefits from the elderly above a given level of income (the "pension clawback") but increasing the level of support for the means-tested Guaranteed Income Supplement. Similarly, changes within the children and youth category are intended to redistribute income within that age group (Ng 1992). A report of a Senate Standing Committee, *Children in Poverty: Toward a Better Future*, presented in January, 1991, includes recommendations to increase the federal minimum wage and to increase child benefits dramatically, but it makes no mention of financing such programs by reducing benefits to the aged.

Policy reports are not easy to track in Canada, but we found three in which the term intergenerational equity was used, though with an intent quite the opposite of that which characterized the discussion in the United States. The first was the final report of a major interdepartmental task force on the Canadian retirement income system (Task Force on Retirement Income Policy 1979). Although the Canada Pension Plan (CPP) and Quebec Pension Plan (QPP) were adopted in 1965, full retirement pensions were delayed for 10 years after the establishment of the plans and, consequently, benefit flows only began to build up after 1976, providing a benefit to future generations that was not available to people currently old. Thus, the task force noted, "given the way in which the C/QPP were phased in—there is a presumption that the future elderly will be relatively better off than are today's elderly. This is the position adopted by this report and obviously argues strongly for improving the financial position of those who are now elderly in order to maintain equity between generations."

A 1982 Canadian government report aimed at a wider public audience, *Better Pensions for Canadians* (Government of Canada 1983), repeated this same concern in a brief, two-page section entitled "Intergenerational Equity." This report recognized that "today's generation should not place an undue burden on future generations through the pension arrangements it established;" but it also argued that "the current generation should treat the elderly today at least as well as it expects to be treated by future generations" (p. 15). A year later, the Report of the Parliamentary Task Force on Pension Reform (House of Commons 1983) devoted three paragraphs to the issue and suggested "a kind of intergenerational golden rule":

> . . . . those now working could build up a moral claim on future pension entitlements by making transfers to the current elderly of at least the same magnitude as they would expect to receive when their time came. . . . Future working generations should be willing to make pension transfers if they know that the beneficiaries of those transfers had, in their time, made similar transfers." (p. 15)

None of these reports suggested that anything more than prudent fiscal planning was called for, and none of them pitted the old against the young in any conflictual context.

Public Opinion

To gauge attention within the general public to the issue of intergenerational equity, we used published information on public opinion survey data from Canadian and American public opinion polling organizations (Gallup of Canada; Gallup of U.S.; Decima of Canada; Harris Poll, U.S.). Not surprisingly, we were able to find no survey questions which ask members of the public whether they are familiar with the intergenerational equity issue. Therefore, we searched for survey questions in each country that addressed attitudes toward programs for aged adults. Our reasoning was that if members of the public had been influenced by the issue, they would not be supportive of programs for the elderly and would want to reduce spending on programs for elderly persons so as to increase spending to programs for children.

Assessing the degree of similarity in attitudes toward the elderly in Canada and the United States is not a simple task. Although polling organizations in both countries have asked respondents about their support for benefits for the elderly, the questions have seldom been identical. In addition, many more such questions have been asked of Americans than of Canadians. Thus, we piece together a comparative portrayal of support for the elderly using disparate questions, questions that have been asked in different years, and fewer questions for Canadians than for Americans.

Canadian public opinion. Canadian public opinion might be expected to respond to U.S. media stimuli. Since three out of four Canadians live within 150 kilometers of the U.S.-Canadian border (Canadian Ministry of Industry 1993), cable and satellite television coverage, as well as Canada's three national television networks, beam U.S. programs onto Canadian television screens. Print coverage is also extensive, with "Canadian" versions of *Time* and *Readers Digest*, and extensive distribution of U.S. magazines in Canada. *USA Today* is distributed in many parts of Canada through newsboxes. The question is whether Canadians have been influenced by coverage of the intergenerational equity debate to the extent that they are not supportive of programs for the old.

Between 1981 and 1986, Canadians were asked if senior citizens should receive more "social services and benefits from the government than they do now" (*Decima Quarterly Report*, Fall 1986). In each year more than three-fourths of Canadians supported more services to the elderly. In another survey, Gallup of Canada (1988) asked respondents in a nationwide survey, "Would you approve or disapprove if old age pensions were increased, but paid only to people who needed them?" Two-thirds of respondents said they approved such an increase.

Are Canadians simply supportive of increased benefits to all social groups in general, or are the elderly special? In 1981, 1983, and again in 1988, Canadians were asked whether the government should do more, less, or about the same for a wide variety of groups, including the elderly. As table 4.3 shows, the elderly constitute one of the most highly supported groups along with the poor and the handicapped. In each of the three years, more than three-fourths of respondents said the government should do more for the elderly. Fewer than half supported doing more for women, immigrants, the unemployed, French Canadians, and English Canadians.

Public opinion in the United States. In the 1980s and early 1990s, United States citizens responded to a variety of questions that gauged their support for benefits directed to the elderly. These questions include whether programs for the elderly should be protected from deficit-reducing measures and whether spending should be increased or decreased for programs for the elderly. Beginning in 1983, the Gallup organization asked U.S. citizens about spending cuts in programs such as Social Security or Medicare in order to reduce the deficit. The percent of the public disapproving of such cuts ranged between 83 percent in 1983 to 88 percent in 1987 (*Gallup Report*, August 1987). Similarly, the Gallup organization reported from surveys conducted in early 1989, that the public was more opposed to proposals trimming Social Security and Medicare benefits than to 13 other deficit reduction proposals described (*Gallup Report*, May 1989).

In surveys conducted from 1984 to 1986 by the National Opinion Research Center (NORC), respondents were asked whether they felt "too much, too little, or about the right amount" was spent on Social Security. In 1984, nearly 85 percent responded with either "the right amount" or "too little." In the 1985 and 1986 surveys, this number rose to over 90 percent (Shapiro and Smith 1985; Davis and Smith 1986).

In a 1986 nationally representative survey of 1209 respondents Cook and Barrett (1992) asked whether respondents thought that benefits should be increased, decreased, or maintained at current levels for seven different social programs. The programs receiving the most support were those primarily aimed at older adults (Medicare, SSI, and Social Security). The percentage of those wanting to increase benefits for these programs ranged from 68 percent for Medicare to 57 percent for Social Security. When the percentage of those wanting to increase benefits is combined with those wanting to maintain benefits (also a show of approval for a program), support for these elderly-related programs climbs above the 90 percent mark.

A Gallup survey conducted in 1989 asked respondents, "If you had a say in making up the Federal budget this year, for which of the

Table 4.3 PERCENTAGE OF CANADIAN CITIZENS WHO PREFER VARIOUS LEVELS OF GOVERNMENT ACTIVITY IN ASSISTANCE TO DIFFERENT GROUPS[a]

Policy Area	Government Should Do More			Government Should Do Same			Government Should Do Less		
	1981	1983	1988	1981	1983	1988	1981	1983	1988
Aid to Senior Citizens[b]	89	81	76	7	13	24	4	6	1
Aid to the Poor	84	78	79	9	15	19	7	7	2
Aid to the Unemployed	36	49	—	22	26	—	42	25	—
Aid to the Handicapped	90	—	42	8	—	—	2	—	—
Aid to Women	62	55	—	19	27	54	19	18	4
Aid to Immigrants	35	27	—	22	27	—	43	46	—
Aid to Aboriginal People[c]	54	45	49	17	24	39	29	31	11
Aid to English Canadians	—	—	22	—	—	71	—	—	7
Aid to French Canadians	—	—	23	—	—	59	—	—	18

Sources: 1988 data are from personal communication with R. Johnston, University of British Columbia, Vancouver, Canada. 1983 and 1981 data are from R. Johnston (1986, p. 210). *Public Opinion and Public Policy in Canada.* Canada: Minster of Supply and Services Canada.

a. Across these years (1981, 1983, and 1988), two different questions were asked. In 1981 and 1983, the question was: "Many different individuals and groups receive social services and benefits from government. I'd like to read a list of some of these groups to you and have you tell me, from your perspective, whether each of these groups should receive more or less social services and benefits from government than they do now. Whould you say (name of group) should receive more or less social services and benefits from the government than they do now?" In addition to the groups listed in the table, the 1981 and 1983 question also asked about the physically handicapped. In 1988, the question was: "I am going to read a list of groups. For each group, could you tell me if you think government should do more, do less, or do about the same for the group as it does now?" In addition to the groups listed in the table, the 1988 question also asked about farmers, small business owners, ethnic minorities, and single parent families.

b. In 1988, the category was "the elderly."

c. In 1988, the category was "native people."

following programs should spending be increased, for which should spending be decreased, or for which should spending be kept the same?" When the choice was "programs for the elderly," 50 percent said spending should be increased, 45 percent said spending should be kept the same, and only three percent said spending should be decreased (2 percent had no opinion) (*Gallup Report*, May 1989).

In 1987, The National Opinion Research Center (Opinion Roundup, 1987) asked what respondents thought the government's responsibility should be in a number of domains. Eighty-eight percent of respondents agreed it was the government's responsibility to "provide a decent standard of living to older people," and 83 percent agreed that it was the government's responsibility to "provide health care for the sick." These items received more approval than such items as "provide a decent standard of living for the unemployed" (51 percent), "reduce income differences between the rich and poor" (39 percent), and "provide a job for everyone who wants one" (35 percent).

Cook and Barrett's U.S data (1992) also allow for a comparison between support for senior citizens and other groups. Respondents were asked to rank groups according to whom they thought should receive additional assistance from the government. The groups ranked first and second were the poor disabled elderly and the poor elderly. Respondents ranked poor children next, then poor disabled adults, poor female heads of households, and finally, poor unemployed men. Similar to the Canadian data are the high ranking of the elderly and the low ranking of unemployed people.

Despite the rise in salience of the intergenerational equity issue in the U.S. media, academic writings, and political debate, the U.S. general public appears committed to supporting publicly financed programs that assist the old. This general public support appears to be as true in the U.S. as it is in Canada, where intergenerational equity has not emerged as an issue.

EXPLAINING THE DIFFERENCES

Why are the United States and Canada so different in the salience of intergenerational equity as an issue in the media, academic discourse, and political debate? We examine four alternative explanations: values, poverty status of young and old, resource allocation mechanisms, and political processes. We then explore possible reasons why, in contrast, public opinion is overwhelmingly in favor of programs for the old in both countries.

Value Differences

Could it be that Canadians hold values of beneficence that override concerns about intergenerational equity as defined in the conflictual U.S. sense? In fact, many Canadians have a self-image that, compared to the United States, theirs is a "kinder, gentler society." Nonetheless, further examination casts doubt on the importance of value differences as an explanation for greater U.S. preoccupation with intergenerational equity.

The debate as to any potential distinctiveness in societal values between Canada and the United States and as to the possible sources of these values has constituted one of the major topics of Canadian sociology (Brym 1989). The principal theorist fueling the debate has been an American, sociologist Seymour Martin Lipset (1963, 1986, 1990). The Lipset thesis rests most heavily on historically conditioned value differences between Canada and the United States.

The bases of value differences according to Lipset are five (this summary is based on Brym 1989). First, the nature of the physical terrain and geography required greater state supported intervention and centralized control in Canada than in the "lone frontiersman" approach which was possible in the United States; second, the continuing threat from the United States, as an expansionary revolutionary society, led to an emphasis on control over the population which held any possible liberal-democratic tendencies in check; third, the American Revolution led the least liberal populace of the new nation to flee to Canada, giving Canada a strong conservative impulse; fourth, religious differences between the two countries saw greater "Protestant ethic" influences toward individualism in the United States, compared with the more hierarchical and authoritarian values of Anglicanism and Catholicism; fifth, the failure of American expansionism, including the U.S. failure to conquer Canada in the War of 1812, as well as the suppression of liberal-democratic rebellions in both Upper Canada and Lower Canada (roughly, Ontario and Quebec) in 1837, reinforced conservatism. According to Lipset, the major value differences between Canada and the United States were set more than 100 years ago through a series of historical events having much to do with the revolutionary aspects of American society.

Many scholars have expressed strong reservations about Lipset's disregard of regional variations (Matthews 1983) and about his selectivity and overinterpretation of data (Brym 1989: 29–30; Truman 1971). According to a number of these scholars (e.g., Matthews 1983), Lipset's most recent attempts to counter criticism that he ignores tremendous regional variability in his book *Continental Divide* (1990), strain credulity.

Lipset's contentions about values concerning government and the economy are relevant to the generational equity debate. He sees Canada as midway between the United States and European countries in regard to individualism versus collectivism, citing data on the percentage of wealth in government hands and the extent of government ownership of industry. The political process in Canada is, according to Lipset, aptly characterized as social democratic (1990: 141), and he cites cross-national public opinion polls supporting the notion that Americans are more individualistic than Canadians (Lipset 1990: 142).

Other data challenge the strength of Lipset's analysis. For example, in an examination of public opinion about social welfare programs in eight countries (West Germany, France, Sweden, Denmark Australia, the United Kingdom, Canada, and the United States), Coughlin (1980) reports that Americans and Canadians are more similar to each other than to the citizens of any of the other countries in their commitment to collectivism (p. 18). Coughlin found that citizens of the two countries shared a similar mix of collectivist and individualist mass ideologies, with Americans' individualistic leanings being only somewhat stronger. Some argue that the similar ideology in the two countries results in similar proportions of the gross national product spent on social welfare programs. For example, Schwarz (1981) compared countries based on general government transfer payments as a percentage of gross domestic product in 1977 and found that of 22 OECD countries, Canada and the U.S. were ranked right near each other on this measure. Canada ranked 17th and the U.S. ranked 18th (p. 103).

Some commentators even see a few indications of a shift towards greater individualism in Canada, a drift that Allan Gregg of Decima sees as a major watershed in Canadian public opinion. He offers as evidence an increase in the percentage of Canadians who said individual Canadians were primarily responsible for protecting the environment from a 1986 level of 18 percent to 35 percent by December, 1989 (Gregg and Posner 1990: 96). Moreover, the federal government, which was conservative from 1984 to 1993, increased the emphasis on individualism and on economic competitiveness through a number of policies and programs. However, the popularity of the conservatives began to wane in the early 1990s. In the 1993 Canadian election, in what has been called "the most sweeping turnabout in the entire history of democratic politics" (Ladd 1993: 23), the Progressive Conservatives went from having won 169 of Parliament's 295 seats in the preceding contest to just 2 seats in the 1993 one. The Liberals won 177 of the 295 seats, meaning that the Canadian government is now majority Liberal. The Liberals ran on a platform promising the maintenance of the social safety net and job creation through government stimulus.

Canadians, according to survey data from the 1980s, "think of themselves as far less violent than Americans—as well as harder working, less competitive, better informed, more concerned about the environment and the disadvantaged, and generally more honest" (Gregg and Posner, 1990: 181). The most frequently offered reason why Canadians said Canada is a more caring society than the United States was the quality and availability of health care; about 9 of 10 Canadians specifically say that the Canadian system of universal medicare is better than the U.S. medical care system. While Canadians concede that the stronger economy and lower taxation rate in the United States make the American way stronger or better, two-thirds of Canadians judge the Canadian "quality of life" to be better (Gregg and Posner 1990: 19). Yet, one Canadian sociologist notes, without sympathy, that Canadians are a "caring society" only indirectly. As individuals, Canadians give much less than Americans to charitable causes. According to Bibby, "In a highly specialized Canada, we all officially care. But in practice, we contract it out to the government and the specialists" (Bibby 1990: 114).

Most Canadian social scientists today are hesitant to endorse Lipset's characterization of Canadian-American value differences. Available data, including the public opinion data on support for the elderly we reviewed in an earlier section, the eight-nation survey by Coughlin cited above, and the many critiques of the Lipset thesis, suggest more parallels than differences.

Differences in Poverty Status

An obvious potential explanation for the comparative lack of intergenerational equity concern in Canada, in contrast to the higher concern in the United States, is that there are genuine economic inequities based on age in the United States but not, to the same extent, in Canada. In the United States, part of the argument that there are intergenerational inequities is that, while the aged were once the most likely age group to be poor, they are now less likely to be poor than

Figure 4.1 PERCENTAGE OF PERSONS BELOW THE POVERTY LINE BY AGE
GROUP IN THE UNITED STATES, 1966–1991

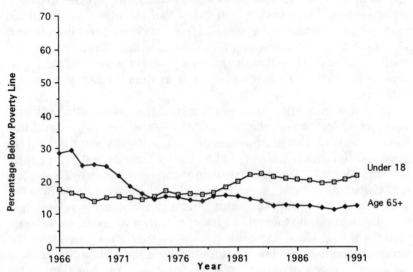

Source: U.S. Bureau of the Census, 1992. *Poverty in the United States: 1992.* Current
Population Reports, Series P-60, Number 185. U.S. Government Printing Office: Washington, D.C.

persons in the general population due to lavish resource allocation
from the public purse, while simultaneously the rate of poverty among
children has increased. One indication of this complex issue is depicted in figure 4.1, which shows the percentage of persons age 18 and
younger and age 65 and older below the poverty line in the United
States over the period 1966–1991.

The most striking feature of the poverty rate over this period is the
dramatic change in the group most likely to be poor. Figure 4.1 shows
a sharp fall in poverty among those age 65 and older and a slight
increase in poverty among those age 18 and younger, resulting in a
large discrepancy between the two groups. The point is that such a
dramatic change might well be expected to contribute to the perception of intergenerational inequity in the United States. In fact, figures
similar to figure 4.1 have been reproduced and discussed in the U.S.
media and in academic publications (e.g., Taylor 1991; Preston 1984a,
b). How different is the pattern in Canada?

Before we turn to the Canadian data, it is important to note that the
definitions of poverty are not exactly the same in the two countries
because they are calculated differently by the U.S. Census Bureau and
Statistics Canada. We believe that those differences are not important

in the context of this chapter because what we want to understand is the extent to which the *patterns* of poverty for children and the elderly in Canada are similar to the patterns in the United States. If they are similar, then we have some cause to rule out differences in poverty status as a possible explanation for the emergence of the intergenerational equity issue in the United States but not Canada. Unfortunately, there is an additional problem in looking at patterns: the figure using U.S. data (figure 4.1) goes back to the 1960s; however, the figures using Canadian data (figures 4.2a, b, and c) only go back ten years to 1981, because before that time Statistics Canada did not publish reports with data specifically on children. Another problem is that Statistics Canada used a different calculation to develop the poverty ("low income") threshold in the 1970s, making comparisons between the 1970s and 1980s difficult to interpret.

The Canadian data are presented separately by family type—first, for children and elderly persons living in families and, second, for lone parents with children under 18 and elderly persons living alone as unattached individuals. Finally, in figure 4.2c we combine all elderly persons living in families with elderly persons living alone (unattached) and compare them to all children—both those living in families with two parents and those living with one parent.

The comparative story is not a simple one, with some similarities and some differences between the two countries.[1] Similar to the U.S. pattern, the condition of the elderly has improved over time, and this is true both for older persons living in families and for unattached elders. Figure 4.2a shows that poverty for the elderly in families dropped from 18.9 percent in 1981 to 8.5 percent in 1991, and figure 4.2b shows that poverty for unattached elderly dropped from 62.8 percent in 1981 to 43.8 percent in 1991. In contrast, poverty among families with children increased from 15.2 percent in 1981 to 18.3 percent in 1991, and over that time poverty among lone parent families with children increased from 49.8 percent to 57.5 percent. Thus, similar to the U.S. pattern, poverty has decreased among the elderly and increased among children.

The difference from the U.S. pattern is that when we combine the elderly in families with elderly who are unattached, the poverty rate among the elderly is slightly higher (1.7 percent) than among children. Although the pattern of increased poverty for children and decreased poverty for the elderly is present, the *overall* pattern shows the two age groups to be in relatively similar economic circumstances.

We conclude, therefore, that one reason concerns about intergenerational equity may not have not arisen in Canada is that the economic

Figure 4.2a PERCENTAGE OF PERSONS IN LOW INCOME FAMILIES BY AGE IN
CANADA, 1981–1991

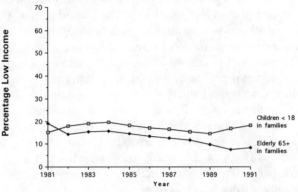

Figure 4.2b PERCENTAGE OF PERSONS WITH LOW INCOME FOR SELECTED
FAMILY UNIT TYPES IN CANADA, 1981–1991

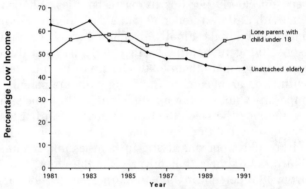

Figure 4.2c PERCENTAGE OF PERSONS WITH LOW INCOME BY AGE IN CANADA,
1981–1991

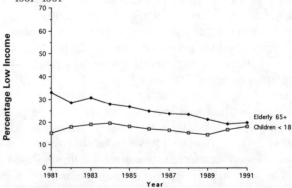

Source: Statistics Canada. *Income Distribution by Size in Canada, 1991*. Catalog Number 13-207. (Text tables III and IV).

inequities only appear when specific population subgroups are examined—that is, children in families versus elderly in families, and lone parents with children versus unattached elderly. Thus, the "target group" against which political action or ideology formation might be directed is not clearly visible. Further, statistics such as those in figures 4.2a, b, and c are seldom published for Canada, and comparisons between the elderly and children are rarely made (for one exception, see Ng 1992).

Social Policies and Programs

Do resource allocation mechanisms help explain differences in the importance of the intergenerational equity issue? This explanation centers on the greater importance of universal programs in Canada and the better balancing of benefits to young and old.

In Canada, there are currently two major universal programs, and until very recently there was a third. One (Medicare) is a health program that covers citizens of all ages. The second (Old Age Security) covers the old. Until 1992, a third (Family Allowances) covered children. In contrast, in the United States the two major universal programs—Social Security and Medicare—serve primarily the old and are treated in the public debate almost exclusively as programs for the elderly.

Old Age Income Security. The income security systems for the elderly in the two countries are discussed in detail in chapter 2 of this volume. The Canadian system has three components. The universal Old Age Security (OAS) program is the most important, accounting for about one-third of retirement income in Canada (Messinger and Powell 1987: 572). OAS provides a standard pension to all citizens and landed immigrants age 65 and older. There is no U.S. counterpart to this universal benefit. The OAS is not as visible to the taxpayer as is the Social Security tax because it is funded out of general revenues. This lack of visibility is plausibly one reason for the reduced salience of intergenerational equity in Canada. People do not perceive themselves as paying during their working years for benefits for the older generation.

The second component of Canada's old age income security system is the Canadian Pension Plan (CPP) and the similar Quebec Pension Plan (QPP). Each is a contributory pension plan to which all workers and their employers contribute. Like the U.S. Social Security program, CPP/QPP benefits depend on an individual's earnings and retirement history but also contain a redistributive component. Quadagno (1989:

357) notes that in the United States the public image of Social Security was manipulated during the early 1980s so that, rather than being seen as a solution to a social problem, it came to be seen as a problem—as a contributory cause of the failings of the U.S. economy. Canadian formulation of the CPP funding problem was not put in such terms. Perhaps as important, CCP/QPP benefits are considerably less generous than U.S. social security benefits (see chapter 2 of this volume).

The third component of Canada's old age income security program is a series of income-tested programs, principally the Guaranteed Income Supplement, that brings low-income pensioners closer to the poverty line. About half of Canada's old age pensioners receive full or partial supplements, which represent about 4 percent of GNP (Messinger and Powell 1987: 576). The U.S. counterpart is Supplemental Security Income (SSI), a means-tested entitlement for the elderly poor as well as for physically and mentally disabled adults under age 65. SSI benefits represent less than one percent of Gross Domestic Product, and are not typically included in the intergenerational equity rancor.

The Family Allowance Program. Until a major legislative change in 1992, the Family Allowance Program provided a benefit to parents on behalf of each child below the age of 18. This was a universal age-specific program which was small by comparison to Canadian government benefits directed toward the elderly, and by no means avoided the emergence of a serious problem of child poverty in Canada. However, despite the small level of benefits to children (and their young adult parents), the sense that the aged were not the only group to receive across-the-board benefits acted to reduce the sense of intergenerational inequity.

A dramatic change occurred in 1992. The Canadian Parliament voted to eliminate family allowances and to create a new system of monthly payment for low-income families. In other words, a universal program for children was transformed into a means-tested program. Since this legislative change was only very recently implemented into action, its effect on public perceptions is not yet clear.

Medicare. Surely a major reason that intergenerational equity issues are less visible in Canada than in the United States is that Medicare is not, in Canada, an age-specific program as it is in the United States. Canada's Medicare provides benefits to every citizen regardless of age. It is estimated that about one-third of all public health care expenditure is directed to the elderly population, amounting to about 2 percent of the GNP (Messinger and Powell 1987: 575).

In the United States Medicare policies provide age-based benefits and account for 2 percent of the Gross Domestic Product (U.S. Congress 1993). In addition, Medicaid, the other major public medical care program in the United States, covers families on welfare, the medically indigent, and the low-income elderly. Only 14 percent of Medicaid recipients are elderly, but this small proportion of Medicaid recipients receives 35 percent of all Medicaid payments; children constitute 42 percent of beneficiaries and receive only 12 percent of payments (Levitan 1990).

Claims are made in the Canadian political arena and in the Canadian media that recent and projected increases in health care costs in Canada constitute a "crisis" for governments and that the cause of increased costs is held to be the aging of the population. While rising health care costs are largely attributed by Canadian academics and by both federal and provincial bureaucrats to inadequate controls on physician and hospital spending (the latter seen as highly controlled by physicians), these costs do provide a focal point for media attention to the aging of the population. Popular newspaper accounts, and even some government reports, sometimes couple policy discussions of increased health care costs to population aging.

It is one thing, however, to "blame the aged," and another to pit the aged against the young. While Canadians have frequently fallen into the trap of blaming the aged, or population aging, for rising health care costs (McDaniel 1987), this is not linked to deprivation of the young. Rather, it is viewed in a more general context of perceived fiscal mismanagement by government. The overall level of discontent with health care costs may also be lower in Canada than in the United States, especially among academics and policymakers, because, as a percentage of Gross National Product, Canadians spend about 20 percent less per capita than Americans do for health care, while enjoying slightly lower morbidity and mortality rates as well as smaller social class inequities in health care delivery (Marmor, Mashaw and Harvey 1990).

The Political Process

Does the different nature of the political process account for differences in the importance of the intergenerational equity issue? Important differences in political structure and process exist between Canada and the United States. For a start, at the time of our analyses

Canada had three national political parties with discernible (though small) differences in political ideology. Parties meet in caucuses and the British principle of loyalty to the party is operative (Brym 1989: 61). A result is weaker emphasis on lobbying, as it is difficult for a lobbyist to make a difference by lobbying an individual member of Parliament than might be the case, for example, with lobbying of an American member of Congress.

Major analysts of senior gray power observe that it is much less developed in Canada than in the United States. Pratt, who has studied both U.S. and Canadian seniors' movements, notes that Canadian seniors groups have less influence than their American counterparts, and "are not enfolded into Canada's process of elite accommodations (Pratt 1987: 73). Neysmith (1987: 107) suggests that Canadian seniors may seek power and influence through organizations which are not specifically age-based. Marshall (1993) suggests that high levels of satisfaction by seniors with economic and service conditions may have diffused the potential bases for political organization.

Since issue articulation is enhanced by conflict and its resulting debate, the relative lack of a "senior power" movement in Canada may be one factor for the lower level of discussion of intergenerational equity. Gifford (1990: 248), who has provided the most thorough documentation of senior power in Canada, says that "Although seniors have clear common interests, the movement is not yet at the stage of Canada-wide united action among its organizations, except in a crisis."

Another reason for the difference in focus on intergenerational equity may be the preoccupation in Canada with the federal-provincial division of powers and the even more complicated division of economic responsibility. Foot (1984) estimates that with current programs, it costs 2.5 times as much to support an older Canadian as a young one, but he notes that in Canada support of the young has been primarily a private sector responsibility while that of the old has been primarily a public sector responsibility. He cites a study by McDonald which estimates that 43 percent of age-specific program costs are borne by the federal government, 47 percent by the provincial governments and 10 percent by municipal governments. However, while 58 percent of expenditures for the young were by provincial governments, 72 percent of those to the old were from the federal government. Most age-specific provincial expenditures are oriented to those of working age, while most municipal expenditures are oriented to the young. With the aging of the baby boom, the federal government will see a significant rise in expenditure, while municipal governments benefit.

Population aging is thought by Canadian academics to be manageable within economic growth projections, but to require resource reallocation among governmental sectors. They recognize that posing the question as one of purely public-sector expenditures miscasts it; rather, the issue is the capacity of the nation as a whole, the public and private sectors, to produce the wealth necessary to provide a decent quality of life for all citizens. The pressures of population aging are likely to be seen in political conflict among the different levels of government. The issue is not young versus old, but federal versus provincial versus municipal political jurisdictions.

Explaining Similarity in the Domain of Public Opinion

In the first section of this paper, we reported differences between Canada and the United States in the salience of the intergenerational equity issue in three domains: the media, the academic community, and the policy community. In the domain of public opinion, however, we found no difference.

Despite the fact that U.S. citizens have been exposed to the intergenerational equity debate in the media and in the policy community, the elderly appear to have a special place in public opinion, just as they do in Canada. Why is this? At least two reasons seem to be important. One has to do with the way citizens perceive the need of the elderly. The other has to do with ideology.

Need. Crystal (1982) argues that the public thinks most elderly are ill, poor, disabled, and isolated and that social policies for old people are formulated with these myths in mind. Data from both the United States and Canada support Crystal's claims. A majority of U.S. respondents in a survey conducted by the Harris Organization in 1981 said they believe that persons aged 65 and over do not have enough money to live on, are lonely, and are in poor health (Kearl, Moore, and Osberg 1982). In a 1989 Gallup organization survey, 61 percent of the U.S. respondents said they think that people 60 years and older are "more likely to be poor than other Americans" (Gallup Report, May 1989).

Similarly, in a nationally representative survey by Decima of Canada in 1988, almost 70 percent of Canadian respondents said they think senior citizens do not have enough money to meet their needs (*Decima Quarterly Report*, Winter 1988). The Canadian public's view holds when broken down by region, ethnicity, age, education, employment status, annual income, gender, and community size.

Ideology. Coughlin (1980) suggests that social welfare programs for the elderly tap ideologies in a different way from the way that programs for other groups tap ideologies. Values of individualism give way to values of collectivity when programs benefiting the aged are considered:

> We can understand the nearly universal popularity of old-age pension
> . . . programs as a result of the predominance of the collectivist component in mass ideology and the almost complete circumvention of competing individualist values and beliefs. While it is logically possible to argue that principles of self-reliance and individual initiative ought to extend to these areas of social policy, in actual fact very few hardnosed advocates can be found who publicly counsel denying a monthly allowance to the aged . . . solely to preserve ideological purity (p. 121).

The point is that in both Canada and the United States, citizens appear to hold an ideology of collectivity and solidarity when it comes to programs for the old.

CONCLUSION

Generational equity seems not to have emerged as a significant issue in Canada. We found virtually no record in Canada of attention in the media, in academic publications, or in policymaking communities. Where the term intergenerational equity was used in three government reports, the connotation was totally different from the U.S. connotation (i.e., an "intergenerational golden rule" was recommended whereby current workers build up a "moral claim" on future pension entitlements "by making transfers to the current elderly of the same magnitude as they would expect to receive when their time came") (House of Commons, 1983: 15). In the United States, on the other hand, the issue received attention in the academic, policy, and media arenas. Why?

Of the four possible explanations which we examined, we argue that at least three have some power as multi-determinants of the differential salience of the issue in the United States and Canada. We have been unable to find support for significant value differences between the two countries and thus conclude that differences in the emergence of the intergenerational equity issue cannot be attributed to differences in societal values.

Rather, we argue that the greater use in Canada of universal programs that provide almost all medical care at all ages may deflect attention away from age-based concerns. Prior to 1992, the Canadian program of family allowances provided a compensating, universal, resource allocation to children (and their young parents) and also perhaps lessened any sense of intergenerational inequity.

In addition, the political structure, and related processes, in Canada are different from those in the United States, and these too may have had an impact in lessening the amount of political discourse about inequities in resource allocation. Interest-group lobbying, other than that done more directly by corporate capital, is less a fact of the Canadian political process than it is in the United States. The greater receptivity to interest-group politics in the United States contributed to the success of AGE in getting intergenerational equity onto the policy table. Our data also suggest the remarkable extent to which this very small organization contributed to the emergence of a high profile issue.

Finally and significantly, economic inequities between children and the elderly are not as clearly visible in Canada as they are in the United States, and in fact they only appear when specific population subgroups are examined.

An additional major conclusion is that the two countries do not differ in public opinion toward support for the elderly. The explanation for this similarity is tentative and based on judgments of perceived need and ideology. This conclusion raises further questions, however. Why is it that the general public in both countries persist in attributing high levels of need to the elderly, when objective data do not support this judgment? The impact of academic research on public opinion seems in this instance to be minimal.

What will be the eventual fate of the intergenerational equity issue in the United States and in Canada? Will crushing "age wars" arise as Dychtwald and Flower (1989) propose? Or will intergenerational equity lose its salience in the various realms we have discussed?

On the one hand, there is some indication that intergenerational equity could actually rise in salience. Presumably, a rise in salience could occur under any of the following conditions:

(1) if intergenerational equity continues to lure the attention of the media, politicians, interest groups, and academics;
(2) if politicians continue to face constricted budgets, resulting in tight competition for scarce resources (i.e., many politicians would prefer to construct a zero-sum game *within* the social welfare domain, instead of choosing between social welfare and other political domains such as defense);

(3) if academics, interest groups, and the media continue to frame the issue in terms of the "demands of the old" versus the "needs of the young;" or

(4) if the debate within the health care sector about rationing of services to the old versus the young is heightened in intensity as American health care reform is implemented.

On the other hand, there is also some indication that the issue could decrease in salience in the United States. A decrease in salience could occur under the following conditions:

(1) if certain interest and lobbying groups that fueled this debate lose momentum, visibility, and power;

(2) if the voices of interest groups opposed to the debate as presently construed combine to change the terms of the debate (e.g., to change the terms from zero-sum calculations to the unity of common interests across generations);

(3) if age-neutral policies and legislation are enacted (e.g., a universal health care program) diverting attention away from policies focused on age; and

(4) if future scholarly research on intergenerational transfers (both monetary and nonmonetary) shows as much flow from the elderly to younger generations as from younger generations to the old.

In fact, a number of these latter conditions are appearing. AGE, for example, has suffered drastic declines in both visibility and power since 1988. In 1988, Durenberger's image took a turn for the worse when he became plagued with ethical, moral, and political troubles (e.g., inappropriate use of campaign and office funds, an impending divorce, alleged extramarital affairs). Durenberger finally left as head of the organization, and AGE had several other leaders, including Richard Lamm, former governor of Colorado. By early 1991, the AGE office was decimated, with only four staff members (one in Washington, D.C., and three in Texas). At about this time, AGE developed a link to a then-new lobby organization of baby-boomers—the American Association of Boomers ("Boomers")—and became the Boomers' research and education foundation. However, by early 1992 the relationship between the two organizations became strained, and AGE was dissolved (Keller 1994). The Boomers have a new research arm called simply Generations.

In addition, we see the emergence of groups attempting to change the terms of the young versus old debate. For example, Generations

United was formed to "dispel the myth of competition for scarce resources and reap the benefits of intergenerational collaboration . . . and interdependence" and to "unite at national, state, and local levels on key public policy issues that address the human needs across all generations" (Generations United, 1990a, 1990b). According to David Liederman, executive director of the Child Welfare League of America who helped to start Generations United, "What we are trying to say is that the fates of the generations are linked. Obviously, I want better programs for kids . . . but they should not come at the expense of seniors, especially the large number of seniors who are poor or near poor" (quoted in Pearlstein, 1993: F1).

Finally, universal health care is a high priority of U.S. President Bill Clinton. His administration submitted a proposal to Congress in late 1993 which will be debated in Congress in 1994, along with a number of congressional proposals, several of which also call for universal health care but with different management strategies.

Intergenerational equity could become increasingly important in Canada if the following conditions were to emerge:

(1) if media coverage of the issue begins to increase, and if coverage of generational issues is portrayed in a provocative way;
(2) if academics begin to take hold of the intergenerational equity issue, and begin to frame the debate on the same terms that it has been framed in the United States; or
(3) if policy analysts also begin to examine specifically how much various age groups get from the government, and explicitly compare the proportion of money spent on the elderly to the proportion spent on children.

We think, however, that intergenerational equity is not likely to emerge as an issue in Canada for the very reasons that it has not yet emerged. That is, the age-neutral universal program of Medicare in Canada helps to mitigate any sense that one group is being helped at the expense of another group. Moreover, the political system in Canada is less responsive to interest groups and lobbying from any one group such as AGE. Nonetheless, the increasing discrepancy between the economic well-being of Canada's senior citizens as compared to children provides a potentially fertile ground for the issue to take hold.

In short, we witnessed the emergence of the issue of intergenerational equity in the 1980s in the United States but not in Canada. In the 1990s we do not think we will see its rise in Canada and we think some indicators point to its possible decline in the United States.

APPENDIX 4.A

Database searching is an interactive process in which the person searching the database designs and modifies the search based on subject terms and other parameters such as data range, language of publication, or geographic area. Because the search process is determined by the searcher's online skills and the intellectual decisions made, the results of database searches are not standardized products. Any use of online search results as a data source should provide the details of the search method, so that the validity of the databases chosen and the search approach used can be assessed.

Databases Selected

The CANADIAN BUSINESS AND CURRENT AFFAIRS (CBCA), database, available through the DIALOG online information service as File 262, covers the time period July 1980 to the present and contained 1,907,570 records as of January 1993. It is updated monthly by Micromedia Ltd in Toronto. The database is the machine-readable counterpart of three printed indexes published by Micromedia: Canadian Business Index, Canadian News Index, and Canadian Magazine Index. The Canadian News Index provides access to 10 newspapers: 7 major dailies from across the country and 3 business newspapers. The Globe & Mail, which purports to be Canada's national newspaper, is one of the newspapers indexed. Approximately 500 magazines are indexed in CBCA. The database is bibliographic, without abstracts, but it does include subject descriptors, or standardized indexing terms, that are added by Micromedia staff.

An additional database, MAGAZINE INDEX, File 47 on Dialog, (containing 2,723,528 records as of January 1993) provides access to North American popular magazines and selected major scholarly journals from 1959 to March 1970 and from 1973 to the present. A review of the list of journals covered suggested that, although the vast majority of the publications were of U.S. origin, at least 11 Canadian magazines were also included.

For U.S. newspapers and magazines, no single database was found that included both of these publication types. The newspaper coverage was split between NEWSPAPER ABSTRACTS, File 603 on Dialog, which indexed 19 major newspapers from 1984 to 1988 (2,625,473 records as of January 1993) and NEWSPAPER & PERIODICAL ABSTRACTS (File 484—3,034,750 records as of January 1993) which included 300 "general interest, professional and scholarly periodicals" from January 1988 to the present and indexing for 25 national and regional newspapers from 1989 to the present. Both newspaper indices include the New York Times.

There are additional full text newspaper databases available in the United States and Canada besides the bibliographic databases searched for this paper; however, the authors decided that the sources searched provided a sufficient indication of the content of the popular press in both countries for the purposes of this paper.

The AGELINE database produced by the American Association of Retired Persons served as a source of publications in both the popular and academic media. The database covers the years 1978 to the present with selected coverage back to 1966. Journal citations account for about two-thirds of the database, with the rest including citations of books, book chapters, and reports. The database provides comprehensive coverage in social gerontology and, as such, was the most appropriate database to use for identifying the academic works. AGELINE contained 34,720 records as of January 1, 1993.

Search Strategy

Each of the online databases used for this research was created by a different database producer. As such, the database structures and indexing languages differed. The approach taken in searching was to initially search as broadly as possible under words or phrases that represented the concepts "the old" and "the young." Both concepts had to be present in the database record for the item to be retrieved. Specific terms frequently used by authors such as "intergenerational conflict" and "intergenerational equity" were also used in the search. If a database had appropriate indexing terms or descriptors available, these were also used. High recall as opposed to high precision was used as a standard in the initial searches to ensure that as many potentially relevant citations as possible were retrieved. Despite the care taken in the search process, it is possible that there are additional publications in both the popular media and academic categories. This may have occurred because particular publications were not included in the databases or because our particular search strategy did not retrieve the items.

The search results were examined separately by two reviewers to determine whether specific citations dealt with intergenerational conflict as it had been defined in the research and whether the publication source was popular or academic in nature. Disagreements were resolved by discussion between the two reviewers.

Notes

Acknowledgment: The authors thank Richard A. Settersten, Jr., Leslyn Curle, and Joanne Daciuk for research assistance in Evanston and Toronto.
1. In an earlier paper (Marshall, Cook, and Marshall 1993), we did not deal adequately with these complexities.

References

Americans for Generational Equity. 1990. *Annual Report*. Washington, D.C.: Americans for Generational Equity.

Bengtson, Vern L. 1990. "Generations and Aging: Continuities, Conflicts and Reciprocities." Presidential address to the Gerontological Society of America, 17 November 1990.

Bengtson, Vern L., Neal E. Cutler, David J. Mangen, and Victor W. Marshall. 1985. "Generations, Cohorts, and Relations between Age Groups." In R. H. Binstock, Ethel Shanas and Associates (eds.), *Handbook of Aging and the Social Sciences*, 2nd ed. New York: Van Nostrand Reinhold, pp. 304–338.

Bibby, Reginald W. 1990. *Mozaic Madness: The Poverty and Potential of Life in Canada*. Toronto: Stoddart.

Brym, Robert J., with Bonnie Fox. 1989. *From Culture to Power: The Sociology of English Canada*. Toronto: Oxford University Press.

Canadian Ministry of Industry. 1993. *The 1994 Canada Year Book*. Ottawa: Ministry of Industry, Science and Technology.

Cook, Fay Lomax, and Edith J. Barrett. 1992. *Support for the American Welfare State: The Views of Congress and the Public*. New York: Columbia University Press.

Coughlin, R. M. 1980. *Ideology, Public Opinion, and Welfare Policy: Attitudes toward Taxes and Spending in Industrialized Societies*. Berkeley: Institute of International Studies.

Crystal, S. 1982. *America's Old Age Crisis*. New York: Basic Books, Inc.

Davis, J. A. 1986. "British and American Attitudes: Similarities and Contrasts." In *British Social Attitudes*," edited by R. Jowell, S. Witherspoon, & L. Brook. Aldershot: Gower, 89–114.

Decima Quarterly Report, Fall 1986 and Winter 1988.

Directory of Online Databases. New York: Cuadra/Elsevier, July 1989.

Dychtwald, Ken and Flower, Joe. 1989. Age Wave: The Challenges and Opportunities of an Aging America. New York: J. P. Tarcher Publicity.

Foot, David K. 1984. "The Demographic Future of Fiscal Federalism in Canada." Canadian Public Policy 10(4): 406–414.

Gallup Canada, Inc., poll conducted 10/12/88 to 10/15/88.

Gallup Report, August 1987, Report No. 263.

Gallup Report, May 1989, Report No. 284.

Garfield, Eugene. 1984. "The 100 Most-Cited Papers Ever and How We Select 'Citation Classics.'" Current Contents 23 (June 4).

Generations United. 1990a. Strategies for Change: Building State and Local Coalitions on Intergenerational Issues and Programs. Washington, D.C.: Generations United.

Generations United. 1990b. Promoting Cooperation Among Americans of All Ages. Washington, D.C.: Generations United.

Gifford, C. G. 1990. Canada's Fighting Seniors. Toronto: James Lorimer and Company.

Gould, Stephanie G. and John L. Palmer. 1988. "Outcomes, Interpretations, and Policy Implications." In John L. Palmer, Timothy Smeeding, and Barbara Boyle Torrey (eds.), The Vulnerable. Washington, D.C.: The Urban Institute Press.

Government of Canada. 1983. Better Pensions for Canadians. Ottawa: Government of Canada, Minister of Supply and Services, Catalogue No. CP 45-28/ 1982e.

Government of Canada. 1982. Better Pensions for Canadians. Ottawa: Government of Canada (Catalogue No. CP 45-48/1982E).

Gregg, Allan, and Michael Posner. 1990. The Big Picture: What Canadians Think About Almost Everything. Toronto: MacFarlane Walter & Ross.

House of Commons. 1983. Report of the Parliamentary Task Force on Pension Reform. Ottawa: Queen's Printer for Canada.

Kearl, M. C., Moore, K., and Osberg, J. S. 1982. "Political Implications of the 'New Ageism.'" International Journal of Aging and Human Development 15(3), 167–183.

Keller, Doris. 1994. Staff, American Association of Boomers. Personal communication.

Kuehne, Valerie S. 1987. "The Rise and Demise of Intergenerational Equity as a Conflictual Issue on the Federal Agenda." Unpublished manuscript, Evanston, Illinois: Northwestern University.

Ladd, Carll Everett. 1993. "Canada's Great Partisan Realignment." The Public Perspective 5: 23–24.

Levitan, Sar A. 1990. Programs in Aid of the Poor. Baltimore: Johns Hopkins University Press.

Lipset, Seymour Martin. 1963. The First New Nation. New York: Basic Books, Inc.

————. 1986. "Historical Traditions and National Characteristics: A Comparative Analysis of Canada and the United States." *Canadian Journal of Sociology* 11(2): 113–155.

————. 1990. *Continental Divide: The Values and Institutions of the United States and Canada.* New York and London: Routledge.

Longman, Phillip. 1982. "Taking America to the Cleaners." *The Washington Monthly* November: 24–30.

Marmor, Theodore R., Jerry L. Mashaw, and Philip L. Harvey. 1990. *America's Misunderstood Welfare State.* New York: Basic Books.

Marshall, Victor W. 1979. "Age Irrelevance or Generational Conflict: Contrasting Images of the Future." In *The Young-Old . . . A New North American Phenomenon.* Proceedings of the 30th Annual Winter Conference, Couchiching Institute of Public Affairs. Toronto: Couchiching Institute, pp. 13–20.

————. 1981. "Societal Toleration of Aging: Sociological Theory and Social Response to Population Aging." In *Adaptability and Aging I.* Proceedings, IX International Conference on Social Gerontology. Paris: International Centre of Social Gerontology, pp. 85–104.

————. 1993. "Services for the Aged in Canada." In Kruger, Arthur M., Morley, David, and Shachar, Arie (eds.), *Public Services under Stress: A Canadian-Israeli Policy Review.* Jerusalem: Magnes Press.

Marshall, Victor W., Fay Lomax Cook, and Joanne Gard Marshall. 1993. "Conflict over Intergenerational Equity: Rhetoric and Reality in a Comparative Context." In Bengtson, Vern L. and Aclenbaum, Vern L., eds., *The Changing Contract across Generations.* New York: Aldine De Gruyter: 119–140.

Matthews, D. R. 1983. *The Creation of Regional Dependency.* Toronto: University of Toronto Press.

McDaniel, Susan A. 1987. "Demographic Aging as a Guiding Paradigm in Canada's Welfare State." *Canadian Public Policy* 13(3): 330–336.

Messinger, Hans, and Brian J. Powell. 1987. "The Implications of Canada's Aging Society on Social Expenditures." In V. W. Marshall (ed.), *Aging in Canada: Social Perspectives, 2nd Edition.* Markham: Fitzhenry and Whiteside, pp. 569–585.

Mitchell, Allana. 1992. "Seniors Gain at Expense of Young, Report Says. Growing Child Poverty May Fuel Debate Over Who Deserves Social Aid." *Globe & Mail* (July 15) A5.

NORC. 1987. "Opinion Roundup: The Role of Government." *Public Opinion* 9(6), 22–29.

Neugarten, Bernice L. 1973. "Patterns of Aging: Past, Present, and Future." *Social Service Review* 47(4): 571–80.

Neysmith, Sheila M. 1987. "Organizing for Influence: The Relationship of Structure to Impact." *Canadian Journal on Aging* 6(2): 105–116.

Ng, Edward. 1992. "Children and Elderly People: Sharing Public Income Resources." *Canadian Social Trends* 25: 12–15.

Palmer, John L., Timothy Smeeding, and Barbara Boyle Torrey, eds. 1988. *The Vulnerable.* Washington, D.C.: The Urban Institute Press.

Pearlstein, Steven. 1993. "The Battle over 'Generational Equity': Powerful Spending, Tax Choices Have the Young Calling for the Old to Get Less." *Washington Post* (February 17) F1.

Pratt, Henry J. 1987. "Aging Policy and Process in the Canadian Federal Government," *Canadian Public Administration* 30(1): 57–75.

Preston, Samuel H. 1984a. "Children and the Elderly: Divergent Paths for America's Dependents." *Demography* 21(4): 435–57.

———. 1984b. "Children and the Elderly in the U.S." *Scientific American* 251(6): 44–49.

Quadagno, Jill. 1989. "Generational Equity and the Politics of the Welfare State." *Politics and Society* 17(3): 353–376.

Schwarz, M. A. 1981. *The Environment for Policy-making in Canada and the United States.* Montreal: C. D. Howe Institute.

Seward, Shirley. 1986. "More and Younger?" *Policy Options* 7(1): 16–19.

Shapiro, R. Y., and T. W. Smith. 1985. "The Polls: Social Security." *Public Opinion Quarterly* 49: 561–572.

Task Force on Retirement Income Policy. 1979. *The Retirement Income System in Canada: Problems and Alternative Policies for Reform,* vol. 1. Ottawa: Government of Canada.

Taylor, Paul. 1991. "Like Taking Money from a Baby: The Young Lose to the Old in the Funding Sweepstakes." *The Washington Post National Weekly Edition,* March 4–10, p. 31.

Tindale, Joseph A., and Victor W. Marshall. 1980. "A Generational-Conflict Perspective for Gerontology." In V. W. Marshall (ed.), *Aging in Canada: Social Perspectives.* Don Mills: Fitzhenry and Whiteside, pp. 43–50.

Truman, T. 1971. "A critique of Seymour M. Lipset's article, 'Value Differences, Absolute or Relative: The English-speaking Democracies.' " *Canadian Journal of Political Science* 4(4): 497–525.

Walker, Alan. 1990. "The Economic 'Burden' of Aging and the Prospect of Intergenerational Conflict." *Aging and Society* 10(4).

Weir, Margaret, Ann Orloff, and Theda Skocpol. 1988. *The Politics of Social Policy in the United States.* Princeton, NJ: Princeton University Press.

Part Two

RESOLVING THE ECONOMIC CONFLICT AMONG GENERATIONS

A TRUCE IN THE AGE WARS? INTERGENERATIONAL JUSTICE AND THE PRUDENTIAL LIFESPAN SOLUTION IN HEALTH CARE

Margaret Pabst Battin

The so-called age wars, while fluctuating in public visibility from one political season to the next, remain a continuing source of friction in policy development concerning domestic issues. Ought the young support the old? Ought there be legislation providing social benefits like health care, income support, social security, senior subsidies, and other sorts of benefits, either through taxes or other transfer policies, which have the effect of supporting the elderly at the expense of younger generations? Or, on the contrary, as Euripides insisted almost 2500 years ago, ought the old "quit this life and clear the way for youth" (*Suppliants*, line 1109)? Ought policies extending the lives of the elderly not be provided, in order to give the young a chance? Ought health care and other benefits simply be withheld—or withdrawn— from the elderly "to clear the way for youth"? Should we let the old die, if they cannot or will not provide health care for themselves? The "age wars," fought over the relative obligations of younger and older generations to each other, are always ready to erupt, and will remain so unless a comprehensive, coherent, defensible solution to the underlying theoretical issue of young against old can be found—a solution, perhaps, that will make possible a genuine truce.

POLICIES AND CONFLICT IN THE AGE WARS

Conflict in the age wars has been perhaps most vividly pursued in the recent friction between two lobbying organizations: AARP, the venerable American Association of Retired Persons, now over 40 years old and with some 32 million members, and the upstart, shakily financed, little-known AGE, Americans for Generational Equity, founded in 1984 by Sen. David Durenberger (see chapter 4 for more detail on AGE). AARP lobbies tirelessly for increased benefits to the elderly in every area from health care to senior housing; AGE had sought to undermine AARP's central assumptions about the desirability of supporting the elderly in the first place. AGE collapsed as an organization in 1991; but the basic point it was attempting to make remains one of considerable philosophical interest.

Two of the most heavily disputed targets in the age wars are the immense federal programs Medicare and Social Security. AARP fights to maintain and strengthen these programs. AGE, in opposition, had insisted they are unjust: since both are financed (either entirely or in part) by taxes—taxes paid by working, hence younger people—but since both benefit only the aged, these programs do not treat differing generations equitably. As AGE saw it, these policies are unfair because the elderly, who receive benefits from these programs, do not (for the most part) contribute to them, and those who pay for them, the young, do not receive benefits. Hence, while AARP claims they are just, AGE insisted they are generationally unjust: a kind of perverse Robin Hood, robbing the poor to give to the rich.

Though they seem insignificant compared to huge federal programs like Medicare and Social Security, small differential policies are also sometimes said to be generationally unjust: senior citizen discounts, lowered bus fares, and reduced admission to National Parks—at least insofar as the lower fees paid by the elderly are subsidized by taxes and/or higher user fees paid by the young. Those supporting the elderly argue that these differential policies are appropriate concessions to the vulnerable position of the elderly. Those concerned with the plight of the young argue that it is not clear—for huge federal programs or for tiny senior citizen discounts—either that the elderly are morally entitled to such benefits or that the young should be required to provide them—especially when doing so seems to undercut their own interests. Why should the young be forced to support the old? Why shouldn't the old be treated with greater concern and respect by the young? These are the battle cries of the age wars.

The dispute over intergenerational justice continues with conflicting claims about the relative sizes of overall outlays to the young and the old. The Congressional Budget Office estimated in 1990 that after military spending and interest payments were factored out, federal expenditures for the elderly totaled nearly half domestic federal spending—some 47 percent. Meanwhile, support for children has been declining, especially in programs like the nutrition program for women, infants, and children (WIC) and the income support program

Aid for Families with Dependent Children (AFDC), and now represents only a fraction of support for the old. The value of AFDC assistance has declined by 40 percent since 1970, according to the Children's Defense Fund, because it has not been adjusted for inflation. Furthermore, it is only poor children who receive any benefits at all, while all old people do, many of whom are well off. As Richard Lamm, former Governor of Colorado and former Chairman of the Board of AGE, points out, "a child in America is much more likely to be poor than someone 65"; he urges that we realize that "our society does have the option of transferring money now going to rich elderly to poor kids."[1]

Of course, not all public programs providing benefits for the elderly are attacked as violations of intergenerational justice. The Catastrophic Health Insurance Act, enacted in 1990 but hastily repealed, would not have involved intergenerational transfers, as it imposed costs on the same age-group as its prospective beneficiaries; instead, it would have involved transfers from well to ill and from rich to poor members of the elderly age-group. AGE took credit for what it called the measure's "generationally neutral" financing mechanism (Lamm 1991, p. 2), which was not however perceived as generationally neutral by the seniors' groups. As they saw it, this measure imposed all the costs on them. It was the seniors' groups that pressured (successfully) for its repeal.

Furthermore, a countercharge can be leveled against those who view programs involving large outlays to the elderly as generationally unjust. Not only are these programs not unjust as they stand, it is argued, but true intergenerational justice would require much *larger* societal expenditures for the elderly in health care programs like Medicare, in income supports like Social Security, and in other kinds of programs. This countercharge points to the treatment of the elderly in other countries, especially those with generous and effective health care and/or social welfare programs, e.g., the Netherlands, Canada, and some of the Scandinavian countries. In contrast to these countries, it is observed, the United States often offers comparatively inferior care in inferior facilities, and fails altogether to provide many sorts of ancillary supports: long-term care, in-home care, psychiatric care, etc., etc. Rather than having the United States restrict outlays to its elderly, this counterargument continues, the United States ought to augment its pool of resources available for health care, either by further contributions or reallocation of other priorities, and services to the elderly should be increased. Indeed, we should be ashamed of the comparatively limited, erratic, poor care we offer the elderly, and

should make every effort to see that it is improved. Age bias is every-
where, and nowhere more shameful than in our wretched care for the
old. In the war between the young and the old, on this view, it is the
old who are mistreated and cheated by the young.

Ought the young support the old? Ought the old be treated more
decently by the young? Are the young and the old caught in a continuing conflict of interests, popularly—and properly—called the age
wars? Not only are these questions already pressing, but they will
grow even more urgent as the population ages (as is the case in all
advanced industrial nations) and the proportion of old and very old
persons increases. This pressure will increase in just two decades,
starting around 2011, as the 85 million "baby boomers" born between
1946 and 1964 reach 65, then 75, then 85 and over. The aging of the
baby boom will produce a substantial shift in the proportion of old
to young in the population and, because older people require more
health care, will make enormous demands on health care resources.
And this, in turn, is likely to exacerbate the already patent political
friction between the young and the old, making still more troubling
the underlying basic questions—unless, of course, an adequate theoretical and practical solution to the problem of intergenerational justice can be found. At least one new group—Generations United—
attempts to reduce the friction, and intergenerational justice is an
explicit objective of the Clinton administration's national health care
plan, but the mere existence of a lobby group or a political goal does
not entail that a theoretically adequate resolution of the basic conflict
in the age wars has been found.

A COHERENT RESOLUTION? THE PRUDENTIAL LIFESPAN APPROACH TO ISSUES OF INTERGENERATIONAL JUSTICE

It is not ordinarily very interesting, either philosophically or rhetorically, to "apply" a "theory" to a "problem." We merely see a single,
limited way of viewing a problem; and alternative theoretical constructions of the problem, or alternative understandings of what the
problem is, are left out of account. Once in a long while, however, the
application of a theory proves genuinely illuminating. This is especially likely when the theory consists largely in a single, central point
that is crucial to conceptualizing the problem in an appropriate way
but has been overlooked. As it happens, there is a theory of sufficient
power for addressing the policy problems raised by the age wars: it is

Norman Daniels' now-classic analysis of the way in which problems of competition among age groups have been traditionally misunderstood, and how—by a single, simple shift—they can be radically reinterpreted. Daniels' discussion, first articulated in his book *Am I My Parents' Keeper?* (1988) is easily described as the most influential and important contemporary treatment of issues in intergenerational justice. It earns that honor by recasting the problem in a simple but thoroughgoing way.

The problem of intergenerational justice, like all problems of distributive justice generally, has been understood as a problem of competition for scarce resources by two or more competitors or groups of competitors: broadly speaking, the young and the old. This is a conception emphasized in the so-called age wars, and reinforced especially by organizations like AARP and AGE. One can also understand the problem in a more complex way as involving mutual competition among a number of groups—infants, children, young adults, the middle-aged, the old, and the old old. But however finely divided, the problem construed in this way is still understood as a competition among different age groups.

It is this central assumption that is challenged by Daniels' approach. While other problems of distributive justice are correctly understood as a competition for resources among competing groups (say, racial, gender, occupational, educational, or other groups), Daniels argues, age groups ought not be understood in this way. This is because persons are not simply members of given age groups in a fixed, permanent way, as they are of racial or gender groups, but pass through different age groups in the course of a lifetime. We do not change our race or gender during our lives, but we do change our age groups: we are first young, then middle-aged, then old. Consequently, the analysis of issues of intergenerational justice cannot properly take place in the terms of mutual competition among groups, though such an analysis would be appropriate for conflict between racial or gender groups.

Instead, Daniels argues in explicating what has come to be known as the Prudential Lifespan approach, we can best reach an understanding of what justice requires by considering what policies we would choose if we understood ourselves as persons destined to pass through a series of age-stages in the course of our lifetimes. Here, Daniels appeals to the theory of justice developed by John Rawls (1971), according to which issues of distributive justice can be settled by considering what principles prudent persons would agree to have govern a society of which they are members, if they were required to agree to these principles without knowing their own personal characteristics and hence without knowing what principles would favor themselves—or, in Rawls' terminology, what rational self-interest-maximizers would consent to in the "original position," when they are behind the "veil of ignorance" about the individual characteristics they have as a product of the "natural lottery."

This Rawlsian strategy, applied (as Rawls himself never does) to public policy, poses direct questions about policy issues. What differential allocation of resources between young and old would you consent to, if you wished to maximize your own interests but did not know your own age? What specific public programs would you accept? Medicare, with its extensive allocations to the elderly, but without provision for the young? WIC, even though its resources are very, very small? A world with both? It might seem that Medicare would be attractive to you if you are old or approaching old age, WIC if you are young, and a world with both attractive to no one really interested in maximizing *self*-interest. Yet more careful reflection, stimulated by the device of the original position and the veil of ignorance, may produce quite a different answer.

The prudential lifespan approach, thus, considers how the prudent allocator would assign health care resources available to her over her lifetime, given that she cannot know at what point she currently finds herself in that lifetime. She will choose, Daniels conjectures, a policy which emphasizes expenditures for health care in youth but deemphasizes expenditures for the elderly. This is a prudent choice because passage through the younger life-stages is prerequisite to reaching older ages. If one understands one's interests as furthered by having a normal range of age-relative opportunities, which of course presuppose also having continued life, then one will choose a savings scheme which will most enhance one's chances of reaching old age. Prudent allocators are aware that medical care is more efficient in the treatment of the young (except perhaps the worst-off newborns, whose realistic chances of survival are very small) than in treatment of the elderly, both because the young are likely to have fewer coexisting conditions and deteriorative processes, and because their natural recovery processes are better. But because care in youth is prerequisite to reaching old age and because it is more efficient in youth, prudent allocators in a situation of scarcity will agree only to policies which provide adequate care in youth—that is, care sufficient to ensure survival in reasonably good health—but which concede, if scarcity requires, to limitations after that. Of course, emphasizing expenditures for health care in youth but deemphasizing them for the elderly need not entail that the dollar amount allocated to youth is greater than that for the elderly. On the contrary, because the likelihood of ill health increases as age increases and because ill health becomes increasingly expensive to treat, the dollar amount the prudent allocator assigns to older ages may actually be greater than that allocated to childhood. What is crucial is the *proportion* of a given age's health care needs that are met. (This applies only to real needs, not to various kinds of desired but nonessential health care.) The prudent allocator will choose policies that cover 100 percent of childhood's health care needs, even if that means that only, say 50 percent or 75 percent or even 25 percent of the expected health care needs of older ages will be covered.

Hence, prudent allocators will reject Medicare, if it is not supplemented by companion programs for the young, because it provides care only to the elderly. Provided there are guarantees of redistribution to the young, on the other hand, they will accept proposals like Daniel Callahan's (1987, 1990, 1993) call for age-rationing, which would limit care for the elderly primarily to comfort care but would not provide expensive life-sustaining therapy for those who are dying. They would even entertain more radical policies tolerating voluntary euthanasia or voluntary physician-assisted suicide, provided there were protections against abuse and guarantees that funds for care would be redistributed to the young, under the assumption that an earlier, more humane exit, voluntarily chosen by those terminally ill persons who so wished, would also yield savings of resources for further medical care.[2] All these policies would operate to increase the chances for each individual of survival into old age. Thus, they benefit *both* the young and the old: they benefit the young by increasing their chance of survival and maintaining their normal age-relative opportunity range, and they benefit the old by having already increased the chance of reaching advanced age and hence retaining the opportunities that continuing life provides. Allocation plans that use resources differentially at ages where they are most efficient benefit everyone over their lifetimes, if full care cannot be provided at all ages, and hence will be most attractive under stable institutions to rational self-interest maximizers, since these parties know they will benefit from and cannot be the losers under such distributive schemes. Older persons are not rationed "against," even though allocations to them would be reduced. On the contrary, older persons will already have realized substantial benefits from this system, including the current benefit of having had an increased chance of reaching old age.

DISADVANTAGES OF THE LIFESPAN APPROACH

That Daniels' prudential lifespan account has already become a classic in the few short years since its publication does not mean that it
is immune to objection; on the contrary, the objections leveled against
it are numerous (see also chapter 6 of this volume).[3] They include, to
review just some of the objections more frequently voiced and to add
several less frequently discussed, the following six claims.

First, age groups are not the same as age cohorts. Daniels addresses
this problem, suggesting that it requires only "fine tuning." But it
remains unclear how well the prudential lifespan approach can account for the often very different characteristics and circumstances of
different age cohorts, as e.g. the comparatively small cohort born during World War II and the huge baby boom cohort born just following
it. Substantial differences in characteristics and circumstances of
these two temporally close cohorts may mean that their "age-relative
normal opportunity range" will be different and perhaps that health
care will play a different role in protecting it.

Second, startup problems would be involved in putting the prudential lifespan theory into practice. The attraction of the lifespan account
trades on the advantages to the person who is now old of having had
better prospects for becoming so; but of course these advantages are
not available to the person who is already old (and hence to be allocated less care) at the time any such policy is put into practice.

The third objection points out that the prudential lifespan account
presupposes an ideal world, involving practices operating against a
background of just institutions, when the actual institutions of the
real world are often demonstrably unfair. Hence, a policy that would
be just in an ideal world may, on the contrary, reinforce injustice in
the real world. Daniels (1988, p. 96) recognizes that his argument
"does not readily or easily extend to non-ideal contexts," and specifically insists that it does not automatically justify age-rationing of the
sort said to characterize the British National Health system. However,
this does not answer the question of whether the prudential lifespan
account can be useful in the real world at all.

Fourth, the prudential lifespan account will not resolve problems
in intergenerational justice in the same way in areas other than health
care, since it cannot be supposed in other areas that allocations early
in life are prerequisite to adequate function later in life. For example,
while survival early in life is prerequisite to survival later in life,
literacy early in life is not prerequisite to literacy later on: even an

adult can learn to read. A person who has stopped living in child-hood, however, cannot take it up again at a later point in the normal lifespan. Thus the account's emphasis on early-life allocations will not be preserved in other contexts.

Fifth, the prudential lifespan account presupposes that personal identity persists over time. The rational allocator who develops a pru-dential savings plan favoring heavier allocations early in life in order to increase the chance of later life saves for this later period under the assumption that he or she will be the same person as earlier. Other-wise, the self-interest-maximizer would have little reason to care whether some later, other person survived her.

Sixth and finally, the prudential lifespan account presupposes Rawls' theory of justice, and hence is open to the more general com-munitarian and other critiques of that theory.

Despite its limitations, the Rawls-Daniels approach has influenced a number of writers. For example Daniel Callahan, in his hotly dis-cussed defense of age-rationing first put forward in *Setting Limits* (1988) and explored in several later books (1990, 1993), argues from (and also toward) a communitarian rather than liberal and individu-alistic perspective, but nevertheless accepts many of the assumptions and conclusions already evident in Daniels' work: for instance, that health care is more efficient at earlier ages, that it is meaningful to examine the pattern of health care allocations over a lifetime, and that health care allocations ought to be just, and not, say, the product of market forces. Callahan argues for a reformed—indeed, transformed—social conception of what it means to be old, one which would deem-phasize mere continuation of life and instead place more emphasis on the roles of older persons in preparing to turn their concerns over to the next generation. Indeed, Callahan thinks the young should become the focus of older persons' lives, not their own physical continuation; the old can achieve real permanence not through "medicalizing," "modernizing" attempts to stave off death, but through continuity with the young. Callahan argues powerfully against maintaining very heavy health care allocations to the elderly, insisting that it is neces-sary to "set limits" to the resources expended to prolong life in very old age. But he also hopes that this view will be accepted by those older people and their society generally who reinspect and alter their assumptions about the significance and purpose of old age. Callahan's defense of age-rationing has received a great deal of criticism as well as support, and when interpreted least charitably, it is made to sound much like Euripides' remark that the old "ought to quit this life and clear the way for youth." Yet what Callahan actually argues is not so much that the elderly should be involuntarily denied care they actually want, but that a rethinking of the meaning of old age will lead them not to desire such care after all.

There are also new voices on the horizon exploring such claims. For instance, Nancy Jecker (1991) proposes still another reconceptualization of the issue. Like Daniels, she employs a Rawlsian framework, but she reminds us that relationships between age groups are not the same as relationships between generations, and stresses the motivational aspects of Rawls' account. Though they are different generations, for example, the teenage parent may not be very different in age-group from the child, while siblings within a given family may be members of very different age-groups. Jecker rejects Daniels' strategy of considering prudential self-interest, thus apparently undercutting the rationale for a lifespan approach, and instead proposes a modification of the underlying Rawlsian motivational assumption that we are concerned primarily, after ourselves, with the one or two generations succeeding us—that is, our children and grandchildren. We are also concerned, she holds, with the one or two generations preceding us—that is, our parents and grandparents. Parties in the original position are descendents of grandparents and parents, and are also actual or potential progenitors of children and grandchildren. But since they are behind the veil of ignorance, they do not know of what generation they are members or at what time period they live. Consequently, they will choose principles protecting the interests of both prior and succeeding generations generally. Since the criterion for justice between generations is what would be chosen in the original position, justice includes principles benefiting both the young and the old. This "benevolent chooser" model holds that the "affection and love between generations in a family furnishes the underpinnings for justice between generations" (Jecker 1992) and represents an attempt to join traditional concerns for justice with feminist concerns for care in a single account.

While communitarian accounts like Callahan's or feminist-influenced ones like Jecker's seem to threaten the central components of the prudential lifespan notion, and may seem to reintroduce conceptions of justice as involving claims between competing groups, I do not think they are successful in doing so. Daniels' central notion remains a genuine contribution to the resolution of the issue.

Nevertheless, it might seem that the prudential lifespan account, however ingenious as a solution to the theoretical issues in intergenerational justice, must be of little use in resolving practical political problems, since after all—due to the inherent limitations of employing a Rawlsian strategy—it would seem unable to yield detailed, specific policy recommendations and that retreat to a modified model like Callahan's or Jecker's is necessary. There is little way for policymakers in the real world to approximate the condition of detachment from one's own characteristics, both as an individual and as a member of an age, race, gender, or other subgroup, as Rawlsian contractarianism requires in determining what principles would count as just. Rawls, of course, does not make actual policy recommendations, nor does he suggest that his theory could be applied in this direct way. Actual real-world policymakers, after all, are not in the original position and cannot place themselves behind the veil of ignorance; they are real, not hypothetical persons, who do know their own ages, health histories, socioeconomic situations, and so on. They can attempt not to take their own special interests into account, but this is not to achieve a view that is genuinely independent of individual characteristics. Thus, they could hardly expect to resolve the conflict, for example, between AARP and AGE.

Not surprisingly, most discussions of intergenerational justice and of age-based policies in health care tend to assume the point of view of the middle-aged, regarding the very young and the elderly as other, different groups; this is because they are for the most part written by people who are no longer very young and not yet very old. As a matter of ordinary psychology, it is nearly impossible for a person who is middle-aged to adopt the point of view of someone who is either very young or very old; we who are middle-aged do not accurately recollect youth (and its very limited view of its own interests), and we have no way of knowing, as Parfit (1984) discusses in theory and Brock (1988) points out in practice with reference to persons with senile dementia, whether we accurately anticipate the view we will have in old age. (Among other things, Brock points out, we are unable to tell before it comes upon us whether moderate dementia would be bad: we know it is bad from our present view, of course, but we cannot say how we will experience it then.) Furthermore, we tend to discount benefits or harms in the distant future compared to benefits or harms in the near future, as well as to discount even more greatly those in the distant past. Yet a genuinely age-neutral view would not do so. In general, the impossibility for real policymakers of adopting a genuinely age-neutral view might seem to suggest that the prudential lifespan approach, however attractive theoretically, is unsuited for actual policy construction.

Nevertheless, despite the various general objections that can be raised against the prudential lifespan account or its Rawlsian roots, it remains extraordinarily influential, at least in philosophical if not policy circles. As Harry Moody suggests (1988, p. 36), it is "the best way yet proposed for us to think about justice between age-groups." Its root idea, that *age groups ought not be thought of as competitors but rather as stages through which each individual passes*, remains intuitively attractive—regardless of whether the world is nonideal, of whether institutions are stable, or whether one accepts any portions of Rawls' thesis at all. Thus, this theory provides the most plausible avenue for exploring and resolving practical political problems like the conflict between AARP and AGE or the question of other public programs. In what follows, I explore what the prudential lifespan account can and cannot offer in addressing political friction like this.

ADVANTAGES OF THE LIFESPAN APPROACH

Despite its general and substantial problems, the lifespan approach makes a number of contributions to the discussion of intergenerational justice and to the resolution of policy issues. And it does provide concrete answers to several of the most important issues under discussion. Eight principal points come to mind.

First, the prudential lifespan approach provides a clear, positive answer to the central political issue: whether intergenerational transfers are *per se* unjust. They are not. The mere fact that Medicare disbursements to the elderly are at least partly financed by payroll taxes on those of working age does not entail that they are, in the rhetoric of some of the more vocal opponents of this program, "social theft," even if the payouts to specific individuals are larger than what they paid in. Rather, at least in the context of a larger, stable scheme, they can be seen as the efficient use of one age group's savings for its own later use, in which current savings are lent to a holder who will later repay it when needed at a very favorable interest rate. The solution to intergenerational problems does not lie in tracking the current locations of each individual's own dollars, but in observing the operations of the scheme over time and one's return on dollars invested at an earlier point.

Second, the lifespan approach shows that our current public policy situation—the spotty pattern of Medicare Part A, Medicare Part B, Medicaid, WIC, AFDC, Social Security, military and civil service retirement plans, and so on—is problematic, since it does not form a considered, rationally chosen plan of prudential savings for the society as a whole. A prudential saver would not choose policies that make substantial allocations for his old age but provide little health care in childhood or youth; nor would a prudential saver choose a conglomeration of erratically cobbled-together programs not based on a unified, coherent, consistent lifespan plan. Here again, what the lifespan approach points to is not merely the current pattern of allocations, *but the operations of a distributive scheme over time.* Thus, the lifespan approach forces us to take a long-term look at both current and proposed future policies, not a merely current allocation scheme.

Third, the lifespan approach shows that the relationship between age groups cannot be regarded in the conventional way. It is not a competitive relationship between distinct groups vying for the same resources; rather, it should be seen as a relationship characterized by a "solidarity of interests" between different current age groups. For the middle-aged to view the elderly as having interests *different* from their own is for them to forget that they too will be elderly, and that they too will have the interests the currently elderly now have. Of course, there will be slight variations in interests for different age cohorts, depending on such things as the relative sizes and historical circumstances of various cohorts passing through the lifespan. But it is always to be remembered that the middle-aged are the future elderly, just as the currently young are the future middle-aged and are also the (more remotely) future elderly. The currently young have the *same* interests as the currently elderly—for instance interests in humane nursing-home care and advances in geriatric medicine—but simply have not yet reached the point where these interests are likely to come into play. If the currently young thwart these interests, for instance by dismantling the programs that serve them, they themselves will (eventually) suffer the consequences.

Fourth, the prudential lifespan approach also provides new ways of assessing the justness or unjustness of various societies, including our own. This involves examining allocations among age groups relative to a given level of scarcity, assessed with reference to the efficiency of such schemes. For example, while comparatively lavish allocations to the elderly are warranted in a society like the Netherlands, which already provides near-saturation care to the young, much starker policies can be understood in marginal societies where survival of the young—and hence the whole group—is at stake. For instance, though the Eskimo practice of abandoning the elderly on ice floes to die (a practice that can be described as allocating *no* resources to the health care or support of the elderly) may seem to be the most just resolution of distributive issues for a society in a genuinely precarious economic position, such a practice would be unconscionable in a richer society able to support both the young and the old. In our own society it would reflect mere stinginess, not the demands of justice under extreme scarcity. The lifespan approach also provides ways of assessing differential practices in other contemporary societies: for instance, the British practice of tacitly age-rationing dialysis and other care, described by Aaron and Schwartz (1984), and the former East German practice of permitting emigration of only the elderly from East to West Berlin, clearly a strategy for limiting health care and income support to the old.

This, as a fifth point, raises questions about the size of the resource pool and whether and on what basis it can be expanded. Many discussions of intergenerational justice and the specific policies at issue, like Medicare or Social Security, trade on the standard scarcity assumption that the pool of resources cannot be significantly expanded. But of course, in anything other than a truly marginal survival society, this is merely a political assumption reflecting the assignment of other social priorities or, as is evident currently, political fears about such strategies as raising taxes. If the size of the health care resources pool were expanded enough to provide saturation care for all persons in all age groups, this would clearly solve one part of the problem, though it would then introduce a renewed version of the problem of intergenerational justice—focusing on whether the increased costs should be borne by the currently working generation or could justly be displaced onto future generations, for example by increasing the federal deficit. While the prudential lifespan approach can answer the question of the morality of imposing obligations on future generations—it will say that there is nothing in principle wrong with doing so or with the intergenerational transfers this involves, providing any increases in deficit work to the greatest benefit of the least well off and do not risk the financial collapse of the nation (which, of course, would mean the collapse of those stable institutions on which intergenerational justice depends)—it cannot answer the question of how large the overall pool of resources should be or how other social priorities should be adjusted. But it can point out that there is nothing fixed about the size of the current pool, and no fundamental limit beyond which it cannot be allowed to expand.

Sixth, the prudential lifespan approach reminds us that not only ought we not consider the size of the pool fixed, but that we ought to reflect on the justness or unjustness of other alternatives that we ordinarily do not consider. The United States tends to think only of policies which involve withholding or withdrawing of treatment as ways of limiting care; that is why age-rationing may seem a plausible solution to problems of intergenerational justice. But we do not reflect, as I've said earlier, on whether liberal policies permitting voluntary, earlier choices of death, as in physician-assisted suicide or active euthanasia in terminal illness or extreme old age, might not also be favored by prudential savers. By permitting (not requiring!) voluntary choices of death for those terminally ill persons within a society who prefer an earlier, easier dying process, redistribution of resources to earlier age groups is ensured, and the chances of every person reaching old age in good health, where choices about suicide and euthanasia do not arise until a later date, are increased for all.

Seventh, among the most important contributions of the prudential lifespan model is the light it sheds on our usual approaches to problems of intergenerational justice like the conflict between AARP and AGE, or the political friction over public programs for either the young or the old. Our usual approaches to policymaking are political, rooted in the assumption that mutual pursuit of one's own interests in a democratic society will result in reasonably just compromises. But democratic solutions to political conflicts over intergenerational justice, unlike conflicts between other parties, cannot be fair. This is because in intergenerational conflicts, unlike others, the parties cannot be on equal political footing. As AGE correctly pointed out, while seniors' groups wield very considerable political influence ("Gray Power," as it is sometimes called), children, especially poor children, have little or no political representation: they cannot organize, they cannot conceptualize or publicize their problems, and they cannot vote. Unless members of other age groups speak for children (and thus, on the usual competitive model presupposed in political process, speak against their own interests), children are without a voice in any democratic process. Thus, although they are among the appropriate claimants to health care—indeed, they have the highest priority among claimants for health care, since childhood or youth is the age-group in which the prudential saver would invest the greatest amount of care—children are politically disenfranchised and unable to secure their own needs.

The model of democratic resolution of intergenerational issues is based on the notion of competition among age groups, the very notion the prudential lifespan approach rejects. On the contrary, not only are the competing parties of unequal power, but they should not be understood as *competing* at all. What is not clear, however, and is unlikely to be clear to practicing policymakers, is how to represent in a democratic society that "solidarity of interests" across age groups which the lifespan approach urges us to recognize instead.

This is what Generations United attempts. This group is a national coalition of over 100 organizations, cochaired by two groups concerned with the elderly, the National Council on Aging and the American Association of Retired Persons, and two groups concerned with the young, the Children's Defense Fund and the Child Welfare League. In coming together in this way, these groups reject the forced choice between young and old. AARP is a major supporter of this new coalition, and AGE, with its divide-and-conquer policies, no longer survives.

Eighth and finally, the prudential lifespan approach also lets us see the problem with our current health care situation more clearly. The problem is one that results from partial age-group coverage only. It is partial coverage of a curious sort: as Marmor (1988, p. 6) has remarked of Medicare, "No other industrial democracy has compulsory health insurance for its elderly citizens alone, and none started public health insurance with such a beneficiary group." And as Cook and coauthors observe, the age wars have not occurred at all in Canada, which has had universal health coverage for all age groups from the start of its program (see chapter 4 of this volume). It is clear that partial coverage of the sort that the United States endures is viewed as increasingly politically problematic, especially by the young and middle-aged who perceive themselves to be paying for this program but getting no coverage from it. The remedy, in the eyes of an increasing proportion of the population, is to extend coverage to the young and the middle-aged—that is, to expand from partial national health care to a full national program with coverage for all age groups. Indeed, achieving intergenerational justice is part of the rationale behind the Clinton administration's national health plan, and its promise of universal coverage. But while a national health plan offering universal coverage may well solve the problem, it does not accurately diagnose it.

WHAT THE LIFESPAN APPROACH REVEALS

After all, we must consider whether the current arrangement—partial coverage on an age-based criterion—is *unjust*, and if so, whether it represents a violation of the requirements of intergenerational justice. It is essential to ask this question—even if the prospects for achieving full national health care, with coverage for all age groups, seem reasonably good—since questions of distributive justice are always a function of a given level of scarcity and that level might well change. Some observers think the intergenerational equity issue will wane, but it should not be allowed to slip from public view before an adequate theoretical resolution is achieved. After all, even if full national health care currently seems within reach and the current level of scarcity mild enough to support it, we can always imagine a society's taking an economic turn for the worse: and with it, reintroducing the same distributive issues about intergenerational justice in health care all over again. If the nation faced economic catastrophe, and retrenchment on health care seemed the only way to save it, what programs, for what age groups, would have to be deleted? This question could be particularly pressing for a country that assembled a national health program by patching together an assortment of different programs for different age groups, economic levels, and persons with special eligibilities, as the United States has sometimes seemed likely to do: one program, Medicare, for the elderly; another, the VA, for veterans; another, Medicaid, for the poor; yet another, the Indian Health Service, for Native Americans, plus an assortment of new programs for, say, children and pregnant women, for the employed, for the unemployed, for the uninsurable, and so on, supplemented by a variety of state-based backup plans. If the United States were to approach national coverage in this way, rather than by adopting a unified program, it would produce a system vulnerable to encroachment in specific programs whenever budget pressures increased. It will remain a problem if such programs as the Indian Health Service or the VA remain distinct. Similarly, depending on their internal structure, state-by-state programs might also be vulnerable to the same pressures. A unified national health program is not vulnerable in the same way, though internal priorities for funding various classes of patients may raise some of the same problems. It is in a patchwork program that it is particularly essential to resolve the issues of justice in advance, to prevent selective erosion in ways that cannot be defended.

Well, then: Is a system of the sort we have now, in which there is partial age-group coverage for the elderly but not for the young, unjust? Is it as I have asked, a violation of intergenerational justice to provide extensive outlays for the elderly but little or nothing for the young? On the conventional interpretation, reading the issue as one of competition among age groups, the answer is yes, the current system is unjust; but under the theoretically more sophisticated prudential lifespan approach, the answer is no. Startup inequities aside, the current system is not on the surface unjust: on the contrary, it treats all persons equally by providing care in their old age. Persons who are now young or middle-aged are not deprived of care that others, unfairly, get; rather, they all get care, but not until they are old. But that does not mean there is no problem, nor that the current policy is one rational self-interest maximizers in the original position would accept. The problem is, instead, one of efficiency, not, at least on the face of it, one of justice. Since health care is less efficient in old age and since health care in old age does not guarantee survival through earlier years, a program attempting to distribute health care resources over a lifetime in this way would be, to put it succinctly, ass-back-wards. If the objective of justice in this application is to maximize the life-prospects of all, not some at the expense of others, health care should be provided to the young first (excluding the worst-off new-borns, for whom health care cannot make a real difference in life prospects), then the middle-aged, and the elderly last of all. It is this policy that most greatly increases the prospects for survival into old age, and hence most greatly benefits the elderly as a group. However, this is not an argument for withholding care from the elderly unless scarcity is so severe that the resources pool cannot be expanded, and it is not an argument for merely casual acceptance of the assumption that only some groups can be served. Unlike that of the Eskimo, our society is not an economically marginal one, and the more plausible explanations for our assumption that we cannot expand the pool involve stinginess, inflexibility, and political cowardice.

The real import of the observation that the problem with our current partial coverage is a problem of efficiency, rather than justice, is the discovery that what seem to be matters of intractable intergenerational conflict over allocations of health care to different age groups are not intractable and are not really conflicts. In what is described as the problem of "intergenerational justice" there is no basic problem of justice after all, but only a set of practical issues about how to distribute health care so that it is most efficient and how to maintain distributive institutions so that they are stable over time. Current allocations can be said to be unjust only in the Rawlsian sense that rational self-interest-maximizers behind the veil of ignorance would not agree to them. But they would not agree to them because they are inefficient, not because they are unfair or skewed in any other way. The practical recommendations such a conclusion yields may sound idealistic, but AGE and AARP should have shaken hands, sat down at the table, and gotten to work in figuring out just how much health care for the young will maximize prospects for the elderly as well—

that is, gotten to work at figuring out what would be the most rational distribution of health care along the human lifespan. Indeed, this is what Generations United is actually attempting to do: to promote intergenerational programs and to keep each generation aware of the stake it has in the welfare of the others. Putting true intergenerational justice into practice also means reminding each other that such policies enhance not only the life-prospects of the young but of the elderly as well, especially if start-up problems are resolved by temporary special treatment for the current elderly who cannot have been benefited in youth.

Thus, the problem of "intergenerational justice" in the age wars is something quite different from what it originally seemed. Of course, this is a limited result, applicable only to health care, because it is only in health care that earlier, more efficient care in youth is prerequisite to later survival and hence enhances the prospects for the old as well as the young. The prudential lifespan approach will not as readily resolve issues about Social Security or other income supports, nonmedical supportive care, senior citizen discounts, reduced bus fares, or cheap admission to National Parks. But that there is no basic conflict of justice and indeed no basic conflict of values in one very major area of current and potential public expenditure—health care— means that at least in this one area, we need not appeal to political solutions, since in any case they would not resolve the issue, and we can even dream of the prospect of mutual agreement and the development of widely satisfactory policy.

So who was right, AGE or AARP? Both were, I think, though both saw only part of the picture. AARP and the other seniors' groups were right in holding that age bias is pervasive and that treatment of the elderly is inadequate: more adequate provision should be made not only for medical care but for nursing home care, long-term care, and so on. But AGE was right that the elderly currently get the lion's share of public allocations, and that children, especially poor children, are deprived in comparison to the benefits provided the elderly. Both were wrong in thinking of the issue as a zero-sum game. Both sides were also wrong in their solutions to the problem, to remove support from one group in order to satisfy the other. Furthermore, neither appeared to acknowledge that the problem is produced by government's only partial entry into an area of social provision. If it is to provide any of its citizens, young or old, with care, the government must do so as part of a comprehensive, rationally defensible, efficient program for all age groups, and it is morally indefensible—even if not unjust—for it to provide the spotty, erratic, and above all inefficient kinds of programs we see now. Thus, the prudential lifespan approach leaves a curious legacy in resolving the age wars: While it resolves the theoretical issues about intergenerational justice, it leaves a great deal of practical work for a group that has got it right, like Generations United, and provides a compelling argument for a comprehensive national health plan ensuring care for persons of all ages.

Notes

1. *The Washington Post*, October 15, 1990, page A10.
2. See Battin (1987) for a defense of this claim.
3. See Moody (1988, esp. pp. 38ff) for a useful review.

References

Aaron, Henry J., and William B. Schwartz. 1984. *The Painful Prescription: Rationing Hospital Care.* Washington, D.C.: Brookings Institution.

Battin, Margaret P. 1987. "Age Rationing and the Just Distribution of Health Care: Is There a Duty to Die?" *Ethics* 97 (January): 317-40.

Brock, Dan. 1988. "Justice and the Severely Demented Elderly." *The Journal of Medicine and Philosophy* 13 (1, February).

Callahan, Daniel. 1987. *Setting Limits: Medical Goals in an Aging Society.* New York: Simon & Schuster.

_____. 1990. *What Kind of Life? The Limits of Medical Progress.* New York: Simon & Schuster.

_____. 1993. *The Troubled Dream of Life, Living with Mortality.* New York: Simon & Schuster.

Daniels, Norman. 1988. *Am I My Parents' Keeper? An Essay on Justice Between the Young and the Old.* New York: Oxford University Press.

Euripides. *Suppliants,* in *Plutarch's Moralia,* tr. Frank Cole Babbitt. Cambridge: Harvard University Press, 1928.

Jecker, Nancy S. 1991. "Justifying Justice Between Generations." Paper in progress, University of Washington Medical School.

Lamm, Richard D. 1991. "The Brave New World of Public Policy." Speech to the National Press Club, Washington, DC, Jan. 11, 1991. Printed in *Center Issues,* University of Denver.

Marmor, Theodore H. 1988. "Reflections on Medicare." *The Journal of Medicine and Philosophy* 13 (1, February): 6.
Moody, H. R. 1988. "Generational Equity and Social Insurance." *The Journal of Medicine and Philosophy* 13 (1, February).
Parfit, Derek. 1984. *Reasons and Persons*. Oxford: Clarendon Press.
Rawls, John. 1971. *A Theory of Justice*. Cambridge, Mass.: Harvard University Press.

Chapter Six

TRANSCENDING INTERGENERATIONAL EQUITY

Robert H. Binstock

The climate of U.S. politics and public discourse is increasingly hostile to older people. In the early 1990s public resources are perceived as scarce. The need to "reduce the deficit" is a rhetorical mainstay of domestic politics. "Containing health care costs" is widely considered to be one of the major goals of our society.

Population aging is commonly viewed as exacerbating each of these problems, and others as well. About 30 percent of the annual federal budget, nearly $450 billion in fiscal 1992, is expended on benefits to older persons.[1] Persons age 65 and older, who constitute 12.6 percent of our population, account for one-third of the nation's annual health care expenditures (U.S. House of Representatives 1989, p. 4), or about $270 billion out of a total $809 billion in 1992 (Sonnefeld et al. 1991). Because this elderly population is growing, absolutely and proportionally—from about 32 million persons today to an estimated 69 million (23 percent of our population) in the year 2040 (Taeuber 1990)—there is much anxiety about costs of governmental benefits to older people, now and in the future.

In this context many issues of so-called intergenerational equity portray older people in conflict with younger cohorts of Americans, and as a growing and unsustainable burden that will undermine our national well-being. The costs of health care for older persons, for instance, have been depicted as "a great fiscal black hole" that will absorb an unlimited amount of our country's resources (Callahan 1987, p. 17).

How did this political context of hostility to older persons develop? How accurate and useful is the intergenerational equity construct? This chapter analyzes the emergence of issues of intergenerational equity, suggesting that they are spuriously constructed on the basis of inaccurate old age stereotypes, superficial reasoning, and unrealistic extrapolations from existing public policies. It also illustrates how the constructs of intergenerational equity—such as "justice between age groups" in the allocation of health care—may divert us from seeking more useful, alternative issues to confront in dealing with our domestic social policy dilemmas.

COMPASSIONATE AGEISM AND THE "OLD AGE WELFARE STATE"

Public policy issues concerning older Americans have been framed for a long time by an underlying ageism—the attribution of the same characteristics, status, and just deserts to a heterogeneous group that has been artificially homogenized, packaged, labeled, and marketed as "the aged."[2] Ageism, in contrast with racism, has provided many benefits for older persons (Kutza 1981).

Prior to the late 1970s the predominant stereotypes of older Americans were compassionate. Elderly persons were seen as poor, frail, socially dependent, objects of discrimination, and above all, deserving (see Kalish 1979) . For some 40 years—dating from the Social Security Act of 1935—American society accepted the oversimplified notion that all older persons are essentially the same, and that all are in need of governmental assistance. Our governments acted on this perception by adopting and financing major old-age benefit programs, and tax and price subsidies for which eligibility is not determined by need. Through Social Security, Medicare, the Older Americans Act, special tax privileges for being age 65 or older, "senior citizen discounts," and a variety of other measures, elderly persons were exempted from the screenings applied to welfare applicants to determine whether they qualify for public help.

During the 1960s and the 1970s, just about every issue that advocates for the elderly could identify as affecting some subgroup of the older population became a governmental responsibility: nutritional, legal, supportive, and recreational services; housing; home repair; energy assistance; transportation; help in getting jobs; protection against being fired from jobs; special mental health programs; a separate National Institute on Aging; and so on. In the mid 1970s a congressional committee identified 134 federal programs benefiting older citizens, overseen by 49 committees and subcommittees of Congress (U.S. House of Representatives 1977).

By the late 1970s, if not earlier, U.S. society had learned the catechism of compassionate ageism and expressed it through a variety of governmental policies that created an "Old Age Welfare State."[3] We had rejected proposals for universal national health insurance, for example, but—through Medicare—were willing to establish national health insurance for elderly people (Marmor 1970).

THE EMERGENCE OF THE AGED AS SCAPEGOAT

Since 1978, however, the long-standing compassionate stereotypes of older persons have undergone an extraordinary reversal (Binstock 1983). Older people have come to be portrayed as one of the more flourishing and powerful groups in American society, and attacked as a burdensome responsibility. The immediate precipitating factor was a so-called crisis in the cash flow of the Social Security system that emerged within the larger context of a depressed economy during President Carter's administration (Estes 1983).

Two additional factors contributed importantly to this reversal of stereotypes. One was tremendous growth in the amount of federal dollars expended on benefits to aging citizens, which had come to be more than one-quarter of our annual budget and comparable in size to expenditures on national defense. Journalists (e.g., Samuelson 1978) and academicians (e.g., Hudson 1978) began to notice and publicize this phenomenon. By 1982 an economist in the U.S. Office of Management and Budget had pointed up the comparison with the defense budget by reframing the classical trade-off metaphor of political economy from "guns vs. butter" to "guns vs. canes" (Torrey 1982).

A second element in the reversal of the stereotypes of old age was dramatic improvements in the aggregate status of older Americans, in large measure due to the impact of federal benefit programs. Social Security, for example, has helped reduce the proportion of elderly persons in poverty from about 35 percent three decades ago (Clark 1990) to 11.4 percent today (Radner 1991). The success of such programs has improved the average economic status of aged persons to the point where journalists and social commentators can now, with superficial accuracy, depict older people, on average, as "more prosperous than the general population" (Tolchin 1988).

Throughout the 1980s and into the 1990s the new stereotypes, readily observed in popular culture, have depicted older persons as prosperous, hedonistic, politically powerful, and selfish. For example, a cover story in *Time*, entitled "Grays on the Go," was filled with pictures of senior surfers, senior swingers, and senior softball players. Older persons were pictured as America's new elite—healthy, wealthy, powerful, and "staging history's biggest retirement party" (Gibbs 1988).

A dominant theme in such accounts of older persons is that their selfishness is ruining the nation. The *New Republic* highlighted this motif early in 1988 with a cover displaying "Greedy Geezers." The table of contents "teaser" for the story that followed (Fairlie 1988) announced that "The real me generation isn't the yuppies, it's America's growing ranks of prosperous elderly." This theme has been echoed widely since. The epithet "greedy geezers" has become a familiar phrase in journalistic accounts of federal budget politics (e.g., Salholz 1990). Early in 1992, *Fortune* declaimed that "The Tyranny of America's Old" is "one of the most crucial issues facing U.S. society" (Smith 1992).

These images have laid a foundation upon which the aged have emerged as a scapegoat for an impressive list of American problems. As social psychologist Gordon Allport observed in his classic work, the *ABC's of Scapegoating:* "An issue seems nicely simplified if we blame a group or class of people rather than the complex course of social and historical forces" (1959, pp. 13-14). Practitioners of this scapegoating include academicians, policy analysts, politicians, and advocates for various causes, as well as journalists.

THE AGED AND AMERICA'S PROBLEMS

Demographer Samuel H. Preston (1984) and advocates for children (e.g., Carballo 1981) have blamed the political power of the elderly for the injustices experienced by youngsters who have inadequate nutrition, health care, education, and insufficiently supportive family environments. Former Secretary of Commerce Peter Peterson (1987) has suggested frequently that a prerequisite for the United States to regain its stature as a first class power in the world economy is a sharp reduction in programs benefiting older Americans.

In 1989 a distinguished "executive panel" of American leaders convened by the Ford Foundation designated older persons as the only group of citizens that should be responsible for financing a broad range of social programs for persons of all ages, including infants. In a report entitled *The Common Good: Social Welfare and the American Future*, the panel recommended a series of policies, costing a total of $29 billion (Ford Foundation 1989). And how did the panel propose that this $29 billion be financed? Solely by taxation of Social Security benefits. In fact, every financing alternative considered in the report implied that elderly people should be the exclusive financiers of the panel's package of recommendations for solving social problems in our nation. Apparently the Ford panel felt that the reasons for this assumption were self-evident; it did not even bother to justify its selection of these financing options as opposed to others.[4]

Perhaps the most serious scapegoating of the aged has been with respect to health care. A widespread concern about high rates of inflation in health care costs has somehow been refocused from the health care providers, suppliers, administrators, and insurers—the parties responsible for setting the prices of care—to the elderly persons for whom health care is provided, even though about two-thirds of the growth in health care costs is due to the general and health-sector-specific rates of inflation, and less than one-tenth to population growth (Sonnefeld et al. 1991; also, see Mendelson and Schwartz 1993).

The suggestion that health care should be rationed on the basis of old age began to develop, through implication, in 1983. In a speech to the Health Insurance Association of America, economist Alan Greenspan, now chairman of the Federal Reserve Board, stated that 30 percent of Medicare funds are expended annually on 5 to 6 percent of Medicare insurees who die within the year. He pointedly wondered, "whether it is worth it" (Schulte 1983).

In 1984 Richard Lamm, then Governor of Colorado, was widely quoted as stating that older persons "have a duty to die and get out of the way" (Slater 1984). Although Lamm subsequently said he had been misquoted on this specific statement, he has been delivering the same message repeatedly since leaving office, in only somewhat more delicately worded fashions (e.g., Lamm 1987, 1989a, 1989b, 1990). John Silber, the 1990 Democratic candidate for governor in Massachusetts, carried forth Lamm's torch by proclaiming that "When you've had a long life and you're ripe, then it's time to go" (Butterfield 1990).

The topic has spread to a number of forums during the past few years. Philosophers have been generating principles of equity to undergird "justice between age groups" in the provision of health care (Daniels 1988; Menzel 1990), rather than, for instance, justice between rich and poor, or justice among ethnic and racial subgroups. Conferences and books have explicitly addressed the issue with titles such as *Should Health Care Be Rationed by Age?* (Smeeding et al. 1987). Biomedical ethicists have turned to examining the economics of terminal illness (Veatch 1988) and "assisted suicide" in old age (Battin 1987).

Late in 1987 this theme received substantial popular attention with the publication of *Setting Limits: Medical Goals in an Aging Society,* by Daniel Callahan (1987), a biomedical ethicist. Callahan depicted the elderly population as a "demographic, economic, and medical avalanche . . . that could ultimately (and perhaps already) do [sic] great harm" (p.20). Callahan's remedy was to urge that life-saving health care be denied—as a matter of public policy—to persons in their late 70s or early 80s (p. 171).

The significance of Callahan's book lies in the extraordinary national attention it received, despite a great many flaws in its economic, political, and philosophical arguments (see Binstock and Post 1991). It was reviewed in national magazines, the *New York Times*, the *Washington Post*, the *Wall Street Journal*, and just about every relevant professional and scholarly journal and newsletter. Callahan has continued to present and defend his point of view in a subsequent book (Callahan 1990), journal articles, and a number of public forums throughout the country. It appears that proposals for rationing health care on the basis of old age are rather firmly embedded in public discourse concerning U.S. health care policies.

EQUITY AS AN "INTERGENERATIONAL" CONSTRUCT

These various problems and responsibilities for which elderly people have become a scapegoat have been thematically unified as issues of intergenerational equity, a construct stimulated by the efforts of Americans for Generational Equity (AGE), a Washington-based interest group that was highly visible in the late 1980s (see chapter 4 for further discussion).

Central to AGE's credo was the proposition that today's older people are locked in an intergenerational conflict with younger age cohorts regarding the distribution of public resources. The appeal that this intergenerational construct has had for advocates for children, the homeless, education, rebuilding the nation's infrastructure, combatting drug abuse, and other domestic concerns can be appreciated by examining table 6.1, which shows the distribution of federal outlays for fiscal year 1992. The proportion of gross federal outlays devoted to domestic discretionary spending was only 14.1 percent.[5] Nearly half of the budget went for mandatory programs, and expenditures through Social Security's Old Age Insurance (OAI) (excluding survivors, and disability insurance) and Medicare constituted 46 percent of that half

Table 6.1 FEDERAL OUTLAYS, BY CATEGORY, FISCAL YEAR 1992

Spending Category	In Billions of Dollars	As a Percentage of Gross Domestic Product
Defense Discretionary	313	5.4
International Discretionary	20	0.3
Domestic Discretionary	214	3.7
Mandatory Spending	708	12.1
Deposit Insurance	67	1.1
Net Interest	201	3.4
GROSS TOTAL	1,523	26.0
Offsetting Receipts	− 64	− 1.1
Desert Storm Contributions	− 5	− 0.1
NET TOTAL	1,454	24.8

Source: Congressional Budget Office, U.S. Congress, *The Economic and Budget Outlook: Fiscal Years 1993–1997* (Washington, D.C.: U.S. Government Printing Office, 1992), p. 50.

(U.S. Congress 1992, p. 56). If one adds in the portions of Medicaid, SSI, food stamps, and social service programs that provide benefits to older persons, over half the mandatory spending is on elderly people. And other mandatory programs that include older people—such as retirement and disability for federal civilian and military employees (excluding veterans benefits)—bring the proportion of mandatory spending on benefits for the aging to about 60 percent. This perspective makes it easy to understand why proponents of various social causes view the old-age lobby as a prime competitor for a limited budgetary pie.

Although AGE has faded from the scene, its theme of intergenerational conflict has been adopted by the media as a routine perspective for describing many social policy issues. During the 1990 budget negotiations between the President and Congress, for example, a headline in the *Washington Post* (1990, p. 1) proclaimed: "Older Voters Drive Budget; Generational Divide Marks Budget Battle." The theme has also gained currency in elite sectors of American society. The president of the prestigious American Association of Universities, for instance, has warned that: "[T]he shape of the domestic federal budget inescapably pits programs for the retired against every other social purpose dependent on federal funds, in the present and the future" (Rosenzweig 1990, p. 6).

The notion that there is a war between generations has also captured the mindset of powerful members of Congress. For example, as

Congress ended its 1989 session, Representative Dan Rostenkowski, Chairman of the House Ways and Means Committee, observed: "One of the most unhappy results of our ongoing budget gridlock has been an uneven contest between the very young and the very old. . . ." He said that "the sad story of the 1980s," was that "the old have gotten more while the young have gotten less" (Tolchin 1989a). The record does not bear out Rostenkowski. There were no legislative choices or contests during the decade between "the very young and the very old," and the old did not get "more." But the very fact that he was willing to characterize congressional activity in the 1980s in these terms reflects the general trend through which the framework of intergenerational equity has become accepted as a perspective for describing trade-offs in health and social welfare policies.

TRANSCENDING INTERGENERATIONAL EQUITY

The very description of the axis upon which equity is to be judged tends to circumscribe the major options available for rendering justice. As issues of intergenerational equity become axioms of public rhetoric, they tend to shape our policy choices, even though the issues may be constructed on the basis of misinformation and spurious, unwarranted assumptions. Moreover, issues of intergenerational equity divert our attention from other ways of viewing trade-offs and options available to us that may be more accurate and propitious.

If, alternatively, we can perceive issues that express equity in ways that transcend intergenerational trade-offs (see e.g., Heclo 1988; Kingson 1988; Kingson et al. 1986; Neugarten and Neugarten 1986; Wisensale 1988), those alternative issues may generate a series of new practical choices for public policy and private institutional arrangements in the decades ahead. It is not within the scope of this chapter to examine each issue of intergenerational equity that has emerged to date. But it is feasible to treat briefly two examples of such issues in order to indicate that they are poorly constructed and empirically flawed: complaints about the political power of the aged, and concerns about increasing dependency ratios. And it is possible to treat a third issue area at greater length: the ways in which issues of allocating health care resources are presently expressed in terms of proposals to ration the health care of older people.

The Political Power of the Aged

Fundamental to the theme of intergenerational equity are the notions (1) that the political power of elderly Americans has created an Old Age Welfare State, and (2) that this power is now sufficient to prevent any policy changes that will reduce benefits to older persons. Media stereotypes reinforce these notions by portraying older people as a monolithic bloc of voters that promotes and defends its self-interests successfully, and by depicting old-age-based organizations as one of the most powerful clusters of interest groups in American politics. In the fall of 1990, for example, when President Bush and congressional leaders agreed on a budget proposal that included changes in Social Security benefits and taxes, a *New York Times* reporter predicted a political explosion because: "America's older citizens are among the nation's most potent constituencies. They vote at higher rates than most other Americans. . . . In addition their organizations, lead [sic] by the American Association of Retired Persons, swing great weight on Capitol Hill" (Oreskes 1990, p. 12). Examination of the aging in American politics indicates that these nuggets of conventional wisdom are very oversimplified.

Although older persons constituted from 17 to 21 percent of those who actually voted in recent national elections (U.S. Senate 1988, p. 11), table 6.2 shows that the votes of older persons usually distribute among candidates in about the same proportions as the votes of other age groupings of citizens. The 1992 election was unusual in that Bill Clinton fared much better among older voters than among younger voters. Yet, it should be noted that the support of older people for President Bush was roughly the same as that of younger age groups, and precisely the same as the overall average for Bush. Data from various polls suggest that the comparatively large plurality for Clinton among older voters—and their relatively low support for Ross Perot— might be explained by the relative reluctance of older people to accept Perot as a serious candidate. Although older voters tend to switch their allegiance among Democratic and Republican candidates in about the same patterns as most other voters, research has consistently shown that older persons have a greater attachment to traditional political institutions. A greater reluctance to support an Independent candidate such as Perot is consistent with this tendency. In 1980, when John Anderson was an Independent candidate, support for him ranged from 8 percent to 11 percent among the younger age groups, but only from 4 percent to 5 percent among the older age groups.

Table 6.2 NATIONWIDE VOTE DISTRIBUTION, BY AGE GROUPS AND GENDER, IN ELECTIONS FOR U.S. PRESIDENT, 1980, 1984, 1988, 1992

	The 1980 Vote			The 1984 Vote		The 1988 Vote		The 1992 Vote		
	Reagan	Carter	Anderson	Reagan	Mondale	Bush	Dukakis	Clinton	Bush	Perot
Percent of All Voters										
all ages	51%	41%	7%	59%	40%	53%	45%	43%	38%	19%
18–29 years old	43	44	11	59	40	52	47	44	34	22
30–44 years old	55	36	8	57	42	54	45	42	38	20
44–59 years old	55	39	5	60	40	57	42	41	40	19
60 years & older	54	41	4	60	40	50	49	50	38	12
Percent of Men										
all ages	55	36	7	62	37	57	41	41	38	21
18–29 years old	47	39	11	63	36	55	43	38	36	26
30–44 years old	59	31	4	61	38	58	40	39	38	22
44–59 years old	60	34	5	62	36	62	36	40	40	20
60 years & older	56	40	3	62	37	53	46	49	37	14
Percent of Women										
all ages	47	45	7	56	44	50	49	46	37	17
18–29 years old	39	49	10	55	45	49	50	48	33	19
30–44 years old	50	41	8	54	45	50	49	44	38	18
44–59 years old	50	44	5	57	42	52	48	43	40	17
60 years & older	52	43	4	58	42	48	52	51	39	10

Source: *New York Times*/CBS News Poll, "Portrait of the Electorate," *New York Times*, November 5, 1992, p. B9.

Among journalists it is a common view that the votes of older people distribute distinctively in the context of state and local referenda that present specific issues, rather than candidates, for balloting—such as propositions to cap local property taxes or to finance schools. In this view, the assumption is that the self-interest of older people will transcend other considerations—say, in voting against propositions to finance schools because they have do not have children in school (see Binstock 1992). Yet, in such referenda, old age is not a statistically significant variable associated with the distribution of votes (Button and Rosenbaum 1989; Chomitz 1987).

These data should not be surprising, since there is no sound reason to expect that a cohort of perons would suddenly become homogenized in "self interests" and political behavior when it reaches the "old age" category (see Simon 1985). Diversity among older persons may be at least as great with respect to political attitudes and behavior as it is in relation to economic, social, and other characteristics (Hudson and Strate 1985). For instance, a recent analysis comparing age group attitudes toward public policy issues during the 1980s found that "older people are nearly indistinguishable from younger adults (both middle-aged and younger categories) on most issues—including aging policy issues" (Day 1990, p. 47).

But don't politicians behave as if older persons vote as a bloc in response to issues? Aren't they heavily influenced by the so-called gray lobby (Pratt 1976) represented by the American Association of Retired Persons (AARP), which has a membership of more than 30 million persons age 50 and older? It is certainly evident that no politician goes out of his or her way to offend the aged. But there have been numerous cases in recent years, enumerated below, when Congress has enacted legislation that has adversely affected the presumed interests of the aged.

In fact, the scholarly literature indicates that organized demands of older persons have had little to do with enactment and amendment of the major old-age policies such as Social Security and Medicare. Rather, such actions are attributable for the most part to the initiatives of public officials in the White House, Congress, and the bureaucracy who have focused on their own agendas for social and economic policy (Cohen 1985a, 1985b; Derthick 1979; Hudson and Strate 1985; Iglehart 1989; Jacobs 1990; Light 1985). The impact of old-age-based interest groups has been confined largely to relatively minor policies that have distributed benefits to professionals and practitioners in the field of aging rather than directly to older persons (Binstock 1972; Binstock et al. 1985; Estes 1979; Fox 1989; Lockett 1983).

At present, the old-age interest organizations are functioning as what political scientist Hugh Heclo (1984) terms an "anti-redistributive veto force" in American politics. Even in this so-called veto role, however, the force of old-age interests has not been uniformly successful.

A number of public policy decisions, conventionally perceived as adverse to the self-interests of older persons, proved to be politically feasible in the 1980s through changes in Medicare, Social Security, and other programs. Medicare deductibles, copayments, and Part B premiums have increased continuously. Old Age Insurance benefits have been made subject to taxation. The legislated formula for cost-of-living adjustments (COLAs) to OAI benefits has been rendered less generous. The Omnibus Reconciliation Act of 1981 narrowed five benefit and eligibility provisions of Social Security, which had a direct adverse effect on OAI recipients. The Tax Reform Act of 1986 eliminated the extra personal exemption that all persons 65 years of age and older had been receiving in filing their federal income tax returns. The politics of enacting and repealing the Catastrophic Coverage Act in 1988 and 1989 respectively, clearly illustrated that older persons are not a homogeneous monolith, either politically or in terms of self-interests (see Crystal 1990; Holstein and Minkler 1991). And most recently, despite the protests of old-age interest groups, the Omnibus Budget Reconciliation Act of 1993 raised to 85 percent the proportion of Social Security benefits subject to taxation for individuals with incomes of over $34,000 and for couples with incomes of over $44,000, and cut back on Medicare reimbursements to health care providers (U.S. Congress 1993).

Despite these facts, the image of so-called senior power persists because it serves certain purposes. It is used by journalists as a tabloid symbol to simplify the complexities of politics. It is marketed by the leaders of old-age-based organizations who have many incentives to inflate the size of the constituency for which they speak. And it is attacked by those who would like to see greater resources allocated to their causes, and by those who depict the selfishness of the aged as the root of many problems (e.g., Carballo 1981; Levy and Murnane 1992; Longman 1987).

Increasing Dependency Ratios

"Increasing dependency ratios," conventionally expressed as the size of the retired population relative to the working population, has become a metaphor for anxieties about the economic burdens of population aging. This construct grossly distorts the issues involved because it is largely an artifact of an existing policy, Social Security, which taxes the paychecks of workers. It does not capture the range of major elements that determines whether a society is economically capable of supporting dependents within it, or the many different sources—including general revenues—through which government could fund such support.

The most fundamental problem with the dependency ratio construct lies in using the number or proportion of workers in a society to assess the productive capacity of the economy. Productive capacity is a function of a variety of factors—at least including capital, natural resources, balance of trade, and technological innovation, as well as number of workers.

More specific flaws in common use of dependency ratios express the ubiquitous impact of ageism in the framing of issues. Age categories are used to estimate the numbers of workers and retirees—rather than actual and projected labor-force participation rates—even though the two approaches can yield substantially different results. In addition, the focus on retirees as "the dependent population" ignores the fact that many retired older persons are economically independent. It also ignores children and unemployed adults of any age who are economically dependent; for instance, research has indicated that a decline in "youth dependency" during the decades ahead may well moderate or even dominate the economic significance of projected increases in "elderly dependency" (Crown 1985; Habib 1990; Schulz et al. 1991).

Discussion of increasing dependency ratios has generated several assumptions that may be unwarranted. One is that we will need far more workers in the decades ahead than projected from current age norms for entering and retiring from the labor force. A second is that older persons who retire in the context of contemporary policies, many of whom engage in unpaid productive activities (Committee on an Aging Society 1986), will want and be able to work for pay in the future if incentives to retire and the ages associated with them are marginally adjusted. And a third is that there will be employer demand for such workers.

Policies pursuant to these assumptions would not only be based upon a poor understanding of what it is that enables an economy to support dependents, but they might also be based upon misperceptions regarding incentives and disincentives that influence the decisions of older workers regarding work and retirement. For example, it is commonly proposed that the ages of eligibility for Social Security retirement benefits be moved upward, beyond the minor increases that will be phased in gradually in the next century. Yet, we know today that two-thirds of current Social Security beneficiaries choose to retire early, before age 65, even though it means that they receive reduced benefits; we also know that poor health, and the availability of private pension income are powerful influences on decisions to retire early (see Quinn and Burkhauser 1990; Schulz 1988, esp., ch. 3).

Perspectives on Rationing the Health Care of Older People

Denying health care to people solely because they have attained a specific older age would be a substantial departure from existing practices and philosophies. To be sure, health care in the United States has long been rationed informally on the bases of social class and ability to pay (Churchill 1987; Hiatt 1987), the immediate availability of resources (Blank 1988), and the individual conditions and characteristics of patients. However, suggestions for rationing the health care of people who are members of a demographically identified category— be it by age, race, ethnicity, religion, gender, or other characteristics— start us down the clichéd "slippery slope" to a moral abyss.[6] Any of us is vulnerable to social constructions that classify us as unworthy. Any of us is subject to becoming a scapegoat.

As drastic as proposals to deny health care to older people are—in ethical, moral, and social terms—no persuasive arguments have been made to justify them. The economic justifications for old-age-based rationing rest on unwarranted assumptions and are poorly developed. The philosophical constructs and rationalizations are unattractive and far from compelling. And some pleasant policy scenarios, through which the funds saved from rationing would be reallocated to "wish lists" of worthy, underfunded causes, are unrealistic. Although providing adequate health care for an increasing number of older persons will certainly present us with complex challenges, constructive steps can be taken to meet the health care needs of an aging society without policies that establish old-age-based health care rationing.

The Pseudo-Economics of Rationing Proposals.   A basic premise underlying rationing proposals is that ever-increasing American health care expenditures are bringing about an economic "crisis," and that some form of rationing is an inevitable, if not a preferred, solution. As Callahan has framed the issue, "How does the use of age as a standard for limiting health care compare with other unpleasant methods of limitation? We need to pit the methods of rationing against each other, not against the ideal world in which we all wish we lived" (Callahan 1987).

But is there an economic crisis, current or impending, engendered by health care expenditures? Advocates of health care cost containment warn, rhetorically, that we cannot economically sustain increasing health care expenditures. Why not? What are the inevitable dire consequences that would ensue for our nation (as opposed to for specific health care payers and providers) if health care expenditures continue to grow?

It is not at all clear, for example, that escalating health care costs has hurt the global position of the U.S. economy. Despite the current laments about the economic decline of the United States, our share of the World Gross Product (WGP) has held constant at 23 percent since the mid-1970s (Nye 1990). In theory, of course, it could be argued that the American economy might have an even stronger position in the world if it were not for the proportion of our wealth spent on health care costs. A fashionable expression of this perspective is the complaint made by some corporate executives and health care policy analysts that the competitiveness of American business firms is hurt because about 10 percent of payroll expenses in our medium and large industries goes to employee health insurance (McNerny 1990). But these health insurance fringe benefits merely substitute for either larger wages and salaries, or other types of fringe benefits that would be used as alternative components in the total package of employee compensation. As health economist Uwe Reinhardt notes, "It does not make sense to pick out one of these components and blame it for problems American business faces in pricing its products" (Reinhardt 1990).

Robert Reischauer, Director of the Congressional Budget Office, has observed that spiraling health care costs depress wages and exacerbate the problems of uninsured workers in having access to care. At the same time, however, he concludes that the net effects of health care spending on the economy "are hard to disentangle; growth could be increased or decreased, depending on what consumers get when they pay for medical care" (1991, p. 10). The critical issue, in his view, is eliminating waste.

Health care cost-containment is not an end in itself, and is not mandated by any "iron law" of economics. As many economists have pointed out, there is no inherent reason why 12 percent, 13 percent, or more of our GNP cannot be expended on health care (Schwartz and Aaron 1985). The proportion of our national wealth that we can and ought to invest in health care is not a technical issue of economics, but a value judgment to be resolved through politics.

Even if we assume that reducing or curbing the growth of health care costs is a high priority for our nation, what sorts of financial savings might be achieved through rationing measures, such as categorically denying life-saving care to older persons? Would these savings be of any fiscal significance? How would they compare in magnitude to savings that might be achieved through other, less morally troublesome measures?

For a number of years, about 28 percent of annual Medicare expenditures has been on those Medicare insurees who die within a year (Lubitz and Riley 1993). Suppose we were to deny care to prospective high-cost decedents (although, clinically, it is rarely possible to make highly reliable prospective distinctions between high-cost survivors and decedents)? Even if it were ethically and morally palatable to implement a policy that denied treatment to such high-cost Medicare patients, and thereby eliminate "wasteful" health care, the dollars saved would be insignificant in the larger context of national health care costs.

High-cost Medicare decedents annually account for about 3.5 percent of Medicare expenditures (see Lubitz and Prihoda 1984; Scitovsky 1984, 1988). In 1993, when Medicare expenditures were estimated to be $143 billion (Congressional Budget Office 1993, p. 41), a policy that denied them treatment would have saved about $5 billion. Viewed in isolation, this is substantial. But saving such an amount would have a negligible effect on the overall situation, reducing 1993 national health care costs from $900 billion to about $895 billion.[7]

It would be easy enough to argue that so-called "waste" on health care for older persons is dwarfed by other expenditures that, from a political point of view or as a matter of personal values, can be labeled as undesirable or frivolous, and that should have limits set for them—federal subsidies for tobacco; luxury items such as furs and jewelry; and even the health care of cats and dogs. Orthopedic and heart surgery on household pets can cost from $1,500 to $4,000. In 1987, Americans spent nearly $6 billion on veterinary services, including CAT scans and pacemaker implants (Nordheimer 1990).

But even if we agree that *human* health care costs need to be reduced, how do the "wasteful" expenditures that might be saved by rationing the care of older persons compare with other areas of waste and potential savings in our health care system? The bureaucratic aspects of our health care system alone provide a promising arena for saving unnecessary expenditures.

The proportion of U.S. health care spending consumed by administration is at least 117 percent higher than in Canada; if health care administration in the United States had been as efficient as in Canada in 1987, the savings to our system would have ranged from $69 billion to $83 billion (Woolhandler and Himmelstein 1991). The Health Insurance Association of America estimated that about $60 billion in fraudulent or abusive private and governmental insurance claims were paid in 1989 (Rosenthal 1990). Joseph Califano, Jr., former Secretary of Health, Education, and Welfare, estimates that more than $25 billion a year could be saved by electronic processing, standardizing, and simplifying reimbursement claims and audit procedures (Califano 1991). Medicare pays about $600 million to $1 billion a year in reimbursement claims that have already been paid by private insurers or should have been (Pear 1990). Compare these figures with the $5 billion expended on high-cost Medicare decedents in the last 12 months of their lives.

Philosophical and Political Rationalizations. As these few examples indicate, there is no economic imperative to ration. Suggestions that older persons are not worthy of life-saving care need to be viewed and evaluated in terms of the political and moral preferences they express and reflect. But the preferences that have been put forward, and various arguments to justify them, are far from persuasive.

Among the proponents of old-age-based rationing, Callahan in particular has offered a philosophical construct to suggest that older persons would benefit if our society were to deny them life-saving care. He argues that such rationing would enable older persons to find a meaningful societal context for decline, suffering, and death: "[T]he meaning and significance of life for the elderly themselves is best founded on a sense of limits to health care. . . . The old would have to understand that the intent behind a policy of limiting care would be the welfare of the elderly and of younger generations, and that it was affirmative toward old age and not simply mean spirited" (1987, p. 200).

This new meaning of aging envisioned by Callahan requires older persons to adhere to a communalistic value of serving the interests of the young through politics, and by working directly with young persons on a one-on-one basis. He does not address seriously the question of how such a communalistic philosophy would take hold in the context of a highly individualistic American political culture. Nonetheless, he believes that individuals would derive satisfaction from "knowing that because of the limits on research and health care delivery devoted to life extension for the elderly, a continuing high growth rate for the health-care budget had ceased to be inevitable" (Callahan 1987, p. 155). Really? Would even the administrator of the federal government's Health Care Financing Administration take death-bed satisfaction in the knowledge that the growth rate for the federal health-care budget had slowed?

Callahan, Lamm, and other proponents of denying health care to older persons also justify their views by appealing to the common good. They argue that the resources saved would be applied to the education and health care of children, governmental health insurance for an estimated 37 million uninsured Americans, housing for home-less people, rebuilding the nation's transportation infrastructure, pre-serving and reclaiming our environment, and a host of other worthy social objectives. In a similar, though narrower vein, they suggest that the funds saved from denying efforts at life-saving cures for elderly people might be reallocated to long-term care and palliation for chron-ically ill and disabled aged patients. Even as older persons become socialized to the notion that they will be denied life-saving health care, it is argued, they can look forward to the months and years still available to them as ones that can be finished out relatively free of pain and avoidable suffering.

Such justifications ignore the political realities of national policy-making. Even if the resources saved from denying life-saving care for older persons could be sufficient to tackle these "better causes" in adequate fashion (which they are not), little in American political experience suggests that funds saved from financing one cause are likely to go to other, preferred and pre-designated causes. Did any of us think, when Secretary of Defense Richard Cheney canceled con-tracts for the further development of the A-12 Navy attack plane in 1991, that the more than $2 billion saved through this decision would be used for program expansions in prenatal care, immunization of children, or Head Start?

The notion that funds conserved from denying health care to older people would be earmarked and reallocated for long-term care is po-litically naive. New federal programs get financed from explicit policy initiatives formulated to deal with them, not from decisions to elim-inate existing commitments. Even President Clinton's 1993 proposal for reforming U.S. health care, as broad and sweeping as it was, did not suggest that *new* health care benefits would be financed from the savings he expected to achieve through the plan. Rather, for each new benefit there was an explicit proposal regarding who would pay for it (White House Domestic Policy Council 1993).

Constructive Approaches.   Rationing health care on the basis of old age would not accomplish much, but it could cause great harm. If American society were to categorically deny life-saving interventions for older persons, we would gain little in the way of national economic strength, save a negligible proportion of our health care costs, and do little to improve our health care system and to further other worthy social causes. Yet, such rationing would fracture moral barriers, unnecessarily end the lives of many elderly persons, and could substantially depress the outlook and quality of life for all of us as we approach the "too old for health care" category. Perhaps such a norm could even nourish, to reach a significant scale, the present phenomenon of preemptive suicide.

Fortunately, there are many alternative steps we can take to make our health care of older persons, and our health care system generally, less wasteful and more sensible. A good starting point for a constructive approach is to clear up some common misperceptions of what is happening in the world of health care for older Americans.

One recurring assumption in discussions of rationing is that patients of advanced age are poor candidates for complicated medical interventions, that they do not benefit from many treatments as well as younger adults. Yet, substantial evidence on a wide variety of medical interventions shows that old age, in itself, is not a good predictor of success or failure. The important predictors are the underlying clinical conditions and functional statuses of patients (Jahnigen and Binstock 1991).

Patients in their 60s, 70s, and even 80s, for example, unquestionably benefit from such procedures as renal dialysis, and heart, liver, and kidney transplantation sometimes more so than younger patients (Evans 1991). Indeed, the desires of organ transplant surgeons to achieve success motivate them to select for surgery those older patients they regard as most likely to benefit substantially. Some advanced procedures undertaken with older patients, such as kidney transplants, often cost less per additional life year than other treatments for kidney disease (Evans 1991).

A related, persistent theme impelling proposals for old-age-based rationing is the assertion that costly, futile, and therefore wasteful efforts are made frequently to keep alive older patients through the use of expensive high-technology medical interventions, and against the patients' wishes. For some years the press has provided dramatic accounts of organ transplants and other forms of surgery on elderly persons, as well as sagas of legal issues involving the extended ordeals of older patients who linger on the edge of death in hospitals and nursing homes, sustained only by mechanical breathing ventilators or nutrition obtained intravenously or through tube feeding.

But a majority of the funds expended on health care for aged people in the United States is not for dramatic technological interventions. Only a very small proportion of elderly nursing home patients, for example, receive life-sustaining technologies; from 2 to 5 percent receive nutritional support, and the proportion receiving other life-sustaining technologies is even smaller (Office of Technology Assessment 1987). Yet, nursing homes account for 21 percent of health care expenditures on older persons. A wide range of health care goods and services—prescription drugs, dental care, home health care, vision and hearing aids, and medical equipment and supplies—totals 16 percent of expenditures, and outpatient and inpatient physician fees are 22 percent. The remaining 41 percent is for payments to hospitals (U.S. House of Representatives 1989).

Studies in both the United States (Scitovsky 1984, 1988) and Canada (Roos et al. 1987) indicate that aggressive medical interventions are comparable across adult age groups in the last years of life. The greatest difference between younger and older adults with respect to expenditures associated with dying, in both countries, is that elderly people are far more likely to incur expenses for nursing homes and home care services.

Certainly, reforms in the practice of American medicine could help to reduce the frequency of unfortunate situations in which older patients become subject to inappropriate, painful, and/or needlessly costly treatments. Such circumstances often arise through lack of adequate prior discussions among physicians, patients, and the patients' family members, as well as through poor prognostic information. Patients' values and the nonmedical aspects of their lives can receive much greater attention than they have.

Physicians will need to struggle continuously to balance the heroic and humanistic models of medical practice as we become, increasingly, an aging society (Cassel and Neugarten 1991). The heroic model, in its most simplistic caricature, portrays physicians as preoccupied with how they can hold death at bay, without considering whether a death is appropriate, acceptable, or premature. In the humanistic model, the primary goal is to improve the patient's quality of life, with an emphasis on interventions that place a low burden of pain and suffering on the patient and often are relatively inexpensive.

Adjustments in the practice and goals of medicine, however, will not eliminate high-cost (and sometimes futile) treatments, situations in which patients are subjected to needless suffering, and cases that present ethical and moral issues that are difficult to resolve. Fortunately, our society is struggling actively with the ethical and moral dilemmas generated by the ever-improving capacity of the medical profession to treat life-threatening situations.

About 40 states have enacted statutes that authorize the use of legal instruments known as "advance directives." The federal Patient Self-Determination Act now requires hospitals and nursing homes to determine whether newly admitted patients have executed such instruments, and to inform them of their right to do so. One type of advance directive is the "living will," through which each of us can attempt to envision and describe the clinical conditions and medical care situations in which we would prefer to die rather than have interventions undertaken that would extend our lives. Surveys indicate that 15 to 20 percent of American adults have signed living wills (Lewin 1990). Another type is the "durable power of attorney," through which we can designate a specific person to make health care decisions for us should we become unable, or deemed incompetent, to do so for ourselves.

Living wills and durable powers of attorney are far from foolproof instruments. It is difficult for any of us to envision, prospectively, the range of clinical realities that may beset us. Moreover, specific treatment decisions will be tempered in most cases by medically, ethically, and legally appropriate courses of action as perceived by health care providers and their employing organizations. Nonetheless, such advance directives can help maintain patient autonomy, reduce suffering in the context of futile or very marginal interventions, and cut down on undesired and fruitless health care expenditures.

Our struggles to deal with ethical and moral dilemmas in health care are also proceeding through the adjudication of cases. The Supreme court's ruling in the case of Cruzan v. Missouri (1990) upheld the principle that patients have a "right to die" when such a right has been statutorily expressed by their state governments, and when the circumstances of the case meet the criteria set forth by the state. Neither the Cruzan decision nor any other case, however, will eliminate legal disputes over issues concerning termination of medical care. In fact, a recent case in Minnesota involved a reversal of the situation in the Cruzan case. A hospital wanted to terminate what it regarded as futile care for an 87-year-old woman, but the court ruled in favor of the patient's husband who asserted that she had long ago expressed a strong preference, because of her religious convictions, to

live in such circumstances (Cranford 1991). Our courts will undoubtedly go on dealing with new types of dilemmas generated by specific
cases.

At the same time there are broader struggles that can be undertaken
to change our American health care system. By focusing more of our
efforts on such fundamental issues—excessive prices, waste, and ine-
quitable distributions of care—we can improve our use of health care
resources for elderly people, as well as reform our system generally.
President Clinton's 1993 proposal for reforming American health care
has done much to draw public attention to such issues (White House
Domestic Policy Council 1993).

We can use the power of government to provide health insurance
for an estimated 37 million persons who currently have none. We can
expand public insurance for long-term care in nursing homes and in
residential settings, for patients of all ages who have chronic diseases
and disabilities. And, as government regulation has begun to demonstrate in the past few years, we can control prices charged by hospitals and physicians.

We can also turn our attention to relatively unpublicized areas of
health care expenses and waste. Governmental power can be used to
limit excess profits generated by pharmaceutical and medical equipment and supply companies, and to discourage practices that lead to
overuse of high-priced therapeutic and diagnostic procedures, particularly those of unproven value. We can also develop a much better
picture of the private health insurance industry, which is largely un-
regulated by the federal government, to try to answer some basic
questions: How substantial are profits in the industry, and at what
cost to the public good? How do the costs of administering private
health insurance claims (estimated by some analysts to exceed 20
percent) compare with such costs incurred in the public sector (estimated by some to be as low as 2 percent) (Pear 1991)? What arrangements could reduce fraud and abuse in health insurance claims?
Could medical malpractice insurance be restructured to reduce costs
in the health care industry?

Although such reforms in our health care system might improve its
effectiveness and efficiency, they are far from being panaceas. And
our ongoing struggles to refine medical practice and to resolve legal
issues will not eliminate our need to deal with many challenges and
dilemmas in providing health care for our aging population. The limitations of these constructive and practicable steps, however, hardly
mandate the use of a measure so extreme as the denial of life-saving
health care on the basis of an old-age category.

Justice between Age Groups or between Rich and Poor?   Although cost-containment presently appears to be an end in itself in the United States, anxieties that escalating costs must lead, through public policy, to acute health care rationing on a scale far greater than ever before— may be unfounded. As Moody (1991) has observed, situations that justify "rationing," as opposed to allocation, are characterized by both a scarcity of supply and a widely shared sense of crisis.

There may be a sense of crisis about costs, but health care resources, in general, are certainly not growing scarcer. Rather, they are expanding (Sonnefeld et al. 1991). It is primarily for patients dependent upon public insurance, and the uninsured and underinsured, that resources are scarce and for whom informal rationing takes place. The state of Oregon, for example, has made a political decision to limit its expenditures on Medicaid. With federal approval it has implemented a rationing scheme that gives a priority ranking to health care procedures, and reimburses for the care of poor patients only as far down the list of priorities as a predetermined Medicaid budget will be able to provide reimbursement (Office of Technology Assessment 1992).

If we can put aside our preoccupation with intergenerational constructs of justice, perhaps we will see that it is the capacity of patients to pay for charges—out-of-pocket or through third-party reimbursements—that has a great deal to do with the allocation of care. It is not a scarcity of health resources that poses a problem, but an unwillingness and/or incapacity of our political system to allocate them through some means other than economic and social stratification.

"Justice between rich and poor" may be a better metaphor than "justice between age groups" for the dilemmas of equity we confront in the allocation or rationing of care. With the issue framed on this axis, the specific policy options we might generate and consider would more likely reflect the true trade-offs that take place in the allocation of health care resources. After two decades of socialization to the "rights" or "entitlements" provided through Medicare and Medicaid, it could well be that Americans—reassured that they are not paying for waste and excess profits—will not want to impose a ceiling on health care expenditures and/or will not be willing to acquiesce to rationing practices that such a ceiling might impose (see Aaron and Schwartz 1984).

Walzer (1983) has argued that notions of justice throughout history have varied not only among cultures and political systems, but also among spheres of activities and relationships within any given culture or political system. Nothing requires us to devise or accept separate spheres of justice within the health care arena, either spheres separating age groups or spheres separating the relatively wealthy from the relatively poor. We may prefer to delineate the health care arena as a single sphere of justice within which no such distinctions are made. Reinhardt (1986, p. 29) has explained the choice very clearly: "If the American public, and the politicians who represent it, really cared about the nation's indigent, they ought to be able to exploit the emerging surplus of health care resources to the advantage of the poor."

*   *   *

These perspectives on old-age-based health care rationing—and the briefer treatments of the political power of the aged, and increasing dependency ratios—are examples of how contemporary social policy dilemmas can be perceived in terms that express neither compassionate and dispassionate ageism, nor intergenerational conflicts. Whether such perceptions are more accurate or even more propitious ways to frame issues is certainly open to debate. They have been offered to illustrate that preoccupations with stereotypes, conventional wisdom, and existing policies and institutional arrangements can divert us from seeking alternative ways to anticipate and deal with the implications of population aging and other societal challenges.

It is especially important that we examine the principles of equity implicit in the choices that we frame. If we allow our thinking to be confined by an agenda of intergenerational equity, we may very well find ourselves engaged in policy debates on issues of age-group conflict that are far worse than those we have experienced to date—deliberately trading off the value of one human life against another. Ultimately, the principles of equity that we use to describe issues will be far more important than data and policy analyses for shaping the quality of life and the nature of justice in our society.

Notes

1. This percentage is calculated on the basis of federal outlays, by category, estimated for fiscal year 1992 (U.S. Congress 1992), as modified by more detailed information from Sonnefeld et al. (1991), U.S. Senate (1991), and U.S. Social Security Administration (1991).

2. This definition of *ageism* (Binstock 1983) is intended to include positive as well as negative stereotypes regarding older persons, and is therefore more inclusive than that offered by Robert N. Butler, who originally coined the term and defined it as a "preju-

dice of the middle-aged against the old . . . a deep seated uneasiness on the part of the young and middle-aged" (Butler 1969, p. 243).

3. The term *Old Age Welfare State* was coined by John F. Myles (1983).

4. For a journalistic parallel to this perception of older persons as the appropriate financiers of the common good, see Beatty (1990).

5. Some policy analysts would argue that Social Security and Medicare expenditures should not be included in calculating the percentage of the federal budget available for domestic or any other category of discretionary programs. Their reasoning is based on the fact that the revenues funding Social Security and much of Medicare are dedicated to the purpose of paying benefits under those programs, and therefore should not be included in the total pool of funds available for allocation between mandatory and discretionary spending purposes. From this perspective one would deduct from mandatory outlays all expenditures on OASDI and on Part A of Medicare, thereby reducing substantially the total pool available for spending choices, and also increasing substantially the percentage of outlays on domestic discretionary programs.

6. Proponents of old-age-based rationing suggest that their notions pose no moral threat by arguing that since we all join the demographic category of old age (if we are lucky), using it to discriminate is unlike discrimination based on other categories—such as race, ethnicity, religion, and gender—because the practice affects us all equally. It is hard to understand, however, how equal application of a morally reprehensible policy would transform it into a just policy.

7. Among high-cost Medicare patients over a 12-month period, 50 percent tend to be decedents and 50 percent, survivors; see Lubitz and Prihoda (1984) and Scitovsky (1984).

References

Aaron, H. J., and W. B. Schwartz. 1984. *The Painful Prescription: Rationing Hospital Care*. Washington, D.C.: The Brookings Institution.

Allport, G. W. 1959. *ABC's of Scapegoating*. New York: Anti-Defamation League of B'nai B'rith.

Battin, M. P. 1987. "Choosing the Time to Die: The Ethics and Economics of Suicide in Old Age." In *Ethical Dimensions of Geriatric Care*, edited by S. Spicker (161–189). Dordrect, Holland: D. Reidel.

Beatty, J. 1990. "A Post-Cold War Budget." *The Atlantic Monthly* 256(2): 74–82.

Binstock, R. H. 1972. "Interest Group Liberalism and the Politics of Aging." *The Gerontologist* 12: 265–280.

————. 1983. "The Aged as Scapegoat." *The Gerontologist* 23: 136–143.

————. 1992. "Older Voters and the 1992 Presidential Election." *The Gerontologist* 32: 601–606.

Binstock, R. H., M. A. Levin, and R. H. Weatherley. 1985. "Political Dilemmas of Social Intervention." In *Handbook of Aging and the Social Sci-*

ences, 2nd ed., edited by R. H. Binstock and E. Shanas (589–618). New York: Van Nostrand Reinhold.

Binstock, R. H., and S. G. Post, eds. 1991. *Too Old For Health Care? Controversies in Medicine, Law, Economics, and Ethics.* Baltimore, MD: The Johns Hopkins University Press.

Butler, R. N. 1969. "Age-ism: Another Form of Bigotry." *The Gerontologist* 9: 243–246.

Blank, R. H. 1988. *Rationing Medicine.* New York: Columbia University Press.

Butterfield, F. 1990. "Silber Taps Public's Anger To Run a Strong Race in Massachusetts." *New York Times* (27 July): A6.

Button, J. W., and W. A. Rosenbaum. 1989. "Seeing Gray: School Bond Issues and the Aging in Florida." *Research on Aging* 11(2): 158–173.

Califano, J. A. Jr. 1991. "More Health Care for Less Money." *New York Times* (14 May): A15.

Callahan, D. 1987. *Setting Limits: Medical Goals in an Aging Society.* New York: Simon and Schuster.

————. 1990. *What Kind of Life? The Limits of Medical Progress.* New York: Simon and Schuster.

Carballo, M. 1981. "Extra Votes for Parents?" *The Boston Globe* (17 December): 35.

Cassel, C. K., and B. L. Neugarten. 1991. "The Goals of Medicine in an Aging Society." In *Too Old for Health Care? Controversies in Medicine, Law, Economics, and Ethics,* edited by R. H. Binstock and S. G. Post (75–91). Baltimore, MD: The Johns Hopkins University Press.

Chomitz, K. M. 1987. "Demographic Influences on Local Public Education Expenditures: A Review of Econometric Evidence." In *Demographic Change and the Well-Being of Children and the Elderly,* edited by Committee on Population, Commission on Behavioral and Social Sciences Education, National Research Council (45–53). Washington, D.C.: National Academy Press.

Churchill, L. R. 1987. *Rationing Health Care in America: Perceptions and Principles of Justice.* Notre Dame, Indiana: University of Notre Dame Press.

Clark, R. L. 1990. "Income Maintenance Policies in the United States." In *Handbook of Aging and the Social Sciences,* edited by R. H. Binstock and L. K. George (382–397). San Diego, CA: Academic Press, Inc.

Cohen, W. J. 1985a. "Securing Social Security." *New Leader* 66: 5–8.

————. 1985b. "Reflections on the Enactment of Medicare and Medicaid." *Health Care Financing Review, Annual Supplement:* 3–11.

Committee on an Aging Society. Institute of Medicine and National Research Council. 1986. *America's Aging: Productive Roles in an Older Society.* Washington, D.C.: National Academy Press.

Cranford, R. E. 1991. "Helga Wanglie's Ventilator." *Hastings Center Report* 21(4): 23–24.

Crown, W. 1985. "Some Thoughts on Reformulating the Dependency Ratio." *The Gerontologist* 25: 166–171.

Cruzan v. Director, Missouri Department of Health. 1990. 110 S. Ct. 2841.

Crystal, S. 1990. "Health Economics, Old-Age Politics, and the Catastrophic Medicare Debate." *Journal of Gerontological Social Work* 15(3/4): 21–31.

Daniels, N. 1983. "Justice Between Age Groups: Am I My Parents' Keeper?" *Milbank Memorial Fund Quarterly/Health and Society* 61(3): 489–522.

———. 1988. *Am I My Parents' Keeper? An Essay On Justice Between the Young and the Old*. New York: Oxford University Press.

Day, C. L. 1990. *What Older Americans Think: Interest Groups and Aging Policy*. Princeton, NJ: Princeton University Press.

Derthick, M. 1979. *Policymaking For Social Security*. Washington, D.C.: The Brookings Institution.

Estes, C. L. 1979. *The Aging Enterprise*. San Francisco, CA: Jossey-Bass Publishers.

———. 1983. "Social Security: The Social Construction of a Crisis." *Milbank Memorial Fund Quarterly/Health and Society* 61: 445–461.

Evans, R. W. 1991. "Advanced Medical Technology and Elderly People." In *Too Old for Health Care? Controversies in Medicine, Law, Economics, and Ethics*, edited by R. H. Binstock and S. G. Post (44–74). Baltimore, MD: The Johns Hopkins University Press.

Fairlie, H. 1988. "'Talkin' 'bout My Generation." *The New Republic* 198(13): 19–22.

Ford Foundation. Project on Social Welfare and the American Future, Executive Panel. 1989. *The Common Good: Social Welfare and the American Future*. New York: Ford Foundation.

Fox, P. 1989. "From Senility to Alzheimer's Disease: The Rise of the Alzheimer's Disease Movement." *The Milbank Quarterly* 67: 58–102.

Gibbs, N. R. 1988. "Grays on the Go." *Time* 131(8): 66–75.

Habib, J. 1990. "The Economy and the Aged." In *Handbook of Aging and the Social Sciences*, 3rd ed., edited by R. H. Binstock and L. K. George (328–345). San Diego, CA: Academic Press, Inc.

Heclo, H. 1984. "The Political Foundations of Anti-Poverty Policy." IRP Conference Paper on *Poverty and Policy: Retrospect and Prospect*, 6–8. Madison, WI: Institute for Research on Poverty.

———. 1988. "Generational Politics." In *The Vulnerable*, edited by J. L. Palmer, T. Smeeding, and B. B. Torrey (381–411). Washington, D.C.: Urban Institute Press.

Hiatt, H. H. 1987. *America's Health in the Balance: Choice or Change?* New York: Harper & Row, Publishers.

Holstein, M., and M. Minkler. 1991. "The Short Life and Painful Death of the Medicare Catastrophic Coverage Act." In *Critical Perspectives on Aging: The Political and Moral Economy of Growing Old*, edited by M. Minkler and C. Estes (189–208). Amityville, NY: Baywood Publishing Company, Inc.

182   *Economic Security and Intergenerational Justice*

Hudson, R. B. 1978. "The Graying of the Federal Budget and Its Consequences For Old Age Policy." *The Gerontologist* 18: 428–440.
Hudson, R. B., and J. Strate. 1985. "Aging and Political Systems". In *Handbook of Aging and the Social Sciences*, 2nd ed., edited by R. H. Binstock and E. Shanas (554–585). New York: Van Nostrand Reinhold.
Iglehart, J.K. 1989. "Medicare's New Benefits: Catastrophic Health Insurance." *New England Journal of Medicine* 320: 329–336.
Jacobs, B. 1990. "Aging in Politics". In *Handbook of Aging and the Social Sciences*, 3rd ed., edited by R. H. Binstock and L. K. George (349–361). San Diego, CA: Academic Press, Inc.
Jahnigen, D. W. and R. H. Binstock. 1991. "Economic and Clinical Realities: Health Care for Elderly People." In *Too Old for Health Care? Controversies in Medicine, Law, Economics and Ethics*, edited by R. H. Binstock and S. G. Post (13–43). Baltimore, MD: The Johns Hopkins University Press.
Kalish, R. A. 1979. "The New Ageism and the Failure Models: A Polemic." *The Gerontologist* 19: 398–407.
Kingson, E. R. 1988. "Generational Equity: An Unexpected Opportunity To Broaden the Politics of Aging." *The Gerontologist* 28: 765–772.
Kingson, E. R., B. A. Hirshorn, and J. M. Cornman. 1986. *Ties That Bind: The Interdependence of Generations.* Washington, D.C.: Seven Locks Press.
Kutza, E. A. 1981. *The Benefits of Old Age.* Chicago: University of Chicago Press.
Lamm, R. D. 1987. "A Debate: Medicare in 2020." In *Medicare Reform and the Baby Boom Generation*, edited proceedings of the second annual conference of Americans for Generational Equity, 30 April–1 May, pp. 77–88. Washington, D.C.: Americans for Generational Equity.
————. 1989a. "Columbus and Copernicus: New Wine in Old Wineskins." *Mount Sinai Journal of Medicine* 56(1): 1–10.
————. 1989b. "Saving a Few, Sacrificing Many—At Great Cost." *New York Times* (8 August): 23.
————. 1990. "Again, Age Beats Youth." *New York Times* (2 December): E19.
Levy, F., and R. J. Murnane. 1992. "Orphans of the Ballot Box." *New York Times* (6 February): A15.
Lewin, T. 1990. "With Court Leading the Way, Living Will Gains New Life." *New York Times* (23 July): A1 & A13.
Light, P. 1985. *Artful Work: The Politics of Social Security Reform.* New York: Random House.
Lockett, A. 1983. *Aging, Politics, and Research: Setting the Federal Agenda for Research on Aging.* New York: Springer Publishing Co.
Longman, P. 1987. *Born to Pay: The New Politics of Aging in America.* Boston MA: Houghton Mifflin Co.

Lubitz, J., and R. Prihoda. 1984. "The Use and Costs of Medicare Services in the Last Two Years of Life." *Health Care Financing Review* 5(3): 117–131.

Lubitz, J., and G. Riley. 1993. "Trends in Medicare Payments in the Last Year of Life." *New England Journal of Medicine* 328: 1092–1096.

Marmor, T. R. 1970. *The Politics of Medicare*. London: Routledge and Kegan Paul.

McNerny, W. J. 1990. "A Macroeconomic Case For Cost Containment." *Health Affairs* 9(1): 172–174.

Mendelson, D. N., and W. B. Schwartz. 1993. "The Effects of Aging and Population Growth on Health Care Costs." *Health Affairs* 12(1): 119–125.

Menzel, P. T. 1990. *Strong Medicine: The Ethical Rationing of Health Care*. New York, NY: Oxford University Press.

Moody, H. R. 1991. "Allocation, Yes; Age-based Rationing, No." In *Too Old For Health Care? Controversies in Medicine, Law, Economics, and Ethics*, edited by R. H. Binstock and S. G. Post (180–203). Baltimore, MD: The Johns Hopkins University Press.

Myles, J. F. 1983. "Conflict, Crisis, and the Future of Old Age Security." *Milbank Memorial Fund Quarterly/Health and Society* 61: 462–472.

Neugarten, B. L., and D. A. Neugarten. 1986. "Age in the Aging Society." *Daedalus* 115(1): 31–49.

New York Times/CBS News Poll. 1992. "Portrait of the Electorate." *New York Times* (5 November): B9.

Nordheimer, J. 1990. "High-tech Medicine At High-rise Costs Is Keeping Pets Fit." *New York Times* (17 September): 1.

Nye, S., Jr. 1990. *Bound to Lead: The Changing Nature of American Power*. New York: Basic Books, Inc.

OMB Watch. 1990. *Long-term Care Policy: Where Are We Going?* Boston, MA: Gerontology Institute, University of Massachusetts at Boston.

Oreskes, M. 1990. "Social Security: A Tinderbox Both Parties Handle Gingerly." *New York Times* (28 September): 12.

Pear, R. 1990. "U.S. Would Force Private Insurer To Pay Claim Before Medicare." *New York Times* (21 December): 1.

——————. 1991. "Medicare Prognosis: Unwieldy Growth Fueled By More Fees and Beneficiaries." *New York Times* (10 March): 4E.

Peterson, P. 1987. "The Morning After." *The Atlantic* 260(4): 43–69.

Pratt, H. J. 1976. *The Gray Lobby*. Chicago: University of Chicago Press.

Preston, S. H. 1984. "Children and the Elderly in the U.S." *Scientific American* 251(6): 44–49.

Quinn, J. F. and R. V. Burkhauser. 1990. "Work and Retirement." In *Handbook of Aging and the Social Sciences*, 3rd ed., edited by R. H. Binstock and L. K. George (307–327). San Diego, CA: Academic Press, Inc.

Radner, D. B. 1991. "Changes in the Income of Age Groups, 1984–1989." *Social Security Bulletin* 54(12): 2–18.

Reinhardt, U. 1986. Letter of June 9, 1986 to Arnold S. Relman. *Health Affairs* 5(2): 28–31.

————. 1990. "Health Care Woes Of American Business: Reinhardt Response." *Health Affairs* 9(1): 174–177.

Reischauer, R. D. 1991. Statement Before the Committee on Ways and Means, U.S. House of Representatives, 9 October.

Roos, N. P., P. Montgomery, and L. L. Roos. 1987. "Health Care Utilization in the Years Prior to Death." *Milbank Memorial Fund Quarterly/Health and Society* 65: 231–254.

Rosenthal, E. 1990. "Health Insurers Say Rising Fraud Is Costing Them Tens of Billions." *New York Times* (5 July): 1.

Rosenzweig, R. M. 1990. Address to the President's Opening Session, 43rd Annual Scientific Meeting, the Gerontological Society of America. Boston: 16 November.

Salholz, E. 1990. "Blaming the Voters: Hapless Budgeteers Single Out 'Greedy Geezers.' " *Newsweek* (29 October): 36.

Samuelson, R. J. 1978. Aging America: Who Will Shoulder the Growing Burden? *National Journal*, 10: 1712–1717.

Schulte, J. 1983. "Terminal Patients Deplete Medicare, Greenspan Says." *Dallas Morning News* (26 April): 1.

Schulz, J. H. 1988. *The Economics of Aging*, 4th ed. Dover, MA: Auburn House Publishing Co.

Schulz, J. H., A. Borowski, and W. H. Crown. 1991. *Economics of Population Aging: The "Graying" of Australia, Japan and the United States.* New York: Auburn House Publishing Co.

Schwartz, W. B., and H. J. Aaron. 1985. "Health Care Costs: The Social Tradeoffs." *Issues in Science and Technology* 1(2): 39–46.

Scitovsky, A. A. 1984. "The High Cost of Dying: What Do the Data Show?" *Milbank Memorial Fund Quarterly/Health and Society* 62: 591–608.

————. 1988. "Medical Care in the Last Twelve Months of Life: The Relation Between Age, Functional Status, and Medical Care Expenditures." *Milbank Memorial Fund Quarterly/Health and Society* 66: 640–660.

Simon, H. A. 1985. "Human Nature in Politics: The Dialogue of Psychology With Political Science." *American Political Science Review* 79: 293–304.

Slater, W. 1984. "Latest Lamm Remark Angers the Elderly." *Arizona Daily Star* (29 March): 1.

Smeeding, T. M., M. P. Battin, L. P. Francis, and B. M. Landesman, eds. 1987. *Should Medical Care Be Rationed By Age?* Totowa, NJ: Rowman & Littlefield.

Smith, L. 1992. "The Tyranny of America's Old." *Fortune* 125(1): 68–72.

Sonnefeld, S. T., D. R. Waldo, J. A. Lemieux, and D. R. McKusick. 1991. "Projections of National Health Expenditures through the Year 2000." *Health Care Financing Review* 13(1): 1–27.

Taeuber, C. 1990. "Diversity: The Dramatic Reality." In *Diversity in Aging: Challenges Facing Planners & Policymakers in the 1990s*, edited by S. A. Bass, E. A. Kutza, and F. M. Torres-Gil (1–45). Glenview, IL: Scott, Foresman and Co.

Tolchin, M. 1988. "New Health Insurance Plan Provokes Outcry Over Costs." *New York Times* (2 November): 1.

———. 1989a. "Lawmakers Tell the Elderly: 'Next Year' on Health Care." *New York Times* (23 November): 10Y.

———. 1989b. "House Acts to Kill '88 Medicare Plan of Extra Benefits." *New York Times* (5 October): 1.

Torrey, B. B. 1982. "Guns vs. Canes: The Fiscal Implications of an Aging Population." In *American Economics Association Papers and Proceedings* 72: 309–313.

U.S. Congress. Office of Technology Assessment. 1987. *Life-sustaining Technologies and the Elderly.* Washington, D.C.: U.S. Government Printing Office.

———. 1992. *Summary: Evaluation of the Oregon Medicaid Proposal.* Washington, D.C.: U.S. Government Printing Office.

U.S. Congress. Congressional Budget Office. 1992. *The Economic and Budget Outlook: Fiscal Years 1993–1997.* Washington, D.C.: U.S. Government Printing Office.

———. 1993. *The Economic and Budget Outlook: An Update.* Washington, D.C.: U.S. Government Printing Office.

U.S. House of Representatives. Select Committee on Aging. 1977. *Federal Responsibility To the Elderly: Executive Programs and Legislative Jurisdiction.* Washington, D.C.: U.S. Government Printing Office.

———. 1989. *Health Care Costs For America's Elderly, 1977–88.* Washington, D.C.: U.S. Government Printing Office.

U.S. Senate. Special Committee on Aging. 1988. *Developments In Aging: 1987,* vol. 1. Washington, D.C.: U.S. Government Printing Office.

———. 1991. *Developments in Aging: 1990,* vol. 1. Washington, D.C.: U.S. Government Printing Office.

U.S. Social Security Administration. 1991. *Social Security Bulletin, Annual Statistical Supplement, 1991.* Washington, D.C.: U.S. Department of Health and Human Services.

Veatch, R. 1988. "Justice and the Economics of Terminal Illness." *Hastings Center Report* 18(4): 34–40.

Walzer, M. 1983. *Spheres of Justice.* New York: Basic Books, Inc.

Washington Post. 1990. "Older Voters Drive Budget: Generational Divide Marks Budget Battle" (15 October): 1.

White House Domestic Policy Council. 1993. *The President's Health Security Plan.* New York: Random House.

Wisensale, S. M. 1988. "Generational Equity and Intergenerational Policies." *The Gerontologist* 28: 773–778.

Woolhandler, S., and D. U. Himmelstein. 1991. "The Deteriorating Administrative Efficiency of the U.S. Health Care System." *New England Journal of Medicine* 324: 1253–1258.

Part Three

POLICY DIMENSIONS OF ECONOMIC SECURITY FOR THE ELDERLY

BALANCING INTERESTS AND CONTROLLING RISKS ACROSS WORKERS AND RETIREES

Carolyn L. Weaver

Barring some significant, unforseen developments in fertility, mortality, or immigration, the population of the United States is destined to age very rapidly beginning just 20 years from now, when the first wave of the baby-boom generation moves into retirement. According to the intermediate projections of the Social Security Board of Trustees, the proportion of the population age 65 and older will jump from 12–13 percent, the level expected to prevail through 2010, to 20 percent in 2030; the ratio of workers to beneficiaries is thus projected to fall by one-third—from three workers per beneficiary to two workers per beneficiary—in the span of just two decades.[1]

Not only will more people than ever before reach retirement, but also more retirees than ever before will live to be very old. The U.S. Bureau of the Census reports that the proportion of the population age 85 and older, now just 1.3 percent, will increase four-fold, reaching 5.1 percent by 2050 (U.S. Department of Commerce 1989). Without a reversal of the trend toward early retirement, Americans will spend a larger and larger share of their lives in retirement.

Neither public mechanisms for transferring income over time, such as Social Security, nor private mechanisms, such as employer-provided pensions or intrafamily transfers, will be immune to these developments. Public and private systems alike will feel the pressures of a potentially dramatic increase in the per capita cost of income support for the elderly.

The debate over income security policy that will surely unfold in the years ahead is likely to differ in some important respects from the debate of the past. For most of this century, income security policy has been a term of art associated with federal income transfers to the elderly. The recipe for enhanced income security has been a simple one: increase Social Security benefits, liberalize program eligibility, expand coverage—and shift the cost to future workers and taxpayers.

During the 1960s and early 1970s, average monthly benefits increased 54 percent in real terms for retired workers and a whopping 85 percent for widows of decreased workers. Over the same period, 1960–1975, the number of Social Security beneficiaries rose from 14 million to 31 million and the proportion of the elderly receiving benefits jumped from 60 percent to 90 percent. To top it all off, Medicare was enacted in 1965, making hospital insurance protection available to millions of elderly people who had made no contribution toward its cost, and indexing of cash benefits was introduced in 1972, building in automatic, annual increases in benefits to reflect changes in the cost of living.[2]

Social Security spending exploded. Between 1960 and 1975, expenditures more than tripled in real terms, rising from $49 billion to $157 billion in constant 1989 dollars. By 1975, Social Security accounted for 21 percent of the federal budget (24 percent including Medicare), up from 13 percent in 1960.

This recipe for income security worked remarkably well—provided we focus on the interests of present rather than future generations. During the great expansion of Social Security, which began in earnest in the 1950s, poverty rates among the elderly plummeted and the income and wealth of the elderly rose appreciably, while payroll taxes remained deceptively low. As a recently as 1975, the payroll tax (employer-employee combined, OASDHI) was 11.7 percent on the first $14,100 of earnings. This amounted to a tax bill of $1,650 for the worker with maximum earnings, or $3,740 in real 1989 dollars. Today, the tax is 15.3 percent on the first $57,600 ($135,000 for the Medicare portion of the tax), which translates into a tax bill of $10,770 for the high-wage worker—more than double the 1975 level in real terms, yet substantially less than what will be necessary to meet projected benefits when today's young workers retire.

That Social Security could provide so much income to retirees at such a relatively low cost to workers was not due to any inherent superiority of Social Security relative to private pensions or to other means of transferring income over time. Rather, it was due to the unique ability of pay-as-you go financing to create, during a finite and now passing time, huge wealth transfers to retirees. These transfers were not sustainable in the long run.

Since Social Security did not have to accumulate assets to meet accruing liabilities, the government could accumulate very large long-range liabilities without owning up to the cost. All the revenues collected—during periods of prosperous economic growth, rapidly expanding coverage, and artificially high ratios of workers to beneficiaries—could be spent on current retirees rather than invested in real capital to help meet the cost of benefits for future retirees. Retirees received benefits substantially larger than the taxes they had paid, and many workers paid taxes substantially less than necessary to pay for the benefits they would become entitled to receive. While Social Security was still a young system, pay-as-you-go financing provided a relatively painless way of redistributing income from younger to older people.

At some point, pay-as-you-go systems have to mature, and the U.S. Social Security system is at that point. Coverage is basically universal and people are paying taxes over their full working lives; the implicit rate of return on taxes is thus fast approaching its long-term sustainable rate—roughly 1–2 percent in real terms, which is substantially below the return to real private capital.[3] With a stable set of tax rates, the intergenerational wealth transfers disappear. People have to pay for what they get—and then some. Research by Michael Boskin et al. (1987) indicates that workers age 45 or younger will not get their "money's worth" from Social Security (meaning that they will not receive the actuarial equivalent of taxes paid); in fact, they can expect to experience fairly substantial wealth losses when they retire.[4]

In this environment—an aging Social Security system with high current taxes, superimposed on an aging population—"income security" is taking on a whole new meaning. Increasingly, Social Security and other federal programs are being seen from an intergenerational perspective in which the interests of one generation must be balanced against the interests of the others. It is becoming ever more clear that policies designed to "guarantee" a level of support for one group deny income security and predictability to other groups.

An essential truth with which Social Security reform (no less than the reform of other income security programs) must contend is that risks cannot be eliminated for people in retirement *and* for younger workers planning their retirement. They can only be rearranged across generations (through redistributive policies that may or may not promote "income security)" or reduced (through policies designed to secure contract terms or to promote diversification). Policies that promote the interests of today's retirees at the expense of today's workers and children—tomorrow's elderly—cannot reasonably be said to promote income security and they are not likely to survive in the long term.

In the remainder of this chapter, I discuss two issues of particular concern in income security policy: first, the advance funding of Social Security as it relates to the security of public retirement benefits; and second, federal regulation of private pensions as it relates to the security of private retirement benefits. The intergenerational consequences of public policy will be the focus of the discussion.

SOCIAL SECURITY AND ADVANCE FUNDING

As a result of legislation enacted in 1983, and generally robust economic growth since then, the Social Security and Medicare (old-age and survivors insurance, disability insurance, and hospital insurance) trust funds are running large annual surpluses and accumulating substantial interest-bearing reserves. Total assets stand at $330 billion, roughly seven times their level in 1985, and are expected to top $1 trillion within a decade. The much discussed Social Security surplus is $47 billion annually ($50 billion including Medicare), the equivalent of almost $1 billion weekly.[5]

Ironically it was not until Senator Moynihan proposed cutting the payroll tax and substantially reducing the size of the reserves that attention really focused on how the surplus receipts were being invested and what the implications were for future workers and retirees.[6] Under present law and procedure, virtually all monies not needed to pay benefits are held in special issue U.S. government bonds, which are, quite literally, IOUs from one part of the government to another.

Thanks to Senator Moynihan, we now have a lively debate over whether this policy makes sense. Are the Social Security surpluses being saved and invested to lighten the burden of benefits for baby-boom retirees? If not, how can government policy be restructured to enhance income security for future workers and retirees?[7]

The stakes are high. Social Security is slated to spend $20 trillion, in present value terms, over the next 75 years ($32 trillion including Medicare). In the two-decade period spanning the retirement of the youngest and oldest members of the baby-boom generation, 2010 to 2030, the number of people on the benefit rolls is projected to swell by 25 million, or close to 50 percent, while the number of covered workers remains almost flat. Benefit costs in relation to taxable payroll are thus projected to jump by close to 50 percent.

Failing to advance fund Social Security amounts to putting our heads in the sand—leaving the full liability of future benefits to be met as it comes due by tax increases on future workers. The alternative—meaningful advance funding—involves taking steps now to increase national saving and economic growth in recognition and anticipation of this liability, allowing for lower ultimate tax rates.

But there are two practical problems with the way the government is advance funding Social Security. First, there is no mechanism in the law to ensure that the surpluses are, in fact, saved, meaning that real resources are transferred from present to future generations. When surplus monies are "invested" in government bonds, the trust funds are credited with a bond and the Treasury gets the cash. From the standpoint of the Treasury, these monies are indistinguishable from any other monies and are available to finance the general operations of the government. If Congress uses these surpluses to relax fiscal restraint in the rest of the budget—reducing federal income taxes or increasing spending on other programs—there is no meaningful advance funding or investment policy. There is simply a hidden reallocation of taxes toward payroll tax financing of the general operation of government today and toward general fund financing of Social Security (to meet the ever-growing interest payments to the trust funds) tomorrow.[8]

The risk to present and future workers is clear: the substantial excess taxes now being paid could end up funding an increase in current consumption rather than contributing to meaningful economic saving. If this were to happen, the long-run burden of Social Security would be no lighter than if the system had been pay-as-you-go financed all along. The $5 trillion reserve fund ($1 trillion in 1989 dollars) projected for the next century would then represent nothing more than Social Security's claim on the general fund of the Treasury, with no real capital backing up that claim.

The second problem is that nothing ensures that the surpluses, if saved, will be saved on an ongoing basis. Congress can increase benefits and meet part of the cost by depleting reserves rather than by raising taxes or cutting other benefits.[9] As reserves accumulate, the political pressures will be strong to do just that. There are many "particularly deserving" groups—whether aged widows, two-earner families, "notch babies," the incapacitated near-elderly, or nonworking spouses. Using the reserves in this way, or indeed, using them to bail out the Medicare program, would undermine saving just as surely as any mishandling of the federal budget today.

Unlike private pensions, which must comply with the funding requirements of ERISA (the Employee Retirement Income Security Act), Social Security has no funding requirements with which it must comply. The system can legally run deficits and deplete reserves without regard to the security of future benefits.

What can be done to improve the chances that the surpluses are productively saved and invested, reducing the risks to future workers and taxpayers? Some have argued for allowing the government to begin investing directly in a variety of public and private investments. While this alternative holds some appeal, its central drawback is that the government has weak incentives to allocate surplus monies to their highest valued uses. Investment decisions would be politically determined and resources would flow toward politically favored projects. One can easily imagine the list of disallowed investments, right alongside the list of preferred investments. Rate of return would undoubtedly suffer relative to a strategy in which investment decisions were competitively determined.

If our goal is to increase saving and investment, to ensure a competitive rate on return to investments, and ultimately to ensure that the funds are still there in 30 or 40 years, we need to find ways to: (1) draw on the competitive market process to direct investment funds toward their highest valued uses; and (2) secure the rights of workers (future retirees) to the proceeds of these investments.

For example, suppose the surplus revenues in the trust funds could be rebated to workers for direct deposit into individualized retirement accounts, along the lines of IRAs, with restrictions against withdrawal before retirement. (This is what Congressman Porter has in mind with his proposal to "privatize" the surpluses.)[10] Such a policy would basically solve the investment problem in that it would allow for real saving and real capital investment, but without involving the federal government in direct management and control of vast sums of private resources. (Keep in mind that the assets of the Social Security trust funds already exceed those held by the nation's top 10 private pension funds combined, including GM, Ford Motor Company, and AT&T.)[11] Investment decisions would be fully decentralized and competitively determined. At the same time, individuals—directly involved in their retirement savings decisions—would accumulate legally enforceable claims to future benefits.

Alternatively, suppose workers were permitted the right to contract out of Social Security (at least the earnings-related portion) if they were covered by a comparable employer-sponsored pension. This is basically the way the British Social Security system works. This too would solve the investment problem, although indirectly, since by law private pensions must be funded and assets must be prudently invested.

Admittedly, these are not tinkering proposals. Either one would necessitate a restructuring of benefits relative to taxes, not just a change in investment procedures. But, the pay-as-you-go method of financing adopted decades ago doesn't make sense with the demographic bulge our nation faces in the 21st century. Nor does advance funding make sense the way the government is doing it—without any assurance of real saving. The role of the private sector can and should be expanded to lighten the demands on future workers and taxpayers and to improve our chances of meeting, at the least possible cost, the retirement income needs of baby-boom retirees as well as those that will come along behind them.

Another direction for reform, more modest in scope, is to simply scale back long-range benefits and lower the payroll tax. The idea here would be to encourage rather than mandate private savings, thereby leaving more of the retirement decision to the individual. With less income taxed away for the purpose of retirement saving, and less offered by the government in the way of future benefits, individuals and families would have increased flexibility—and incentive—to structure their savings to meet their needs. There would be greater freedom to decide when to save as well as how to save.

Long-range benefits can be trimmed through any number of modest changes, including increasing the age at which full retirement benefits are payable (speeding the transition from 65 to 67 or raising the age to 68 or 70), indexing the retirement age to longevity, or raising the age at which early retirement benefits are payable. Simply revising the way benefits are computed for new retirees would generate substantial savings while still allowing for real benefit growth over time.[12]

If properly designed, this option could reduce the great imbalance between Social Security expenditures and payroll tax income in future decades, ameliorating Social Security's funding and investment problems as well as some of the implied pressures on the federal budget. At the same time, it would return the system more nearly to a pay-as-you-go basis without leaving the full liability implied by today's benefit structure to be met as it comes due.

In evaluating proposals to scale back or reform Social Security, it is important to realize that Social Security is just one piece—albeit a large one—of the U.S. retirement income system. Private pensions (which were just emerging in the 1930s when Social Security was created), life and retiree health insurance, homeownership and other forms of private savings, along with earnings and other public pensions are all important aspects of the financial well-being of future workers and retirees.

It is also important to realize that the Social Security system is insolvent in the long run. Based on the "best guess" projections of the Social Security trustees, in the year 2050, when today's children are beginning to retire, the assets of the Social Security (OASI and DI) trust funds will be exhausted and benefit costs will exceed payroll tax income by $200 billion annually in real 1989 dollars. Taking Medicare into account leads to a projected deficit of $700 billion annually. Under the trustees' "pessimistic" cost assumptions, 40 percent of Social Security benefits (and 60 percent of Social Security and Medicare benefits) in the year 2050 cannot be met with the tax rates now in the law.

Those who think that tax increases are the answer must contend with the fact that Social Security is *already* the largest and most costly component of the domestic federal budget; the payroll tax necessary to fund *current* benefits imposes a heavier tax burden on most American taxpayers than the federal income tax. In 1977 and again in 1983, Congress enacted major payroll tax increases—on the order of $300-$400 billion in the 1980s alone—and in neither instance was long-range solvency secured. Bringing benefit costs back into line with available resources is a necessary first step toward a sustainable income security policy.

PRIVATE PENSIONS AND GOVERNMENT REGULATION

Just as Social Security reform must contend with the interests of both present and future retirees, so must the reform of policies affecting private pensions. The federal government presently regulates virtually all aspects of private pensions—from the design of the pension contract and the funding and investment of pension assets to the insurance of pension benefits. New pension regulations, written and enforced by three different federal agencies, and new pension laws come onto line every year. While many of these regulations, and indeed many of the proposals for new regulations, are premised on bolstering the security of pension benefits, their indirect effect may well be to undermine retirement income security.

Private pensions are an important source of income for millions of U.S. retireees. In 1987, close to one-third of elderly houshohlds (9 million people in total) received income from a private pension. (Over 40 percent received income from some type of employer pension, including military and civilian government pensions.) The average pension payment was $5,200 annually.[13]

Pensions are also an important part of retirement income planning for millions of U.S. workers. Sixty-six million people, or 55 percent of the civilian work force, are covered by some type of private pension plan (EBRI Databook 1992). (Among full-time workers in medium and large firms, the coverage rate is close to 90 percent.) New pension contributions exceed $100 billion annually, and pension fund assets exceed $2 trillion.

The defined benefit pension plan, while declining in popularity, remains the primary pension of American workers. Defined benefit plans offer annuities at retirement that are generally based on years of service and salary. This contrasts with defined contribution plans, which guarantee the return of contributions plus interest earnings. (Defined contribution plans include 401(k), profit sharing, thrift-savings, and money purchase plans.) Roughly two-thirds of workers covered by pensions have a defined benefit plan as their primary plan, with the balance covered by some type of defined contribution plan.[14]

What does the future hold for private pensions? At one level, the future of private pensions looks quite good. With substantially more people covered by pensions now than when today's retirees were young, substantially more people can expect to retire with at least some pension income in future decades. Researchers estimate that on the basis of current contributions, two-thirds of the full-time work force will retire with a pension and that these pensions will replace about one-quarter (23 percent) of pre-retirement earnings (Ippolito 1986). Employer-sponsored pensions have met the test of time—having survived the Great Depression and a barrage of federal regulations—and, quite likely, are here to stay.

At a deeper level, though, there is reason for concern. The federal government has the capacity, through its tax and regulatory policies, to undermine the growth and evolution of the private pension system, and evidence is accumulating that it may be doing just that.[15]

There is nothing magic about private pensions that gives them enduring value. Pensions are simply one financial arrangement among many for transferring resources over time, from working years to retirement. Houses, savings accounts, public retirement programs, life insurance, IRAs—even our children—perform the same basic function. Alter the net benefits of pensions relative to other savings arrangements and people will alter the amount of resources they devote to them.

The unique feature of defined benefit pensions is that they shield participants from investment risk near retirement and allow workers to target, in advance, particular income goals.[16] Rather than having to rely on good investment decisions or a rally in the stock market or in real estate, for example, workers covered by defined benefit pensions gain eligibility for a benefit that replaces a predetermined amount of earnings. The group annuity feature of defined benefit pensions, moreover, provides a type of insurance (against the risk of living "too long") that is generally more expensive if purchased individually on the open market, as may be necessary to annuitize the lump-sum proceeds of defined contribution plans or traditional savings accounts.

With sufficient flexibility in design, defined benefit pensions have value to employers too—as potentially potent management tools. Through the financial incentives and disincentives inherent in these pensions, workers can be encouraged to remain with a firm during their productive years and to retire as older workers. Defined benefit pensions, in other words, are a type of long-term employment contract that can reduce labor turnover and increase productivity.[17] With such a contract in place, firms can pay higher wages or make investments in their workers, such as in costly on-the-job training, that they otherwise would not make. Both workers and employers stand to gain from the turnover reducing/productivity increasing aspects of defined benefit pensions.[18]

Restrict the flexibility of workers and employers to structure mutually beneficial pension contracts or increase the cost of offering pensions, and resources will flow into other financial and nonfinancial arrangements.

There's another reason we value—and demand from our employers—pensions. It's their favorable tax treatment relative to ordinary savings. Pension contributions and accrued interest escape taxation until the time of distribution, making pensions a relatively less expensive means of saving for retirement.

To see the value of this, consider a worker who saves 10 percent of his earnings in an ordinary savings account (or, say, invests it in a CD); he owes income tax on this amount as well as on any interest earnings. If, instead, he has his employer set aside 10 percent in a company pension (possibly invested in the same CD), no taxes are owed until retirement. Saving through a tax-favored company pension allows the worker to accumulate interest at a pre-tax rate of return, which results in substantial tax savings even before factoring in the lower marginal tax rates he is likely to face on income received in retirement. Richard Ippolito, chief economist at the Pension Benefit Guaranty Corporation, estimates that the value of these tax savings is equivalent to a 25 percent increase in after-tax retirement income for middle-income workers (Ippolito 1986).[19]

Eliminate or reduce this tax advantage and part of the foundation of employer pensions will disappear. Pensions will be more costly and we will do less retirement savings through them.[20]

So how can federal regulation jeopardize the well-being of future workers and retirees? Consider the regulations governing vesting and participation, which reduce the pension penalties for workers who leave firms prematurely. The hope of policymakers would be that the regulations increase pensions for mobile or transient workers without affecting pensions for other workers. But these regulations increase the cost of defined benefit pensions and seriously restrict the ability of employers to use them to control turnover; the net gains to defined benefit pensions are reduced, making them less likely to be offered. People who already have jobs covered by pensions (and manage to keep those pensions) benefit at the expense of those who do not.[21]

Or consider the regulations governing the PBGC, which establish a mandatory federal insurance program for companies offering defined benefit plans and charge premiums that are only partially (and imperfectly) adjusted to reflect risk differences among plans. Premiums are generally too low for high-risk plans and too high for low-risk plans. In addition, firms are not required to bear the full cost of actions, such as pursuing risky investment strategies, that increase the risk of loss to the PBGC. These regulations encourage unsuccessful firms to adopt defined benefit plans while discouraging new firms from setting them up and successful ongoing firms from keeping them. The result may well be more risk among defined benefit pensions.[22]

The decision to adopt a pension plan in the first place is the one decision regarding pensions that still can be made exclusively by employers and their employees. All proposals for new government regulation must be weighed against the reality that as pensions become more costly—and less beneficial from the standpoint of either employees or employers—they are less likely to be offered.

Already there is evidence that federal policies designed to bolster pension security may be adversely affecting the retirement income system, reducing both the proportion of the work force covered by defined benefit plans and the rate of new plan formation. Between 1980 and 1989, the number of workers whose primary plan was a defined benefit plan fell from 30 million to 27 million while the number whose primary plan was a defined contribution plan more than doubled, reaching 15 million workers; the proportion whose primary pension plan was a defined benefit plan thus fell from 83 percent to 63 percent.[23] The trend toward defined contribution plans is observed in all sectors of the economy. While the jury is still out on precisely why this trend is occurring, there is a growing body of research suggesting that government regulation is a major contributing factor (Clark and McDermed 1990; Gustman and Steinmeier 1992; and Ippolito, forthcoming).[24]

There is also evidence of a decline in the pension participation rate—that is, the proportion of covered workers who actually participate in their company's pension plan (including both defined benefit and defined contribution plans). The percent of covered workers participating in a pension plan dropped from 81 percent in 1979 to 76 percent in 1988, thus reducing the percent of the civilian work force participating in a pension plan from 46 percent to 42 percent.[25] Here too there is concern that government tax and regulatory policy may be paving the way.

Some, no doubt, will respond to these developments by proposing more government regulation: for example, mandating that all companies offer pension plans to their employees. This approach is misguided. While a pension mandate would solve the coverage problem, it would do so by creating two new problems. First, it would compel companies to establish plans that may not be in the best interests of their workers. Recognizing that workers must pay for their pensions, the regulation would force some workers, particularly low-wage workers, to save more for retirement—and enjoy less take-home pay—than they would desire. These workers are likely to respond by taking actions that minimize the costs that are imposed in this way, but in so doing will limit the effectiveness of the regulation. Low-wage people forced to save too much through their pensions, for example, will rationally increase their borrowing (or reduce other saving) to restore their desired consumption patterns, thus negating part of the purpose of the regulation which presumably is to increase consumption opportunities in retirement.[26]

Second, as with any mandated benefits program, a pension mandate would likely hurt the employment opportunities of low-wage workers. Superimposing a pension mandate on top of minimum wage laws (and any other wage or fringe-benefit mandates that might apply at the federal and state level) could easily result in a minimum level of compensation for low-skill workers that exceeded the value of their output. Firms would rationally respond by laying off and/or creating fewer new jobs for low-skilled workers. The more "adequate" the minimum pension, the greater the adverse effects on employment are likely to be.

The government, in other words, may be able to ensure that people who work have pensions, but it cannot simultaneously ensure that workers keep their jobs or that the pensions they receive are worth more than they cost. Policies designed to remake private pensions, through costly government regulation, to offer "something for everyone" run the very real risk of undermining income security for those most vulnerable to income fluctuations.

Unfortunately, there appears to be more pressure, not less, for using the political process to reshape the private pension system. Increasingly, regulations have as their goal income redistribution rather than simply securing the terms of the pension contract or ensuring the adequacy of pension assets. Pension regulations, however, are inherently limited in their ability to influence the distribution of income and thus to deliver the sought-after benefits.

The Social Security system, it should be noted, already addresses many of the problems reformers are attempting to achieve through private pensions. For example, Social Security is virtually universal in its coverage, benefits are weighted heavily toward low-income people; and benefits are fully portable among employers (i.e., workers suffer no loss of pension wealth in moving from one job to another). Proposals to make private pensions more like Social Security—for example, by mandating portability or higher benefits for low-wage workers—carry large economic costs and highly uncertain benefits.

Private pensions are not, it should be stressed, the end all and be all of retirement income planning in the 21st century. Nor are pensions the answer for everyone. They are simply a part—albeit an important part—of a *well-diversified* retirement income system. Private pensions, as we know them, are unlikely to ever be a major source of income for people who work outside the home only part-time or sporadically or on a volunteer basis; for example, the homemaker or the disabled or chronically unemployed person. For them, Social Security, private insurance and saving, family support, and public assistance will be important. For the great bulk of people who do work—and work full time—pensions can be expected to remain important, provided they are nourished by the proper tax and regulatory environment.

Tax and regulatory policy governing pensions (as well as other financial instruments) should be designed to encourage competition, diversity, and flexibility in contract design. This would permit pensions to evolve to meet the diverse and changing interests of employees and employers, both now and in the future. Federal policy should also be as neutral as possible in the way it affects our decisions to save today or tomorrow or to save through this vehicle or that. Such a policy would permit individuals to provide for their retirement at the least possible sacrifice during their younger years—and do so through well-diversified portfolios of financial and nonfinancial assets—as they seek to maximize their consumption opportunities over their lifetimes. All sources of wealth and income carry risks and our public policies and private decisions should be structured to control those risks through diversification.

*   *   *

I would note in closing that the efficiency of the retirement income system would be enhanced if the tax advantages now available to people who save through company pensions were made available to other people attempting to save for retirement. (This was basically the idea behind IRAs as they were originally conceived.) Such a policy creates a broadly available means of savings for retirement that escapes the double tax on savings. In addition, it creates some healthy competition for company pension plans. Many of the detailed regulations governing the distribution of benefits, allowable investments, and other rules designed to protect plan participants would be unnecessary in a world in which workers had viable alternative means of saving.

The promise of "income security" through Social Security, no less than through other public and private programs, is a qualified promise; it involves contingencies and risks. The uncertainties inherent in long-term benefit promises—and in the cost of those promises—cannot be eliminated; they can only be reduced through well-designed government policies. As the retiree bulge of the 21st century approaches, policymakers would be well advised to focus less on policies designed to increase benefit promises and more on policies designed to control the risks.

Notes

1. Unless otherwise noted, data drawn from Board of Trustees (1993) based on the Trustee's intermediate (II-B) assumptions.

2. For a comprehensive review of the history of Social Security expansion, see Weaver (1982). For data, see *Social Security Bulletin* (1990), Myers (1991), and Board of Trustees (1993).

3. In the long run, the average rate of return on Social Security taxes is determined by the real rate of growth of taxable wages. Because of the redistributive nature of the

benefit formula, rates of return are higher for low-wage workers and lower for high-wage workers.

4. Estimates for workers (with nonworking spouses) with median earnings. See Boskin et al. (1987).

5. Calendar Year 1993 data. Data supplied by Office of the Actuary, Social Security Administration (January 12, 1993).

6. Senator Moynihan's proposal, which applies to OASDI only, would reduce the OASDI tax rate for the years 1991-2015 and increase it thereafter. By 2050, the tax rate would be 30 percent higher than scheduled under present law. Senator Moynihan would also increase the amount of wages subject to the Social Security tax, negating the effect of the tax cut for high-wage workers. See Senate bill S. 11, introduced on January 14, 1991.

7. For a series of essays on the funding of Social Security, the investment of trust fund assets, and the arguments for and against advance funding or pay-as-you-go financing, see Weaver (1990).

8. The alternative, what might be termed the "best case scenario," is where the surplus funds are used to retire outstanding publicly held government debt (or to reduce the amount of new debt issued to the public). Private investors could then substitute new private securities for the government debt they relinquished, thus increasing the funds available for private investment. For a careful explanation of the way in which advance funding can indirectly add to the nation's real capital investment, see Feldstein (1976).

Unfortunately, at the present time, it is not possible to observe the size and composition of the budget to determine (with certainty) whether the Social Security surpluses are being spent or saved. It would be necessary to know what the size and composition of the budget would have been in the absence of the trust fund buildup, or the budget excluding Social Security would have to be in balance. For example, if the budget excluding Social Security were kept in balance, we would know that the surplus receipts in the trust fund were having no effect on taxing and spending decisions in the rest of the budget and thus were being channeled into retiring outstanding debt.

9. Under the Gramm-Rudman-Hollings budget control law, as revised in 1990, there are a set of complex provisions which appear to protect the Social Security reserves from unfinanced benefit increases or tax cuts. These protections are more apparent than real, however. For examle, a key procedural hurdle—the requirement of a super-majority vote in the Senate—is waived for legislation originating on the floor rather than in committee. In addition, expansions of Social Security spending do not trigger any automatic spending reductions. See *Congressional Record* (1990).

10. For a summary and evaluation of Rep. John E. Porter's proposal, see General Accounting Office (1990).

11. For data on private pension plans, see "The Top 200 . . ." (1989).

12. The benefit formula used to compute benefits for people when they first go on the rolls is indexed to wage growth in the economy, which typically exceeds the rate of inflation. (Once people are on the rolls, benefits are increased annually based on changes in the consumer price index.) This proposal would involve moving (either completely or in part) to price indexing of the benefit formula.

13. In the aggregate, private pensions accounted for 20 percent of income to retirees (including those without pensions) age 65–74. Unless otherwise noted, pension data is drawn from Turner and Beller (1990).

14. See "Changing Roles of Defined Benefit and Defined Contribution Plans" (1992).

15. For three informative studies on the economics of pension regulation, see Ippolito (1986 and 1987) and Clark and McDermed (1990). See also Utgoff (1990).

16. For a more complete discussion of the unique features of DB pensions and an assessment of their value to workers, see Bodie (1990) and Ippolito (1986).

17. On pensions as implicit long-term contracts, see Lazear (1979) and Ippolito (1986). See also Clark and McDermed (1990) and Quinn et al. (1990).

18. Workers stand to gain in ex ante sense. After the fact, of course, some workers would prefer to have negotiated a different contract—for example, workers who join a company expecting to stay with it for many years, voluntarily accepting the wage-pension package offered, and who subsequently leave after only a brief spell. Obviously, they would prefer to get all the benefits that accrue to full service workers, including on-the-job training and a full pension.

19. For more on the tax treatment of pensions, see Ippolito (1990) and Congressional Budget Office (1987).

20. Of course, the government can also affect private pensions through tax policy elsewhere. Reducing marginal income tax rates, for example, reduces the relative advantages of tax-free accumulation through pensions and thus reduces the demand to shelter current earnings in this way. Likewise, tax policy with respect to IRAs will affect employer-provided pensions.

21. For more on this, see Clark and McDermed (1990).

22. See, in particular, Ippolito (1987 and 1989), and Bodie (1993).

23. See "Pension Evolution in a Changing Economy" (1993).

24. Two other factors include the shift in employment away from large unionized firms in the manufacturing sector where DB plan coverage has been highest and the introduction of 401 (k) plans, which present employees and employers with a closer substitute for DB plans. The shift in the composition of jobs does not raise the same concerns as government regulation since in this case changes in underlying market conditions are affecting pension outcomes through their impact on the supply of and demand for pensions; there need be no inefficiencies involved.

25. For data, see "Pension Coverage. . ." (1989). Part of the decline in participation rates may be due to the increasing prevalence of DC plans (induced by regulation) and the voluntary choice of workers not to participate in these plans.

26. For a similar argument applied to the integration rules governing the offset of pensions for Social Security, see Utgoff (1990). On mandated benefits generally, see Kosters (1988).

References

Board of Trustees of the Federal Old-Age and Survivors Insurance and Federal Disability Insurance Trust Funds. 1993. *1993 Annual Report*. Washington, D.C.: U.S. Government Printing Office.

Bodie, Zvi. 1990. "Pensions and Retirement Income Insurance." *Journal of Economic Literature* 28 (1, March): 28–49.

Bodie, Zvi, and Robert C. Merton. 1993. "Pension Benefit Guarantees in the United States." In *The Future of Pensions in the United States*, ed. R. Schmitt. Philadelphia: University of Pennsylvania Press.

Boskin, Michael J., Laurence J. Kotlikoff, Douglas J. Puffert, and John B. Shoven. 1987. "Social Security: A Financial Appraisal Across and within Generations." *National Tax Journal* 40 (1, March): 19–34.

"Changing Roles of Defined Benefit and Defined Contribution Plans." 1992. *Employee Benefit Notes* 13 (9, December). Washington, D.C.: Employee Benefit Research Institute.

Clark, Robert L., and Ann A. McDermed. 1990. *The Choice of Pension Plans in a Changing Regulatory Environment.* Washington, D.C.: American Enterprise Institute.

Congressional Budget Office. 1987. *Tax Policy and Pensions and Other Retirement Saving.* Washington, D.C.: Government Printing Office (April).

EBRI Databook on Employee Pensions. 1992. Washington, D.C.: Employee Benefit Research Institute.

Feldstein, Martin. 1976. "The Social Security Fund and National Capital Accumulation." In *Funding Pensions: Issues and Implications for Financial Markets,* Conference Series No. 16. Boston: Federal Reserve Bank of Boston.

General Accounting Office. 1990. *Social Security: Analysis of a Proposal to Privatize Trust Fund Reserves.* GAP/HRD-91-22. (December).

Gustman, Alan, and Thomas Steinmeier. 1992. "The Stampede to Defined Contribution Plans." *Industrial Relations* 31 (Spring): 361–369.

Ippolito, Richard A. 1986. *Pensions, Economics, and Public Policy.* Homewood, Ill: Dow Jones-Irwin.

————. 1987. "Pension Security: Has ERISA Had Any Effect?" *Regulation* (2): 15–22.

————. 1988. "A Study of the Regulatory Impact of ERISA." *Journal of Law and Economics* (April).

————. 1989. *The Economics of Pension Insurance.* Homewood, Ill.: Irwin.

————. 1990. *An Economic Appraisal of Pension Tax Policy in the United States,* Homewood, Ill: Irwin.

————. Forthcoming. "Toward Explaining the Growth of Defined Contribution Plans." *Industrial Relations.*

Kosters, Marvin H. 1988. "Mandated Benefits—On the Agenda." *Regulation* (3): 21–27.

Lazear, Edward P. 1979. "Why Is There Mandatory Retirement?" *Journal of Political Economy* 87 (December): 1261–1284.

Myers, Robert J. 1991. "Summary of the Provisions of the Old-Age, Survivors, and Disability Insurance System, the Hospital Insurance System, and the Supplementary Medical Insurance System." Mimeographed (January).

"Pension Coverage and Benefit Entitlement; New Findings from 1988." 1989. *EBRI Issue Brief, No. 94.* Washington, D.C.: Employee Benefit Research Institute (September).

"Pension Evolution in a Changing Economy." 1993. *EBRI Special Report, No. 141.* Washington, D.C.: Employee Benefit Research Institute (September).

Quinn, Joseph F., Richard V. Burkhauser, and Daniel A. Myers. 1990. *Passing the Torch: The Influence of Economic Incentives on Work and Retirement.* Kalamazoo, Mich.: W. E. Upjohn Institute for Employment Research.

Social Security Bulletin: Annual Statistical Supplement, 1989. Washington, D.C.: U.S. Government Printing Office.

"The Top 200: Who's Who Among Corporate Pension Funds." 1989. *Business Week* (6, November), 173–174.

Turner, John A., and Daniel J. Beller, eds. 1990. *Trends in Pensions.* U.S. Department of Labor, Pension, and Welfare Benefits Administration.

U.S. Department of Commerce. Bureau of the Census. 1989. *Current Population Reports, Series P-25, No. 1018: Projections of the Population of the United States by Age, Sex, and Race: 1988 to 2080.* Prepared by Gregory Spencer. Washington, D.C.: U.S. Government Printing Office.

Utgoff, Kathleen P. 1990. "Proliferation of Pension Regulations." *Regulation* (Summer): 29–38.

Weaver, Carolyn L. 1982. *Crisis in Social Security: Economic and Political Origins.* Durham, N.C.: Duke University Press.

————, ed. 1990. *Social Security's Looming Surpluses: Prospects and Implications.* Washington, D.C.: American Enterprise Institute.

————. 1993. "Government Guarantees of Private Pension Benefits: Current Problems and Likely Future Prospects." Presented at conference on "Public Policy Towards Pensions," sponsored by the Association of Private Pension and Welfare Plans the Center for Economic Policy Research, Stanford University, Washington, D.C., Oct.

Chapter Eight

THE NEEDY OR THE GREEDY? ASSESSING THE INCOME SUPPORT NEEDS OF AN AGING POPULATION

Marilyn Moon and Patricia Ruggles

Ensuring the economic well-being of older Americans has been a high priority of public policy since the 1930s. Nonetheless, the rising share of the federal budget devoted to Social Security (now over 20 percent) and other programs serving the elderly has become an increasingly controversial element of the domestic policy debate. Can we and should we continue to support our elderly so fully as America's population ages?

Fears about the public burdens of maintaining Social Security, especially as the baby boom ages, have spurred calls for reducing or even eliminating the program. Supporters of change argue that we cannot afford to continue as we have. The costs will become too large and our economy will not be able to support such generosity. And ironically, the success of public programs in raising the income levels of older Americans is often used to support the argument for cuts; the presumption is that help is no longer needed. Sometimes the claim is an absolute one—that the elderly are no longer needy. In other cases, the argument is a comparative one—that funding should be channeled to other, needier groups.

A chapter on income security policy in an era of an aging population could thus take many different directions. We focus here on current and future needs for public programs to support the incomes of older Americans. We leave it to others to debate how generously we will be able to afford to support older Americans in the future, and whether other groups are in greater need or are being penalized by our generosity to the elderly. We are convinced by the arguments of Aaron, Bosworth, and Burtless (1989), and others that, while Social Security burdens in the future will be an economic concern, our economic growth should allow us to meet those needs and more. The issue is not a lack of absolute resources, but rather a question of how we choose to allocate those resources that will be available. The intergenerational questions can be politically tendentious and pose substantively difficult tradeoffs. (See Part II of this volume.)

THE ECONOMIC STATUS OF OLDER AMERICANS

By any measure of economic well-being, the circumstances of older Americans have improved substantially over the past three decades. Average incomes and assets for persons over 65 have risen dramatically. Public programs for income security have played a major role in these gains. Social Security represents the most successful antipoverty program ever undertaken in the United States, and the Supplemental Security Income program offers relatively generous benefits to the poorest of the elderly. The introduction of Medicare and Medicaid in 1965 helped alleviate the tremendous burdens of health care costs that face this portion of our population.

Incomes for those 65 and older have risen steadily, from a median per capita income of $3,408 in 1975 to $10,174 in 1990. After controlling for inflation, this represents a gain of 22 percent in the purchasing power of this age group. Moreover, in the 1980s the elderly's income growth outstripped increases in income for other, younger subgroups of the population. While average before-tax incomes for elderly families still lag behind those of younger families, after adjusting for differences in family size and tax liabilities, the disposable (post-tax) incomes of older Americans compare favorably with those of the young. In fact, some researchers have claimed that the overall well-being of the elderly now is on a par with or even exceeds that of younger families (Danziger et al. 1984; Smeeding 1986).

But to comprehend fully the ability of elderly individuals to meet their needs, it is crucial to look beyond averages and to understand the diversity of the resources held by this group. While it is perfectly correct to say that the elderly as a group have shown impressive gains, that is not the same as arguing that each elderly individual experienced such gains. For example, some of the increase in well-being seen in comparing mean incomes across time reflects the changing composition of the elderly population. Each year individuals turning age 65 join the elderly "category," and the incomes of these newly elderly individuals have tended on average to be higher with each succeeding year. At the same time, some of the oldest old, who tend to have lower incomes, die. Thus, even if there were no real (inflation-adjusted) growth in the income of any specific elderly individual each year, these demographic changes would yield steady improvements in reported average income levels (Moon 1988). Individuals within the elderly population display much slower rates of income growth than does the group as a whole.

The poverty rate, which focuses attention on those at the bottom of the income distribution, has also declined for the elderly in recent years, again implying that well-being in general has improved. The share of the elderly in poverty dropped from 25 percent in 1968 to 11.4 percent in 1989 and 12.9 percent in 1992. In 1982, for the first time, the official rate of poverty among the elderly was lower than that for the rest of the population, and that gap has widened since then. The largest declines in poverty rates for the elderly occurred before 1975, however, and the rates have remained relatively flat since 1984 (Bureau of Census 1993).

Some researchers have gone further and suggested that poverty rates are still lower (Smeeding 1984) when the benefits of noncash programs are taken into account in computing rates of poverty. Such analyses have even prompted some policy analysts to declare poverty a thing of the past for persons age 65 and older (Anderson 1978). The biggest impact on poverty rates occurs when health expenditures by Medicare and Medicaid are added to income. Computing the cash value of these benefits is problematic, but analysts have most often used estimates based on the insurance value of the benefits to different demographic groups. Since the elderly are very heavy users of health care services, the insurance value of medical care for them is much larger than for those in other groups. Thus, their poverty rates fall the most when these benefits are counted as income, reflecting the peculiar result that the sicker your demographic group is likely to be, the better off you will be judged if medical benefits are counted as income.

But not all analysts are sanguine about these statistics. Many take issue with the simple approach of adding Medicare and Medicaid to income for this group without also adjusting the poverty thresholds to which incomes are compared. Such efforts make a substantial difference in the poverty rates. A recent critique of the official Census approach by Weinberg and Lamas (1992) suggests that instead of reducing the poverty rate from 11.4 percent in 1989 to 8.6 percent, the appropriate rate would instead rise to 21.4 percent in poverty. Their approach would not add in the value of Medicaid and Medicare but would instead subtract out-of-pocket spending.

Further, in her book on problems with the measurement of poverty, Patricia Ruggles (1990) argues that statistics on rates of poverty are understated overall and that those for the elderly may be particularly misleading. First, lower poverty lines are used for one- and two-person households with heads over age 65, even though those distinctions now make little sense in terms of the consumption patterns and needs of the elderly. Just eliminating this distinction would result in a substantial increase in the elderly poverty rate. Ruggles estimated that in 1986 it would have raised the rate from 12.4 to 15.3 percent, well above the rate for the population as a whole, and the impacts would be similar today.

Further, the measures of poverty we use for all persons have lagged behind the growth in our living standards in general. Updating these measures would also result in more persons being classified as poor, with a disproportionate increase in the number of elderly who are designated as poor. Under these alternatives, the rate of poverty for the elderly would again be higher than the rate for the population as a whole, and would approach the poverty rates for the elderly seen in the mid-1960s. If all of these changes were made in the poverty thresholds, almost one-third of those aged 65 or more would be counted as poor.

Poverty rates for the elderly are particularly sensitive to the level of the poverty thresholds used because a very large number of older persons have incomes just above the official poverty lines. In 1992, 4.0 million individuals 65 or older were counted as poor under the official measure, but another 2.3 million had incomes of no more than 25 percent above the poverty threshold. And if the cutoff for being counted as poor were raised to 150 percent of the official poverty threshold, 27.6 percent of the elderly—about 10.7 million persons—would have been counted as poor. The number of elderly below 150 percent of the official poverty thresholds is about 25 percent greater today than it was in 1983 (Ruggles and Cullinan 1984). A large portion of the elderly remain in the near poor category; they have not "escaped" very far above the poverty level.

Smeeding (1986) has focused particular attention on this just-above-poverty category—a group he calls the "Tweeners." Such individuals are ineligible for means tested programs, and are particularly vulnerable to economic hardships. A severe illness, for example, could wipe out the fragile economic base of these older Americans—particularly for those elderly who depend on earnings to supplement their incomes. And, this vulnerable group now extends to some individuals below the poverty thresholds, because Supplemental Security Income and Medicaid eligibility do not cover all the poor.

It is true that the elderly do hold more assets, on average, than other families with low and moderate incomes, but even if these assets are taken into account, relatively few of today's low-income elderly would be counted as well-off. More than half of the elderly with incomes below 150 percent of the poverty threshold also had less than $10,000 in total asset holdings, for example (Ruggles and Williams 1989).

Finally, in recent years the pattern of income growth has increased this dispersion rather than lessened it. While growth between 1967 and 1979 was disproportionately greater for the lowest income groups among the elderly, the opposite was true between 1979 and 1984 (Radner 1987). For example, the one-fifth of elderly families with the lowest incomes experienced a decline in real income of $640 on average between 1979 and 1984, as compared to a $7,727 increase for elderly families in the top fifth. And this increasing dispersion, which parallels increases in inequality across all age groups, continued in the second half of the 1980s (Ruggles and Stone 1991; Cutler and Katz 1991). Over the period 1979 to 1990, income for the bottom quintile of elderly couples rose by 16.2 percent compared to 26.5 percent growth in the top quintile (Moon 1993).

The dichotomy between the wealthiest and the poorest older Americans creates new challenges and belies the notion that we have conquered problems of economic security for this age group. A better understanding of the sources of the dichotomy and implications for the future can help shape more realistic public policies.

GROWTH IN WELL-BEING AND PROSPECTS FOR THE FUTURE

Although not all groups among the elderly have benefited equally, it remains true that on average today's elderly are better off in economic terms than were the elderly of 30 years ago. Rising well-being over time has occurred for many reasons. For individuals, economic status after age 65 depends upon a combination of events and choices, only some of which are truly under their own control. Across a lifetime, people make decisions about whether to invest in themselves with education and training, whether to save and make other investments, and whether to have families.

They are also subject to a broad range of unforseen events that can have enormous consequences. For example, the size of their own cohort group and those that precede and follow them affect economic status. Changes in technology influence the pace of growth in our economy and the relative values of different types of goods and services and the occupations associated with producing them. The hardships imposed by illness and injury can also dramatically change the financial outcomes at retirement.

The future economic status of the elderly will similarly depend on many unknown factors. Life expectancy, health status, age of retirement, savings behavior, the overall health of the economy, and public policy changes will all play a role. If the trends of the last decade were simply taken as projections into the next, we would expect to see continued steady growth in average incomes of the elderly, continued improvement relative to the working population, and a general trend toward somewhat lower poverty rates. In turn, we could also expect higher levels of assets and less reliance on relatives.

Evidence from the 1950–1980 Censuses (Ross, Danziger, and Smolensky 1987) and from wealth surveys taken between 1962 and 1984 (Wolff 1987) indicate that the next generation of elderly (i.e., those born between 1920 and 1935, and reaching age 65 between 1985 and 2000) will be considerably better off as they age than their older counterparts. This age group (ages 25 to 40 in 1960) had the good fortune to be in their prime working years during the period of maximum earnings growth of the halcyon 1960s, to find the value of their homes soaring during the inflation of the 1970s, and to be in the maximum liquid asset position to capture most fully the benefits of high real interest rates and the stock market boom of the early to mid-1980s.

There are several reasons for caution in assuming ever-rising increases in economic status for the elderly, however. First, the rate of growth of Social Security benefits is likely to slow somewhat in the near future. Second, income from private pensions, which has shown rapid growth in recent years, now seems to be leveling off. Third, the changing age composition of the elderly will also affect the extent to which incomes grow over time. If this population grows more as a result of longer life spans than because of new "entrants" to the 65 and over category, income growth will tend to be slower. Finally, there will be increasing demands placed on the elderly, particularly in the form of health expenditures. These benefits and burdens will not necessarily be equally shared across the elderly population.

Growth by Source of Income. The growth in incomes of the elderly in recent years does not stem from just one component; rather, most sources of income for the elderly have grown substantially. Changes in the share of income from various sources offer insight into the factors behind the rapid growth in the average incomes of the elderly, and allow us to assess the probability that such growth can be expected to continue. For example, over the last 28 years Social Security benefit increases have played an important role in income growth, (Yeas and Grad 1987; Grad 1992). As shown in figure 8.1, the most dramatic growth occurred in pensions and asset incomes. These sources not only grew in absolute dollars, they constitute a considerably larger share of the pie over time. Earnings and the "other" category, which includes public assistance, are considerably less important than they were in 1962.

A number of extraordinary factors affected the rapid rate of growth in inflation-adjusted Social Security benefits through the 1970s. The 1972 Social Security Amendments led to a dramatic increase in benefits in 1973. In addition, the so-called "double-indexing flaw" in benefit calculations increased benefits to new retirees at an unusually rapid rate. The correction of that flaw has helped slow new benefit increases. Slower wage growth in the 1980s will also affect future retirees. Total benefits from the OASDI program as a share of national personal income reached a peak in 1983 and have been on a downward trend since then (Ways and Means 1990). Thus, Social Security is not likely to be as strong a source of growth in the future.

Private pensions have expanded rapidly in recent years, reflecting not only higher awards over time but also an expansion in the proportion of retired individuals receiving such pensions. On average, however, private pension income is still less than 10 percent of the elderly's total income. The growth in this latter component is expected to level off in the near future and remain an important income source for only a minority of the elderly. Further growth in coverage by private pensions is expected to move at a slower pace, since much of the growth in employment in the United States is now in the service

Figure 8.1 SOURCES OF INCOME FOR THE AGED

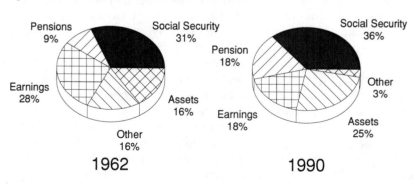

Source: Yeas and Grad 1987; Grad 1992.

sector, an area where fringe benefits tend to be less generous on average than in manufacturing (Zedlewski et al. 1990). Consequently, average income growth will likely slow in the future from this source of income as well.

The dramatic decrease in the contribution of wage and salary income implicitly protects the elderly relative to others during periods of unemployment. But it also means a lost opportunity to adjust income to changing needs over time as well. The young can adjust to other changes in resources by working more or seeking higher paying employment; that flexibility is often not available to older persons.

Another aspect of labor force participation is the advantage it offers to older persons who do work. Those in the highest income categories often have continued some labor force participation (Congressional Budget Office 1989). Moreover, the phenomenon of people returning to the paid labor force after withdrawing from their main job and drawing retirement benefits has increased somewhat in recent years. These part-time workers are supplementing their incomes and helping keep incomes of the younger elderly higher—a factor that may become more important over time.

The old fears about the ravages of inflation are not as critical as before the introduction of Social Security cost-of-living adjustments (COLAs). Clark et al. (1985) argued that over the period 1969 to 1974 the elderly were not on average harmed by inflation. But the data for this analysis ended before the high rates of inflation of the late 1970s, which were followed by increases in poverty rates.

Since 1980, lower rates of inflation have enhanced a number of sources of income for the elderly. For example, because of the way that Social Security is adjusted for inflation, there is a lag in the yearly increase. That is, the cost-of-living adjustment reflects the rate of inflation over a one-year period prior to the actual adjustment date. In periods of rising inflation, the elderly usually fall a little behind in real benefit growth. But, in a period when the rate of inflation is falling, such as the years 1980 to 1984, the elderly "catch up." The stable, low rates of inflation since then have served to protect this purchasing power.[1] This protection, however, is certainly dependent upon continuing COLA protections for Social Security, an area where policies may well change in the future.

Public assistance, now in the form of Supplemental Security Income (SSI), has become a less and less important contributor to the well-being of the elderly—in part because of the rising incomes of those age 65 and over. Another important factor is the low participation rate in SSI by the elderly; public assistance remains unable to reach all low-income families, and only about half of those eligible for SSI are thought to participate in the progam. And finally, although SSI benefits are indexed for inflation, federal benefits remain below the poverty level, so that even some elderly persons in poverty have incomes too high to qualify for the program.[2]

Another element of economic well-being, wealth, is generally reflected in the asset incomes of the elderly. Asset stocks have advantages in addition to the income they generate; control over a stock of resources and the implicit advantages of, for example, owning one's own home also enhance well-being. The image of the elderly as income poor but asset rich is considerably exaggerated, however. Generally, those with the highest incomes also control the most wealth. And, older persons with modest means are likely to hold much of their wealth in housing—an asset that is difficult to liquidate to meet short-term needs and may carry substantial burdens in the form of high taxes or maintenance costs as well. Financial assets, which can be readily used to meet short-term needs, are very unequally distributed across the elderly population. In 1985, the median value of financial assets for the elderly in the top fifth as ranked by income was about $60,000, but only about $4,000 for the bottom fifth (CBO 1989). In fact, more than one-third of elderly persons and families with incomes below the poverty line reported total assets of less than $1,000 (Ruggles 1990). One recent study predicts that growth in wealth will be substantial in the future (Zedlewski et al. 1990). What is not clear is whether that growth will extend down to the most vulnerable of the elderly.

Demographic Influences. In the 1990s, growth in the numbers of persons 65 and over will be concentrated in the 85 and over category, reflecting increased life expectancies. Individuals reaching retirement age will have been born in the 1930s, a period when birth rates were very low. For example, between 1990 and the year 2000, the population between the ages of 65 and 74 will grow by only 1.2 percent, while the age 85 and above group will grow nearly 34 percent (Ways and Means 1992). Thus, the very old will grow as a proportion of the elderly and their lower average incomes are likely to help hold down overall rates of growth in income as compared to the 1970s. These oldest Americans are least likely to work and their pensions, Social Security, and other incomes are unlikely to increase markedly over time. At best, they will keep pace with inflation.

Burdens from Health Spending. Another continuing challenge to the well-being of older Americans is the burden of health care spending by individuals. Despite the introduction of Medicare (for the elderly) and Medicaid (for those with low incomes) in 1965, the percent of income spent on out-of-pocket, unreimbursed health care costs by persons over age 65 is at an all-time high and is projected to increase further. As figure 8.2 indicates, whether compared to mean or median income, this spending represents a critical burden for the elderly.[3] Incomes have risen rapidly for this age group, but out-of-pocket health costs have simply risen faster.

Analyses of the acute care portion of these expenses reveal considerable burdens on those with low or moderate incomes. Feder, Moon and Scanlon (1987) estimated that in 1986, elderly persons with a hospital stay and incomes of less than $10,000 spent 18.3 percent of income, on average, out of their own pockets for acute health care services. Since this is an average, it understates the burden for a considerable minority of this group. Smeeding, in his study of Tweeners (1986), stressed the low rates of private health insurance purchased by this group, leaving them vulnerable to very high potential health care liabilities.

Figure 8.2 HEALTH CARE SPENDING AS SHARE OF INCOME, PERSONS 65 +

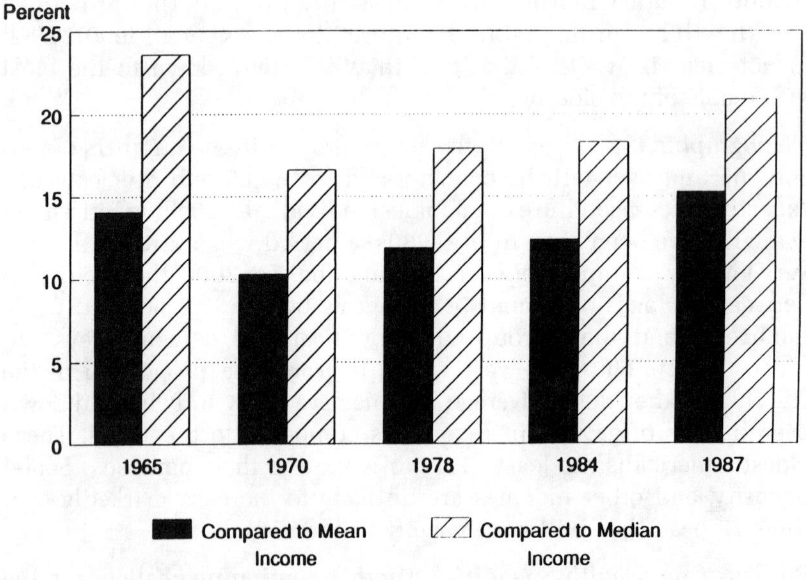

Source: Moon (1993).

As serious as these considerations are, the costs of long-term care hold the potential for even more devastating reductions in economic status for older families. The burdens imposed by these costs are harder to evaluate, however, because institutionalized individuals are generally not included in surveys that capture income or expenditures. An individual may pay, on average, $25,000 to $30,000 for a year's stay in a nursing home. Medicare pays virtually nothing and Medicaid will only cover these costs once an individual has spent down all his assets. Then, even with expanded protections in recent years, the spouse remaining in the community will likely be placed in severely straightened circumstances. It is in these circumstances that even middle-class elderly families find it impossible to meet their health care needs.

The likelihood of incurring costs from both acute and long-term health care needs rises steadily with age—in reverse proportion to ability to pay. It is the elderly woman living alone who is most at risk of needing long-term care services (Doty, Liu, and Weiner 1985). And the outlook for the future is not particularly reassuring. Rivlin and Wiener (1988) suggest that only a minority of older families will ever be able to afford to protect themselves against long-term care expenditures.

The Distribution of Well-Being. These changes also suggest that the disparity in incomes *within* the elderly is likely to worsen—as indeed it has since 1979 (Ways and Means 1992). If Social Security becomes less important as a source of income and if life expectancies continue to expand, for example, the status of the oldest old, who depend largely on Social Security benefits, will lag further behind that of other elderly families whose sources of income (such as from assets) continue to grow. Moreover, current public policy suggests that programs aiding those with lower incomes are unlikely to expand. Finally, a long trend toward increasing inequality in families of all ages suggests a pattern that is likely to continue to affect the elderly for the indefinite future. The findings of greater concentration in wealth holdings reported above also raise questions about whether this trend will continue, leading to further inequality in total well-being.

Sources of well-being also vary by age group within the elderly population (Grad 1992). For the oldest old, Social Security and asset income account for nearly four-fifths of the annual resources available (CBO 1989). For the younger elderly, earnings are much more important. But since incomes decline steadily with age as well, dollar amounts of Social Security to the youngest age group are nearly as large as for the oldest age group, although they account for a much smaller share of total income. The oldest old have lower incomes and less flexibility to adjust their incomes over time for needs such as health care expenses.

Another important unknown in how we view the well-being of the elderly is their status relative to other groups. Although predicting income growth for the elderly is difficult in and of itself, it is even harder to predict how such growth will compare with income changes for younger working families. If the trends discussed here hold and the economy experiences relatively rapid real growth in the next decade, the status of the elderly relative to the young could again decline. More likely, however, is that the economic position of the elderly will stabilize relative to their younger counterparts. The relative status of the elderly is likely to be important in any political debates over who would pay for Medicare, since many of the potential policy alternatives involve tradeoffs between burdens on the old and the young.

Overall, the outlook appears to continue to be good for most of the elderly, although future improvements are likely to come at a slower pace than in recent years. Nonetheless, a substantial minority of the elderly still have incomes that are at best barely adequate to meet their needs, and many elderly remain vulnerable to major losses in periods of poor health. Bold statements that we have solved the income problems of older Americans or have gone too far in providing protection are not universally valid now and unlikely to be so in the foreseeable future.

FUTURE POLICY ISSUES

Policies toward the elderly must balance the growing perception that the burdens of programs such as Social Security and Medicare are excessive with the reality of continuing economic needs for many older Americans. The increasing diversity in the economic status of our older citizens may further contribute to pressures for changing publicly provided income support programs. But unless decisions are made with great care, policy changes may further disadvantage the neediest elderly. For example, in the late 1980s and now in the 1990s, advocates of freezes in the Social Security Cost of Living Adjustment (COLA) often argue that older Americans are doing better than the young so cutbacks would not be painful. Such claims rest on the new stereotype of a uniformly affluent older population. But since Social

Security is much more important as a share of income for lower-income individuals than for those who truly are well-to-do, the burdens of a COLA reduction would fall disproportionately on those least able to absorb the cuts.

The important challenges for policy thus will be to address the income diversity among the elderly in a meaningful way. Some policies have begun to do so. For example, taxation of Social Security benefits as part of the 1983 Amendments represented a change aimed at individuals with relatively high incomes from all sources. Similarly, the Tax Reform Act of 1986 offered the lowest tax relief to higher income seniors—a group that has historically enjoyed low tax liability. The Medicare Catastrophic Coverage Act also attempted to relate a major benefit to income levels. Although it was repealed, this idea is one that will continue to arise as indeed it has in recent budget proposals. And more recently, the Omnibus Budget Reconciliation Act of 1993 further increased taxation of Social Security for those with incomes over $34,000 per year.

The entitlements conference held in Philadelphia in December of 1993 as a follow-up to budget reduction activities of the U.S. Congress underscores that this issue is likely to expand rather than diminish in importance. Many policymakers seem to accept as "inevitable" that further changes in Social Security will be necessary in the near future.

As part of the policy debate, it will become increasingly appealing to subdivide the "elderly." Indeed, to some extent that has already been occurring with new attention being paid to the very old. But a number of important caveats ought to govern such policy discussions.

1. *Changing the Concept of the Aged.* It is now common to subdivide individuals 65 and over into the young old and the old old—although the specific dividing line remains blurred. In this case the justification is often to focus on the specific needs and concerns of the older group. In other areas we have begun to think about raising the original age at which people are thought to be "elderly." Eligibility for full benefits for Social Security will rise from age 65 to 67 in 2022. New policy discussions suggest that perhaps it should rise further—to age 68 or 70, for example. Debate several years ago over the reauthorization of the Older Americans Act included consideration of whether the age cutoff for receiving services should be raised from 60 to 70. These age increases are intended to reduce benefits or eligibility—and thus program costs—over time.

What about targeting enhanced benefits on the old old? Again the question arises of whether such efforts will truly achieve their goals of providing income or other support for the most vulnerable group. On average, such individuals are not as well-off as their younger counterparts. But why should age itself trigger special benefits? Cost-of-living adjustments and the savings behavior of at least the current generation of elderly suggest that individuals' incomes do not deteriorate very much over time, absent some major event such as widowhood (Holden, Burkhauser, and Feaster 1987). And although ill health or the death of a spouse are more likely to occur at advanced age, it is the event and not the age that is the trigger. Indeed, young widows are more likely to be in poverty than older ones, partly because of the age cut-offs already built into our income support programs.

What about the issue of retirement per se? Traditionally, we have welcomed the retirement of older persons from the labor force to make room for younger workers or simply to allow them to enjoy their leisure time. Employers are often anxious to have their employees retire early. But is age still a relevant factor for retirement? Or should we even more dramatically tilt policy to encouraging longer years of labor force participation? This would argue for further changes in Social Security's benefit formula to encourage workers to remain in the labor force. But again, such a policy might especially disadvantage lower-income workers, whose job skills and earnings are likely to decline more rapidly with age.

The justification for many of these new age distinctions rests largely on the increased life expectancy of older persons. But a complicating factor that is not always taken into account is the question of whether health status is also improving for older Americans. And here the evidence is still unclear. Some findings suggest that longer lives are not necessarily healthier lives (Poterba and Summers 1985). If that is the case, a two-year increase in life expectancy does not necessarily imply that age of retirement or eligibility for special programs ought to automatically be advanced by two years as well. Other, new studies are beginning to suggest that disability by age many now be declining (Manton, Corder and Stallard 1993).

Moreover, the old issue of diversity arises again here. While many individuals are in vigorous health at age 65, others are not. And we are even beginning to recognize that early retirees less than age 65 face some specific problems of their own, such as affording health insurance coverage before they become old enough to qualify for Medicare.

Overall, the evidence is strong that both within the elderly group and in comparisons between the elderly and others, age alone is not a strong predictor of economic status. Dispersion in well-being among the elderly, and even among age-based subgroups within the elderly, is about as great as among the rest of the population. Age may thus be losing its usefulness as an indicator of need.

2. *Recognizing Special Needs*. One of the most appropriate potential replacements for age as a general indicator of need is health status. Health status can affect the ability of older persons to work. Over time it can serve as a drain on resources, eating into assets and lowering income from that source. And at any one point in time, health status crucially affects what resources are needed to provide a reasonable level of living. Thus, health status measures might be more appropriate indicators of resource needs over time than age.

While age is used as a proxy for need in the case of old old, for example, health status addresses the relevant concerns directly. Similarly, using health status directly means that the needs of the younger elderly who may not be able to work could also be met. While age could sometimes be used as a proxy for health needs, that ought to occur at a considerably older age than 65, and perhaps even older than 75 or 80. But such presumptions imply that other indicators should also be used.

What does this imply for policy? First, it suggests that any changes raising the age of eligibility for various programs such as Medicare ought to make provisions for the younger old who are disabled and in need of support. For example, a substantial minority of the young old would be severely disadvantaged by increasing the age of eligibility for Medicare. Extensions and liberalization of disability rules might then be in order. The burdens associated with poor health vary considerably depending on several other factors, including job skills, type of occupation, and the presence or absence of a spouse or other family support. Again, these issues should be dealt with directly in assessing need and benefit eligibility. The major objection to such additional protections would arise because raising the age of eligibility for benefits is a proposal based more on the justification for finding ways of cutting costs than on improving the appropriateness of Social Security benefits.

Another way in which health status might be used instead of age is in setting proverty lines or other standards of need. These standards are not abstract principles, but rather serve as the basis for policy. For example, recent federal legislation requires that states offer additional out-of-pocket spending protections through Medicaid to poor Medicare beneficiaries (the "qualified Medicare beneficiary" program). Rather than making distinctions by age for poverty thresholds or other standards, using health status or health needs adjustments would offer a better way of identifying persons with differing needs. In this example, a disabled older person would thus receive greater protection from health care expenses than a healthy Medicare beneficiary with similar economic resources, for example. Difficulties arise in finding workable definitions for such new proverty thresholds, however.

3. *The Role of Government in Redistribution.* If, as many analysts have suggested, future budget constraints will require improved targeting of resources to meet the needs of older Americans, and if many of those needs are likely to remain in the years to come, a strong role for government in the redistribution of resources will be essential. Private pensions, higher wages over time, and increased savings by the young simply do not address the problems of the vulnerable elderly. Nor do efforts to enhance these activities through tax benefits; such economic incentives never trickle down far enough to help those in need.

"Privatization" proposals, often based on the premise that individuals could do better for themselves if they were outside Social Security and Medicare and instead investing on their own, are extremely short-sighted. Those at the very top of the income distribution and who face no catastrophic health costs or other events would undoubtedly do better. That is, some persons could obtain higher returns on investments in the private sector. But Social Security is not now and never has been exactly equivalent to private pensions since it represents a *combination* of retirement investment (the pension portion), disability coverage, and protection against low earnings years, job loss and other uncertainties across a lifetime of work. Ignoring these last two functions requires the benefit of hindsight to know that you are one of the lucky few who have no problems with disability or employment.

For example, a male aged 20 in 1986 had a 19.1 percent chance of becoming disabled by age 60 in the United States (HIAA 1989) and Social Security is an important safety net. Moreover, these privatization approaches are explicitly intended to deny any redistribution of resources from those who do succeed to those who have fewer resources. Part of the "benefits" of privatizing programs like Social Security is to avoid sharing of resources. It is thus not surprising to find that high income workers could be better off. Only public spending can successfully alter the distribution of income in favor of those who are needy. This can be done both through social insurance programs that offer protection for individuals from the uncertainties of a lifetime of work experiences, or through programs that directly target aid on the neediest of our senior citizens.

Which type of government benefit is better? Which is most likely to meet the needs of the vulnerable elderly without "breaking the bank?" While well-designed programs relying on either universal or targeted approaches can be imagined, we believe that the issue of popular support for universal social insurance programs versus welfare-based systems is an important practical consideration in trying to implement such programs.

While much of this chapter argues that a large number of elderly persons remain vulnerable, even though some elderly are doing quite well, that does not necessarily lead to the conclusion that universal programs like Social Security are undesirable or unnecessary. First, a substantial part of the well-being of those in the middle of the distribution is due to Social Security and indirectly to Medicare. In addition, there are political dangers in emphasizing targeting of benefits by standard means testing. Participation rates are often low in welfare programs because of both the stigma of being on welfare and the lack of political support to keep benefits high enough to make them worthwhile supplements to income. And if the means-tested limits are set high enough to keep the program more popular, the savings would be quite small. Better targeting alone, therefore, is not the best solution.

It is true that targeted programs are usually less expensive than universal ones, at least in terms of the immediate cost of their benefits. Because more universal approaches—even those, like Social Security, that involve some substantial redistribution of resources—are much more popular than "welfare" programs, however, taxpayers may support much higher levels of spending for such programs without protest. Lower spending levels are not necessarily a good thing in and of themselves; if there is a social consensus in favor of universal programs, and people are willing to pay the taxes needed to support such programs, they may in some sense be less costly than more targeted programs with lower overall spending but also lower levels of taxpayer support.

In some cases targeting is clearly appropriate—not all potential beneficiaries face the same level of need for all goods and services, and some programs may be largely irrelevant to specific categories of potential recipients. Indeed, even the redistribution from higher-income workers to lower-income retirees that occurs within the Social Security program could be seen as a form of benefit targeting. But when targeting is appropriate, we would favor more attention to determining how cutoffs and eligibility will be assessed. Dramatic changes that would save substantial amounts of money in the short run sacrifice the subtlety that might lead to reasonable policy changes.

Reliance on age as a proxy for differential needs is increasingly outmoded. We would emphasize the development of more appropriate standards, focusing particularly on the issues of most relevance to an aging society: ability to continue working and the demands placed on resources by declining health. Benefits should be targeted not to those of a specific age, in other words, but to those who really do experience differential needs.

Moreover, even where targeting is appropriate, it is important not to set our standards so low that even the vulnerable elderly are excluded from programs designed to provide help. A "middle ground" makes more sense for eligibility and benefit determinations. We need not be constrained by a "welfare" approach to targeting that limits help to those who are poor under the official definition (which is particularly low for the elderly, as we have discussed). Many of the elderly are still vulnerable, even if they are a little higher up in the income scale, because they face extraordinary health care costs and because they have special needs related to health status. Any movement from universal to more restrictive standards for public programs serving this group must take such needs into account.

Notes

1. This sensitivity to inflation rates also means that the specific years chosen for analyzing changes in economic status also matter substantially. Older persons seem to have done very well if we look only at the 1980s. If the cut were 1975 and beyond instead, the gains would be less.

2. About half the states provide supplements to the federal SSI program, although even in many of these states benefit levels for many recipients remain below the poverty level.

3. While the comparison here is with mean private health spending, mean income may not be appropriate since its distribution is so highly skewed. The comparison to median income, which more accurately represents a "typical" elderly person's income, is more appropriate.

Bibliography

Aaron, Henry, Barry Bosworth, and Gary Burtless. 1989. *Can America Afford to Grow Old?* Washington, D.C.: Brookings Institution Press.

Anderson, Martin. 1978. *Welfare.* Stanford, CA: Hoover Institution.

Bureau of the Census. 1990. *Money Income and Households, Families and Persons in the United States: 1989.* Series P-60, No. 168.

Clark, Robert, George Maddox, Ronald Schrimper, and Daniel Sumner. 1985. *Inflation and the Economic Well-Being of the Elderly.* Baltimore: John Hopkins Press.

Congressional Budget Office. 1989. *The Economic Status of the Elderly.* Washington, D.C., May.

Cutler, David M., and Lawrence F. Katz. 1991. "Macroeconomic Performance and the Disadvantaged." *Brookings Economic Papers,* 1991–92, pp. 1–74.

Danziger, Sheldon, Jacques van der Gaag, Eugene Smolensky, and Michael Taussig. 1984. "Income Transfers and the Economic Status of the Elderly." In *Economic Transfers in the United States,* ed. by Marilyn Moon. Chicago: University of Chicago Press.

Doty, Pamela, Korbin Liu, and Joshua Wiener. 1985. "An Overview of Long Term Care." *Health Care Financing Review* (Spring): 69–78.

Feder, Judy, Marilyn Moon, and William Scanlon. 1987. "Nibbling at Catastrophic Costs." *Health Affairs* 6 (Winter): 5–19.

Grad, Susan. 1992. *Income of the Population 55 or Older, 1990.* Social Security Administration, Office of Policy. Washington, D.C.: USGPO, June.

Health Insurance Association of America. 1989. *Source Book of Health Insurance Data 1989.* Washington, D.C.: author.

Holden, Karen, Richard Burkhauser, and D. J. Feaster. 1987. "The Timing of Falls into Poverty After Retirement: An Event-history Approach." Mimeo, University of Wisconsin.

Manton, Kenneth, Larry Corder, and Eric Stallard. 1993. "Estimates of Change in Chronic Disability and Institutional Incidence and Prevalence Rates in the U.S. Elderly Population from the 1982, 1984, and 1989 National Long Term Care Survey." *Journal of Gerontology* 48: S153–S166.

Moon, Marilyn. 1993. *Medicare Now and in the Future.* Washington, D.C.: Urban Institute Press.

Moon, Marilyn. 1988. "The Economic Situation of Older Americans: Emerging Wealth and Continuing Hardship." In *Annual Review of Gerontology and Geriatrics,* Volume 8, ed. by George Maddox and M. Powell Lawton. New York: Springer Publishing Co.

Poterba, James and Lawrence Summers. 1985. "Public Policy Implications of Declining Old-Age Mortality." Presented to the Brookings Institution Conference on Retirement and Aging, May 2, 1985 and revised.

Radner, Daniel. 1987. "Money Incomes of Aged and Nonaged Family Units, 1967–84." *Social Security Bulletin* 50: 9–28.

Rivlin, Alice and Joshua Wiener. 1988. *Caring for the Disabled Elderly.* Washington, D.C.: Brookings Institution.

Ross, Christine, Sheldon Danziger, and Eugene Smolensky. 1987. "Interpreting Changes in the Economic Status of the Elderly, 1949–79." *Contemporary Policy Issues* 5: 98–112.

Ruggles, Patricia. 1990. *Drawing the Line: Alternative Poverty Measures and their Implications for Public Policy.* Washington, D.C.: Urban Institute Press.

Ruggles, Patricia and Paul Cullinan. 1985. "The Contribution of Transfer Payments to the Incomes of the Elderly." Mimeo, Urban Institute, Washington, D.C.

Ruggles, Patricia and Charles F. Stone. 1992. "Income Distribution Over the Business Cycle: the 1980s Were Different." *Journal of Policy Analysis and Management* 11 (Fall).

Ruggles, Patricia and Roberson Williams. 1989. "Longitudinal Measures of Poverty: The Role of Assets." *Proceedings of the Social Statistics Section.* American Statistical Association, December.

Smeeding, Timothy. 1982. *Alternative Methods For Valuing In-Kind Transfer Benefits and Measuring their Impacts on Poverty.* Technical Report 50, S.S. Bureau of the Census. Washington, D.C.: USGPO.

Smeeding, Timothy. 1986. "Nonmoney Income and the Elderly: The Case of the 'Tweeners'." *Journal of Policy Analysis and Management* 5 (Summer): 707–24.

Ways and Means, Committee on. 1992. *1992 Green Book: Background Material and Data on Programs Within the Jurisdiction of the Committee on Ways and Means.* Washington, D.C.: USGPO.

Weinberg, Daniel and Enrique Lamas. 1992. "Some Experimental Results on Alternate Poverty Measures." Mimeo. Washington, Bureau of the Census. December.

Wolff, Edward. 1987. "Estimate of Household Wealth Inequality in the U.S., 1962–83." *Review of Income and Wealth* 33: 231–56.

Yeas, Martynas and Susan Grad. 1987. "Income of Retirement Aged Persons in the United States." *Social Security Bulletin* 50: 5–14.

Zedlewski, Sheila, Roberta Barnes, Martha Burt, Timothy McBride, and Jack Meyer. 1990. *The Needs of the Elderly in the 21st Century.* Washington, D.C.: Urban Institute Press.

Chapter Nine

KINDER AND GENTLER: A COMPARATIVE ANALYSIS OF INCOMES OF THE ELDERLY IN CANADA AND THE UNITED STATES

Michael C. Wolfson and Brian B. Murphy

The conventional wisdom is that Americans are wealthier than Canadians. In the regularly published series by the OECD, for example, the 1988 Canadian GDP per capita (the most commonly used statistical indicator) was at 95 percent of the U.S. figure. Moreover, with a fully mature Social Security system, many analysts consider the United States to have a more generous system of public old age pensions. In aggregate, U.S. public pensions in 1985 amounted to 7.2 percent of GDP compared to 5.4 percent in Canada (OECD 1988a). On the other hand, a great deal of concern has been expressed in the context of the recently concluded Canada-U.S. Free Trade Agreement about U.S. firms being more competitive than their Canadian counterparts due to lower labor costs. If this concern is well founded, one explanation would be that American workers are *not* as well paid. Not surprisingly, the picture is more complex than either of these conflicting descriptions suggests.

DATA AND METHODS

The basic sources of data are the major income distribution surveys in the two countries—Statistics Canada's Survey of Consumer Finances and the U.S. Census Bureau's March supplement to the Current Population Survey. In both cases we rely on the detailed microdata files containing the raw data for 1988. U.S. dollar amounts have been converted to Canadian dollars using the 1988 purchasing power parity of 1.25 (OECD 1989).

The analysis is based on families (defined as individuals living in the same household who are related by blood, marriage or adoption; unattached individuals are included as one-person families). There

were almost exactly ten times as many such families in the U.S.—
100.2 million compared to 10.16 million in Canada. Most of the results
for elderly families focus on either unattached individuals or married
couples without any other relatives in the household.

A crucial step in any international economic comparison is the
method of converting from one national currency to the other. A convenient and frequently used method is simply to apply the exchange
rate. However, this can be seriously misleading, as has been shown by
the development of purchasing power parities (PPPs). PPPs are, in
effect, price indices designed for intercountry rather than intertem-
poral comparisons. They are based on a commonly defined basket of
goods priced in both countries. The Canada-U.S. exchange rate has
fluctuated from a low of $.72 to a high of $.88 since the early 1980s,
i.e., one U.S. dollar buying between $1.14 and $1.39 Canadian dollars.
In 1988 the U.S. dollar bought 1.23 Canadian dollars. The PPP, meanwhile, has remained within a percentage point of 1.25 (Dryden, Reut,
and Slater 1987).

The relative prices of different commodities that underlie PPPs provide an important backdrop to comparisons of incomes in the two
countries. The most recent systematic data are from 1985 and show
that Canadian prices for dairy products, meat, alcoholic beverages,
tobacco products, clothing and footwear, and household equipment
and operation have PPPs considerably higher than the overall 1.25
PPP; on the other hand, fuel and power related to housing, medical
care and health services, and education, recreation and culture have
PPPs that are significantly lower (by at least 10 percentage points in
each direction, respectively—Dryden, Reut, and Slater 1987).

In addition to these differences in relative prices in the two countries, residents spend their incomes somewhat differently. U.S. residents spend more than their Canadian counterparts on clothing and
footwear, medical care and health services, transport and communication, personal care, and restaurants. While private spending on
education is about the same in the two countries, Canadians spend
more on publicly provided educational services.

Media headlines regarding relative prices in Canada and the United
States single out tobacco products, alcoholic beverages, gasoline, some
clothing items, and some appliances as being particular bargains for
Canadians in the United States. The far more rigorous PPP data show,
however, that this is only a partial picture. Part of the U.S. price
advantage has been a more competitive environment for consumer
goods. Where Canada has significantly different prices, this is often
the result of deliberate government policies such as farm price stabi-

lization and support, "sin taxes" on alcohol and tobacco, high excises on transportation fuels, universal quality public education, and universal public health care insurance.

ARE U.S. FAMILIES RICHER?

Before considering the comparative position of the elderly in the two countries, it is important to examine the broader context of all families. Based on PPPs, average family before-tax income (based on the two household surveys) was about 2.2 percent higher in the U.S.— $38,900 compared to $38,000 in Canada—in line with the conventional wisdom.[1] After tax, the gap is slightly smaller—$31,700 in the U.S. compared to $31,100 in Canada.

However, *median* family income was *lower* in the United States— by about 4.4 percent before tax, at $30,700 in the U.S. compared to $32,000 in Canada, and by about 1.0 percent in after-tax dollars. What can explain this apparent contradiction as to which country's families are better off? The short answer is that the United States has more poor families, and has middle-income families with lower average incomes than their Canadian counterparts. But the wealthy in the United States are more numerous, and their high incomes bring the U.S. average family income above the corresponding Canadian average.

Consider the following scenario in the spirit of Jan Pen's (1973) "A Parade of Dwarfs (and a Few Giants)." Families in both countries line up in ascending order of their before-tax incomes. The queues on each side of the border are arranged so that they are exactly the same length. Thus, if a family p percent along the way in one country looks over its shoulder to the corresponding family in the other country, that family will also be p percent along the queue. U.S. incomes are converted to Canadian dollars using the PPP, and each family's height is adjusted to be proportional to their income. The question is then, at which parts of the two parallel queues will Canadian families find themselves taller or shorter than their U.S. counterparts?

Figure 9.1 graphs these comparative levels of income in the two countries. The first 60–65 percent of Canadian families have higher after-tax incomes than their U.S. counterparts, while the reverse is true for the top 35–40 percent of families. The bottom tenth of families in Canada have after-tax incomes more than 50 percent higher than the bottom tenth of U.S. families, while the top tenth of U.S. families

Figure 9.1 AVERAGE AFTER-TAX INCOME DISTRIBUTION, CANADIAN AND U.S.
FAMILIES, 1988

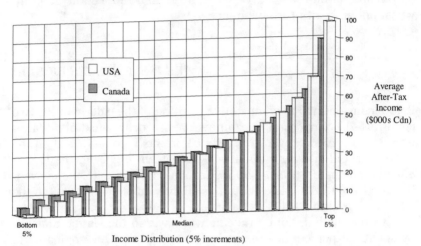

have incomes that average 10 to 14 percent higher than the top tenth
of Canadian families.[2] A purely relative analysis, using the conventional Lorenz curve, shows that U.S. income inequality is consistently
higher.

In principle, these differences could be affected by differences in
the age structure of the population. In fact, however, the two countries
have very similar family breakdowns by age of head, family size, and
after-tax income. There are somewhat greater differences in kinds of
families between the two countries. But the income inequality picture
is not significantly affected when these differences are taken into
account (see appendix 9.A).

In summary, while the United States is richer on average, family
incomes are more unequally distributed than in Canada. Moreover,
taking account of differences in both the exchange rate and in purchasing power, the lower and middle classes in Canada had higher
real incomes than their U.S. counterparts in 1988. (These higher real
Canadian incomes in the lower and middle income ranges would be
even higher than those of their U.S. counterparts if account were also
taken of publicly provided health care and education.)

Another perspective on the comparative income distributions in
the U.S. and Canada is given by looking at income ranges defined
relatively in terms of each country's median family income, rather

than dividing the population into percentiles. Table 9.1 shows the distribution of families along the income spectrum classified this way—with income adjusted for family size and composition.[3] This form of tabulation is convenient because it shows the extent of the low-income population according to a widely used definition— namely, the proportion of families with adjusted incomes below half the adjusted median. According to this common definition, the United States had about a 50 percent larger proportion of low-income families (20.8 percent versus 13.5 percent in Canada). In other words, if the United States had Canada's proportion of low-income families, there would be over seven million fewer U.S. families counted as low-income, a reduction of about one-third.

U.S. low-income families were also further below the low-income line than their Canadian counterparts—with a gap nearly one-third again as large. On average, U.S. low-income families were about $4,000 below their respective low-income lines while Canadian low-income families were about $3,100 below theirs (from tabulations not shown in this text). At the same time, Canada had relatively more low-middle income families with incomes just above the 50 percent adjusted median low-income line—18.8 percent versus 14.7 percent in the U.S. with incomes between 50 percent and 75 percent of the

Table 9.1 PROPORTIONS AND AVERAGE FAMILY SIZE BY ADJUSTED INCOME RANGES, CANADIAN AND U.S. FAMILIES, 1988

Income Ranges Relative to Adjusted Median Income	Percent Distribution of Families		Average Family Size	
	Canada	U.S.	Canada	U.S.
Low-Income				
Under 50%	13.5	20.8	1.97	2.22
Low-Middle				
50%–75%	18.8	14.7	2.28	2.39
Middle-Income				
75%–100%	17.7	14.4	2.74	2.50
100%–125%	16.6	12.7	2.83	2.54
125%–150%	11.9	11.0	2.68	2.53
High-Income				
150%–175%	8.6	8.3	2.61	2.47
175%–200%	5.0	5.7	2.52	2.42
200%–225%	4.8	6.6	2.52	2.42
225%–300%	1.7	3.0	2.41	2.36
300% and over	1.4	2.8	2.25	2.10

Note: Income ranges are expressed as percentages of median adjusted after-tax family income. The median was adjusted using a .40/.30 equivalent adult unit (EAU) scale.

median (all income figures adjusted for variations in family size). At the other end of the income spectrum, the U.S. had almost twice Canada's proportion in the highest income range. Almost 3 percent of U.S. families had incomes over three times the family size-adjusted median (i.e., about $110,000 for a couple with two children), while the Canadian fraction was half that, at 1.4 percent.

A different perspective on the distribution of income comes from the "disappearing middle class" debate. While it is not yet widely appreciated, this phenomenon of "polarization" is quite different from inequality as generally understood (Wolfson 1989, 1994; Foster and Wolfson 1991).[4] One indicator of polarization, or equivalently the size of the middle class, is the share of the population with family incomes close to the median. Canada has a somewhat higher proportion of middle-income families; about 46 percent of families have (adjusted) after-tax incomes between 75 percent and 150 percent of the median compared to 38 percent in the U.S. As a result, the U.S. distribution of family income is not only more unequal, it is also more polarized.

Finally, as regards overall comparisons of the distribution of income in the two countries, it has been claimed that there are significant regional differences within both. Specifically, Baer, Grabb, and Johnston (1991) claim that the significant cleavages in North America are Quebec within Canada, and the Old South within the United States. Once these regions are taken out, the rest of Canada and the United States are much alike. Their analysis is based principally on social structure and attitudinal survey results. However, if there were such a pattern, we would expect it to show up in the income distribution data as well.

Figure 9.2 shows the income distributions for the four geographic regions in question.[5] These curves clearly show that the Old South is a significantly poorer region than the rest of the United States, and Quebec is similarly poorer than the rest of Canada. However, the more interesting result is the implicitly greater tolerance of poverty and inequality in the United States. While the curve for the Old South starts out at the bottom end of the income spectrum with the lowest levels of income, it rises most steeply, until the richest Southerners have essentially the same incomes as the rest of their U.S. counterparts. On the other hand, even though Quebec has generally lower incomes than the rest of Canada for the lowest quarter of the income spectrum, Quebec adjusted family incomes are not only higher than those in the Old South, but are also higher than those in the rest of the United States.

Figure 9.2 THE THREE NATIONS OF NORTH AMERICA?

Family Incomes
($000s Cdn)

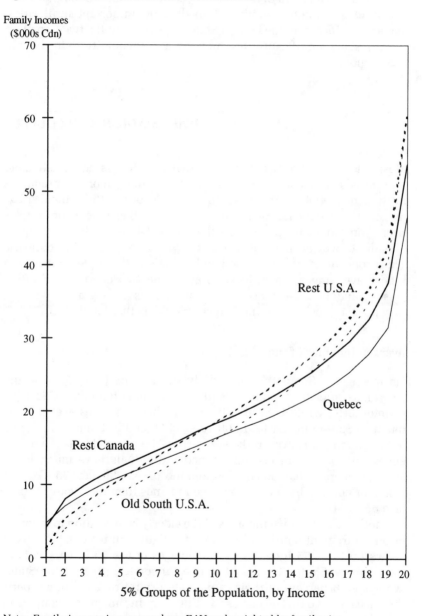

5% Groups of the Population, by Income

Note: Family income is expressed per EAU and weighted by family size.

After taking account of the generally lower incomes in the Old South and in Quebec, both regions of Canada show important similarities, and are distinct from the United States. Specifically, the two Canadian regions show significantly less poverty and inequality than the two U.S. regions.

ELDERLY SINGLES AND COUPLES

Most elderly and "near elderly" families are either single unattached individuals or married couples without any children or other relatives in their households. As shown in table 9.2 for the three highest age ranges, the proportion of families that are either singles or couples rises from about 60 percent in the 55- to 64-year-old age group in Canada to over 86 percent in the 75 + age group in both countries. The proportions of unattached individuals and couples within the higher age ranges are quite similar in the two countries. For this reason, and because these are homogeneous demographic groups, they are the focus in the income comparisons that follow.

Average Incomes of the Elderly

On average, U.S. unattached elderly individuals (age 65 to 74 and 75 +) have after-tax incomes about $1,000 higher than their Canadian counterparts, while U.S. elderly couples have incomes averaging as much as $5,000 higher ($31,200 versus $26,300 in Canada, in the 65 to 74 age range). However, the similarities are as notable as the differences. In both countries, unattached individuals have much lower average incomes than do couples, and the "older old" (age 75 +, either single or couple) have lower average incomes than the "younger old" (age 65 to 74).

Another way to judge incomes of the elderly is in relation to incomes of pre-retirement families. Based on the figures in table 9.2, table 9.3 shows post-age 65 incomes as percentages of age 55 to 64 incomes. For example, 65- to 74-year-old couples' incomes in the United States average 80.8 percent of their immediate pre-retirement counterparts (i.e., ages 55 to 64). The corresponding drop in income for couples in Canada is somewhat sharper. Similarly, U.S. age 75 + couples—at 72.3 percent of 55- to 64-year-old couples—show a somewhat smaller drop in after-tax incomes than their Canadian counterparts. Canadian

Table 9.2 AFTER-TAX INCOMES BY AGE AND FAMILY TYPE, CANADIAN AND
U.S. FAMILIES, 1988

Age of Head	Family Type	Percent Distribution of Families within Age Group		After-Tax Income ($000s Cdn)	
		Canada	U.S.	Canada	U.S.
0–24	All	100.0	100.0	16.5	15.8
	Single	61.8	60.9	12.1	12.1
	Couples	16.8	10.0	26.8	28.1
	Others	21.5	29.1	21.0	19.3
25–44	All	100.0	100.0	33.0	33.3
	Single	25.2	29.7	19.0	21.5
	Couples	13.5	10.5	39.6	46.0
	Others	61.3	59.7	37.3	37.0
45–54	All	100.0	100.0	41.0	42.2
	Single	18.4	22.2	20.4	22.0
	Couples	16.0	18.2	40.1	43.5
	Others	65.6	59.6	46.9	49.3
55–64	All	100.0	100.0	33.8	35.9
	Single	25.9	28.1	16.3	18.6
	Couples	34.7	37.5	34.6	38.6
	Others	39.5	34.4	44.5	46.9
65–74	All	100.0	100.0	23.6	26.4
	Single	38.7	39.2	14.3	15.3
	Couples	41.6	42.3	26.3	31.2
	Others	19.7	18.5	36.3	39.1
75+	All	100.0	100.0	18.6	20.6
	Single	55.9	56.2	12.5	13.4
	Couples	30.4	30.2	23.8	27.9
	Others	13.7	13.7	32.3	34.3

elderly singles, on the other hand, have incomes that drop by smaller percentages than those of their U.S. counterparts.

While these proportions are cross-sectional rather than longitudinal, they do give a rough indication of the average "replacement ratios" realized by the elderly in each country. The replacement ratio indicates the extent of the drop in income the elderly can expect upon and during retirement. The ratios in table 9.3 indicate that in both countries there is a 19 to 24 percent drop in relative income for couples upon retirement, and a further 7 to 8 percent drop as the couples age one decade. The sharpest declines, however, are for surviving spouses (most often women) of a couple. If these cross-sectional data are taken as indicative of the longitudinal realities, then a widow can expect an

Table 9.3 AVERAGE INCOMES OF ELDERLY COHORTS AS PERCENTAGES OF THE AVERAGE INCOMES OF THE PRE-RETIREMENT COHORT (AGE 55 TO 64), CANADIAN AND U.S. FAMILIES, 1988

Age of Head	Family Type	Canada	U.S.
65–74	single[a]	87.7	82.3
	single[b]	41.3	39.6
	couple	76.0	80.8
75+	single[a]	76.7	72.0
	single[b]	36.1	34.7
	couple	68.8	72.3

a. As a proportion of the corresponding 55–64 *single* average income.
b. As a proportion of the corresponding 55–64 *couple* average income.

income after age 75 of about one-third her pre-retirement couple's income in either country.

It is difficult to estimate proper longitudinal replacement ratios, particularly on a family rather than on an individual basis, and on a basis that takes account of all sources of income and taxation. Wolfson (1987) provides detailed estimates of such replacement ratios for Canada. He shows that the lowest 20 percent of the pre-retirement career average earnings distribution can expect very high net rates of replacement—on the order of 100 percent or higher. The reason is that federal public pension transfers dominate post-65 income guarantees, while provincial Social Assistance programs provide the basic "safety net" income guarantees at ages below 65. These latter benefit guarantees are lower than the federal public pension guarantees. In the middle 60 percent of the pre-retirement career average earnings distribution, the picture shifts. One-third of the population can expect a net replacement rate of 85 percent or less. This latter result critically depends on the indexing assumption for the Old Age Security Pension and the Guaranteed Income Supplement, a point to which we return later. Similar estimates for the United States appear unavailable.

Sources of Income for the Elderly

The largest source of income of the elderly (age 65 +) in both countries is public pensions. Public pensions are a larger proportion of GDP in the United States than in Canada, so we might expect that average dollar levels per elderly family would also be higher. However, as shown in table 9.4, the average level of public pension income for both elderly age groups (65 to 74 and 75 +) and for both family types (singles and couples) is *higher* in Canada. The main factor that ac-

Table 9.4 NUMBERS AND AVERAGE INCOMES ($000s CDN) BY SOURCE, FAMILY TYPE, AND AGE, CANADIAN AND U.S. ELDERLY AND NEAR-ELDERLY FAMILIES, 1988

Item	Country	Unattached Individuals			Married Couples		
		55–64	65–74	75+	55–64	65–74	75+
Families	Canada	0.37	0.40	0.47	0.49	0.43	0.25
(Millions)	U.S.	3.70	4.22	5.23	4.94	4.55	2.81
Source of Income							
Total Income	Canada	19.6	15.9	13.4	43.7	29.5	26.4
	U.S.	24.1	16.9	14.4	49.1	35.8	31.1
Labor Income	Canada	10.9	1.2	0.1	32.1	4.6	1.9
	U.S.	15.1	2.6	0.7	34.9	8.7	3.5
Investment Income	Canada	4.8	6.0	4.9	7.7	11.6	10.6
	U.S.	6.1	7.2	6.5	11.1	15.3	14.6
Government Income	Canada	3.5	8.5	8.3	3.1	12.9	13.6
	U.S.	2.4	7.0	7.1	2.9	11.6	12.8
Pensions	Canada	1.8	7.9	7.7	1.6	11.9	12.8
	U.S.	2.0	6.8	7.0	2.4	11.2	12.6
Other	Canada	1.7	0.6	0.6	1.5	1.0	0.7
	U.S.	0.4	0.2	0.1	0.5	0.4	0.2
Other Income	Canada	0.4	0.2	0.1	0.7	0.4	0.3
	U.S.	0.4	0.1	0.1	0.1	0.1	0.1
Income Taxes	Canada	3.3	1.6	0.9	9.1	3.2	2.6
	U.S.	5.4	1.6	1.0	10.4	4.6	3.2
Income After Tax	Canada	16.3	14.3	12.5	34.6	26.3	23.8
	U.S.	18.6	15.3	13.4	38.6	31.2	27.9

counts for this apparent contradiction with the aggregate figures is that over one-third of OASDI benefits, the dominant component of public pensions in the United States, is paid to individuals under age 65 (U.S. Committee on Ways and Means 1988, Table 15, p. 29).[6] In contrast, less than 10 percent of Canadian public pension payments are paid to the nonelderly.[7] Moreover, the elderly are relatively more numerous in the United States—12.1 percent compared to 10.7 percent in Canada; for the 75+ age groups the figures are 5.0 and 4.1 percent, respectively (OECD 1988a).[8]

In contrast to the situation with public pensions, U.S. seniors have higher average incomes from private sources than Canadian seniors. They have $1,000 to $4,000 more per year from working, and similarly larger incomes from investments and private pensions. In turn, the higher incomes U.S. seniors receive from working might account for the lower average public pensions in the United States just noted, due to the workings of Social Security. We return to this point shortly.

Income Sources by Income Range

The adage "beware of the mean" is appropriate in these comparisons of income sources of seniors in the two countries. As we saw earlier, the U.S. distribution of income is generally more unequal and more polarized. More importantly, even though average incomes are higher in the United States, the first 60–65 percent of Canadian families have higher (before- and after-tax) incomes than their U.S. counterparts. In order to address these kinds of points for the elderly, tables 9.5 and 9.6 give further details by income range. As in table 9.1, the income ranges are expressed as percentages of the median adjusted after-tax family income for all families (not just seniors). Even though U.S. seniors have higher average incomes, the United States has from 6 to 24 percentage points higher incidence of low-income elderly families (depending on the age group and family composition). For example, 11.1 percent of U.S. married couples with family head age 65 to 74 had "low incomes," while the percentage for corresponding Canadian families was 5.4. For single individuals age 65 to 74 the percentage with low incomes was much higher in the United States—37.8 percent compared to 16.6 percent in Canada.

Table 9.5 also shows that in Canada, the incidence of low income declines after age 65, while in the United States it increases. This is perhaps ironic, given the much more explicit debate in the United States than in Canada over intergenerational equity. This in turn was fuelled in part by feelings that the U.S. elderly were quite well off compared to other priority social policy concerns, particularly child poverty (see chapters 3 and 4 in this volume).

Not only is there a higher proportion of elderly families with low incomes in the United States, but the average depth of low income is up to $1,500 greater (average income $10,300 in Canada and $8,800 in the United States). At the same time, there are relatively more U.S. elderly families in the highest tabulated income range (over 1.5 times the adjusted all-family median). Thus, the pattern of higher inequality and higher incidence of low income in the United States as compared to Canada applies to the elderly as well as overall.

Table 9.5 also shows the percentages of families with nontrivial attachment to the labor force (indicated by receipt of more than $500 Cdn of labor income). Overall, Canadian senior unattached individuals and couples are considerably less likely to be working than their

Table 9.5 NUMBERS, AVERAGE INCOMES, AND LABOR FORCE STATUS BY AGE, FAMILY TYPE, AND ADJUSTED INCOME, CANADIAN AND U.S. ELDERLY AND NEAR-ELDERLY FAMILIES, 1988

Age of Head	Family Type	Income Range[a]	Families (%) Canada	U.S.	Average After-Tax Income ($000s Cdn) Canada	U.S.	Percent Working[b] Canada	U.S.
55–64	Single	0–50	33.0	32.4	5.9	5.2	22.4	21.8
		50–100	32.8	29.2	12.9	13.6	48.5	67.0
		100–150	18.4	18.5	21.2	22.5	70.6	78.1
		150+	15.8	19.8	39.3	44.5	85.5	87.6
		All	100.0	100.0	16.3	18.6	49.8	58.5
	Couple	0–50	9.4	8.9	7.4	7.2	27.0	38.5
		50–100	27.1	22.2	19.2	19.8	66.3	68.9
		100–150	29.5	26.2	30.5	31.9	84.4	84.2
		150+	34.0	42.7	58.0	59.0	96.8	93.4
		All	100.0	100.0	34.6	38.6	78.3	80.7
65–74	Single	0–50	16.6	37.8	7.4	6.4	1.6*	5.6
		50–100	63.4	33.6	12.1	13.2	5.7	21.5
		100–150	12.4	16.8	21.2	22.1	15.5	35.3
		150+	7.7	11.8	36.3	39.9	42.3	39.3
		All	100.0	100.0	14.3	15.3	9.0	19.9
	Couple	0–50	5.4	11.1	10.3	8.8	8.1*	14.4
		50–100	54.6	35.7	18.6	19.2	17.9	28.7
		100–150	25.1	27.1	30.3	31.5	32.3	42.0
		150+	14.9	26.0	53.6	56.8	55.8	53.5
		All	100.0	100.0	26.3	31.2	26.7	37.2
75+	Single	0–50	19.9	44.2	7.5	6.5	—	1.7*
		50–100	68.4	35.8	11.5	12.7	1.2*	4.9
		100–150	7.2	11.8	21.2	22.0	7.0*	10.1
		150+	4.6	8.3	35.0	41.1	6.5*	16.6
		All	100.0	100.0	12.5	13.4	1.6*	5.1
	Couple	0–50	3.4	17.4	9.6	9.5	—	4.2*
		50–100	69.2	41.8	18.0	18.8	3.7*	12.4
		100–150	16.9	20.9	30.3	31.2	13.2*	19.3
		150+	10.5	19.9	56.2	59.7	37.1*	35.7
		All	100.0	100.0	23.8	27.9	8.7	17.1

Notes:
Dash (—): no sample for working population.
* Sample size of working population very small.
a. After-tax income ranges expressed as percentages of median adjusted after-tax family income.
b. Fraction of family units with labor income accounting for more than $500 Cdn of after-tax income within age/family type/country/income range.

Table 9.6 AVERAGE INCOMES ($000s CDN) BY AGE GROUP, FAMILY TYPE, AND ADJUSTED INCOME, CANADIAN AND U.S. ELDERLY AND NEAR-ELDERLY FAMILIES, 1988

Age of Head	Family Type	Income Range (%)	Canada					United States				
			Labor	Public Pensions	Other Transfers	Invest-ments	Income Taxes	Labor	Public Pensions	Other Transfers	Invest-ments	Income Taxes
55–64	Single	0–49	1.0	1.4	2.8	0.6	0.1	1.7	2.8	0.5	0.8	0.7
		50–99	5.7	2.5	1.7	4.4	1.7	9.3	2.1	0.4	3.6	2.0
		100–149	16.4	1.7	0.8	6.3	4.4	19.4	1.5	0.4	6.4	5.6
		150+	36.1	1.3	0.3	12.8	12.0	41.7	0.9	0.3	18.3	18.0
	Couple	0–49	1.7	2.0	2.9	0.9	0.1	3.3	3.3	0.3	1.6	1.5
		50–99	10.4	2.5	2.3	5.3	2.2	12.0	3.6	0.4	6.1	2.4
		100–149	24.9	1.6	1.3	8.0	6.0	25.6	2.8	0.6	8.6	5.7
		150+	64.2	0.7	0.8	11.3	19.8	59.1	1.4	0.5	17.2	19.4
65–74	Single	0–49	0.0	6.4	0.6	0.5	0.2	0.1	5.6	0.1	0.6	0.0
		50–99	0.4	8.3	0.6	3.4	0.6	1.6	7.4	0.1	4.4	0.4
		100–149	2.0	7.8	0.5	14.2	3.6	4.8	7.5	0.4	11.5	2.2
		150+	9.7	8.0	1.3	26.0	9.3	10.2	7.8	0.5	30.4	9.7
	Couple	0–49	0.1	7.1	1.8	1.4	0.1	2.2	7.5	0.2	1.6	2.7
		50–99	1.3	12.4	0.8	4.5	0.6	2.5	11.6	0.2	5.2	0.3
		100–149	4.3	11.8	1.2	16.3	3.8	6.7	11.9	0.5	14.4	2.0
		150+	18.7	12.0	1.1	33.3	12.8	22.0	11.6	0.8	36.1	14.1

75+	Single	0–49	0.0	6.9	0.3	0.3	0.0	5.8	0.1	0.5	0.0
		50–99	0.0	8.1	0.6	2.9	0.3	7.7	0.2	4.6	0.2
		100–149	0.4	6.9	1.1	16.0	1.2	8.2	0.2	13.6	1.5
		150+	1.5	6.6	0.5	36.5	4.7	8.7	0.2	36.4	9.2
	Couple	0–49	0.0	7.8	0.9	0.9	0.1	8.1	0.1	1.1	0.0
		50–99	0.1	13.1	0.7	4.2	0.8	12.7	0.1	5.4	0.2
		100–149	1.7	12.5	0.6	18.5	2.2	14.0	0.3	15.7	1.2
		150+	14.3	13.1	1.0	43.7	13.7	15.1	0.2	44.6	14.3
Labor Income <$500 Cdn (the "nonworking" elderly)											
65–74	Single	0–49	0.0	6.5	0.6	0.5	−0.1	5.7	0.1	0.7	0.0
		50–99	0.0	8.5	0.5	3.4	0.0	7.9	0.1	5.2	0.2
		100–149	0.0	8.0	0.6	15.9	0.0	8.4	0.4	14.6	1.5
		150+	0.0	8.3	1.4	35.3	−0.2	8.6	0.3	37.3	7.5
	Couple	0–49	−0.1	7.2	1.9	1.4	−0.3	7.7	0.2	1.4	0.0
		50–99	0.0	13.1	0.7	4.7	−0.1	12.8	0.2	6.1	0.1
		100–149	0.0	12.5	1.3	19.3	0.0	13.0	0.6	18.6	1.1
		150+	0.0	13.5	1.6	48.7	−0.1	14.0	1.2	46.0	8.6

Note: Income ranges expressed as percentages of median adjusted after-tax family income.

U.S. counterparts—by about 10 percentage points. This is in line with the higher average amounts of labor income among U.S. seniors.

The greater incidence of low income amongst U.S. seniors is consistent with the view that the U.S. public pension system is not as generous as Canada's at the low end of the income spectrum. This is because the U.S. public pensions are dominated by benefits that are tied to average pre-retirement earnings. Even though these earnings-related benefits are calculated according to a progressive formula of nominal replacement rates, very low average pre-retirement earnings will still result in very low public pensions. The U.S. benefit formula was as follows: 90 percent of average earnings up to an annual amount of $3,828, 32 percent of the next $19,236, and 15 percent of the next $4,662, for a maximum pension of $10,300 on maximum pensionable earnings of $27,726 in 1988. Subject to an "earnings disregard," in 1988, Social Security benefits were reduced by 50 percent of employment income for recipients under age 70. In addition, subject to both an income and an asset test, elderly with minimal other sources of income are eligible for SSI, which varies by state and amounts to at least $4,248 and $6,384 for individuals and couples living independently. Thus, in Canadian dollars, U.S. public pensions range from $5,310 (lowest SSI of an independent elderly individual) to $12,875 (maximum individual old age retirement pension assuming normal retirement age) to $19,313 (maximum for a couple).

The earnings-related Canada and Quebec Pension Plans (C/QPP) provide pensions with a lower nominal replacement rate and a lower maximum pension than with U.S. Social Security—25 percent of average pre-retirement earnings up to a maximum retirement pension of $6,517 on maximum pensionable earnings of $26,500. However, the C/QPP pensions are accompanied by the Old Age Security (OAS) pension demogrant, which provides $3,788 for every person age 65 + (except for adjustments for recent immigrants), and the Guaranteed Income Supplement (GIS), which provides maximum annual benefits of $4,501 and $5,863 for individuals and couples, respectively. The GIS, unlike SSI, has no means test, but is subject to a general 50-cent reduction for each dollar of other income (excluding OAS but including C/QPP). Unlike Social Security, in 1988 neither C/QPP or OAS were subject to reductions on account of earnings.[9] Thus, Canadian public pensions range from a minimum of $8,289 (maximum GIS plus OAS for an unattached individual) to $16,698 (couple with partial GIS, two OAS benefits, and one maximum C/QPP).

Even though a casual examination of the benefit formulae of the two countries' earnings-related public pensions would leave the impres-

sion that the U.S. system provides higher replacement rates in the
middle pre-retirement income ranges, this is incorrect because it fails
to take account of the OAS elderly demogrant in Canada. These characteristics of the public pension programs, in turn, account for the
similarities in average incomes from public pensions between Canada
and the United States within all age, family type, and income ranges
(often only a few hundred dollars difference).[10]

This trend is also apparent for the "nonworking" population shown
at the bottom of table 9.6.[11] There is not a large difference in average
public pensions between the two countries for those not working.
There is some difference between the overall and the nonworking
population in terms of average income from public pensions, with the
latter having public pensions averaging as much as $1,500 higher in
both countries.

The similarities are somewhat curious given the nominal incentive
effects of the two countries' public pension systems with respect to
contemporaneous earnings. Leaving aside personal income taxes, the
only significant marginal tax on earnings in Canada comes via the
GIS at a 50 percent rate, which applies to the first $10,000 of earnings
(less any C/QPP benefits). In the U.S. system, a 100 percent rate is
applied by SSI on earnings up to roughly $5000, and a 50 percent rate
applies to Social Security earnings over $8,400. Thus, throughout
most of the lower-middle range of earnings, the U.S. public pension
system in 1988 typically imposed equal or higher effective marginal
tax rates than the Canadian system. Yet, U.S. elderly generally had
higher incomes from working and from investments and private pensions in all income ranges. The implication is that culture and community norms, or perhaps fears regarding inadequate health insurance,[12] play a much greater role in determining labor force
participation among seniors than the conventional price variables of
mainstream economic theory.

PRIVATE PENSIONS AND SAVING

Private pension arrangements and individual saving constitute a significant portion of the incomes of the elderly. They also form a major
focus for public policy. In this section we give a brief comparative
overview of the private pension and savings arrangements in Canada
and the United States.

As shown in table 9.4, these income sources (called "investment income") amount on average to 40 to 50 percent of after-tax income for the elderly. However, they are skewed toward the upper income ranges. This is indicated in table 9.6, where income from "investments" (private savings and pensions) constituted about 25 percent of after-tax income for couples age 65 to 74 with adjusted incomes between 50 and 100 percent of the median—about half the elderly in this demographic group (see table 9.5). For the "poor" among the elderly (those with adjusted incomes less than 50 percent of the median), private savings arrangements typically provided closer to 10 percent of disposable income for the various elderly demographic groups. In contrast, for the top income range in table 9.6 (those with adjusted incomes over 150 percent of the median), investments (including private pension benefits) accounted for over two-thirds of disposable income. Canada and the United States are broadly similar in the average importance of these private arrangements as sources of post-retirement income, and in their unequal distribution.[13]

Regarding the period prior to retirement, the question most often asked about private pension plans relates to their "coverage." For example, what proportion of the labor force is covered by or participating in an employer-sponsored pension plan or similar arrangement? For public sector employees, coverage is close to 100 percent in both countries. However, in the private sector, the figure is considerably higher in the United States (46 percent) than in Canada (28 percent) (Turner and Dailey 1991, Table 2.2). These coverage ratios have been stable and perhaps even declining marginally during the 1980s, following considerable growth since the post-war period.

In any case, it is important to bear in mind that these "point in time" coverage figures need not have a very strong correlation with pension benefits that will be received after retirement. A year of covered service can translate into a wide range of post-retirement benefits depending on the benefit formula of the pension plan, whether the benefit ever becomes vested, how the value of the accrued benefit is updated in response to inflation, and how portable the benefit is if the employee changes jobs. This range includes no benefit at all. Thus, conventional coverage statistics, despite their popularity, are a poor guide to what we might expect in the future from private pension plans as sources of post-retirement incomes.

Canada and the United States provide an interesting set of similarities and contrasts with regard to the regulatory milieu for private pension plans and savings arrangements. When thinking about these sources of retirement income, the usual focus is private pension plans, most often employer-sponsored. These plans also have the greatest degree of regulation. But for many individuals in both countries, private tax-assisted saving is at least as important. In this latter category, we include explicit retirement savings arrangements like IRAs (Individual Retirement Accounts) in the U.S. and Registered Retirement Savings Plans (RRSPs) in Canada. It is also important to include owner-occupied housing which, for most individuals entering retirement, is their largest source of wealth.[14]

The regulatory milieux for private pension plans in both countries must address the same basic tensions. One derives from the voluntary nature of these plans. Public policy wishes to assure that private pension plans are as fair and adequate as possible, especially given that public pensions in both countries, by themselves and by design, provide inadequate incomes for all but the poor. A significant volume of privately arranged post-retirement income is essential if middle- and high-income workers are to come close to maintaining their pre-retirement living standards into retirement. However, if regulation is too burdensome, employers can simply refuse to offer the plans. Thus, for example, neither country has mandated any significant degree of inflation protection for private pension plans, even though this issue has been on their pension reform agendas for well over a decade.

The second major tension in private pension plan regulation is between the costs to the treasury of tax assistance, and the desire to assure the financial solvency of pension funds. Private retirement savings arrangements constitute one of the two largest tax expenditures in both countries (the other is the tax treatment of owner-occupied housing—relative to the benchmark of a comprehensive income tax base). Larger volumes of tax-deductible contributions to pension funds translate into larger forgone tax revenues. At the same time, they improve the security of employees' future pension entitlements. Both countries face this tension; both give very generous tax treatment to private pension plans but impose a series of limits to protect tax revenues; and both have a complex network of regulations that seek to protect employees' rights to receive the monies embodied in the defined benefit pension promises made by the plans.

In addition to these broad similarities in private pension arrangements in the two countries, there are a number of more specific similarities. For example, both countries have vesting rules that require employees' accrued pension benefits to "lock in," roughly speaking no later than by the end of ten years of service. In other words, if the employee leaves the job after this time, the benefit must take the form of a pension payable only after retirement age. Also, both countries have inducements for married employees to take their pensions in the form of joint and survivor benefits.

There are also a number of differences. One is nondiscrimination. The United States generally requires employers who offer a pension plan at all to offer substantially the same plan to all employees of the firm. This regulation appears to be one way public policy seeks to expand coverage by private plans. Canada has no such regulation. A second difference is the methods used to assure the financial solvency of pension funds. The United States has a Pension Benefit Guarantee Corporation that acts as an insurer for pension funds. Canada has no such arrangements nationally, though the Province of Ontario does. These are both complex areas of regulation, and it is not clear that they contribute in any major way to significant differences in the broad results in the two countries.

Perhaps more interesting are the differences in the forms of the limits on tax deferrals, and the legal and statutory style of the regulations. Our basic claim is that the U.S. congressional system generally leads to more rule-based, complex and less coherent regulation than the Canadian parliamentary system. In Canada, first with the "Carter" Royal Commission on Taxation Reform (1966), and then in the late 1970s with the renewal of the pension reform debate (Ministry of Finance 1979), it was observed that the tax treatment of retirement saving was much more generous for employees than for the self-employed. The result has been the gradual adoption of an integrated and comprehensive system of tax limits. The U.S. system, on the other hand, embodies a complex set of contribution or benefit limits which, if compared in terms of the commuted value of the retirement annuity they permit, would be seen to vary widely across different groups of workers.

Arguably (and admittedly a bit simplistically), this reflects the more pluralistic law-forming process in the United States. Members of Congress can often successfully tack amendments on bills that have very narrowly focused targets, as part of the horse-trading and deal-making of shifting coalitions. The professional public service has only the most limited power to try to ensure consistency and coherence. In contrast, in the Canadian parliamentary system amendments to tax legislation are a very closely guarded prerogative of the Minister of Finance, where Finance Ministry officials have a dominant role. The broad ideological predilections of the governing political party are influential in both countries, for example, in the general directions of fiscal stringency and redistributional impacts. Smaller technical details are also generally well handled by professional staffs in both countries. It is at the intermediate level of the structure and coherence of a related set of laws or regulations that there seems to be a significant difference, certainly as exemplified by limits of tax-assisted retirement saving.

Another facet of these differences is in the degree of regulatory detail. The tax code with respect to pension plans is far lengthier in the United States than in Canada, and includes worked examples. There appears to be a felt need to spell out the implications and the ramifications of the law or regulation in great detail. Canada, in contrast, has more of a tradition of relying on general guidelines plus a professional "wise person" to resolve details of interpretation as they arise. This is embodied in the "Director of Registrations" position within Revenue Canada. This official has considerable authority regarding the registration of employer-sponsored pension plans. Officials in both the Federal and Provincial governments are also responsible for implementing and enforcing the regulations on the funding of pension plans.

Unfortunately, there are virtually no data to assess the comparative impacts of these differences in regulatory milieu. One test would be to examine the extent of ad hoc updating of pensions in pay to compensate for erosion by inflation. Our hypothesis is that such improvements have been more frequent in Canada, due to the more informal relationships between plan sponsors and the regulatory authorities in Canada, and to a somewhat greater shared value that pensions are a form of deferred wage and part of an "implicit pension bargain." In contrast, in the United States where the "law is the law," plan sponsors have been more aggressive in their actuarial assumptions and hence in gaining access to the unanticipated pension fund surpluses generated by inflation and high real interest rates, at the expense of their retirees. While there are some surveys of plan sponsors that report such ad hoc updating, the samples are typically biased and unrepresentative, so no meaningful comparisons are possible.

THE FUTURE

A major difference in the Canadian and U.S. *public* pension systems is their expected evolution.[15] While the Canadian system may appear "kinder and gentler" in 1988, will it still be so when the baby boom generation reaches age 65 in about 2025? Unfortunately, this is not at all clear. The question turns critically on the ways pension benefits will be updated. Based on current legislation in the two countries, it can be expected that Canadian public pensions will decline relative to those in the United States. The major U.S. public pension benefit is Social Security, which is tied closely to earnings levels. Thus, with real per capita economic growth, future U.S. pensioners will automatically share in the increased wealth, since their pensions are largely earnings-related. These provisions are longstanding and relatively stable parts of the U.S. legislation.

The situation in Canada is more complex, as several counteracting forces will be at work. Canada's public pension system is younger and is still maturing, particularly the earnings-related C/QPP—introduced in 1966 and phased in over 10 years. Thus, individuals in their late 80s in 1988 received no C/QPP benefits at all, whereas future seniors at all ages will receive benefits in relation to their pre-retirement earnings. Also, with the dramatic increases in female labor force participation, the numbers of elderly women receiving C/QPP retirement (not just survivor) benefits will increase significantly. However, the C/QPP earnings-related pensions are not the most important part of the Canadian public pension system. The Old Age Security (OAS) demogrant and the Guaranteed Income Supplement (GIS) combined are 70 percent larger than C/QPP in aggregate dollar terms (about 120 percent and 50 percent of C/QPP benefits respectively).

Murphy and Wolfson (1991) provide a series of detailed projections of these pension programs, and examine factors such as the expected maturation of the C/QPP, increasing female labor force participation, population growth, and the indexing provisions of the OAS and GIS. These two major elements of the pension system are indexed to the CPI, so that any real economic growth will cause them to shrink relative to average wages and relative to the C/QPP. Taking a scenario where the current legislation remains unchanged through to 2036 (when the trailing edge of the Canadian baby boom attains age 66), and real per capita economic growth averages one percent per annum, the projections indicate that the proportion of the elderly with "low income" (defined exactly as earlier—less than 50 percent of median adjusted income) will quadruple.

Such projections assume no policy response during the intervening years; and this may be considered unlikely. If U.S. legislation remains unamended, Social Security will continue to play roughly the same role for the elderly relative to their pre-retirement situation in the future as it does now. Of course, with a growing proportion of elderly in the population, Social Security will increase as a percentage of the total economy, and this may emerge as an increasing source of pressure to reduce benefits (though this pressure is already offset to some extent by the legislated two-year increase in the normal retirement age). In Canada, the pressures would most likely be in the opposite direction, to raise pension benefits significantly relative to existing legislation. Arguably, the latter pressures could be stronger, since increasing (relative) poverty amongst the elderly in Canada would be occurring in conjunction with real economic growth. This same kind of real economic growth in the United States would tend to mitigate concerns about the increasing share of the elderly in the total population, and hence Social Security in the economy.

CONCLUSIONS

The conventional wisdom is: first, that the United States is generally a wealthier country than Canada, and second, that the United States has a larger and more generous system of public pensions. The second point is supported by OECD aggregate figures showing U.S. public pensions one-third again as large a share of GDP as Canadian pensions. This second point is further reinforced by the fact that Social Security was instituted 30 years earlier than the Canada and Quebec Pension Plans and is more mature. However, the underlying data show both of these impressions to be misleading.

In fact, the first 60–65 percent of Canadian families had *higher* average after-tax incomes than their U.S. counterparts in 1988, after converting currencies using purchasing power parities. Canada's public pensions are also more generous for the poorest among the elderly, and for those who had middle-level incomes prior to retirement. U.S. family incomes are more unequally distributed. There are relatively more low-income families based on a commonly used measure of low income, a proportionately smaller middle-income group, and a larger proportion of well-to-do families.

Thus, U.S. society is at a different point on the presumed trade-off between the size of the pie and the way it is divided. The majority of Canadian families are absolutely better off, while a minority of high-income U.S. families are better off than their Canadian counterparts. This is true of families generally and of the elderly in particular.

Notes

We gratefully acknowledge helpful comments on an earlier draft of this paper from a workshop at Yale sponsored by the U.S. Donner Foundation. The views expressed here should not be taken to reflect those of Statistics Canada or the Government of Canada. We, of course, remain responsible for any errors or infelicities.

1. This 2.2 percent difference in average family incomes is not quite as large as the 5 percent difference in per capita GDP converted using exchange rates noted earlier. A reconciliation of the two comparisons is given in appendix 9.A.

2. This is an understatement due to the top-coding of very high income amounts on the U.S. microdata file; see appendix 9.A.

3. The adjustment is to divide each family's income by a scale factor based on family size and composition. This scale factor is computed as the sum of 1.0 for the first adult in the family, plus 0.4 for each subsequent adult, plus 0.3 for each child, plus 0.1 if it is a lone parent family (i.e., the first child in a lone-parent family is treated like a second adult with a value of 0.4). These kinds of scale factors are known as equivalence scales. Based on these equivalence scale adjustments, median adjusted family after-tax incomes in Canadian dollars were $17,830 and $18,280 in Canada and the United States respectively. Appendix 9.A provides further discussion regarding the slightly higher U.S. adjusted median figure.

4. Conventional inequality measures like the Gini coefficient and any other measure consistent with Lorenz curve rankings of income distribution can be shown always to rank polarized (e.g., bimodal) distributions as more equal. Hence, the two concepts are not equivalent. In fact, much of the confusion in the "disappearing middle" debate can be ascribed to a failure to use appropriate statistical measures.

5. Note that these curves are based on family size-adjusted family incomes weighted by the number of family members. This is the last form of income distribution presented and explained in appendix 9.A.

6. SSI, the next largest component, amounts to about 5 percent of aggregate OASDI, and about half of adult SSI beneficiaries are under age 65 (Ways and Means 1988, p. 533).

7. Certain C/QPP benefits (orphans, survivors under 65, disability) as well as the Spouse's Allowance benefits are paid to persons under age 65. Persons age 60 to 64 have recently become able to commence their C/QPP retirement benefits before the normal age of 65, but this was negligible in 1988.

8. These population patterns are expected to reverse by the turn of the century, with Canada projected to have a consistently higher percentage of its population age 65 + and 75 +. The OECD projects Canada having a slightly lower share of GDP spent on public pensions even when Canada's elderly population is a larger fraction of the total population (OECD 1988b, Tables 3.1 and 3.2). This latter finding suggests that on per capita terms, the Canadian public pension system is less generous than that in the United States. The key point is that a larger proportion of Canadian public pensions go to the elderly than in the United States.

9. However, both OAS and C/QPP are fully included in income for tax purposes, whereas only up to 50 percent of Social Security is taxable. Also, starting in 1989, OAS benefits are reduced by 15 percent of income in excess of $50,000, while in 1990 the reduction rate for earnings under Social Security dropped from 50 percent to 33 percent.

10. Note that the income averages in table 9.5 are lower than the minimum guarantees in Canada. This is due in part to: the 65 to 74 population includes couples where one spouse is under age 65; less than 100 percent of eligible families apply for benefits; and problems of under-reporting on the survey.

11. Some have negative labor income, due to losses on self-employment.

12. About half of the "somewhat poor" (i.e. above U.S. poverty line but below Statistics Canada's LICOs) of the U.S. elderly are at risk because of incomplete health care insurance, which most then top up by private unsubsidized medigap insurance (Holden and Smeeding 1990).

13. More detailed tabulations of the underlying microdata files are, of course, mechanically feasible. However, questions of data quality—both underreporting and misreporting—suggest that such disaggregations would not bear much analytical weight.

14. Unfortunately, the income distribution data used in this study do not provide the basis for estimating the income from this form of wealth, namely, imputed rent. As shown in Wolfson (1979), for example, it is very significant particularly for the elderly.

15. There are no particular reasons to expect significantly different evolution of private saving arrangements. In both countries, they will likely continue to provide about the same relative volume of retirement income with the same skewed distribution. There is no evidence that the increases in coverage in the post-war period will have a major effect over the next quarter to half century, especially for the bottom half of the income spectrum.

APPENDIX 9.A
FURTHER DETAIL ON INCOME DISTRIBUTION DIFFERENCES
BETWEEN CANADA AND THE UNITED STATES

The "parade of dwarfs (plus a few giants)" shown in figure 9.1 is the basis for observing that the first 60–65 percent of Canadian families were better off than their U.S. counterparts. Since this result may be counter to the conventional wisdom, it is important to assess its reliability. Two issues deserve further discussion.

The first is that GDP per capita valued at exchange rates in 1988 was 5 percent higher in the United States, and mean family income valued at PPP was only 2.2 percent higher. Several explanations for this difference are possible. One is the 2 percent difference between the exchange rate (1.23 Canadian dollars per U.S. dollar) and PPP (1.25) in 1988; another is the difference between household spending as a proportion of GDP between the two countries (individual final consumption at 65.2 percent of GDP in the United States compared to 56.5 percent in Canada in 1985; Schultz 1991); a third is the 4 percent larger average family size in Canada (2.51 versus 2.41 persons per "nuclear" family).

These factors can be applied as follows. First, U.S. GDP per capita would have been 7 percent rather than 5 percent higher had it been converted using PPP rather than the exchange rate. But since it is distributed among 4 percent more families than persons, GDP per family (rather than per capita) converted at PPP (rather than the exchange rate) would have been only on the order of 3 percent higher in the United States than in Canada. Finally, the individual final consumption portion of GDP (a proxy for family income) was about 15 percent higher as a share of GDP in the United States (mainly due to higher U.S. private spending on health care), so that "family" GDP per family converted at PPP would be on the order of 18 percent higher in the United States. (In line with this last factor, U.S. labor income was about 10 percent higher as a share of GDP than in Canada—60 percent versus 55 percent.)

Clearly, this is far higher than the 2.2 percent difference observed from the household surveys. Other possible factors are (1) differences in the survey universes (e.g., institutionalized population, military— probably 1–2 percent at most); (2) employer-paid costs of health insurance, which should not be included from the household survey point of view but are included in the GDP individual final consumption figures; (3) differences in the overall PPP and the PPP for individual final consumption; (4) top-coding of income sources over $200,000 on the public use microdata tape for the United States; and (5) differences in the extent and composition of underreporting in the two surveys. This lack of agreement between the two major sources of comparative data should be borne in mind when judging the figures presented in the main text, though it is unlikely to affect the main results.

The second issue deserving further discussion is the contrast *within* the household surveys of the two countries. While *average* family income was 2.2 percent higher in the U.S., *median* family income in the U.S. was 4.2 percent lower. This is clearly explained by the greater inequality, polarization, and incidence of low income in the United States.

However, these differences can be questioned from a welfare point of view. In particular, the higher average incomes in Canada in the first 60–65 percent of the income spectrum may be supporting larger families. Income per family may be a misleading measure if average family sizes differ, which they do overall by about 4.1 percent (2.51 persons per family in Canada versus 2.41 in the U.S.). Table 9.A.1 gives further details on this point. It shows not only the average before- and after-tax incomes in each 20th of the income distribution, but also the average family size, the average adjusted family size (based on the .40/.30 equivalence scale), and the group cut-points. At the lower end of the income spectrum (first 25 to 30 percent), Canada does have smaller families, both in absolute size and in terms of equivalent adult units, but it has larger families in the remaining 70 to 75 percent of the distribution. The difference in average family sizes, though, is attenuated by the equivalence scale adjustment— average "adjusted" family size is 2.6 percent larger in Canada (1.54 versus 1.50) compared to 4.1 percent unadjusted. In any case, it is useful to construct a more welfare-oriented version of the "parade of dwarfs."

We do this in two steps. First, each family's income is divided by its equivalence scale—the number of equivalent adult units (EAUs) it contains. For example, the income of a two-adult + two-child family would be divided by 2.0 (= 1.0 + 0.4 + 0.3 + 0.3). Table 9.A.2 shows the results of reordering all families in the two countries by family income per EAU (both before- and after-tax), and then dividing them into 20ths. Average "adjusted" before-tax incomes are now $24,100 in Canada and $25,800 in the U.S., compared to $38,000 and $38,900 unadjusted—6.5 percent lower rather than the 2.2 percent unadjusted average family income difference cited in the main text. The corre-

Table 9.A.1   SELECTED STATISTICS BY PERCENTILE RANKINGS FOR U.S. AND CANADIAN FAMILIES, 1988 RANKINGS BASED ON UNADJUSTED BEFORE- AND AFTER-TAX INCOMES

Percentile Group	Average Income ($000s Cdn)		Average Family Size		Average EAU		Cut-Points ($000s Cdn)	
	Canada	U.S.	Canada	U.S.	Canada	U.S.	Canada	U.S.
Before Tax								
1 1–5%	4.0	2.0	1.25	1.70	1.09	1.23	6.6	4.8
2 6–10%	8.2	6.0	1.30	1.63	1.10	1.21	9.4	7.2
3 11–15%	10.4	8.3	1.40	1.70	1.14	1.23	11.5	9.6
4 16–20%	12.7	10.9	1.71	1.80	1.25	1.27	14.1	12.5
5 21–25%	15.7	13.7	1.90	1.92	1.33	1.32	17.0	15.0
6 26–30%	18.3	16.5	2.00	2.04	1.36	1.36	19.7	17.9
7 31–35%	21.0	19.3	2.16	2.03	1.42	1.36	22.5	20.8
8 36–40%	24.1	22.3	2.14	2.09	1.41	1.39	25.5	23.8
9 41–45%	27.2	25.4	2.40	2.21	1.50	1.43	29.0	27.1
10 46–50%	30.5	28.9	2.44	2.35	1.52	1.48	32.0	30.7
11 51–55%	33.8	32.3	2.72	2.39	1.61	1.49	35.6	34.1
12 56–60%	37.2	36.2	2.72	2.50	1.61	1.53	39.0	38.1
13 61–65%	40.9	40.3	2.79	2.63	1.64	1.58	42.8	42.7
14 66–70%	44.9	45.0	3.06	2.75	1.74	1.62	47.1	47.5
15 71–75%	49.4	50.0	3.20	2.84	1.79	1.65	51.7	52.8
16 76–80%	54.1	56.1	3.17	3.00	1.78	1.71	56.8	59.8
17 81–85%	60.2	63.7	3.36	3.01	1.85	1.72	63.7	68.1
18 86–90%	68.1	73.7	3.43	3.16	1.89	1.78	73.0	80.1
19 91–95%	80.1	89.8	3.46	3.20	1.90	1.8	88.7	102.6
20 96–100%	119.8	137.0	3.59	3.22	1.96	1.82	1200.0	552.5
All	38.0	38.9	2.51	2.41	1.54	1.50		

After Tax									
1-5%	1	4.0	1.4	1.25	1.71	1.09	1.23	6.6	4.6
6-10%	2	8.1	5.8	1.28	1.64	1.10	1.21	9.2	6.9
11-15%	3	10.1	8.0	1.35	1.65	1.12	1.22	11.1	9.0
16-20%	4	12.1	10.2	1.55	1.70	1.19	1.24	13.3	11.4
21-25%	5	14.5	12.6	1.75	1.89	1.27	1.31	15.6	13.7
26-30%	6	16.8	14.9	1.98	1.92	1.35	1.32	17.9	16.1
31-35%	7	18.9	17.3	2.03	1.98	1.37	1.34	20.1	18.5
36-40%	8	21.2	19.7	2.22	2.09	1.44	1.38	22.4	21.0
41-45%	9	23.6	22.3	2.31	2.17	1.47	1.41	24.9	23.6
46-50%	10	26.1	24.9	2.53	2.23	1.55	1.44	27.3	26.3
51-55%	11	28.5	27.7	2.60	2.42	1.57	1.50	29.7	29.1
56-60%	12	31.0	30.7	2.78	2.50	1.64	1.53	32.3	32.2
61-65%	13	33.7	33.8	3.00	2.62	1.71	1.57	35.2	35.5
66-70%	14	36.7	37.4	3.16	2.76	1.77	1.63	38.3	39.4
71-75%	15	39.9	41.4	3.16	2.87	1.77	1.66	41.6	43.6
76-80%	16	43.4	46.0	3.20	3.02	1.79	1.72	45.4	48.7
81-85%	17	47.8	51.6	3.36	3.08	1.85	1.75	50.5	54.9
86-90%	18	53.7	58.8	3.39	3.21	1.87	1.80	57.3	63.4
91-95%	19	62.4	69.9	3.62	3.26	1.96	1.82	68.9	78.0
96-100%	20	88.9	98.8	3.67	3.43	1.99	1.91	625.0	400.2
All		31.1	31.7	2.51	2.41	1.54	1.50		

Table 9.A.2 SELECTED STATISTICS BY PERCENTILE RANKINGS FOR U.S. AND CANADIAN FAMILIES, 1988 RANKINGS BASED ON BEFORE- AND AFTER-TAX INCOMES ADJUSTED FOR EAU

Percentile Group		Average Income ($000s Cdn)		Average Family Size		Average EAU		Cut-Points ($000s Cdn)	
		Canada	U.S.	Canada	U.S.	Canada	U.S.	Canada	U.S.
Before Tax									
1–5%	1	3.6	1.5	1.72	2.34	1.25	1.43	6.0	3.6
6–10%	2	7.0	4.9	2.17	2.27	1.40	1.42	8.0	5.9
11–15%	3	8.8	6.8	1.91	2.06	1.32	1.36	9.6	7.7
16–20%	4	10.3	8.6	1.99	2.17	1.36	1.40	11.0	9.5
21–25%	5	11.7	10.4	2.20	2.29	1.43	1.45	12.4	11.3
26–30%	6	13.2	12.2	2.49	2.38	1.53	1.48	14.0	13.2
31–35%	7	14.9	14.2	2.69	2.43	1.60	1.50	15.8	15.1
36–40%	8	16.7	16.1	2.70	2.57	1.60	1.55	17.5	17.0
41–45%	9	18.3	18.1	2.75	2.49	1.62	1.52	19.2	19.0
46–50%	10	20.1	20.1	2.78	2.54	1.64	1.54	21.1	21.3
51–55%	11	22.0	22.2	2.83	2.54	1.65	1.54	22.8	23.3
56–60%	12	23.7	24.5	2.87	2.57	1.67	1.56	24.6	25.6
61–65%	13	25.5	26.9	2.83	2.55	1.66	1.56	26.6	28.2
66–70%	14	27.7	29.6	2.79	2.63	1.65	1.59	29.0	31.2
71–75%	15	30.1	32.6	2.70	2.46	1.62	1.53	31.3	34.3
76–80%	16	32.8	36.1	2.72	2.47	1.63	1.54	34.5	38.1
81–85%	17	36.2	40.5	2.61	2.46	1.60	1.53	38.1	43.4
86–90%	18	40.4	46.6	2.52	2.36	1.57	1.50	43.0	50.4
91–95%	19	47.3	56.1	2.52	2.37	1.57	1.51	52.9	63.1
96–100%	20	72.4	88.3	2.39	2.18	1.52	1.45	857.1	369.3
All		24.1	25.8	2.51	2.41	1.54	1.50		

After Tax	#									
1–5%	1	3.6	1.1	1.73	2.34	1.25	1.43	6.0	3.4
6–10%	2	6.9	4.7	2.17	2.32	1.40	1.44	7.9	5.7
11–15%	3	8.6	6.5	2.04	2.12	1.36	1.38	9.3	7.4
16–20%	4	9.9	8.1	2.01	2.12	1.36	1.38	10.5	8.9
21–25%	5	11.1	9.7	2.26	2.30	1.45	1.45	11.7	10.4
26–30%	6	12.3	11.2	2.47	2.41	1.52	1.49	12.8	12.0
31–35%	7	13.4	12.8	2.68	2.43	1.60	1.50	14.0	13.5
36–40%	8	14.6	14.3	2.68	2.51	1.60	1.53	15.2	15.1
41–45%	9	15.8	15.9	2.78	2.50	1.63	1.53	16.5	16.7
46–50%	10	17.2	17.5	2.76	2.47	1.63	1.52	17.8	18.3
51–55%	11	18.4	19.1	2.89	2.55	1.68	1.55	19.0	20.0
56–60%	12	19.6	20.9	2.87	2.52	1.67	1.54	20.4	21.8
61–65%	13	21.1	22.8	2.76	2.53	1.63	1.55	21.8	23.7
66–70%	14	22.6	24.7	2.72	2.54	1.63	1.55	23.4	25.7
71–75%	15	24.3	26.9	2.68	2.51	1.61	1.54	25.2	28.1
76–80%	16	26.3	29.4	2.64	2.46	1.61	1.53	27.5	30.8
81–85%	17	28.6	32.4	2.57	2.45	1.58	1.54	29.9	34.3
86–90%	18	31.5	36.5	2.60	2.45	1.60	1.54	33.3	39.0
91–95%	19	36.5	42.7	2.52	2.41	1.57	1.53	40.2	47.4
96–100%	20	52.9	61.5	2.38	2.20	1.52	1.46	446.4	260.6
	All	19.8	20.9	2.51	2.41	1.54	1.50		

Table 9.A.3   SELECTED STATISTICS BY PERCENTILE RANKINGS FOR U.S. AND CANADIAN FAMILIES, 1988 ORDERING BASED ON BEFORE- AND AFTER-TAX INCOMES ADJUSTED FOR EAU AND WEIGHTS ADJUSTED FOR FAMILY SIZE

Percentile Group		Average Income ($000s Cdn)		Average Family Size		Average EAU		Cut-Points ($000s Cdn)	
		Canada	U.S.	Canada	U.S.	Canada	U.S.	Canada	U.S.
Before Tax									
1-5%	1	4.6	1.9	2.74	3.61	1.59	1.84	6.7	3.7
6-10%	2	7.9	5.0	3.11	3.54	1.71	1.84	8.9	6.1
11-15%	3	9.9	7.1	2.91	3.21	1.67	1.75	10.8	8.1
16-20%	4	11.7	9.1	3.09	3.32	1.73	1.79	12.4	10.0
21-25%	5	13.2	11.0	3.36	3.38	1.82	1.81	14.1	12.0
26-30%	6	14.9	12.9	3.55	3.31	1.89	1.79	15.7	13.9
31-35%	7	16.5	14.9	3.53	3.47	1.88	1.85	17.3	15.8
36-40%	8	18.1	16.7	3.54	3.47	1.89	1.85	18.8	17.6
41-45%	9	19.7	18.6	3.57	3.43	1.91	1.84	20.6	19.6
46-50%	10	21.3	20.6	3.55	3.32	1.90	1.81	22.1	21.6
51-55%	11	22.9	22.6	3.60	3.40	1.93	1.84	23.7	23.6
56-60%	12	24.4	24.7	3.67	3.35	1.95	1.83	25.3	25.8
61-65%	13	26.1	27.2	3.47	3.31	1.88	1.82	27.2	28.2
66-70%	14	28.2	29.6	3.49	3.34	1.89	1.83	29.3	31.0
71-75%	15	30.3	32.4	3.32	3.21	1.84	1.79	31.5	34.0
76-80%	16	33.0	35.7	3.36	3.16	1.86	1.78	34.5	37.6
81-85%	17	36.2	39.9	3.22	3.11	1.82	1.76	38.0	42.6
86-90%	18	40.2	45.8	3.17	3.02	1.80	1.74	42.8	49.5
91-95%	19	46.8	54.8	3.07	2.95	1.77	1.72	52.2	61.6
96-100%	20	70.1	83.3	2.92	2.72	1.71	1.64	857.1	369.3
	All	24.8	25.7	3.31	3.28	1.82	1.79		

After Tax									
1–5%	1	4.5	1.4	2.75	3.59	1.59	1.83	6.7	3.5
6–10%	2	7.7	4.7	3.21	3.58	1.75	1.85	8.7	5.8
11–15%	3	9.5	6.7	3.07	3.30	1.71	1.77	10.3	7.7
16–20%	4	11.0	8.6	3.16	3.28	1.75	1.77	11.6	9.4
21–25%	5	12.2	10.2	3.37	3.37	1.83	1.85	12.8	11.0
26–30%	6	13.3	11.8	3.50	3.48	1.87	1.81	13.9	12.5
31–35%	7	14.4	13.3	3.54	3.37	1.89	1.85	15.0	14.1
36–40%	8	15.5	14.8	3.56	3.47	1.89	1.83	16.1	15.6
41–45%	9	16.8	16.3	3.52	3.40	1.92	1.81	17.4	17.1
46–50%	10	17.9	17.8	3.58	3.34	1.93	1.81	18.4	18.6
51–55%	11	18.9	19.4	3.63	3.32	1.88	1.82	19.5	20.2
56–60%	12	20.1	21.1	3.48	3.33	1.91	1.81	20.8	22.0
61–65%	13	21.4	22.9	3.54	3.31	1.86	1.82	22.1	23.8
66–70%	14	22.9	24.8	3.40	3.33	1.85	1.79	23.6	25.7
71–75%	15	24.4	26.9	3.34	3.21	1.82	1.77	25.3	28.0
76–80%	16	26.4	29.3	3.24	3.13	1.82	1.76	27.5	30.7
81–85%	17	28.6	32.2	3.23	3.10	1.82	1.75	29.9	34.0
86–90%	18	31.4	36.1	3.19	3.04	1.76	1.74	33.2	38.5
91–95%	19	36.2	42.1	3.04	2.99	1.71	1.64	39.8	46.4
96–100%	20	51.3	59.1	2.90	2.69	1.82	1.79	446.4	260.6
All		20.2	21.0	3.31	3.28				

sponding difference in after-tax incomes per EAU is 5.6 percent compared to 1.9 percent without adjustment. In addition, the crossover points where U.S. families appear better off has moved down to just below the half-way mark. Median after-tax incomes adjusted in this way were $17,800 in Canada compared to $18,300 in the United States.

However, from a welfare point of view this is still not the whole story. Essentially, the figures in table 9.A.2 are counting an unattached individual and a 10-person family equally—they each contribute one observation to the income distribution parade. A better indication would be given if the unattached individual counted for one observation, but the 10-person family counted for 10 observations. These 10 observations would each be treated as if they had the benefit of the whole of the family's EAU adjusted income (i.e., income adjusted for the number of equivalent adults in the family). Table 9.A.3 shows the results of this preferred calculation. With these adjustments, about half of all Canadian individuals are absolutely better off than their U.S. counterparts—not a dramatic difference from numbers discussed in the text.

References

Baer, D., E. Grabb, and W. Johnston. 1991. "The Three Nations of North America: National Character, Regional Culture, and the Values of Canadians and Americans." Dept. of Sociology, University of Western Ontario. Mimeo.

Dryden, J., K. Reut, and B. Slater. 1987. "Bilateral Comparison of Purchasing Power Parities Between the United States and Canada." Supplement to the Oct.–Dec. issue of *Consumer Prices and Price Indexes*, Statistics Canada, Ottawa.

Foster, J., and M. C. Wolfson. 1991. "Inequality and Polarization—Concepts and Recent Trends." Analytical Studies Branch, Statistics Canada, Ottawa. Mimeo.

Holden, K. C., and T. M. Smeeding. 1990. "The Poor, the Rich, and the Insecure Elderly Caught in Between." *Milbank Quarterly* 68(2).

Ministry of Finance. 1979. *Report of the Task Force on Retirement Income Policy*. Ottawa.

Murphy, B. B., and M. C. Wolfson. 1991. "When the Baby Boom Grows Old: Impacts on Canada's Public Sector." *Statistical Journal of the United Nations Economic Commission for Europe* 8(1).

OECD. 1989. *Main Economic Indicators*. OECD Department of Economics and Statistics, Paris.

————. 1988a. *Social Expenditure Trends and Demographic Developments*. OECD report of the Meeting of the Manpower and Social Affairs Committee at Ministerial Level, Paris, July.

————. 1988b. *Reforming Public Pensions*. OECD Social Policy Studies, No. 5, Paris.

Pen, J. 1973. "A Parade of Dwarfs (and a Few Giants)." In *Wealth, Income and Inequality*, edited by A. B. Atkinson. Middlesex: Penguin.

Royal Commission on Taxation. 1966. Ottawa: Queens Printer.

Schultz, B. 1991. "Comparative International Studies of Real Expenditures Based on Purchasing Power Parities." Prices Division, Statistics Canada. Mimeo.

Turner, J. A., and L. M. Dailey. 1991. *Pension Policy: An International Perspective*. U.S. Department of Labor, Pension and Welfare Benefits Administration. Washington, D.C.: US GPO.

U.S. Committee on Ways and Means. 1988. Background Material and Data on Programs Within the Jurisdiction of the Committee on Ways and Means. Washington, D.C.: U.S. Government Printing Office.

Wolfson, M. C. 1979. "Wealth and the Distribution of Income, Canada 1969–70." *Review of Income and Wealth* (June).

————. 1987. "Lifetime Coverage: The Adequacy of Canada's Retirement Income System." In *International Comparisons of the Distribution of Household Wealth*, edited by E. N. Wolff. Oxford: Clarendon Press.

————. 1989. "Inequality and Polarization: Is There a Disappearing Middle Class in Canada?." *Proceedings of the Statistics Canada Symposium on Analysis of Data in Time*. Ottawa, October.

————. 1994. "When Inequalities Diverge." Paper presented to the American Economics Association, January, Boston, forthcoming *American Economic Review—Papers and Proceedings*, May.

Chapter Ten

ON BEING OLD AND SICK: THE BURDEN OF HEALTH CARE FOR THE ELDERLY IN CANADA AND THE UNITED STATES

Morris L. Barer, Clyde Hertzman, Robert Miller,
and Marina V. Pascali

The fact that Americans spend significantly more than Canadians on health care, but are far less content with what they are purchasing, has become an important factor in policy discussions focusing on health care reform in the United States. The marked contrast in satisfaction with their respective health care systems among residents of Canada and the United States has been graphically portrayed in recent years (Blendon et al. 1990; Blendon and Taylor 1989; Blendon and Donelan 1990; Blendon 1989). Most strikingly, only 10 percent of the U.S. population indicated that "On the whole, the [health care] system works pretty well," while the corresponding Canadian proportion was 56 percent (Blendon 1989). The absolute size of the 'satisfaction gap' is even greater among respondents 65 and over. In the United States, 15 percent of the elderly felt that their system 'works pretty well' ; in Canada the share was 66 percent (unpublished data provided by the Institute for the Future). The 'gap' is smaller for respondents who are 'very satisfied' with the system, but the difference remains consistent and considerable (unpublished data, *Three Nations Study*, 1989; provided by the Institute for the Future).

In table 10.1 we show the proportions of the respective populations who indicated that they were 'very satisfied' with a variety of health care services. These data suggest that in each country the elderly tend to be more satisfied than their younger counterparts. But the largest differences in reported satisfaction are found among the elderly populations. Particularly striking is the difference among the elderly in the proportions satisfied with 'health care services.' The Canadian elderly who had recently been hospitalized expressed particular satisfaction with that aspect of their health care system.

What these data do not provide is insight into the underlying causes of the wide gaps in degree of satisfaction. A leading candidate may be

Table 10.1 PERCENT OF THE PUBLIC WHO REPORTED THEY WERE "VERY
SATISFIED" WITH SERVICES, BY TYPE OF SERVICE

	Canada		United States	
	Total	65 and over	Total	65 and over
Health Care Services	67	77	35	40
Most Recent Doctor's Visit	62	77	54	60
Most Recent Hospital Stay	71	93	57	68

Source: *Three Nations Study*, 1989, unpublished cross tabulation, provided by Institute for the Future, Menlo Park, California.

the different impacts of health care services on the financial security of the elderly in the two countries. The financial exposure of the elderly in Canada and the United States for hospital, medical, and pharmaceutical services provides a striking portrayal of the contrasting impact of 'being old and sick' in the two countries.

HEALTH CARE ENTITLEMENT IN CANADA

Since 1971 Canada has provided universal coverage to its entire population for medically necessary services provided in hospital or by physicians. In addition, all provinces provide some form of coverage for long-term care and pharmaceutical costs.

Each Canadian provincial health ministry holds virtually sole responsibility for managing the major components of health care. Funding for hospital, physician, and some long-term care services is shared by the federal government through transfers of taxing authority (tax points) and cash to the provincial governments. The costs of pharmaceutical benefits are entirely the responsibility of the provinces. The private insurance industry cannot offer hospital or medical care coverage, although it can provide supplementary and amenity (e.g., private hospital room) coverage. Patient financial participation is minimal. There are no 'user fees' (deductibles or coinsurance) for hospital or medical care. Alberta and British Columbia are the only provinces that use health insurance premiums, although the universality provision underlying all provincial plans prevents even these provinces from denying care to those whose premium payments may be in arrears.

As we note in more detail below, coverage for the elderly in Canada is, if anything, even more generous. For those residents over 65, the

Alberta medical premiums are waived, and patient copayments in a number of provincial pharmaceutical programs are reduced or eliminated.

HEALTH CARE ENTITLEMENT IN THE UNITED STATES

Canadian universal coverage stands in marked contrast to the patchwork of health care coverage provided by the American 'system,' the dominant effect of which has been to leave a significant component of the population with no coverage, and many more carrying a burden of substantial financial risk.

Public entitlement to health care benefits in the United States is provided through the Medicare and Medicaid programs, which differ from the Canadian public financing in a number of important ways. In particular, Medicare in the United States is limited to a certain segment of the population (the elderly and some disabled persons), it does not cover all medically necessary hospital and physician services, and it requires substantial beneficiary copayments. Medicare is administered by the federal government and financed largely through compulsory payroll taxes (hospital coverage) and federal contributions from general revenues (medical coverage).

For individuals or services not covered by Medicare, health care benefits may be purchased through employer-based insurance plans or private insurers. Individuals unable to afford health insurance may qualify for a variety of state-sponsored means-tested programs which assess eligibility on the basis of income, resources, and a complex set of family and personal characteristics used to categorize level of need.

Almost all (96 percent) of the elderly American population is covered by Medicare and about 77 percent purchase supplementary health insurance (P. W. Ries, personal communication, 1991). Health care benefits may also be obtained through state-administered Medicaid programs which provide coverage for elderly individuals who have depleted both income and assets on health care costs.

THE 'COSTS' OF UNIVERSALITY

As one might expect, a dramatic divergence in health care cost experience has emerged along with the two countries' divergent approaches to entitlement since 1971. But despite the more complete and comprehensive coverage in Canada, the American has emerged as the more expensive system. By 1989, Canadians were devoting 8.9 percent of their GNP to health care services (Canada, Health and Welfare Canada, preliminary unpublished data, 1991). The equivalent American figure was 11.6 percent (Lazenby and Letsch 1990), and preliminary indications are that the gap is still growing.[1] Put differently, if the United States had spent the Canadian share of economic activity on health care in 1989, close to $150 billion would have been saved and available for other uses. This increasing relative commitment to health care in the United States has not, at least to date, been reflected in improved health status (Evans, Barer, and Hertzman 1991).

The difference in cost experience has been shown elsewhere to rest entirely with three types of activity: hospital care, medical services, and administration. More specifically, the share of GNP going to *medical* services has not increased in Canada since 1971. The difference in Canadian/American experience is attributable to relatively more rapid growth in physician fees in the United States (Evans et al. 1989). For *hospital* care, the difference has been found to rest with more intensive daily service provision in the United States and higher provider-related administrative cost (Newhouse et al. 1988; Woolhandler and Himmelstein 1991). But the most dramatic difference in costs has emerged within the insurer-related *administrative* component where, in 1987, Canada spent 0.1 percent of GNP while the United States spent about 0.6 percent.

Ironically, Canada's relative success with cost control has emerged *because* of its approach to providing universal coverage. A single government agency in each province acts as insurer but also takes on the negotiation and payment for the largest program components. Provincial Ministries (or Departments) of Health negotiate provincial medical fee schedules (and, increasingly, global medical expenditures), global hospital budgets, and retain 'majority' control over capital acquisitions (Barer and Evans 1992). Furthermore, administrative activity is largely centralized within those ministries.

TAKING CARE OF THE ELDERLY

As noted above, this general picture of coverage and financial participation for the Canadian population holds as well for the elderly. In fact, when Canadians turn 65 years of age, their entitlements increase.

The premiums in Alberta disappear. More significantly, all provinces provide some form of noninstitutional pharmaceutical coverage for the elderly and, in those provinces where programs exist for the entire population, deductibles and copayments decline markedly at age 65. In addition, each province has developed its own system for chronic or long-term care. Although some of these systems are more developed than others, all facilitate movement across a spectrum of levels of institutional and community care. The funding of these 'long-term care systems' is derived from a combination of public budgets and private out-of-pocket payments, where the latter are tied to a de facto elderly minimum retirement benefit, and are intended to pay in part for room and board.

In contrast, public entitlement to non-means-tested health care coverage in the United States begins at age 65 with Medicare, extends only to hospital and medical care, and involves considerable private financial participation. Coverage for pharmaceuticals and long-term care for those 65 and over varies considerably across states and is generally means-tested. No state covers nursing home stays other than through the Medicaid program, which requires the recipient to prove that s(he) has virtually no non-housing assets, and a below-poverty level of income.

In the following sections, we describe in more detail the implications of hospital, medical, and pharmaceutical care for the financial security of the elderly in the two countries.

COVERAGE AND COSTS FOR THE ELDERLY IN CANADA

There are no deductibles or copays for medical services in Canada. Provincial medical plans are financed largely from general revenues. Medical premiums for the elderly exist only in British Columbia, and can be as high as $35 (single), or $62 (couple) per month (1991 rates). But there is a relatively generous system of reduced charges tied to income. For the most indigent, premiums are less than $2 per month. In general there are no user fees for services provided by physicians.

There are no hospital premiums or user fees for elderly acute hospital care anywhere in Canada. Room and board charges for continuing hospital care following an acute episode take effect under varying conditions in different provinces. A general principle is that these are levied at the point where the institution is deemed to be the patient's permanent residence. For example, in the province of Manitoba, a 70-

year-old admitted to acute care with a stroke will be provided with 'free' acute care coverage until such time as the attending physician determines that no further physical recovery is likely but the patient still requires in-hospital care. At that point the patient becomes responsible for room and board charges amounting to 85 percent of the OAS/GIS/provincial supplement[2] which, in 1991, is equivalent to leaving a minimum $130.85 'comfort allowance' for the elderly with the least income. Residential charges in most provinces are set as a fraction of the elderly's minimum income (never more than 85 percent of OAS/GIS/provincial supplement, where applicable),[3] and are designed to leave the lowest income patients with a 'living allowance' which for 1991, ranges from about $110 to $130 per month. In a few of the provinces and territories, there are no charges for the hospital-based extension of acute episodes.

The extent and nature of patient financial participation in the ambulatory use of pharmaceuticals is more varied. This is most likely due to the fact that the provinces bear full financial responsibility for 'pharmacare' programs, whereas the evolution of the provincial medical and hospital programs was governed by uniform terms and conditions necessary for federal government cost sharing. Patient financial participation in the ambulatory use of prescribed pharmaceuticals takes the form of combinations of deductibles and copays. The variety of copayment arrangements is presented in table 10.2.

Table 10.2 CHARGES TO SENIOR CITIZENS ENROLLED IN PROVINCIAL DRUG PLANS IN 1991

Province	Beneficiary Charges
British Columbia	75% of dispensing fee up to max. of $125
Alberta	20% copay
Saskatchewan	$50–$75 deductible/year + 25% copay
Manitoba	$96.90 deductible/year + 20% copay
Ontario	NONE
Québec	NONE
New Brunswick	$6.45/Rx up to max. of $150/year
Nova Scotia	20% copay up to max. of $150/year
Prince Edward Island	$4 deductible + dispensing fee
Newfoundland	dispensing fee
Yukon	NONE
Northwest Territories	NONE

Note: Adapted and updated from "Provincial and Territorial Drug Reimbursement Programs Descriptive Summary" (Canada 1990).

The 'most generous' provincial/territorial programs (Ontario, Québec, Northwest Territories, and the Yukon) involve no user fees of any
kind. For 'low users,' the 'least generous' program (Manitoba) involves
an annual deductible of $92.75 as well as a 20 percent copayment for
each prescription. The Prince Edward Island program, which requires
the patient to pay a $4 deductible plus the entire dispensing fee for
each prescription, would appear to be the most financially punitive
for 'high users,' although comparisons of Manitoba and Prince Edward
Island are incomplete in the absence of more detailed information on
the distribution and relative sizes of dispensing and ingredient costs
in the two provinces. In between, we find a variety of combinations
such as that in British Columbia, where those 65 and over are responsible for 75 percent of the dispensing fee to an annual ceiling of $125.

One can piece together an overall picture of financial exposure of
the Canadian elderly for hospital, medical, and pharmaceutical care.
In Ontario, Québec, the Yukon, and Northwest Territories (representing, in total, almost two-thirds of the country's population), the individual patient is at no financial risk for any of these services. In
British Columbia, the combination of *maximum* medical premium
plus *maximum* out-of-pocket pharmaceutical costs amounted to $545/
year in 1991. The mean is much lower (the minimum, for those indigent using no drugs, is about $20 per year). Very high users of phar-
maceuticals in Manitoba or Prince Edward Island incur costs in excess of the British Columbia figure, but these individuals represent
the far right-hand tail of the pharmaceutical cost distribution.

COVERAGE AND COSTS FOR THE ELDERLY
IN THE UNITED STATES

The closest equivalent to Canadian coverage for the American elderly
is the Medicare program. It is a non-means-tested program that provides hospital coverage (Part A) to about 96 percent of the American
population of at least 65 years of age (Part A-eligible). Ambulatory
medical coverage (Part B) may be purchased by those who choose to
enroll (about 99 percent of the Part A-eligible population choose to
enroll for Part B coverage).

Part A-eligible coverage involves no monthly premiums, but there
are extensive user charges. In 1991, patients were responsible for the
first $628 (U.S.) of hospital costs incurred in each 'benefit period'
(defined as the period beginning with an initial hospitalization and

ending only after 60 consecutive nonhospital days). In the event that a hospital stay exceeds 60 days, a daily copayment of $157 is normally incurred for each of the subsequent 30 days. Beyond that, patients may draw on a lifetime 60-day reserve of $314/day copay days (Committee on Ways and Means 1991).

In fact, few patients will remain in acute care for as long as 60 days. More commonly, patients will be transferred to skilled nursing facilities (SNFs) following hospitalization. There they are fully covered for the first 20 days, after which they are responsible for a copay of $78.50/day for the next 80 days.

Those elderly subscribing to Part B (medical) benefits must pay a monthly premium of $29.90, and are responsible for the first $100 of incurred costs and *at least* 20 percent of physicians' 'reasonable charges' beyond that deductible.[4] The Medicare program does not include any ambulatory pharmaceutical coverage. Over 75 percent of the elderly purchase some type of private supplemental insurance policy, the majority of which pay for the deductible and the copayments for those services that Medicare covers (P. W. Ries, personal communication, 1991). The patient must usually pay any extra billing over and above the amount that Medicare deems 'reasonable.' Private supplemental insurance premiums are often substantial, and the average return to these policy-holders in benefits is often no more than 60 percent of the premiums paid for the policies (Rice 1987).

The other major source of public health care benefits for elderly Americans is Medicaid. This is a set of state programs providing coverage for Americans meeting state-determined means-tested eligibility criteria. Eligibility is based on both assets and income, so that individuals generally become eligible for Medicaid benefits only after having exhausted their personal, nonhousing assets and have a disposable income after medical payments that is below, and often much below, the poverty line. As a result, in 1984 only 6.4 percent of the community-dwelling elderly received Medicaid benefits (Ries 1987). This means-tested program is to be distinguished from the Canadian social insurance style programs which are designed to prevent poverty (Marmor, Mashaw, and Harvey 1990). This is done by relating health care charges to income. For example, the hotel charges for extended hospital care are set below the minimum *income* level for the elderly in all provinces except Québec.

In addition to providing hospital and medical coverage over and above that provided through Medicare (for those elderly unable to shoulder the Medicare deductibles and copayments), state Medicaid programs can provide prescription drug entitlements to eligible elderly Americans. Medicaid coverage of prescription drugs is an optional service and states vary on the extent to which this cost is subsidized—Alaska and Wyoming do not offer any form of coverage. Pharmaceutical benefits are also available to the poor, near-poor, or middle-class elderly through some state pharmaceutical assistance programs financed mostly through general funds or lotteries (Soumerai and Ross-Degnan 1990). Since 1977, eleven states have implemented such pharmaceutical assistance programs.

Income restrictions on eligibility for state prescription drug programs (ranging from $6,400–$14,000) are generally less stringent than those imposed by the regular Medicaid program in the state, and most do not impose asset limits or spend-down requirements.[5] Generally, the beneficiary is required to pay an out-of-pocket share, ranging from $1/prescription to 40 percent of prescription costs, to reduce program expenditures and to discourage overutilization. In Illinois there is no copayment but the pharmaceuticals and products covered are severely restricted (Soumerai and Ross-Degnan 1990). The variety of copayments is shown in table 10.3.

The largest of these programs (the Pennsylvania Assistance Contract for the Elderly) is income-tested, not asset-tested, and there are no spend-down requirements. All state residents 65 years or over with annual incomes of less than $12,000 (single) or $15,000 (married) are eligible. Despite these programs, as of about 1991, about 80 percent of the total costs of over-the-counter and prescription drugs were shouldered out of pocket by the elderly in America (Stuart et al. 1991).

While current data sources do not permit creation of a summary out-of-pocket cost estimate for elderly Americans like that described above for Canada, we can develop a rough picture by cobbling together a variety of sectoral estimates. Waldo et al. (1989) report health care expenditures from 'private sources' by sector for 1987. Hospital

Table 10.3 CHARGES TO SENIOR CITIZENS ENROLLED IN SELECTED STATE
PHARMACEUTICAL PLANS IN 1988

State	Beneficiary Copayment
New Jersey	$2/Rx
Maine	up to $10
Maryland	$1/Rx
Pennsylvania	$4/Rx
Illinois	NONE
Connecticut	$4/Rx
New York	up to 40%

Note: Adapted from Soumerai and Ross-Degnan (1991, Exhibit 2).

expenditures totaled $333 per capita; physician expenditures amounted to $393. These estimates combine private out-of-pocket payments and payments from private insurers and other nongovernment sources. Thus they underestimate total out-of-pocket costs for two reasons. First, any premium payments to private insurers will exceed expenditures on medical and hospital care by the amount of their retained earnings and administrative expenses. This is corroborated by Rice (1987) who estimates that the 'loss-ratios' for premiums paid to private insurers were approximately 76 percent in 1986. In other words, 24 percent of insurance company premium dollars is retained for administration and profit. Second, premiums paid to Medicare are not included in the above figures (Waldo and Lazenby 1984).

Additionally, these figures do not include private copayments for Medicare-financed SNF stays, which are short, post-hospital stays. Silverman (1991) reports that the average number of Medicare-covered SNF days of care for ever-users in 1987 was 25.3 days. Since the first 20 days of SNF care involve no copays under Medicare, this leaves 5.3 days, on average, for which the patient would bear the (1987) $65/day copay cost.[6] But only about 1 percent of Medicare enrollees used the Medicare SNF benefit in 1987. Therefore, the average per-enrollee private cost in 1987 would have been about $3.50. This would raise our 'hospital' estimate from $333 to $337.

We know that the 1987 Medicare Part B premium was $180. Furthermore, Waldo (1987) provides a 1987 estimate of out-of-pocket costs for outpatient prescription drugs of $304 for those over 65 years of age. Piecing these figures together produces a 'best underestimate' of average per capita expenditures on hospital, medical, and pharmaceutical services incurred by the elderly, of approximately $1,215 (U.S.). Of course this is an underestimate of the mean for the reasons noted earlier. Furthermore, there will be many elderly for whom private expenditures will be far higher, because costs for all three components are functions of rates of use (they all involve copayments).

Alternative estimates for hospital and medical care, for 1985 and 1990, can be pieced together using data from the Committee on Ways and Means (1991). This source reports 1985 average out-of-pocket expenses (copays, balance-billing and premiums) for hospital and medical care under the Medicare program, of $627. The equivalent figure for 1990 is $1,002. Subtracting the pharmaceutical component from our 'best underestimate' above yields a figure for 1987 of $906. The $627 and $1,002 exclude average payments by the elderly for private supplementary coverage. Even so, our 'underestimate' appears to be in the right 'ballpark.'

UNCLE SAM RETIRES IN VICTORIA: AN ELDERLY AMERICAN IN CANADA

Against this picture of costs incurred by the average elderly American, one can speculate as to the costs that same American would have incurred in Canada. Assuming the individual in question chose to retire in Victoria (or elsewhere in B.C.), (s)he would have been responsible for an annual medical care premium of not more than $240 in 1987. In addition, if (s)he had used the average number of prescriptions as reported by Waldo (1987) for elderly Americans in 1987 (17 prescriptions), and we assume the dispensing fee on each prescription was $5, (s)he would have incurred ambulatory pharmaceutical costs of $68 (75 percent of dispensing fee), for a total of $308 (Canadian), or about $250 U.S., expressed in 1987 purchasing power parity dollars.

If instead this individual had retired in Prince Edward Island, (s)he would have incurred greater pharmaceutical costs ($153), but would not have been responsible for medical premiums. In all other provinces, the total out-of-pocket plus premium costs would have been less. In fact, this individual would have incurred no such direct costs in a number of provinces and territories.

More recent data, while incomplete, suggest that, if anything, this Canada–U.S. gap in costs assumed personally has increased rather dramatically. By 1991 our retiree would be paying $510 in B.C. or $187 in Prince Edward Island. Because premiums have been eliminated in Ontario, these costs in that province would have fallen to zero. But if (s)he had stayed in the United States, average out-of-pocket pharmaceutical costs for the elderly would have increased to $432 (U.S.) in 1991 (projected), up from $304 in 1987 (Waldo 1987). Furthermore, the Medicare premium doubled over this period, and all the copays increased significantly. In particular, the projected total of out-of-pocket and premium costs for Medicare in 1990 is $1,002, up from $627 in 1985 (Committee on Ways and Means 1991).

Lost in this discussion of 'average cost profiles' is the fact that the Canadian elderly are not exposed to catastrophic financial risk. They are not responsible for any direct payments for medical or hospital care. In addition, most of the Canadian pharmaceutical programs for the elderly involve out-of-pocket ceilings and, in any case, ambulatory prescription costs are the smallest, and most predictable, of the three health care components. Even in those provinces without pharmaceutical cost ceilings, the right-hand tail of the total out-of-pocket cost distribution is well to the left of the *mean* equivalent costs in the United States.

To estimate out-of-pocket costs for high users in Canada, we turned to the British Columbia pharmacare database. It turned out that in 1988/89, 0.5 percent of British Columbia's elderly generated more than $2,200 in ambulatory pharmaceutical billings, and about 2 percent received more than 50 prescriptions. What financial responsibilities would this level of drug use create in provinces with the least generous pharmaceutical coverage? In Manitoba it would have translated into less than $600 per year total out-of-pocket costs for the tiny segment of very high prescription drug users. In Prince Edward Island, 60 prescriptions would also generate out-of-pocket costs of about $600.[7]

In marked contrast, elderly Americans without comprehensive private health insurance face potential economic ruin from hospital, medical, and pharmaceutical costs. In order to qualify for public health coverage beyond that offered by Medicare, they must first deplete both income and assets to pay such costs. The *maximum* imaginable out-of-pocket costs in Canada are in all likelihood less than half the *mean* equivalent costs in the United States.

PATTERNS OF SERVICE USE

In this section we bring together utilization data from the two countries that suggest that, despite the dramatic differences documented above, changes in age-related patterns of *utilization* have been remarkably similar. The differences in the health care systems in the two countries dictate different sources of utilization data. In particular, data from comprehensive provincial administrative data sets in Canada must be compared with data derived from surveys in the United States. Nevertheless, some generalizations are possible.

In figure 10.1 we show physician visits per capita for the United States, taken from the National Ambulatory Medical Care Survey for 1975 and 1985 (Nelson and McLemore 1988). These data are based on records kept by a sample of ambulatory care physicians during a one-

Figure 10.1 U.S. PHYSICIAN VISITS PER PERSON, 1985 VERSUS 1975

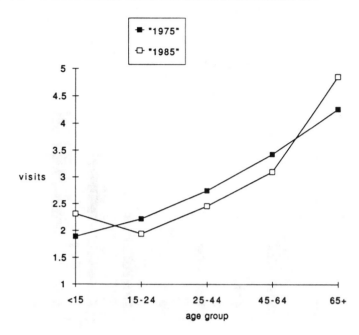

Source: National Ambulatory Medical Care Survey.

week period, and do not include certain types of physicians, or care provided by physicians in institutions. There was an increase in per capita use by the 65-and-over group relative to the rest of the adult population. While per capita visits by persons in this age group increased 13 percent over this 10-year period, visits by persons in the three large adult (or young adult) age categories under 65 decreased by 10 to 13 percent.

A 'pseudo-equivalent' set of representative Canadian age-use curves is shown in figure 10.2. These data, from British Columbia over the period 1974–75 to 1985–86, are based on deflated total medical expenditures per capita by age (Barer et al. 1989).[8] Thus, they involve a different method of estimating utilization, and they incorporate more services than do the American data in figure 10.1 because they include services provided by all physicians, wherever provided. Furthermore, while we are primarily interested in patterns of change, even a comparison of this nature may be compromised if the relative importance of nonvisit billings changed in B.C. over this period. This information is not readily available.

Figure 10.2 DEFLATED PHYSICIAN BILLINGS PER CAPITA, BY PATIENT AGE,
BRITISH COLUMBIA

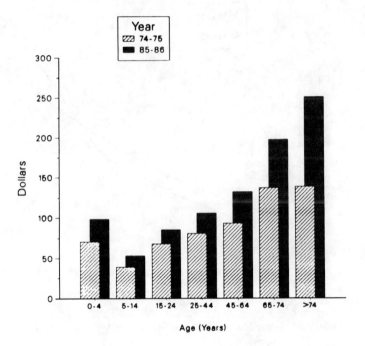

Despite these numerous caveats, the patterns of change in medical utilization for the elderly are remarkably similar. That is, relative to the rest of the adult and adolescent population, utilization per capita increased more rapidly among the elderly in both settings.[9] Similar limited comparisons of age-related changes in hospital utilization are possible. Unlike the medical care data above, where we were forced to compare ambulatory visits with total deflated expenditures, we do have roughly comparable measures of use: separations or hospitalizations per capita. However, in this case the new potential source of contamination is the definition of 'hospital.'

In particular, our U.S. data are taken from various reports on the annual National Hospital Discharge Survey. Since 1965, the National Center for Health Statistics has collected standardized discharge abstracts, for patients with stays of less than 30 days, from a stratified sample of approximately 300 to 400 hospitals representative of the universe of U.S. short-stay general and specialty hospitals. The U.S. statistics reported here exclude discharges of newborn infants but include discharges of women who have given birth (Pokras and Kozak 1984).

In contrast, the published data that we report here for British Columbia are again population-based, and represent separations from acute and rehabilitation care hospital beds. There was no length-of-stay cutoff employed in compiling the statistics. Nevertheless, within each jurisdiction the definitions and inclusions serve to some extent as their own controls, since our primary interest here is in patterns of change over time rather than absolute levels of use.

Figure 10.3 shows age-specific patterns of hospitalization in the United States in 1965 and 1987. Over this period there was a dramatic shift toward greater use of hospital capacity by persons 65 and over relative to the rest of the population (the rate of increase for the 75+ group exceeded even that for those <1 year of age). Since 1983, rates of hospitalization have declined for all age groups, but the rate of

Figure 10.3 U.S. HOSPITALIZATIONS PER 1000 BY AGE GROUP, 1987 VERSUS 1965

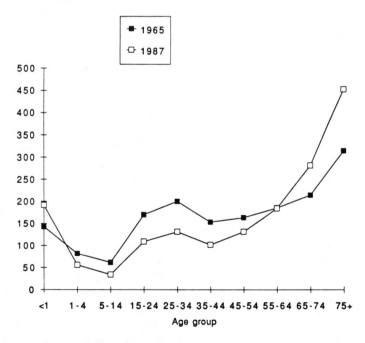

Source: National Hospital Discharge Survey.

decline among the elderly has been considerably lower than for the rest of the population (Pokras and Kozak 1984; Graves 1985, 1987, 1989).

Age-use curves for acute and rehabilitation hospitals in British Columbia are shown in figure 10.4 (Barer et al. 1987). Here we note the similarity in pattern: overall declines in rates of hospitalization, but increases for the elderly. The 'cross-over' point in the B.C. data was found at the 65 to 74 age group, whereas for the U.S. data it occurred in the 55 to 64 group.

In summary, the similar changes in patterns of hospital and medical service use among elderly Americans and Canadians suggest that these Americans are changing their use of services relative to other age groups in a similar way, but are paying more for the privilege and are 'enjoying' it less than their Canadian counterparts. This raises an obvious question about whether the additional financial pain yields any health status gain.

LONGER AND HEALTHIER, OR GRIMMER AND POORER?

One of the few places where one does find apparently comparable data is in the vital statistics of the two countries. Life expectancy at birth in 1985 was 1.7 years higher for Canadian males, and 1.6 years higher for Canadian females. Supplementary life expectancy at age 65 was also higher in Canada: 0.4 years for males; 0.7 years for females (Adams and Nagnur 1988; U.S. Bureau of the Census 1989). However, the latter differentials emerged in the early 1950s, well in advance of the evolution of the Canadian national health insurance programs. American elderly are not living longer. On the other hand, this may have nothing to do with the respective health insurance coverage for the elderly.

Attempting comparisons beyond relatively basic life expectancy data makes comparing utilization data look like a walk in the park. One might expect differential effects of the entitlement programs to be reflected in relative disability rates. However, such data are all survey-based, and are derived from different questions offered in different contexts and at different points in time, in the two countries. What we can cobble together would suggest that there are no large differences in the prevalence of disability among the elderly. Canadian sources suggest disability rates ranging anywhere from 34 percent to 45 percent of the elderly population (Charette 1988; Furrie and

Figure 10.4 HOSPITAL AGE-USE CURVES IN BRITISH COLUMBIA, 1971 AND 1982/83.
(A) MALE SEPARATIONS PER THOUSAND POPULATION (B) FEMALE
SEPARATIONS PER THOUSAND POPULATION

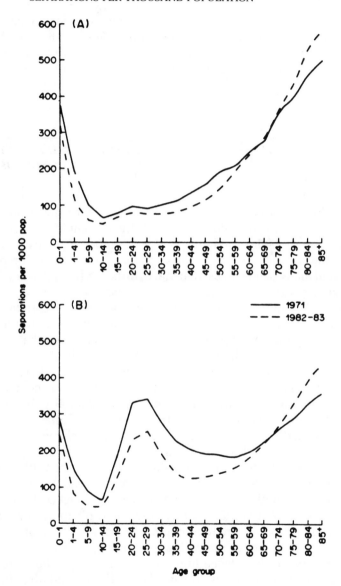

Note: The upper chart (A) shows male separations per 1,000 population; the lower chart
(B) shows female separations per 1,000 population.

Coombs 1990). Two American sources suggest a 'comparable' range of 24 percent to 45 percent in that country (Manton 1989; Meyer and Moon 1988).

While these crude comparisons leave many questions unanswered, they are consistent with an extension of our earlier statement. American elderly are using services in a similar way, paying more for the privilege, 'enjoying' it less, and are no healthier than their Canadian counterparts.

DATA NEEDED FOR BETTER NORTH AMERICAN COMPARISONS

Beyond this rather basic concluding statement, our discussion raises a host of interesting questions for which the current state of comparative data prevents the development of more informed answers. In this concluding section we offer a partial menu of uniform data requirements and data deficiencies that need to be addressed in order to enable better North American comparative work in this area.

Some of the uniform data requirements are simply corollaries of common sense. We need, for example, to have common definitions of the various types of facilities and physician services so that we can be sure we are comparing 'like with like' in medical and hospital utilization. We need common health status measures, derived from analogous sampling strategies, which are collected at comparable points in time. Without these instruments and data, it will continue to be impossible either to compare the relative health status of American and Canadian elderly, or to monitor relative changes in health status, in comparable ways, over time.

Despite the best efforts of various investigators in the United States (Lazenby and Letsch 1990; Waldo 1987; Waldo and Lazenby 1984; Waldo et al. 1989), the American data regarding direct costs of health care to the elderly are awkward to access and difficult to summarize. There is a need for information on premium payments alongside out-of-pocket costs in a form that will allow investigators to estimate the total financing burden placed upon the elderly. As an adjunct to this, it would be extremely useful to have data collected and organized in a way that would facilitate the estimation of the proportion of American elderly who are actually driven to accepting Medicaid because health care costs have exhausted their assets.

Two relatively unexplored frontiers in both countries are the costs of assistive devices and indirect payments for health care through taxes. In both countries a welter of fragmented programs provide assistive devices for the disabled, from prostheses to home renovation for those needing wheelchair accessibility, electric staircases, and other environmental modifications. At present, there is no well-organized information on entitlements, either in Canada or the United States.

The issue of taxation is very important because, although the elderly in Canada pay far less for health care in direct out-of-pocket costs and premiums, we would expect that some of this difference would be made up from the elderly's contribution to health care through income, sales, and other taxes. It should be a relatively simple matter to estimate what proportion of each tax dollar funneled to the federal, provincial or state, and local governments is spent on health care.[10] However, this information would need to be combined with estimates of taxes collected by each of these levels of government from elderly individuals in different ranges of income. When this information is combined with the costs of assistive devices and, in turn, combined with our existing information about hospital, medical, and pharmaceutical costs, it will be possible to reconstruct the total financial burden of medical care in each country in a 'cross-sectional' way. That is to say, it will be possible to estimate the total direct and taxation costs for the average American or Canadian elderly person at a given point in time and also for those whose costs are at the maximum and minimum of the spectrum.

The latter achievement would provide a very useful snapshot of the financial security implications of health care for the elderly. But the most relevant picture would likely be more like a movie: introducing the element of time. We would ultimately like to be able to reconstruct the cost scenarios for a variety of individuals as they age, become sick, and confront disability and dependence. In other words, we need to be able to link information on the financial security implications of acute care, chronic care, home care, assistive devices, drugs, and miscellaneous costs (such as paying security guards to accompany home care workers into inner city neighborhoods in the United States) in order to accurately describe the relative prospects facing the elderly in Canada and the United States when their health begins to fail.

Finally, a heretofore unexplored aspect of the comparative situations of elderly Canadian and American residents is the possible link between health-care-related financial risk, and ill health. Could it be that health care costs for elderly Americans are in part economic-stress-induced by-products of the American health care financial quilt? The data demands of such an investigation are immense. But it is a question worth exploring.

Notes

We gratefully acknowledge the assistance of a number of Canadian provincial and territorial Ministry of Health staff who provided many of the data on which this paper is based. We are also particularly indebted to Roberta Labelle for her help in explaining the complex variations in long term care out-of-pocket costs across Canadian provincial plans, and to Helen Heacock for helping us sort out the provincial pharmaceutical benefit programs. State-side, we owe a particular thanks to Daniel Waldo, Health Care Financing Administration, for assistance with interpreting U.S. statistics, and to Ian Morrison, Institute for the Future, for providing unpublished data on elderly patients' satisfaction with alternative health care systems and services. Finally, without the persistent prodding of Ted Marmor, this chapter would never have happened. We wish to implicate none of the above in any errors or omissions that remain. [By agreement, an almost identical version of this chapter appeared in the *Journal of Health Politics, Policy and Law*, vol. 17, no. 4, pp. 763–782. It has not been updated to reflect developments since submission to that journal. Eds.]

1. Some American analysts have suggested that the comparison of shares of GNP is inappropriate in this context, and that the relevant comparison should be to relative experiences with real per capita costs (Neuschler 1990; Feder, Scanlon, and Clark 1987). This position finds no support either in theory or empirical evidence. See Barer, Welch, and Antioch (1991).

2. The elderly in all provinces are entitled to a minimum income deriving from a variety of federal programs. These include OAS (Old Age Security), GIS (Guaranteed Income Supplement), and provincial need-based supplements (e.g. GAIN (Guaranteed Annual Income for Need)). All residents 65 and over are entitled to OAS, GIS is a federal income-tested supplement, and most provinces administer a variant of a GAIN program. Québec, New Brunswick, Prince Edward Island, and Newfoundland do not offer a provincial need-based supplement (Canada 1989).

3. Charges for long-term care in non-hospital-program facilities can, in some provinces, exceed this maximum for those with sufficient means. See chapter 12 for further discussion of long-term care in the two countries.

4. For physicians who "accept assignment," the maximum charge for which the patient is responsible is 20 percent of the Medicare-approved charge. For physicians not on assignment, the patient is responsible for any difference that may exist between the approved and actual charge, although such physicians may elect to accept the Medicare-approved charge as payment in full.

5. Spending down under Medicaid is a two-step process. First, the individual must meet the assets test: the value of the individual's resources (generally defined as liquid assets) must be less than a state-determined dollar standard. Second, once an individual has depleted virtually all accumulated resources on health care costs, income standards are then considered (Committee on Ways and Means 1991).

6. Of course these figures refer only to "covered" SNF days of care. As Rice and Gabel (1986) noted, the average length of stay in SNFs may exceed Medicare-covered days by

a considerable margin, leaving the patient fully responsible for the costs of uncovered days.

7. We apply British Columbia utilization data to the copayment provisions in the provinces with the most costly programs because utilization data from Manitoba and P.E.I. were not readily available.

8. The B.C. pattern is mirrored in data from other provinces (Gormley et al. 1990; Roch, Evans, and Pascoe 1985).

9. It is interesting that the U.S. survey data show **declines** in use of services for those ages 15 to 64, whereas all age groups increased their medical utilization in British Columbia. This may reflect, although present data do not allow us to confirm it, an increasing gap in rates of use among the insured relative to the less-well-insured in the United States. While Medicare benefits in the United States may be sufficient to remove some access barriers for the elderly, the growing numbers of un- and under-insured cluster in the 15- to 64-year-old groups. Such an interpretation, however, may not be sustained through further investigation. We already know, for example, that physician contact data taken from the National Health Interview Survey do not reveal a similar pattern for 1966–67 to 1981. In fact, adults age 45 to 64 reported greater increases than did those over 75!

10. Neuschler (1990) has provided some preliminary estimates of the relative tax burdens in the two countries. But his analysis does not focus explicitly on tax burdens for the elderly.

References

Adams, O., and D. Nagnur. 1988. *Life Tables for Canada, 1984–1986.* Statistics Canada, Ottawa.

Barer, M. L., and R. G. Evans. 1992. "The Meeting of the Twain: Managing Health Care Capital and Costs in Canada." In *The Changing Health Care Economy: Impact on Physicians, Patients and Innovators,* edited by J. Wennberg and A. Gelijns. Washington, D.C.: National Academy Press.

Barer, M. L., W. P. Welch, and L. Antioch. 1991. "Canadian/U.S. Health Care: Reflections on the HIAA's Analysis." *Health Affairs* 10(3): 229–36.

Barer, M. L., R. G. Evans, C. Hertzman, and J. Lomas. 1987. "Aging and Health Care Utilization: New Evidence on Old Fallacies." *Social Sciences and Medicine* 24(10): 851–62.

Barer, M. L., I. R. Pulcins, R. G. Evans, C. Hertzman, J. Lomas, and G. M. Anderson. 1989. "Trends in Use of Medical Services by the Elderly in British Columbia." *Canadian Medical Assocociation Journal* 141(1): 39–45.

Blendon, R. J. 1989. "Three Systems: A Comparative Survey." *Health Management Quarterly* (First Quarter): 2–10.

Blendon, R. J., and K. Donelan. 1990. "The Public and the Emerging Debate Over National Health Insurance." *New England Journal of Medicine* 323(3): 208–12.

Blendon, R. J., and H. Taylor. 1989. "Views On Health Care: Public Opinion In Three Nations." *Health Affairs* 8(1): 149–57.

Blendon, R. J., R. Leitman, I. Morrison, and K. Donelan. 1990. "Satisfaction With Health Systems in Ten Nations." *Health Affairs* 9(2): 185–192.

Canada. 1989. *Basic Facts On Social Security Programs.* Ottawa: Health and Welfare Canada.

————. 1990. "Provincial and Territorial Drug Reimbursement Programs: Descriptive Summary." Ottawa: Health and Welfare Canada.

Charette, A. 1988. "Special Study On Adults With An Activity Limitation." Technical Report Series, Canada's Health Promotion Survey. Ottawa: Health and Welfare Canada.

Committee on Ways and Means, U.S. Congress, House of Representatives. 1991. *Background Material and Data on Programs Within the Jurisdiction of the Committee on Ways and Means.* Washington, D.C.: U.S. Government Printing Office.

Evans, R. G., M. L. Barer, and C. Hertzman. 1991. "The 20-Year Experiment: Accounting for, Explaining, and Evaluating Health Care Cost Containment In Canada and the United States." *Annual Review of Public Health* 12: 481–518.

Evans, R. G., J. Lomas, M. L. Barer, R. J. Labelle, C. Fooks et al. 1989. "Controlling Health Expenditures—the Canadian Reality." *New England Journal of Medicine* 320(9): 571–577.

Feder, J., W. Scanlon, and J. Clark. 1987. "Canada's Health Care System" (Letter to the Editor). *New England Journal of Medicine* 317: 320.

Furrie, A., and J. Coombs. 1990. *A Profile of Persons With Disabilities In Canada.* Ottawa: Statistics Canada.

Gormley, M., M. L. Barer, P. Melia, and D. Helston. 1990. *The Growth In Use of Health Services 1977/78 to 1985/86.* Regina: Saskatchewan Health.

Graves, E. J. 1985. *Utilization of Short-Stay Hospitals, United States, 1983 Annual Summary.* National Center for Health Statistics. Vital and Health Statistics. Series 13, no. 83. Washington, D.C.: U.S. Government Printing Office.

————. 1987. *Utilization of Short-Stay Hospitals, United States, 1985.* National Center for Health Statistics. Vital and Health Statistics. Series 13, no. 91. Washington, D.C.: U.S. Government Printing Office.

————. 1989. *National Hospital Discharge Survey: Annual Summary 1987.* National Center for Health Statistics. Vital and Health Statistics. Series 13, no. 99. Washington, D.C.: U.S. Government Printing Office.

Lazenby, H. C., and S. W. Letsch. 1990. "National Health Expenditures." *Health Care Financing Review* 12(2): 1–26.

Manton, K. G. 1989. "Epidemiological, Demographic and Social Correlates of Disability Among the Elderly." *Milbank Quarterly* 67(suppl. 2, part 1): 13–58.

Marmor, T. R., J. L. Mashaw, and P. L. Harvey. 1990. *America's Misunderstood Welfare State: Persistent Myths, Enduring Realities.* New York: Basic Books.

Meyer, J., and M. Moon. 1988. "Health Care Spending On Children and the Elderly." In *The Vulnerable,* edited by J. L. Palmer, T. Smeeding, and B. B. Torrey (171–200). Washington, D.C.: Urban Institute Press.

Nelson, C., and T. McLemore. 1988. *The National Ambulatory Medical Survey: United States, 1975–81 and 1985 Trends.* National Center for Health Statistics. Vital and Health Statistics. Series 13, no. 93. Washington, D.C.: U.S. Government Printing Office.

Neuschler, E. 1990. *Canadian Health Care: The Implications of Public Health Insurance.* Washington, D.C.: Health Insurance Association of America.

Newhouse, J. P., G. M. Anderson, and L. L. Roos. 1988. "Hospital Spending in the United States and Canada: A Comparison." *Health Affairs* 7(5): 6–16.

Pokras, R., and L. J. Kozak. 1984. "Adjustment of Hospital Utilization Rates, United States, 1965–1980." National Center for Health Statistics. Vital and Health Statistics. Series 13, no. 81. Washington, D.C.: U.S. Government Printing Office.

Rice, T. 1987. "An Economic Assessment of Health Care Coverage for the Elderly." *Milbank Quarterly* 66: 488–520.

Rice, T., and J. Gabel. 1986. "Protecting the Elderly Against High Health Care Costs." *Health Affairs* 5(3): 5–21.

Ries, P. 1987. "Health Care Coverage by Socio-Demographic and Health Characteristics, United States, 1984." National Center for Health Statistics. Vital and Health Statistics. Series 10, no. 162. Washington, D.C.: U.S. Government Printing Office.

Roch, D. J., R. G. Evans, and D. Pascoe. 1985. *Manitoba and Medicare: 1971 to the Present.* Winnipeg: Manitoba Health.

Silverman, H. A. 1991. "Medicare-Covered Skilled Nursing Facility Services, 1977–1988." *Health Care Financing Review* 12(3): 103–108.

Soumerai, S. B., and D. Ross-Degnan. 1990. "Experience of State Drug Benefit Programs." *Health Affairs* 9(3): 36–54.

Stuart, B., F. Ahern, V. Rabatin, and A. Johnston. 1991. "Patterns of Outpatient Prescription Drug Use Among Pennsylvania Elderly." *Health Care Financing Review* 12(3): 61–72.

U.S. Bureau of the Census. 1989. *Statistical Abstract of the United States: 1989 (109th Edition).* Washington, D.C.

Waldo, D. R. 1987. "Outpatient Prescription Drug Spending By the Medicare Population." *Health Care Financing Review* 9(1): 83–89.

Waldo, D. R., and H. C. Lazenby. 1984. "Demographic Characteristics and Health Care Use and Expenditures By the Aged in the United States: 1977–1984." *Health Care Financing Review* 6(1): 1–29.

Waldo, D. R., S. T. Sonnefeld, D. R. McKusick, and R. H. Arnett III. 1989. "Health Expenditures By Age-Group, 1977 and 1987." *Health Care Financing Review* 10(4): 111–120.

Woolhandler, S., and D. U. Himmelstein. 1991. "The Deteriorating Administrative Efficiency of the U.S. Health Care System." *New England Journal of Medicine* 324: 1253–1258.

Chapter Eleven

LONG-TERM CARE IN THE UNITED STATES: PROBLEMS AND PROMISE

Robert L. Kane

The concurrent trends of an aging population and escalating health system costs have thrust the problem of caring for the elderly who can no longer care for themselves into the policy spotlight. Such care is known as long-term care, to distinguish it from health care directed to preventing or curing illness, although the distinction is not as clear or clean as it might seem at first.

Forecasts for the future suggest that without extensive change the long-term care burden will grow much larger. The long-term care system has historically reacted to external forces, largely around issues of payment and regulation. These forces will continue to exert pressure, which will surely change the nature and shape of services, but the industry has the opportunity to take a more active stance. By offering alternatives and promoting positive steps needed to improve both quality and effectiveness, it may be possible to find a way to meet the projected needs of the next generation of long-term care (LTC) clients without bankrupting the country. The first important step is to recognize that defining LTC correctly is key to wise policy development.

WHAT IS LONG-TERM CARE?

The essence of long-term care is caring for those who have lost at least some capacity to care for themselves. The common theme of LTC is dependence, a reliance on the personal assistance of another person. Generally those who can use some prosthetic device to maintain their functioning are still considered independent for purposes of LTC, even though they may be eligible for disability payments. The range of possible services is wide. They can include food and shelter as well as services. Some LTC is construed to include social activities and stimulation.

Although this chapter and the next discuss LTC in terms of services for the functionally impaired elderly, LTC is not an age-restricted concept. Depending on one's definition, at least as many persons under age 65 need long-term care services as over that age. (If one includes the chronically mentally ill, the numbers of younger persons are even larger.) Nonetheless, the proportion of persons needing LTC increases with age, and forecasts call for more dependent older persons as the population ages (Kemper and Murtaugh 1991).

Nor can LTC be defined by site of care, although popular culture seems to use site of care as a basis for some definitions. Thus, terms emerge like "hospital care" and "ambulatory care" in the acute care sector and "home care," "day care," and "nursing home care" in the long-term care sector. But new technologies and more innovation have made those distinctions dysfunctional. Services that used to be delivered in only one setting can now be offered in several. Long-term care can occur in hospitals, and acute care can be delivered in nursing homes and at home.

Even time may not differentiate LTC from other types of care, despite the implications of the words. LTC is generally considered to last for a prolonged period, but the term "short-term long-term care" has been used by some to describe the often brief post-hospital care delivered in LTC settings, especially since Medicare's prospective payment system for hospitals has increased the pressure for prompt patient discharge. LTC has generally been considered as following acute care, but the boundaries between the two are indistinct. The recent change in how American hospitals are paid has blurred the distinction even more. With the shift to fixed diagnosis-based payments for hospitals under Medicare (the DRG system), there have been incentives to shorten lengths of hospital stay (Kahn et al. 1990). As a result, the determination of a time of discharge from hospital has become arbitrary. With ever-earlier discharges, a new form of care has arisen, post-acute care, ironically very like the recuperative care originally envisioned under Medicare but never effectively implemented under the cost payment approach to hospital reimbursement for lack of incentives to hospitals to use it (Neu and Harrison 1988, Gutterman et al. 1988). Nor does using LTC make one ineligible for acute care. A part of long-term care is the provision of primary health care service; conversely, older persons receiving long-term care frequently need to be hospitalized. Thus, there is no orderly time sequencing for acute and long-term care. They may be alternating or concurrent. It is important to note, however, that the trigger for LTC is often some form of physical or mental dependency that is the residue from an acute care episode. As discussed further, this fact highlights the centrality of acute care coverage in any long-term care coverage system.

LTC is composed of a number of different kinds of services provided by very different kinds of people. Many of the services resemble those that are provided by family when such family members are willing and able to provide them. LTC is much less technological than health care. It uses fewer professional personnel and less sophisticated equipment. It is labor intensive, and the labor is predominantly minimally trained persons, often immigrants. The latter is not surprising, given that much personal care is both physically taxing and aesthetically unpleasant.

The nonprofessional aspects of LTC are reflected in the often quoted statistic that some large proportion of LTC (usually around 80–85 percent) is provided by so-called informal caregivers (i.e., friends and family). This figure is encountered in survey after survey (Kane and Kane 1990). It is also asserted that when formal home-based services are made available through provincial programs in Canada or through demonstration and waiver projects in the United States, families continue to provide much of the care. This statement is true in that the volume of family care remains high, but it may mask some important facts. When formal care is available, the services provided by formal sources are different from those offered by informal caregivers. The latter are largely made up of such activities as housekeeping, money management, transportation, and shopping, whereas the formal services are more likely to offer personal care, such as assistance with bathing (Stephens and Christianson 1986). Both sources are important, as is the need to resist the tendency to view one form of service as a replacement for the other, a tendency more pronounced in the United States than in Canada.

The touchstone of LTC has been the nursing home, an institution with a mixed heritage rooted in both the hospital and the alms house. Because LTC has an institutional prototype, it includes both hotel and nursing services, but its hospital model base places more emphasis on the latter and often fails to recognize the importance of the former for those who may be spending all or most of their remaining days under its roof. Different types of institutions, residential settings, and care programs have evolved, representing different points along the spectrum of relative emphasis on nursing and home. But as older persons age in place, their needs change and the residents of one type of institution begin to more closely resemble those of the other. Because the relationship between type and site of care is tenuous at best, the same levels of disability can be managed in quite varied settings. This fundamental characteristic has been insufficiently recognized in the past and is key to wise policy development in the future as the elderly segments of the population grow and the younger generations who both provide and pay for their care shrink.

THE HISTORICAL CONTEXT OF LONG-TERM CARE IN THE UNITED STATES

Because of the dominant historical role played by the nursing home, much of the policy discussion about LTC deals with either how to address or displace nursing homes. In large measure, the modern nursing home is a creation of federal legislation in the mid-1960s, designed to purchase for the disenfranchised health care similar to that available for the more affluent. The elderly, who had been gradually priced out of the private health insurance market by a process of risk rating rather than community rating, were to be covered by a virtually universal program appended to Social Security—Medicare—while the poor were to be covered by a welfare program—Medicaid. Most expected that the needs of the elderly would be met by Medicare, but the Medicare program was modeled closely on what was available in the private health sector of the time. Hence, its center was the hospital and its epicenter the physician. Other modalities were considered to the extent that they provided services to extend the period of recuperation after hospitalization or offered services that might be used in lieu of such care.

The Medicaid program was intended to fill a similar role for the poor, who were thought of primarily as those eligible for categorical welfare programs (families of dependent children, blind and disabled, chronically disabled, needy elderly). The benefits under Medicaid were made a little broader because its founders recognized that the recipients (a) had no other means of purchasing care and (b) suffered from social as well as physical ills. No one at the time anticipated that Medicaid might be the major payer of long-term care, especially nursing home care.

But Medicaid had a sleeper. It contained a provision that permitted states to include among those eligible for the program persons who became medically needy by virtue of their high medical care costs. When their medical bills exceeded a certain percentage of their monthly income, they could be covered. In a number of states this eligibility criterion became a major vehicle for coverage of older persons with heavy health care expenditures. For many, the largest regular expenditure is nursing home care. Medically indigent elderly, many in nursing homes, became significant items in state budgets. Soon the Medicaid programs were not only major items in the state budgets; they were seen as covering primarily two types of services: care for newborns and nursing home care.

Because the cost of a nursing home can be reasonably well estimated in advance (in contrast to home care, which may vary in intensity over time), it can be used as the basis for determining Medicaid eligibility in advance. Thus, a person in a nursing home where the monthly costs of such care can be calculated to exceed her income (especially if it derives exclusively from a Social Security retirement pension) can be deemed eligible for Medicaid, whereas a person accruing home care costs prospectively will reach the same state only after she has first spent all her own funds. This situation creates another subtle but real incentive to use nursing homes for those at or near medical poverty.

The framers of Medicare and Medicaid did not think much about long-term care at the time. When they did, they pictured chronic care facilities or intensive home care, under whose auspices elderly patients could recuperate after hospitalization at a lower daily cost. Medicare's institutional sites were called "extended care facilities" to emphasize this role of providing post-hospital service. Home health care under Medicare was specifically targeted at those needing intermittent rather than custodial care. The Medicaid program made provisions for "skilled nursing homes," which were intended, as the name implies, to provide care requiring nursing attention. Home care was included in a set of optional benefits. Little thought was given to those needing chronic maintenance, but little had been given to them before.

The two major coverage programs of the mid-1960s brought with them regulations and standards for participation. Two forces shaped the standard setting: the pressure of time and the fear of catastrophes. Faced with the task of creating standards quickly for a modality of care that was largely unfamiliar, federal and state bureaucracies turned to models that were available. One of these was the small hospital. A federal program to support the construction of rural hospitals had created blueprints and standards for construction and staffing, offering a great temptation to envision nursing homes as miniature hospitals, a view not at variance with that of the programs' framers. At the same time, there was a great fear of headline-grabbing catastrophes, especially fires—fear fueled by widespread scandals following introduction of Medicare and Medicaid (Mendelson 1974; Moss and Halamandaris 1977). Thus, the regulations placed strong emphasis on issues of life-safety (wide corridors, fire doors, sprinkler systems), elements already incorporated into the hospital plans. Likewise, staffing requirements were designed to provide an environment more akin to that of a small hospital, with a strong complement of trained nurses to care for patients recuperating from an acute-care hospital episode.

The results were two. First, in the early years few facilities could meet the standards. The Medicaid program was threatened with an embarrassing situation in which it promised coverage but excluded the places needed to provide it. By 1971, bureaucratic ingenuity found a way out of the dilemma by creating a new class of facilities, intermediate care facilities, which would not have to meet such stringent requirements, especially around staffing. Second, the strong emphasis on structural elements, especially life-safety features, meant that many of the original nursing homes, which had emerged from boarding houses, could not be brought up to standard, given the costs of rehabilitation. The modern nursing home thus came to look and function much more like a miniature hospital than a home.

Ironically, today's nursing homes provide little of either attribute implied by their name. There is only minimal nursing attention, especially from professional nurses, and rarely a homelike atmosphere. If anything, the tension between these poles has increased. More stringent standards for charting and documentational expectations of more aggressive care of a progressively more disabled clientele have been juxtaposed against client desires for a more livable environment. This trade-off has come to be called the dilemma between quality of care and quality of life. At its heart, it is an artificial dichotomy.

Because of the evident low quality of life and high cost of nursing home placement, the possibility of developing alternatives became a major policy objective of the 1970s and 1980s. The underlying premise was that care given in the community to persons eligible for nursing home services could prevent, or at least reduce, nursing home admissions. To take advantage of this presumed substitutability, several generations of alternative programs were launched under federal waivers as experiments or demonstration projects. The lessons learned were that, for the most part, community-based programs displaced much less nursing home care than was anticipated and saved even less money.

Two major reasons for the "failure" of the alternatives approach were the general disinclination of persons to use nursing homes as other than a last resort and the concomitant difficulty in targeting those at high risk of nursing home admission (Weissert 1985). For something perceived as inherently negative, like the nursing home, many of those whose dependency level qualifies them for such care will go to great lengths to stay in the community, even at risk to their own best interests and the stress on their families. It is thus correct to say that dependency (or disability) is a good predictor of nursing home use, but its accuracy is still quite low. It becomes a necessary but not sufficient condition to nursing home admission. The difficulty in identifying precisely who will enter a nursing home has made it difficult to target community services to those who might most readily be deflected from such care (Kane 1988). The more persons are treated in the community who would not enter a nursing home even without community care, the less cost-efficient is the alternatives approach.

These were not easy or painless lessons to learn. Despite the failure of the initial series of Medicare experiments (the so-called 222 experiments) using day care and homemaker services to show any appreciable benefits from community-based services (Weissert et al. 1980), a series of demonstration projects was launched in the mid-1970s to test the alternative potential of community-based programs for the dependent elderly (funded under 1115 waivers). The initial reports were enthusiastic. A Government Accounting Office report (GAO 1979) found the evidence for the benefits of these programs in reducing nursing home use so convincing that there should be no further delay in implementing a community-based long-term care strategy. The Department of Health and Human Services was more cautious and argued that a national commitment to this strategy was premature. The compromise was the National Long-Term Care Channeling Demonstration, which operated as a large social experiment in ten sites across the country to test whether enhanced case management with and without community care benefits for Medicaid clients could reduce the likelihood of entry into a nursing home. The results were disappointing for those who had expected large effects. There were few outcome differences between the experimental and control cases in terms of either function or nursing home use (Carcagno and Kemper 1988).

Commitment to this strategy persists, however. Before the Channeling results were available, a new program of community-care waivers had been established under Medicaid, the so-called 2176 waivers. Although these required some evidence of overall cost controls, they were founded on the presumption that community care was cheaper in the long run than care in a nursing home. There is at least some evidence to believe that they have succeeded where channeling failed. Data from Minnesota, which has one of the highest per capita rates of nursing home use in the country, and from Oregon, which has one of the lowest, both suggest an inverse correlation between the costs of community services and nursing home expenditures.

NEW DEVELOPMENTS IN LTC DELIVERY

The preferred modality of long-term care continues to be receiving care at home. But the way LTC is financed in this country can make this difficult even though the care recipient's physical condition may not require institutional placement. In particular, the system often seems to require the presence of informal caregivers as an eligibility condition for receiving formal care at home. The assumption that an informal support system is a precondition for home care needs to be reexamined.

The experience in subsidized housing programs, where informal support is less available and where aging in place has become a dominant theme, for example, suggests that more can be done to deliver care to those living alone, and that even frail older persons can be left alone for extended periods if there is regular oversight (AAHA 1989).

An intriguing development in long-term care is assisted living, which represents a hybrid between the nursing home and simply sheltered residential living. The underlying concept is bringing more individualized services to frail older persons. The general approach should serve to maintain the autonomy of the client to a greater degree. The original efforts were literally home care programs grafted on to sheltered housing, but more recent versions have used purpose-built facilities, where the design maximizes independence. The idea is spreading faster than successful models, however. All sorts of activities are now occurring under this banner. Some are truly attempting to maintain persons who would otherwise need nursing home care, but others are simply marketing a service (Kane and Wilson 1993).

Efforts include introducing adult foster care, which has met with varying success in different places. Although marketing the concept was difficult in Maryland and Hawaii (Braun and Rose 1986, Otkay and Volland 1981), it has thrived in Oregon (Kane et al. 1990). Day care has also been actively promoted as a useful response to many problems, including the care of demented persons. Transportation, however, has proven to be a substantial logistical problem, and the socialization afforded is not universally appealing (Kane and Kane 1987).

Some programs have attempted to reduce institutional care by combining financing for acute and long-term care. The Social Health Maintenance Organization (SHMO) extends coverage beyond prepaid acute care to include at least modest coverage of long-term care. Case management has been a central method to control the use of limited long-term care benefit. Costs are controlled by limiting the proportion of dependent elders who may enroll at any time. Another prepaid approach has used the prototype developed at On Lok in San Francisco's Chinatown. These replications enroll persons at risk for nursing home care and eligible for Medicaid support into a combined program that provides acute and long-term care around a day health care model. Great efforts are made to use primary care and flexible community care to minimize institutional use for either acute or chronic care (Kane et al. 1992). Both of these models have been tried in only limited settings with mixed results. Marketing for both has also been slower than expected, suggesting some resistance to the concepts.

A useful way to assess LTC alternatives is to note that the term "nursing home" implies two functions that are, in fact, completely separable. Though they may be combined in the same institution, that combination is by no means essential.

Nursing homes, in fact, provide only minimal levels of nursing services. Although functionally impaired persons become eligible for subsidized nursing home care because of their need for personal care, the average resident receives less than three hours of cumulative care per day. After persons reach a certain level of disability, home care is inefficient. But this is not because of the nursing services involved. The nursing home is a comparatively good buy because of economies of scale achieved by putting disabled people in residential proximity and minimizing attention to amenities.

The other part of the term "nursing home" suggests housing and hotel functions for people who can no longer maintain an independent household. But care could surely be combined with hotel functions in many different ways to achieve living settings that offer privacy and dignity and yet permit care needs to be met efficiently. It is time we thought more about ways to uncouple the two (Kane and Kane 1991).

The search for alternatives to nursing home care is largely a question of cost. If the housing and hotel functions were financed separately from the care functions, the LTC system could become much more efficient. Disaggregating the traditional model of the nursing home may encourage more individualized care and more private spending while providing a universal program for the health-related personal care that disabled people need. Under such a model, people would defray the costs of their housing at a level that they could afford. While society would maintain its obligation for income maintenance and housing for the indigent, the more affluent could choose to purchase more comfortable housing and amenities. Persons would then have an incentive to save, or even purchase private insurance, because they could buy a better standard of living with the gains.

Regulations for payment and for care could then be recast to reflect the separation between services and housing. This approach should have the salutary effect of changing the procrustean nursing home model, in which the resident is expected to adjust to the routines of the setting in order to receive small amounts of care, to a model in which the tenants of living units receive services to meet their individualized needs and enhance their goals. Rather than fitting the clients to the services, the services would be offered in settings more under the clients' control. Not only should nursing homes not be precluded from participating in these efforts, they should be permitted—even encouraged—to reconfigure their services along such lines.

EVOLVING QUALITY ASSESSMENT AND NEW MODES OF ACCOUNTABILITY

How should quality of care be monitored for LTC, an area characterized by such a wide variety of patients, caregivers, and sites of care? As already noted, the original regulations developed in connection with Medicare and Medicaid regulation placed heavy emphasis on nursing home structure and the process of care. Frustration with this regulatory effort came from both sides of the political spectrum. Some worried that the regulations did not protect enough; others that they were too stringent and limited innovation. In a move to stem the rush to deregulation already established in other sectors, the Congress asked the Institute of Medicine to study the status of nursing home regulation. That report (Institute of Medicine 1986) urged a redirection of effort away from studying charts to greater attention to the clients and their functional outcomes. Such a redirection, which is taking place also with respect to acute care, seems even more crucial for long-term care, where the relationships between the processes and outcomes of care are far less well established and where there is an inherent flexibility in developing mechanisms to achieve desired ends that should be encouraged.

The four features Kane and Kane (1988) have identified as distinguishing quality assessment in long-term care from more familiar milieux highlight the importance of outcome measures.

First, the time horizon over which quality should be assessed is longer than the ever shortening length of a hospital stay and is less precise. It is not always clear when the episode began, and a chronic episode may be punctuated with several acute events, some even requiring hospitalization.

Second, much of the care involved uses little of the sophisticated technology we have come to associate with modern medicine. In the case of long-term care, most of the care is provided by family and friends, and even most of the formal care is rendered by minimally trained aides. Thus, reliance on credentialling may be unproductive and can limit the supply of essential personnel. Also home care may involve several different providers. Putting together a package of coverage may involve dealing with many individuals working for several different agencies and interfacing in various ways with family members. It thus becomes much more difficult to assign specific responsibility for successful activities and especially for the outcomes that result.

Third, there is less opportunity for oversight since much of the care is not given in an institutional setting. The costs of recording, as a function of total encounter costs, would become prohibitive if a support system were required to maintain records in other sites of care at the same level of intensity found in hospitals. There are fewer witnesses to the encounter and thus the only consistent informants are the patient and the provider. Especially in the case of home care, which is often rendered to dependent elderly persons who suffer from various forms of dementia, relying on patient reports may be impossible. Moreover, even cognitively intact patients may feel reluctant to complain for fear of retribution, especially in situations with little external oversight.

Finally, the goals of care are typically directed more towards maintenance of function than cure. It is relatively easy to see when people get better. Assessing maintenance or the slowing of decline depends on having some way of estimating the probable course in the absence of the treatment given. Such an approach requires developing and maintaining large longitudinal data sets along the lines of those proposed for heart disease (Duke 1978). Models for this type of information resource in long-term care are available (Kane et al. 1983).

Long-term care, thus, walks a fine line. On the one hand, there are compelling reasons for advocating strong regulation to protect the dependent clientele and to counter the history of exploitation and misuse. On the other hand, long-term care desperately needs to encourage creative approaches to care and cannot afford to rush to premature closure on the best or even the typically accepted ways to deliver care. Shifting to an emphasis on outcomes would encourage innovation while maintaining control over care standards.

It is, however, not an idea widely adopted yet. Many interpret the lack of concordance between current knowledge about the process and outcome of care as a mandate to press even harder for stricter process and structural standards, and outcomes are more difficult concepts to work with than process. Any outcome-based approach must be understood to require two essential steps: (1) Outcomes imply examining averages rather than single events. The laws of chance mean that even good care can occasionally have poor results. The difference between good and bad care rests on the rate of the two occurrences. (2) Any calculation of outcomes must be corrected for the types of cases being treated. It does not make sense to simply compare raw outcomes because the nature of the clients will have a strong influence on the course of their condition.

In essence, outcomes of care are the product of three major forces: (1) patient characteristics (including both demographics and social factors as well as clinical aspects), (2) the appropriateness of care rendered (basically whether the right diagnosis was made and the appropriate treatment given), and (3) the skill of the practitioner. (It is not enough to do the right thing; it needs to be done well.) The goal of an outcomes system is to separate the effects of patient characteristics in order to test the effects of the latter two. This is accomplished statistically by looking at the patterns of results for many similar cases. For many regulatory purposes it is not necessary to distinguish between appropriateness and skill. But when one wants to improve the state of the art, clarification becomes important. The separation is accomplished by using aggregated data to establish appropriateness by examining the overall relationship between care and results and by looking across providers to distinguish skill by comparing results when appropriate care was given. In long-term care, an outcomes strategy permits comparisons across various modalities, encouraging comparisons and automatically adjusting for patient mix differences.

There is also general agreement on the major outcome categories for LTC: physiologic measures (e.g., blood pressure, decubiti, blood sugar), functional measures (usually some combination of ADLs and IADLs), discomfort, cognition, affect, social interactions and activities, interpersonal relationships, and satisfaction with care and environment. Each of these can and has been reduced to measurement in formats that feature collection of information directly from clients. There is less agreement about how each domain should be valued compared to the others, although some preliminary work suggests there may be more consensus than is usually believed.

INFORMATION TECHNOLOGY CAN HELP

The Omnibus Budget Reconciliation Act of 1987 responded to the Institute of Medicine call for greater attention to outcomes and called for shifts in the approach to nursing regulation. One of the important changes was establishing a minimum data set (MDS) to be used for all assessments of nursing home patients. The MDS will provide a standardized data base, which can form the basis for work to look at changes over time across homes, adjusting for patient characteristics (Morris et al. 1990). Earlier work using a commercial data base has pointed to the feasibility of making outcome conclusions from such a data base (Morris et al. 1987). It is likewise possible to make individual predictions of outcomes from a more purposeful data base (Kane et al. 1983). Although the current MDS does not cover many of the domains deemed appropriate, it does represent an important beginning.

The introduction of the MDS represents an important step forward in collecting systematic information about the status of LTC clients. But the potential for success will rest in part on the extent to which the data collected for outcomes assessment in a regulatory sense is also seen as valuable for patient care (Kane 1990). It is fair to say that information technology may be the most important advance in long-term care this decade (Bock and Kane 1993). The computer allows easy collection and manipulation of information. It permits sharing that information with disparate users. For example, home care can be linked to base stations to permit regular updates.

A very important function is the potential for looking at change over time. Ironically, despite its name, long-term care has tended to look at data about clients more as a series of snapshots than as the motion picture that it is. Frontline workers have little insight into the changes in course that their care makes. This emphasis on change, especially the distinction between observed and expected, is vital to long-term care for accountability and also for promoting morale. In a field where decline is the natural state of things, providing information that shows both the course of clients and the expected course can point to the real differences that good care has made.

Here we can take advantage of the computer's power to transform data. It is now a trivial task to display data in graphic form, even in color. It is thus possible to feed back to the aides caring for clients information about the difference their care has made and hence to give them a sense of accomplishment. Even those with minimal education can understand graphs that show an actual line, an expected line, and the space between them.

Information technology can likewise be used to monitor care and reduce provider burdens. It is feasible today to link individual homes with two-way interactive television. Such a system can be used to provide regular monitoring of client status. It can use programmed histories to ascertain symptoms and can even monitor physiologic data. The same approach can relieve the worried well by offering them an ever-responsive target for inquiries about symptoms, with a built-in provision to contact a health professional if there are significant changes. The same system can be used as a reminder for medications or other therapies. It can serve as an algorithm for care providers, including family members.

Other information technology can be profitably harnessed for LTC. It is now possible to use portable bar code readers to monitor care. Because these readers have a built-in clock, they can be used to monitor the schedules of care in the home, automatically recording when providers arrive and leave and even what tasks were performed. This approach permits a virtually foolproof and tamperproof medication record to assure that the right drug gets to the right person at the right time. These readers can be used to oversee behavioral modification programs such as timed toileting and have the added advantage that they can provide almost instantaneous feedback. With the same activity that charges the battery, these portable readers can download their data into a machine for immediate processing, even to the point of generating graphs of the output.

The fundamental long-term care issue for the United States is to exploit the strengths of the current system for encouraging innovation and cost-effective outcomes while improving the financing system to reduce fragmentation of care and eliminate abrupt thresholds in care financing that inhibit socially cost-effective delivery. In this respect, in particular, we can learn from the Canadians (see chapter 12).

References

American Association of Homes for the Aging (AAHA). 1989. "Aging in place." Southmark Foundation Conference.

Bock, W. H., and R. L. Kane. 1993. "Information Systems in Long-Term Care." In *Advances in Long-Term Care*, edited by P. R. Katz, R. L. Kane, and M. Mezey. New York: Springer Publishing Company.

Braun, K., and C. Rose. 1986. "The Hawaii Geriatric Foster Care Experiment: Impact Evaluation and Cost Analysis." *The Gerontologist* 26: 516–23.

Carcagno, G. J., and P. Kemper. 1988. "The Evaluation of the National Long-Term Care Demonstration: An Overview of the Channeling Demonstration and its Evaluation." *Health Services Research* 23: 1–22.

Duke University Center for the Study of Aging and Human Development. 1978. *Multidimensional Functional Assessment: The OARS Methodology*. Durham, N.C.: Duke University.

Government Accounting Office. 1979. *Entering a Nursing Home—Costly Implications for Medicaid and the Elderly*. Washington, D.C.: United States General Accounting Office.

Gutterman, S., P. W. Eggers, G. Riley, T. F. Greene, et al. 1988. "The First Three Years of Medicare Prospective Payment: An Overview." *Health Care Financing Review* 9.

Institute of Medicine. 1986. *Improving the Quality of Care in Nursing Homes*. Washington, D.C.: National Academy Press.

Kahn, K. L., E. B. Keeler, M. J. Sherwood, W. H. Rogers, et al. 1990. "Comparing Outcomes of Care before and after Implementation of the DRG-Based Prospective Payment System." *Journal of the American Medical Association* 264: 1984–88.

Kane, R. A. 1988. "The Noblest Experiment of them All: Learning from the National Channeling Evaluation." *Health Services Research* 23: 189–98.

Kane, R. A., and R. L. Kane. 1987. *Long-Term Care: Principles, Programs, and Policies*. New York: Springer Publishing Company.

————. 1988. "Long-Term Care: Variations on a Quality Assurance Theme." *Inquiry* 25: 132–46.

Kane, R. A., L. Illston, R. L. Kane, and J. Nyman. 1990. "Meshing Services with Housing: Lessons from Adult Foster Care and Assisted Living in Oregon." Final Report to John A. Hartford Foundation, Division of Health Services Research and Policy, School of Public Health, University of Minnesota, Minneapolis, MN.

Kane, R. A., and K. B. Wilson. 1993. "Assisted Living in the United States: A New Paradigm for Residential Care for Frail Older Persons?" Washington, D.C.: American Association of Retired Persons.

Kane, R. L., and R. A. Kane. 1990. "Health Care for Older People: Organizational and Policy Issues." In *Handbook for Aging and the Social Sciences*, edited by R. H. Binstock and L. K. George, third ed. San Diego: Academic Press.

————. 1991. "A Nursing Home in Your Future." *New England Journal of Medicine* 324: 565–67.

Kane, R. L., R. M. Bell, S. Z. Riegler, A. Wilson, et al. 1983. "Predicting the Outcomes of Nursing-Home Patients." *The Gerontologist* 23: 200–06.

Kane, R. L., L. H. Illston, and N. A. Miller. 1992. "Qualitative Analysis of the Program of All-Inclusive Care for the Elderly (PACE)." *The Gerontologist* 32: 771–80.

Kemper, P., and C. Murtaugh. 1991. "Lifetime Use of Nursing Home Care. *New England Journal of Medicine* 324: 595–600.

Mendelson, M. A. 1974. *Tender Loving Greed*. New York: Alfred A. Knopf.

Morris, J. N., C. Hawes, B. E. Fries, C. D. Phillips, et al. 1990. "Designing the National Resident Assessment Instrument for Nursing Homes." *The Gerontologist* 30: 293–307.

Morris, J. N., S. Sherwood, M. M. May, and E. Bernstein. 1987. "FRED: An Innovative Approach to Nursing Home Level-of-Care Assignments." *Health Services Research* 22: 117–40.

Moss, F. E., and V. J. Halamandaris. 1977. *Too Old, Too Sick, Too Bad: Nursing Homes in America*. Germantown, Md.: Aspen Systems Corp.

Neu, C. R., and S. C. Harrison. 1988. "Posthospital Care before and after the Medicare Prospective Payment System." The RAND Corporation.

Otkay, J. S., and P. J. Volland. 1981. "Community Care Programs for the Elderly." *Health and Social Work* 6: 41–48.

Stephens, S. A., and J. Christianson. 1986. *Informal Care of the Elderly*. New York: Free Press.

Weissert, W. G. 1985. "Seven Reasons Why it is so Difficult to Make Community-Based Long-Term Care Cost-Effective." *Health Services Research* 20: 423–34.

Weissert, W. G., T. T. H. Wan, and B. B. Liveratos. 1980. "Effects and Costs of Day Care and Homemaker Services for the Chronically Ill: A Randomized Experiment." Office of Health Research, Statistics, and Technology, National Center for Health Services Research, Department of Health and Human Services. Hyattsville, Md.: National Center for Health Services Research.

Chapter Twelve

FINANCING LONG-TERM CARE: LESSONS FROM CANADA

Robert L. Kane and Rosalie A. Kane

The common denominator of long-term care (LTC), as noted in chapter 11, is functioning. LTC is directed toward those who cannot provide for themselves at least some of the basic services necessary for daily existence. As stressed repeatedly in the previous chapter, there is no single model—or even set of well-defined models—for providing such care. For this reason, a financing system for LTC should avoid making essentially arbitrary distinctions among different providers and different sites of care. Such distinctions inevitably distort choices by the care receivers and the caregivers—choices that are essential to ensure both quality and efficiency of care. Our purpose here is to examine the differences between the U.S. and Canadian financing systems from this perspective.

TWO APPROACHES TO FINANCIAL COVERAGE

In both the United States and Canada, LTC is a regional (state or provincial) responsibility with some role (largely financial) for the federal government. In both countries, there is, therefore, variation from one locale to another, but generalizations are still possible. All but two small Canadian provinces have opted to include LTC as a universally insured service, financed through federal block grants and additional provincial funds. Both nursing home and home care are covered without deductibles, although the former carries a copayment analogous to an affordable rent. In the main, nursing homes are reimbursed much like acute care hospitals (i.e., they are paid by global budgets or they bill for services at rates set prospectively). Once they have committed to covering the service universally, the Canadian provincial authorities have gone to great lengths to deter the development of a second market. They have effectively prohibited private provision of such care lest the presence of a private market disrupt access.

The American approach is more fragmented. It combines elements of an entitlement program (Medicare[1]) with a welfare program (Medicaid) and rests heavily on the expectation that a substantial portion of the costs will be borne directly by the client (perhaps with help from the family) until that person is impoverished, at which time he becomes eligible for public support as a welfare client.[2] Essentially the United States approach places strong reliance on the individual's ability to meet the challenge of LTC with the government playing a role only after the individual has tried and failed. The government thus becomes the last dollar payor. The Canadian[3] philosophy is just the reverse: Disability is seen as a misfortune, the burden of which should not be enhanced by poverty. Society has a responsibility to share the burden by providing support for needed services. Persons with more resources can purchase or arrange for additional care beyond that minimum but the government is the first payor.

LTC is a family matter. It strikes not only the person needing care but those around who may be called upon to provide it. Poverty induced by struggling to meet the chronic expensive bills for care affects not only the patient but also those in the immediate family, especially the spouse. Spousal impoverishment has become a major concern in the United States, where complicated arrangements have been developed to separate assets and income in order to "protect" the nondisabled spouse.

Case Examples

To offer some sense of what the different approaches to LTC support in the two countries really mean, imagine how several different clients would fare in each:

Case #1. An 82-year-old man with Alzheimer's Disease living with his 78-year-old wife who suffers from chronic arthritis and congestive heart failure. He is confused to the point where he needs constant supervision and assistance with most of the basic activities of daily living. She is mentally alert but has a hard time getting around because of her joint pain and shortness of breath. She needs to have a hip replaced in order to get around more easily and relieve her constant pain. They live on a small private pension and a federal pension; together they provide enough money for food and rent, but not much else.

American version: The care of the husband can be managed at home by purchasing private home health care, but they cannot afford to do this. If they hire help (as long as it is medically necessary), they could apply for Medicaid. In order to determine if they are eligible for assistance, one would compare their monthly income to their monthly medical expenses. In states that have a provision for medical indigence (where the cost of that help exceeds their income), they would be eligible for coverage of the costs of the services that were approved by a case worker. If they get help for the care given at home, the family's income is viewed as what both halves of the couple receive. An option would be for the husband to enter a nursing home. (It might be hard to find a nursing home willing to admit someone who had no means of paying for the care and was not yet enrolled in Medicaid.) The process of establishing Medicaid eligibility is complex. If they have some savings and the husband is institutionalized, half the couple's income and assets is assigned to the husband and available to be spent down to Medicaid eligibility levels; the remainder is assigned to the wife. She would then have to live on her own on half the income they formerly used. Were she to have her hip replaced, the basic costs of the procedure (less one day's hospital stay and 20 percent of the surgeons' and anesthetists' fees and any additional charges they chose to levy over those paid as customary charges by Medicare) would be paid by Medicare (some states now mandate that physicians accept Medicare fees as 80 percent of payment in full). It might also be possible to arrange for Medicare-funded home health care for her post-discharge for gait assistance and training, or she could be admitted to a nursing home to convalesce. If her husband were still living in the community, Medicare would not pay for any care or supervision for him during the time she was in the hospital. She would thus have to make her own arrangements or consider the likelihood that he would have to be placed in a nursing home, probably permanently.

Canadian version: A case manager would assess the family's situation and determine what services would be most helpful to both. Because eligibility is not tied to income or assets and both acute and chronic services are provided with virtually no deductibles or copayments, the decisions are based more on functional problems and personal preferences. Services can be brought into the home at least up to comparable costs of institutional care. If the wife is hospitalized for treatment, care can be brought in the home to allow the husband to stay there until she is well enough to return. Home care after her discharge can include assistance for both of them, because the authority is not linked to recuperation from a hospital event or a self-confined episode of care. On the other hand, the wife may reach a point where she can no longer manage the care of her husband and may opt to have him enter an institution.[4] The decision would be based on his functional abilities and the financial burden would essentially be limited to a modest charge for room and board.

Case #2. A 79-year-old widow who lives alone in a small two-bedroom house, which she owns with no mortgage. She has three children in the area who see her regularly. Her income is limited to a federal pension left to her through her husband. She has a number of chronic problems, including a stroke, which have left her unable to maintain the house without help. She is partially paralyzed on one side and cannot dress herself without help. She walks very slowly with a walker. She is incontinent of urine because she cannot get to the bathroom in time. She has trouble making meals and cannot keep the house clean, although her daughters come in regularly to clean it for her.

American version: This person is not eligible for Medicare coverage for her chronic care because she has no self-limited problem and is not clearly homebound. She would likely be eligible for assistance under Medicaid. She would be allowed to keep her house if she stayed at home; but if she entered a nursing home, the state may have the right to sell the house and use the proceeds to offset the costs of her care. Should she choose to stay at home, a case worker would develop a plan of care that would likely involve some role for her children. The residual need for care after the children had provided what help they were prepared to offer would be used as the basis for a care plan that would include a homemaker and likely a home health aide. Care at home would be covered by Medicaid, but the client would be expected to pay for as much care as she could until the costs exceeded a set proportion of her resources each month. Were she to be admitted to a nursing home, her support from her pension, less a small living allowance, would be used as first dollar coverage for the care.

Canadian version: The services available to her at home would be pretty much the same. Were she to enter a nursing home, she would be able to keep her home and presumably pass it on to one of her daughters. The costs of the nursing home care would be paid directly by the province; but she would be expected to contribute the equivalent of room and board costs, pegged so that she could afford them leaving a more generous living allowance.

Case #3. A 74-year-old married woman was transferred to a nursing home after being hospitalized to repair a fractured hip. She gets physical therapy to assist with her gait training and muscle strengthening. She entered the hospital from her home where she lives with her husband. They are fairly well off. Their private and federal pensions allow them to live at a level about as high as they did when they retired. They own a home and have amassed a sizable estate, which they very much want to leave to a favorite nephew.

American version: Care in the nursing home would likely be covered by Medicare. The decision would be made by fiscal intermediaries who would assess the potential for rehabilitation and the need for convalescent care. It is possible that they would not approve this admission. In that event, the patient (or the couple) would be expected to pay the nursing home bill. She would not be eligible for Medicaid because she and her husband could not pass the income and assets test. Frightened by the experience, they might seek the advice of a lawyer who could help them plan their estate and become eligible for Medicaid by putting their assets into some form of a trust that could be passed on. This trust would remove their assets from their direct control. The arrangement would mean the nephew would probably get the estate without any inheritance tax. (If there was any inheritance unprotected and remaining, most, if not all, of it would be exempt from federal inheritance taxes and most state taxes.) They would still have to accumulate medical costs that exceeded most of their monthly income to become eligible for Medicaid. If the woman stayed in the nursing home for more than 20 days under Medicare coverage (intermediaries would first have to review her case and find cause for the extended stay), she would be expected to pay a copayment equal to about three-fourths of the daily cost. Were she to opt to be treated at home, Medicare coverage of home health care would require that she be homebound.

Canadian version: The woman will be treated in the nursing home as long as she needs rehabilitation. As soon as she is able, she can return home. During her stay in the nursing home she will be charged a room and board charge equal to about a third of the daily rate. If she needs further assistance once she returns to the community, home care can be arranged at no cost to her. The couple's assets would be unaffected. They would still be able to leave their legacy to their nephew but a substantial inheritance tax would be levied. In Canada, this couple's income, including their Canada pension (equivalent to Social Security in the United States) would be fully taxable.

INTERNAL VARIATION

In both the American and Canadian systems there is substantial variation from one location to another. Because long-term care is essentially a provincial matter in Canada, different provinces have approached the problem differently. Those addressing it later have learned from the experience of the pioneers. Beginning with Ontario's financing of nursing home care in 1972 and the broader programs established in Manitoba in 1974 to finance home care and personal care homes (Manitoba's term for nursing homes), there is a trail of replication and adaptation across much of the country. For example, British Columbia developed its program in 1978 (Kane and Kane 1985) and by the early 1980s Alberta and Saskatchewan had equivalent programs (Kane and Kane, forthcoming 1994). Ontario moved progressively to include more home care coverage and has recently proposed major reforms in its long-term care programs to consolidate services, place more emphasis on community services as opposed to nursing homes, and strengthen the role of case management (which will be carried out through yet unspecified single access agencies) (Beer et al. 1990). Quebec has created unified geographic service areas that are supposed to coordinate medical and social care for frail elderly persons (Beland 1986). In many of these programs, the influence of the Manitoba model of community care with active care coordination is evident.

It is important to appreciate that not all provinces have universal long-term care and not all are equally developed. Two Maritime provinces have programs that more closely resemble the situation in the United States in their financing of nursing home care.

The Canadian programs build on a structure that has more institutional beds per capita than in the United States, although the population is somewhat younger.[5] Most provinces are making a shift to place greater emphasis on home care. Some have had established such programs for some time; others have used home care for acute illnesses but are just moving into large-scale community care. The general motivation is a combination of client preference and the hope of saving money by using less expensive care than nursing homes. Virtually every province has targeted those nursing home residents with minimal disabilities as the group most readily displaced by community care.

Canada has a greater proportion of primary care physicians as compared to specialists than does the United States. Perhaps as a result, physicians specializing in geriatrics (geriatricians) seem to have enjoyed a more rapid growth as a specialty there. Although the experience varies from province to province, most provinces have a critical mass of trained geriatricians in their major cities and are more likely to have regional responsibility assigned for geriatric care. For example, Winnipeg, Manitoba, a city of about 500,000, has four hospital centers with geriatric programs. Many of the larger cities in Ontario are developing regional geriatric networks with geographically assigned responsibilities and a plan for coordinating care. Many first generation Canadian geriatricians have come from the United Kingdom and have brought with them a British model of population-based geriatrics. The United States has invested heavily in geriatric training but it has been slow to develop and geriatricians have been used in more entrepreneurial ventures with hospitals seeking to establish a larger share of the elderly client market.

The United States is more populous and more varied in many respects. Its service programs are composed of a mixture of sources. Medicare, the federal entitlement program for acute care, inadvertently covers some chronic care to the extent that it represents a continuation of an acute episode. This program uses a single national standard, although the interpretations may vary from one fiscal intermediary to another. The other large public program for health care is Medicaid, a program for the poor that is jointly supported by federal and state funds. The federal government contributes between half and three-fourths of the costs, depending on the state's economic status. Federal guidelines define minimal standards for eligibility and benefits but states may be more generous and still receive federal matching support up to thresholds. States have thus been the innovators in testing new ways to organize care, especially for long-term care, which has become a dominant component of state Medicaid budgets.

In effect, the Medicaid benefits for older persons are defined by the omissions of Medicare. Because Medicare is basically an acute care program focused on hospitals and physicians (and brief services designed as hospital recuperation), Medicaid is left to cover for the indigent elderly those things uncovered by the universal program. These include predominantly nursing homes, home care, and drugs (as well as Medicare's deductibles and copayments). During the last decade and a half states have embarked on a crusade to find a less expensive alternative to nursing home care. Through a series of waiver programs they have used Medicare and Medicaid funds in attempts to demonstrate that community-based services would reduce the likelihood of institutionalization (Carcagno and Kemper 1988, Weissert et al. 1980, GAO 1979). Several major demonstration projects later, it has become clearer that community care will not displace nursing home care (especially when subjected to the constraints of a time-limited demonstration) (Weissert et al. 1989, Kane and Kane 1987). Rather, the availability of an alternative makes it possible to reduce the supply of nursing home beds and hence their use. In Canada, demonstration projects have not been predominant. Provinces have developed operational programs without an elaborate testing period and have modified them on an ongoing basis. Having the political will to develop operational programs has served well because they have created a constituency of pleased citizens of all ages and (importantly) all incomes.

The states have proven to be the testing grounds for new ways of organizing LTC services in the United States. Under waiver authority, state Medicaid programs have developed case management systems, shifted emphasis to adult foster care, increased home care, established pre-admission screening, and introduced various forms of day care. Oregon is a striking example of a state that has consolidated diverse funding streams to develop a wide array of service options.

The private sector has shown the most innovation in long-term care in the United States. Freed from the dual constraints of publicly funded programs—cost and regulation—it has developed projects in response to perceived consumer demand. Such programs have targeted the upper end of the elderly income distribution: those with money to purchase them can have access to various ways to combine residential programs with needed services. Whether it is a continuing care retirement center or an assisted living center, with sufficient resources it is possible to create an attractive lifestyle that enhances independent functioning but provides the necessary assistance. These options are far less available, however, for those who must rely on public programs, and some of the market-driven innovations have been limited to persons whose disabilities are less severe.

Although it is still not a prevalent commodity, there has been growing interest in private long-term care insurance. The dire fiscal consequences of LTC expenses have been used as selling points to encourage people to protect themselves.[6] However, the young, who could purchase such coverage at low rates, do not feel threatened, and for those already old the cost of coverage approximates the cost of care. The prime target group has thus become the young old, who may feel somewhat vulnerable but are still in a position to spread the risk. The rationale for private insurance is based on one of two factors: either it permits a level of care better than what would be provided under public support or it protects the individual from the consequences of welfare status. The first rationale is best enforced by making the benefits of public programs minimal—a drastic recourse. The second transforms LTC insurance into asset protection; what one is actually buying is security against having to spend down all of one's assets to become eligible for public assistance. There are better ways to protect assets. Indeed, in the United States today there are estate planners who specialize in assisting people to use legal mechanisms to protect their assets while not making them countable for purposes of determining Medicaid eligibility.

Although careful projections suggest that private long-term care insurance is not likely to become a substantial basis for financial protection (Rivlin and Wiener 1988), others maintain that the problem is simply one of establishing the right price. Lacking a great deal of claims history, insurance companies have been conservative in establishing both costs and benefits. The enthusiasts maintain that better policies, at more attractive rates, will attract larger market shares. Thus far, in an era of stringent economic times, few employers have been willing to add long-term care insurance to their employees' benefit packages. At best, they will offer such a product for the employee to purchase as part of a group to obtain a better rate.

Because the rules for insurance are set by states, the long-term care insurance market varies from state to state. Some states have established stringent criteria for benefits, including provisions for inflation and coverage of care provided at home as well as in nursing homes; others permit a wide variety of policies. Of course, long-term care insurance is irrelevant in Canada.

FLOORS VERSUS CEILINGS

Stated simply, the dominant Canadian approach to long-term care provides each person in need of assistance with a package of services that will allow the least affluent to afford basic services without embarrassment. This commitment to universalism also means that the more affluent will be able to take advantage of the same benefits without having to draw heavily upon their income and assets. Those able to purchase more amenities are free to do so but they are not able to use the formal care system to buy a different type of nursing home care privately. Thus, they can get private rooms in nursing homes, bring in better food, live in better housing, purchase additional household help, but they cannot use nursing homes or home health agencies that are unavailable to the rest of the population. The latter constraint is intended to prevent market segmentation. The Canadian approach permits individuals to accumulate an estate, but inheritance taxes are designed to collect a substantial portion of this unearned income. The inheritance tax is not a direct collection for past long-term care support. It is levied regardless of use.

The American approach is quite different. There is strong belief in individual responsibility. The government plays a residual role, interceding after the person has done everything possible to cope with the problem. Thus, an elderly American in need of long-term care would be expected to pay for that care until all personal resources were expended and then convert all assets to cash to provide additional funds. Because one's home is considered a necessity, this asset is usually excluded from calculations of Medicaid eligibility.[7] When a person stays in a nursing home for a period after which return home is unlikely, the home is treated as a liquid asset for spend-down to Medicaid eligibility levels, unless it is occupied by a spouse or a disabled dependent adult child.

When a person reaches a situation where the cost of care exceeds his means, most states will intervene to provide financial assistance. However, the threshold of eligibility varies from state to state. Some states use a ratio of expenses to income (calculated to include liquid assets); others withhold assistance until a person is literally reduced to poverty. This structure becomes even more difficult for couples where one spouse needs long-term care. Because a couple's income is generally treated as joint property, the determination of eligibility may be based on the combined resources of both. Recent steps at the federal level have attempted to provide some protection for the healthy spouse by dividing income for couples for purposes of establishing Medicaid eligibility when one member of the couple is institutionalized, but many couples prefer to try to manage at home with simultaneous care and financial burdens.

Once eligibility for Medicaid is established, the recipient is able to draw upon as many resources as are deemed appropriate to the situation, but the choice of programs and vendors is limited. Some vendors will not treat Medicaid clients because they feel the rates paid are too low or the regulations excessive. Some types of service available in the private market are not covered under Medicaid, particularly creative combinations of housing and services. Some programs for community services authorized by federal waivers to states of the general Medicaid rules have quotas established to prevent increased federal costs.

The income of a person who becomes eligible for Medicaid is still expected to cover as much of the costs as possible. Thus, one sees apparently inconsistent reports that suggest that about two-thirds of persons in American nursing homes are supported by Medicaid but that program pays less than half the national nursing home bill. This is not due to simply a difference in the rates charged to private patients. It is a function of the costs for Medicaid clients paid first from private accounts.

It is important to note that both the American and Canadian long-term programs are built on a foundation of universal coverage for acute care, although in the United States those over 65 are almost the only group universally covered.[8] Availability of acute services is important because the trigger for LTC is usually some form of physical or mental dependency brought on by one or more chronic conditions. It would be very hard to treat part of the problem without access to care for the underlying and accompanying problems.

A difference between the two countries' handling of these universal programs is use of consumer payments. The Canadian version of Medicare operates without deductibles and copayments. At present the Canadians rely on the health professionals and the limited supply of expensive technologies to control cost. In long-term care, as already noted, copayments do apply for nursing home care, but they are fixed at a rate affordable even by those with nothing but government pensions.[9] The latter point applies much less to long-term care, where the level of technology and the commensurate unit cost is low.

The American version relies on copayments as both a source of revenue and a mechanism to control utilization. The rationale is not entirely rational. For example, changes in the way hospitals are paid provide them with strong incentives for early discharge. Nonetheless, Medicare patients are required to pay a copayment to cover hospital costs after several weeks of hospital stay. Likewise, nursing home coverage under Medicare requires a copayment equal to one-eighth of the average cost of a hospital day after the first twenty days. This amounts to about three-fourths of the costs of a typical Medicare-paid nursing home day and hence reduces the effective coverage of nursing home care dramatically, even for the limited amounts presumably provided (up to 100 days in theory, although very few beneficiaries ever receive anywhere near that length of coverage).

Current thinking about Medicaid has not included copayments on the principle that it applies only to those already poor; but some recent proposals have called for them, even at token amounts where the cost of collection exceeds the savings. Most American legislative proposals for universal long-term care coverage are based on some form of copayment, either front-end or back-end. Front-end copays imply a period of care for which the individual is responsible for the bill. If use exceeds that time period the program would pick all or part of the costs. This approach offers a comfortable niche for private insurance, which would face a predictable upper limit of risk. Back-end copays imply coverage for the first portion of nursing home stays, after which point individuals become responsible for the costs until their funds are exhausted. The rationale for this approach is that most nursing home stays are relatively brief. Thus, most people using a nursing home would benefit from coverage of the first part of the stay. Only a small minority of users have very long stays, although they account for much of the total use. These individuals are very likely to spend the rest of their lives in institutions and hence there is no reason why they should not exhaust their personal resources.[10] These proposals for front- or back-ended financing apply to nursing home care but not to home care. They both include further provisions for copayments for services covered that are not applied to home care.

The special treatment of home care is motivated by two factors: (1) There is a general desire to reduce the use of nursing homes by creating incentives for living at home. (2) Nursing home costs include the costs of room and board as well as services. Persons living at home would continue to have to pay for these aspects even if services were provided without charge. Thus, the copays can be seen as more akin to the charges for room and board levied by most Canadian provinces.

FRAGMENTATION AND COORDINATION

Canada

Both the Canadian and American approaches to LTC are separated from acute care, but the level of separation is quite different. Although the ministry responsible for LTC varies from province to province, it is most often the same health ministry that oversees acute care. This cohousing permits shifts in resources (at least theoretically) between the two sectors. At the same time, LTC transcends several purviews. It involves acute care, community and social services, and housing. In Ontario, at present, there is substantial duplication in ministerial responsibility. Both the ministries of health and of community and social services oversee elements of long-term care. The latter is responsible for homes for the elderly, many of which operate nursing home beds that are the jurisdiction of health. The province is working to combine responsibilities and eliminate duplication. The interface between social and medical services at the ministerial level is a bureaucratic problem in other provinces as well. Because LTC transcends many programs, it can readily become ensnared in jurisdictional disputes or, even worse, be left unattended by anyone.

Housing the LTC program within the same ministry as other health care can be seen as both an advantage and a disadvantage. The ability to divert funds (usually by giving priority to growth in the LTC sector) from acute care, which has a much larger budget, is very attractive. Such shifts in program emphasis were evident in the launching of long-term care programs in the 1970s and 1980s (Kane and Kane 1985). The other side of the coin is the concern that LTC may fall too much under the sway of the so-called medical model and lose its emphasis on the clients' social functioning.

Even housing the acute and chronic care programs together does not eliminate duplication. For example, Canadian hospitals frequently operate what are called "extended care units," which perform essentially as nursing homes. Some of these beds are mandated by the province, as is the case in Quebec, where a specific proportion of acute hospital beds were transformed to long-term care use by fiat. Some provinces have used this technique as a means to ration de facto without paying the political price for pulling beds out of use. By converting the beds to long-term care they are filling a social need, but they are filling it at a lower unit cost than would be experienced for acute beds. The result, however, is two parallel systems, one designed for a finite stay and the other for effectively a lifetime. But it is not always easy to separate which patient needs which type of facility at the outset. Hence, some patients begin under the extended care auspices and then transfer to a nursing home. Because extended care is treated as an extension of an acute stay, no copayments are expected, whereas a nursing home stay would require a room and board charge.

The coordination between acute and chronic care is not strong in Canadian provinces despite programmatic efforts to bring it about. Hospital discharge planners do not work any better with community-based case managers than they do in the United States. The duplication of services similar to those available from community institutions within hospitals' special units adds to the lack of coordination. Hospitals often complain about the "bed blockers" who fill their beds and prevent new admissions, but these cases add to overall occupancy at lower unit cost and hence improve hospitals' use of global budget funds. Moreover, in Canada, consumers are less likely to be forced into precipitous decisions about institutional long-term care while still actively ill in the hospital.

It is also possible to encounter separate administrations within a program for community-based LTC and for institutional care. For example, in Manitoba the care coordination that determines eligibility and need for care also oversees home care, but a patient who enters a nursing home falls under the jurisdiction of another agency.

The introduction of care coordinators (or case managers) has shifted the focus of decision-making about post-hospital LTC away from physicians. The care coordinators are empowered to determine the needs for LTC, although they need physician input for the medical elements of the case. Canadian physicians have not welcomed the loss of authority. In some cases, they now complain about being asked to supply information for which they are not paid. In a more positive vein, Manitoba has instituted a paneling program under which all cases recommended by care coordinators for nursing home placement are reviewed by an interdisciplinary panel including (where available) a geriatrician. The panel reviews the case materials and can suggest a more comprehensive medical evaluation when it seems justified.

United States

The American system is fragmented by funding. The American health care system is built on a faith in competition. This approach leads to duplication and redundancy, which produces ready access at the cost of excess capacity. As public payors become concerned about rising costs, often linked to excess capacity, they have moved to restrict the growth of certain aspects of care, especially nursing homes. Each attempt to use LTC requires ascertaining who will pay and for what coverage the patient is eligible. Given the array of governmentally supported programs, it is possible for an individual to be eligible for a slew of different programs, each with its own eligibility criteria and even different start and stop dates. For each public program and private financing opportunity a host of potential providers spring up, each trying to identify a market niche. Unfortunately a program built around a collection of market niches inevitably leaves service gaps. Rather than a planned array of services and providers with distinct responsibility, one faces a cluster of providers, each aiming to maximize their participation in the most desirable part of the market.

Community agencies trying to make use of public funding must contend with different rules and regulations for each. Add to this the intricacies of deductibles and copayments and the system becomes even more mazelike. For many public programs, the complexity requires some type of special labyrinth guides, currently termed "case managers." Private payers are virtually on their own. Although many providers prefer private payment because it is usually at a higher rate, the private payers have no agents to help them locate and obtain services unless they hire case management themselves.

In the United States there is no greater administrative sin than a program using its resources to save money for another program. Politicians and administrators have spent great effort to create the image of multiple sets of books for health and social program costs. Good management has too often become equated with shifting the responsibility from one program to another, especially from public programs to private support. Cost-shifting has been confused with cost control. Canada's single universal payor makes it more difficult to ignore the over-riding issue of total cost.

In the case of long-term care, investment is the key strategy. Thus, more thoughtful discharge planning at the end of a hospitalization can lead to a better decision about LTC. More conscientious primary care for patients in nursing home might delay or avoid hospitalization. But if the sources of support for the initial step differ from those who might benefit, there is no incentive to put in the extra effort. If a patient being discharged from a hospital being paid a fixed amount by Medicare for his care is likely to be sent to care that would be paid for either privately or through Medicaid, neither the hospital nor Medicare has a great interest in improving that decision. At the same time, the hospital has a big stake in minimizing the patient's length of stay. From its vantage point, a day spent making a decision, however wise, is a day wasted.

The difference in entrepreneurial responsiveness is seen in the reaction to payment systems. Many Canadian nursing homes are paid on a global budget, which offers an incentive to minimize care to maximize "profit."[11] However, there is no evidence that such institutions have responded to this temptation. Rather, they seem to be ready to plow whatever resources are made available into more or better care. In stark contrast, American nursing homes are forever seeking the edge. If payment is organized in tiers, they will seek out those persons just over the line, wherever it is drawn. Failure to admit complex cases under a fixed payment system prompted the introduction of case-mix reimbursement in the hopes of making the more clinically complex cases more financially attractive.

Although case management has become the "pixie dust" of American long-term care, being sprinkled liberally wherever one needs an answer as to how any problem can be handled, there is little indication

of a lessening of the centrism of physicians in a process that is noto-
riously outside their sphere of competence. A physician order is still
necessary to admit a patient to a nursing home or to order home health
care under Medicare, and in many states, under Medicaid.

REGULATION

Americans are fond of rules. Despite the irony, the Americans, who
trace their traditions back to a revolution, are much more rule-bound
than the Canadians, many of whose founding fathers fled the revolution. Americans seem to need explicit rules to protect their freedoms,
even when these rules serve to constrain the very freedoms they insisted on protecting. This penchant for specification can be seen reflected in the Bill of Rights, as is the inevitable consequence of protracted legal battles about its interpretation and application.

The nursing home industry is said to be the second most highly
regulated industry in America, just after nuclear power. The combination of publicly supported care delivered largely by proprietary
firms leads inevitably to regulation. The question is less whether than
how to regulate, and especially, how to enforce the rules that have
been established.

Regulation in long-term care faces a special paradox: The dearth of
strong empirical links between specific actions and client outcomes
has led regulators to push for stronger rules about the orthodox ways
of delivering care. The orthodoxy is derived largely by convening
experts, often from the LTC field, who render their best professional
judgments about how care should be given. Often these opinions call
for more intensive professionalization of services, more training, and
fixed ways of delivering care. In essence, in cases of uncertainty establish a dogma. Thus, regulation can become a major impediment to
innovation, and LTC desperately needs innovation.

LTC also demands accountability. The combination of vulnerable
clients being cared for by an industry with a shady past being operated
for a profit demands strict standards of accountability (Mendelson
1974, Moss and Halamandaris 1977, Vladeck 1980). But using stricter
standards without strong evidence of their efficacy, and especially
where the applications require professional judgment about adequacy,
leads to sanctions that are challenged. It seems that the more clinically
important the regulatory element, the more clinical judgment is in-

volved. Therefore, the rules that are enforced tend to be those where measurements are easiest. They also seem to be the most banal; for example, the height of a refrigerator off the floor. The result is a perception of harassment and an adversarial regulatory climate.

The challenge to effective regulation has several important elements: (1) to address the items that are most germane to the well-being of clients, (2) to encourage innovation while assuring accountability, and (3) to be able to effectively correct or prevent problems in care. It is insufficient to simply identify problems; one must be able to intervene. If shortages of LTC resources prevent closing chronic offenders or fear of prolonged litigation deters sanctions, the regulatory system does not work.

The Canadian approach to regulation seems quite different. Rather than operating in an adversarial milieu, Canadian regulators appear to begin from a general position of trust in the providers. Their task is to assure that good care is being provided and to help create a climate in which it can occur. Part of the difference may be attributable to the general intolerance for the entrepreneurial ethos that typifies American business. Although both Canadian and American LTC is heavily proprietary (Canada's less so than America's), there is less tolerance in Canada for the American instinct to find the loophole or the market niche. Strategies that would be second nature for Americans are dismissed as being "not acceptable" in Canada. This substitution of cultural norms for explicit rules may go a long way toward explaining the greater sense of trust in providers exhibited by both clients and regulators.

As a result, Canadian LTC has fewer rules and more informal problem solving. Where American regulators are expressly forbidden from getting involved in seeking answers to problems they uncover, lest they lose their objectivity, their Canadian counterparts are actively engaged in making suggestions.

CONCLUSIONS

Americans and Canadians are neighbors. They share more traits with each other than with many European countries, but they are different nonetheless. Canadian social values lie somewhere between those of Europe and the United States, with Canadians placing greater trust than Americans in professionals and in government. Reich (1987) points to Americans' alternative distrust of big business and big government, seeing each as the solution to the ills of the other. The American distrust of government has created a situation in which the demand for specific protection of individual freedoms has woven a tangled web of rules that seems to threaten the autonomy of all parties.

The Canadian model points to the potential benefits of simplified administration possible with a single payor. Canadian values about the entitlement of disabled persons to assistance regardless of their income or ability to pay will not play as easily in the United States, where both concerns about overuse and a belief that people should first try to help themselves will likely lead to greater reliance on copayments. Even in Canada, there is already some perceptible shift to looking to greater use of copayments as a protection against inappropriate use.

Canada establishes the feasibility of affordable universal long-term care. Part of this cost can be derived from modest transfers from acute to long-term care programs. Most will be borne by some form of taxation (perhaps disguised as insurance although there are more problems with such a strategy[12]). Universal LTC coverage must be laid on a substrate of universal acute care coverage. Some of the current proposals for extending LTC coverage to other than elderly persons need to recognize this dilemma.

The Canadians can thus be said to have demonstrated the advantages of an organized approach to making affordable care accessible. But neither country has begun to effectively explore the possibilities of developing innovative approaches to long-term care that provide the benefits of personalized living situations with the availability of service packages that respond to individual needs. Such a combination implies more than home care, which may not be feasible in many situations. It suggests new combinations of residences and services in ways that offer the two aspects of care implied in the term "nursing home" but designed to actually deliver both (Kane and Kane 1990).

The United States is likely to be a better source of innovative ideas. As a land of demonstration programs, it has been able to develop and test more ideas than it has been able to disseminate. For example, the United States is more actively involved in quality assurance in long-term care and is more likely to develop an approach that will eventually emphasize accountability on the basis of the results of that care. Given the strengths of its diverse constituents, the United States is also more likely to develop formal processes for examining the ways to foster client choice and to recognize the concomitant need for greater client responsibility.

Canadians have proceeded by deciding on the direction in which they wanted to move and starting the journey with the expectations of making midcourse corrections as needed. Once they had sufficient momentum, it was possible to refine the task as new problems were uncovered or the situation became clearer with experience. Americans place greater reliance on mechanisms, especially market mechanisms that speak to incentives. They expect gaming and other efforts to beat the system. They first want to see a system in place that would create (and reinforce) the climate for desired changes in behaviors.[13] Hence, their strong reliance on demonstration projects and general slowness to make major program shifts. But every once in a while they adopt the Canadian approach and introduce a revolution, even in health care (e.g., Prospective Payment for Medicare), and then have to react to the adaptive behaviors they encounter.

Each country can learn useful lessons from the other. The more difficult task is applying them. Ironically, the Canadians, who seem to have come the furthest in establishing an equitable and workable system of long-term care, seem more anxious to learn from the United States than the reverse. Some would suggest that they are too eager to emulate models of care that have been developed in response to perverse incentives. Importing ideas and concepts across the border in either direction will require careful attention to the intellectual import tariff. Each country has enough of its own culture that few ideas can be adopted wholesale from either.

Notes

1. A word of caution about terms: "Medicare" is the name given to programs in both countries. In Canada it refers to the universal health plan. In the United States it refers to a universal health insurance program for persons age 65 and older (and a few others with chronic disabilities).

2. We have facetiously described the American approach to paying for long-term care as universal coverage with a deductible equal to all your assets (except your home and a few thousand dollars) and a copayment equal to all your income (less a few dollars for spending money).

3. Unless otherwise noted, we will use "Canadian" and "American" to refer to general concepts and approaches, which may be implemented somewhat differently in specific provinces or states.

4. One can speculate about the degree to which the demented husband is consulted in either country.

5. The American rate for nursing home beds is about 5 per 100 elderly persons compared to the Canadian rate of about 7.5 beds in homes for special care per 100 elderly

persons, but the Canadian figure covers a wider range of beds, including homes for retarded persons of all ages (also in the U.S. rate for nursing homes), alcohol half-way houses, and other special housing.

6. Although many experts suggest that private insurance will not be an effective deterrent to demands on Medicaid (Rivlin 1988).

7. Some private financing programs have recognized that older persons have a major asset in their homes and have developed packages that entail selling the home and moving to more modest quarters with services or taking out reverse mortgages whereby the person can receive the proceeds from the sale but continue to live in the home as a renter until his death.

8. Persons with end-stage renal disease of all ages are eligible, as are a small group of those who are "permanently and totally disabled."

9. Ontario is considering moving to a graduated copayment.

10. This ignores the impact on a spouse or the right to leave a legacy.

11. Some better term for the excess of revenues less expenses for ostensibly nonprofit enterprises is needed.

12. As soon as the cost of the premium exceeds its value, as was the case with Catastrophic Coverage in the United States several years ago, there will be an outcry by some that they can purchase the benefit cheaper privately. It is easier and politically cleaner to acknowledge the cross-subsidies directly.

13. For a good example of how complex the gaming and counter-gaming can be in American health care planning, see Enthoven and Kronick's consumer choice health plan (Enthoven and Kronick 1989).

References

Beer, C., E. Caplan, G. Morin, and S. Collins. 1990. "Strategies for Change: Comprehensive Reform of Ontario's Long-term Care Services." Division of Community Health and Support Services, Ontario.

Beland, F. 1986. "The Clientele of Comprehensive and Traditional Home Care Programs." *The Gerontologist* 26: 382–88.

Carcagno, G. J., and P. Kemper. 1988. "The Evaluation of the National Long-term Care Channeling Demonstration: I. An Overview of the Channeling Demonstration and its Evaluation." *Health Services Research* 23: 1–22.

Enthoven, A., and R. Kronick. 1989. "A Consumer-Choice Health Plan for the 1990s: Universal Health Insurance in a System Designed to Promote Quality and Economy." *The New England Journal of Medicine* 320

General Accounting Office. 1979. "Entering a Nursing Home—Costly Implications for Medicaid and the Elderly." Washington, D.C.: United States General Accounting Office.

Kane, R. A., and R. L. Kane. 1985. "The Feasibility of Universal Long-term Care Benefits: Ideas from Canada." *New England Journal of Medicine* 312: 1357–63.

————. 1987. *Long-term Care: Principles, Programs, and Policies.* New York: Springer Publishing Company.

————. Forthcoming, 1994. "Lessons from In-home and Community-based Care in Canada." In *Issues in Home Care Financing Reform,* edited by D. Rowland and B. Lyons. Baltimore: The Johns Hopkins University Press.

Kane, R. L., and R. A. Kane. 1985. *A Will and A Way: What Americans Can Learn About Long-term Care From Canada.* New York: Columbia University Press.

————. 1990. "A Nursing Home in Your Future?" *The New England Journal of Medicine* 324: 627–29.

Mendelson, M. A. 1974. *Tender Loving Greed.* New York: Alfred A. Knopf.

Moss, F. E., and V. J. Halamandaris. 1977. *Too Old, Too Sick, Too Bad: Nursing Homes in America.* Germantown, Md.: Aspen Systems Corp.

Reich, R. 1987. *Tales of a New America: The Anxious Liberal's Guide to the Future.* New York: Random House.

Rivlin, A. M., and J.M. Wiener. 1988. "Caring for the Disabled Elderly. Who Will Pay?" Washington, D.C.: The Brookings Institution.

Stephens, S., and J. Christianson. 1986. "Informal Care of the Elderly." New York: Free Press.

Vladeck, B. G. 1980. *Unloving Care: The Nursing Home Tragedy.* New York: Basic Books.

Weissert, W. G., C. M. Cready, and J. E. Pawelak. 1989. "Home and Community Care: Three Decades of Findings." In *Health Care of the Elderly: An Information Source Book,* edited by M. D. Peterson and D. L. White. Newbury Park, Ca.: Sage Publications Ltd, 39–126.

Weissert, W. G., T. T. H. Wan, and B. B. Livieratos. 1980. "Effects and Costs of Day Care and Homemaker Services for the Chronically Ill: A Randomized Experiment." Office of Health Research, Statistics, and Technology, National Center for Health Services Research, Department of Health and Human Services. Hyattsville, Md.: National Center for Health Services Research.

Chapter Thirteen

HOUSING THE ELDERLY: THE DEMOGRAPHIC IMPERATIVE

Langley C. Keyes

Demographic patterns, housing policy history, and an overwhelming predilection for home ownership have produced a very similar overall housing situation for the elderly in the United States and Canada. Unlike health care, for which the differences between the two systems are what captivate attention, in the elderly housing arena what is provocative is the parallelism.

An observer from Great Britain or Sweden would surely be struck by the North American similarities and their collective difference from the history of the Western European countries. With one critical exception, the United States and Canada have a remarkably comparable story to tell about the history, the present profile, and the future challenge of housing the elderly. But that exception has a major potential impact on how each of the countries is likely to handle the challenges to housing policy as the elderly in both countries grow in number and life expectancy.

Since much of this essay focuses on the parallelism between the two countries in housing affecting the elderly, it is organized into four sections with this in mind. The chapter starts with a number of "givens" about the nature of the elderly population, their residential profile, and the housing challenge confronting the two countries in the years ahead. Having set the context for current policy issues, it steps back and briefly discusses the history of elderly housing policy in North America, how both countries got to where they presently are, and the implications of that prologue for the future. The analysis then moves forward to the central paradigm of today's elderly housing challenge: how to manage in a cost effective and humane way the expanding number of elderly households residing in homes that they own. Having established the elderly housing paradigm for the 1990s, the chapter explores the critical difference between the United States and Canada as to how policy is carried out. It is in the area of implementation that differences between the two countries become central to the analysis.

The treatment of long-term care discussed in chapter 12 of this book is singularly important to a comparative discussion of housing policy for the elderly. One cannot understand or make judgments about the housing system for the elderly in either country without acknowledging the workings of its long-term care (LTC) system. In fact, viewed from the perspective of national social policy, LTC for the elderly is simply the extension of the housing and service issue to its logical conclusion in a setting for residential dependency.

THE ELDERLY AND THEIR HOUSING: A PROFILE IN PARALLELISM

The inexorable logic of demography is making and will continue to make the elderly[1] a larger and more significant number of the population profile of the two countries in the decades ahead. Two of the many analyses on the growth of the older population in the United States and Canada make this point succinctly.

For the United States, Struyk et al. (1988, p. 21) report that:

In 1985, 28.6 million people were 65 or older, 12 percent of the total. The elderly population will reach 17.6 percent in 2020 and 21 percent in 2030. In other words, by 2030 the elderly population will be twice as large and account for almost double its current share of the population. The so-called very old population will be 2.6 times larger in 2020 and 2.8 times larger in 2030 than at present.

The Canadian portrait (Schwenger 1988, p. 3) presents the facts somewhat differently, but in a way which has equal applicability to the United States.

Population aging . . . is now occurring rapidly. Well noted has been an aging of the aged population with the greatest relative increase in the oldest old (85 +). This is the group with the greatest proportion of problems, including potential loneliness, poverty, and disability with a much higher rate of institutional care. Old age in [Canada] is predominantly a woman's issue, becoming more so as age increases and, up until recently, at an accelerating rate decade by decade.

Conceptualizing "the elderly" as a category relevant for public policy requires a different mind-set than that required for structuring a problem category like "the poor." (We may always have the poor with us but public policy works with varying degrees of effectiveness to diminish that number.) The elderly are expanding not only in number but also in longevity. Their larger cohorts will demand and require service in the future. This both is inevitable, a consequence of demographic realities, and a cause for celebration, with the old living longer and more independently thanks to science, technology, and better living conditions and habits. The housing challenges confronting elderly people will grow in complexity as that population lives longer. But to the degree the elderly age with a minimum of physical and psychological impairment, the inevitable problems with their housing will be less demanding.

The profile of "the elderly" in all its age categories has a demographic certainty. Unlike estimating which poor families will enter the ranks of the homeless (a cause for debate and conjecture), the number of households entering the ranks of the elderly is a statistical given. But who among them will actually become the frail elderly is a point for discussion and debate. There is good statistical, actuarial, and historical evidence to estimate the frail group's size and shape. These households are already among us, working inexorably along the aging chain. But who among the older will become marginally or totally unable to live independently cannot be known any more than who among very poor families will enter the ranks of the homeless. When frailty will strike a particular household and make it impossible for that household to continue to live independently or even with support is not statistically derivable, as sons and daughters worrying about their aging parents well know.

An increasing number of elderly will be both very old and very frail. There will also be "older" people who are frail and very old elderly who are not. Given these complexities, the critical issue for elderly housing policy is the inexorable logic that more older people means a larger number of households who will have difficulties living independently without a little—or even a lot of—help from their families and friends.

In 1981, 19 percent of Canada's elderly population was over 80. By 2001 that figure will have climbed to 24 percent of the country's senior population (Brink 1984). The impact of this growth on elderly housing planning is evident. "Sixty percent of those persons over 75 years of age have some type of chronic health condition that limits their ability to carry on daily activities" (U.S. Conference of Mayors 1986, p. 2).

Taking care of a house is one of the daily activities that becomes increasingly problematic for many with serious health problems. A recent survey by the American Association of Retired Persons (AARP

1990, p.8) indicates that two-thirds of their respondents "anticipate needing help in the future with outdoor maintenance . . ." and over half see the need for help in the future with "heavy housework."

Both countries then face the same challenge: how to deal with an increasingly large aging population of which a rising percentage will be the very old and very frail. As Struyk et al. intelligently put the issue in *Future U.S. Housing Policy* (1988, p. 13):

> What should public policy be towards this group that will begin to dominate our society shortly after the year 2010? As a starting point the sheer numbers of elderly obviously argue for a cost-effective federal policy that keeps the elderly away from expensive institutional care.
> . . . Housing accommodations for the elderly not only must be afford-able and of adequate quality but also must possess the special features of support services necessary for occupants with functional limitations to live reasonably independently. Housing policy has to deal with both the traditional housing problems and with the provision of support services.

While emphasizing the expanding and aging elderly population, the richness of variation within the category must also be recognized. The elderly are not only different from each other in the physical and psychological burdens that increasing age places on them, they are also heterogeneous in income, class, location, and in the value they attach to their houses and their neighborhoods. What they want, need, and can pay for by way of housing covers a wide spectrum of housing type, location, and cost.

Given these differences, the fact remains that the vast majority of Canada's elderly live in urban centers—with 40 percent of them in cities of 500,000 or more (Brink 1984). In the United States in 1983 about half of those persons 65 and over lived in only seven of the fifty states, most in the Sunbelt (U.S. Conference of Mayors 1986). The saliency of the elderly issue locally is obviously greatest in such locations in both countries. In both countries poor, frail, single women living alone constitute a growing percentage of the elderly population. When focusing on poor families we have increasingly named poverty a "woman's issue." Within the elderly profile, poverty is also a single woman's issue.

In addition to inexorably getting older and more dependent on service, what many of these otherwise different households have in common is that a vast majority of them own their own homes. For the emerging elderly cohorts, the North American dream has been fulfilled. When reviewing the many innovative supported or alternative housing programs on both sides of the border, it is easy to forget that the dominant mode of tenure for the elderly is mortgage-free home ownership. Two-thirds of Canadian elders own their own homes, and 86 percent of them have homes that are mortgage free (Chappell 1990). The comparable U.S. figures are 70 percent owners, of whom 57 percent are unencumbered with a mortgage (Struyk et al. 1988). Thus a majority of elderly households in both countries—regardless of income, location, and health—reside in houses and neighborhoods in which they have lived for a considerable period of time—for many of them it was long enough to pay off the mortgage. The homeowners may have, as a consequence, significant wealth which, if fungible, could greatly benefit their financial situation. This fact has not gone unnoticed; home equity conversions have been explored in numerous ways.

For all the interesting efforts on both sides of the border to provide residential settings for the elderly through public housing or nonprofit institutions, the fact remains that most of the elderly live in "individually chosen homes." In the United States the figure is 91 percent, with only 4 percent living in federal housing for the elderly and retirement communities and 5 percent in nursing homes (U.S. Conference of Mayors 1986). The figures for Canada are comparable. In other words, renting and owning in the private sector is overwhelmingly the status of North American elderly households.

It is critical to emphasize the statistical reality of elderly households living in their own homes because so much of the literature about elderly housing focuses on alternative housing modes. It is easy to focus so much on these modes that the central fact of resident owner becomes obscured.

Moreover, 86 percent of U.S. elderly, a recent survey (AARP 1990) points out, "would like to stay in their own homes and never move. Just 13 percent say they would like to move." That 86 percent is up 8 percentage points from 1986. Sixty-five percent of this recently surveyed group, beyond wanting to avoid moving and hoping to live in a mixed-age neighborhood, anticipate needing help in the future for outdoor maintenance. This is in contrast to 40 percent in the 1986 AARP survey.

An emerging phenomenon in the United States is currently defined by the acronym NORC: Naturally Occurring Retirement Community. In the United States some 27 percent of the elderly live in neighborhoods or buildings where a majority of the residents are 60 or older. This is, in relative terms, a huge number of elderly aging in place. Little is known from research about these clusters of aging households. As Struyk et al. (1988, pp. 144–45) note:

Naturally occurring retirement communities differ in several ways from the planned retirement communities that normally come to mind . . . they are not designed specifically for older people, and they tend to be age integrated, even though they are predominantly occupied by the elderly. The communities are small . . . and they generally are not marketed as retirement communities or considered to be such by their own residents.

To date there has been little systematic examination of how common these naturally occurring retirement communities are in the nation . . . nor have analysts given much thought to exploiting their existence to further help the elderly occupants.

ELDERLY HOUSING HISTORY: THE POLICY DOMAIN

Elderly Housing: A Desired Good

The story of elderly housing is a topic within the general history of housing policy. A number of comparisons of the U.S. and Canadian housing systems have been written which feature these central themes:

1. The relationship between the states and the federal government regarding housing policy is different in the United States from the relationship between the federal government and the provinces in Canada.
2. The U.S. Department of Housing and Urban Development (HUD) plays a much less central role than does the Canadian Mortgage and Housing Corporation (CMHC) in Canada.
3. Social and nonprofit housing are more central to Canada than to the United States.

In both countries the housing policy issues of the elderly have always occupied a privileged position. It is hard to envisage in either country a national politician, policymaker, or vocal neighborhood spokesperson unsupportive of housing for the elderly. While there may be disagreement about the form housing should take, the elderly have great appeal to those who cluster around them. The generational disparity issue never seems to have politicized the domain of elderly housing.

The United States has drawn a much sharper line between the deserving and undeserving poor than has Canada, where the social net is more broadly flung (Katz 1989). Yet even in the United States, where the elderly have historically been considered the deserving poor, elderly housing is literally a "motherhood" issue. Unlike housing for poor families or the mentally handicapped, the not-in-my-backyard (NIMBY) concept does not apply to elderly housing even— in the vast majority of cases—for low-income older Americans.

The privileged public position of elderly housing is such that policymakers are often confronted with the problem of pulling support away from elderly issues in order to focus on the housing needs of other groups—low-income families, the mentally handicapped, etc. On at least one occasion, public housing for the elderly has been the stalking horse for low-income family units. In Massachusetts during the 1980s the state-financed elderly public housing program was made available to localities only if they agreed on a one-to-four split: for every four units of elderly public housing awarded by the Commonwealth, the locality had to take the financing for one family unit. The formula was a success. Communities began to accept family public housing because of their overwhelming desire to get housing for the elderly for their communities.[2]

At the municipal level in both Canada and the United States tax breaks—circuit breakers for elderly homeowners—are perennially popular. Making it financially possible for elderly to remain in their homes—and in the neighborhoods in which they have lived for years—is viewed as a legitimate form of public subsidy. Such relief for poor younger families would raise a cry of favoritism and inequity.

Housing Policy History: A Singular Tale of Two Countries

The history of elderly housing policy in both countries is remarkably similar—emerging as a consequence of the Great Depression which focused the federal government on housing policy in general. The initial North American concerns for elderly housing had to do with the quality and cost of housing and with the development of public housing targeted specifically at the elderly.

Public housing for the elderly, while an interesting topic in both countries and one with many of the same twists and turns, does not house a large percentage of the elderly population in either. While numerically significant—1.5 million senior citizens in the United States live in HUD-supported housing nationwide—as a percentage of the current elderly and future elderly population the category is relatively modest. This small proportion should not obscure the policy concern for those aging in place in such centers. As noted by the U.S. Conference of Mayors (1986, p. 36), "A full 40 percent of the elderly in public housing nationwide are over 75 years of age. . . . As a result many of those elderly housing projects are in danger of becoming nursing homes without services."

Canada's history of federal support for both public housing and nonprofit-sponsored housing for the elderly is quite similar. While not constituting a significant percentage of housing for the elderly, such efforts were a major focus of CMHC activity in the late sixties and early seventies. A 1973 survey of those developments pointed to the strengths and weaknesses of the approach, all of which were mirrored in American studies of elderly public housing. Most of the elderly in the developments were glad to be there but wanted a greater level of social services and support from management for their special needs. The housing was seen as simply bricks and mortar run by management agents unsympathetic to the particular social needs of an elderly population (Canadian Council on Social Development 1973).

In addition to relatively similar levels of financial support from the national government, the two countries have historically focused on the same two traditional concerns about elderly housing: building condition and the amount of income paid by elders for housing. These two topics are a variation of the long-standing North American tendency to define housing problems in terms of the physical condition of buildings, the percentage of income paid for housing and overcrowding. The history has been one of mitigating physical deficiencies and increasing the financial capacity of low-income households to own and to rent.

In the mid-seventies, however, attention in both countries turned from traditional housing problems to greater concern for the relationship between aging occupants of dwellings and their capacity to continue to live independently in the structure:

> In considering the housing needs of the elderly, it is useful to distinguish between the traditional housing problems and the needs associated with health problems and functional impairments. The traditional housing problems (termed here *dwelling-specific* problems) include deficiencies in the dwelling itself, spending an excessive share of income on housing, and living in crowded conditions. These problems can be measured in fairly straightforward ways; they are strongly related to income and little associated with age.
>
> Housing problems associated with the match between the dwelling and the occupants' needs—termed here *dwelling-use* problems—are much less precisely defined. Many dwelling-use problems arise from functional impairments and are best thought of as indicators of *potential* housing problems, because they can be offset through personal help or modifications of the housing unit. . . . Some dwelling-use problems are related to age and physical impairments but not specifically to

income; others, particularly overhousing, are associated with aging and living alone (Struyk et al. 1988, p. 117).

This paradigmatic shift, a focus on use rather than building condition or financial capacity to pay, provides the framework for a more detailed analysis of current policy deliberations concerning the future of the North American elderly and their housing—a topic to which I now turn.

THE CURRENT POLICY PARADIGM

The Convergent Policy Challenge

Whether viewed from the level of federal, state/provincial, or municipal government, how public policy *ought* to deal with its aging population is conceptually similar in the United States and Canada. An internal consensus (overwhelming consensus if contrasted with health care issues in the United States, for example) also exists in each country among advocate groups, policy makers, politicians, and senior citizens themselves that the housing policy in good currency:

1. provide the elderly with a range of choices enabling them to stay in their homes and neighborhoods as long as they wish and can physically and mentally do so;
2. support aging in place as the preferred option of most elderly; means should be found to adjust the structure of current housing and the services provided to it to facilitate such place-based strategies;
3. provide sheltered or supported housing as an alternative to nursing homes for those who can no longer cope with their current residential setting, however physically modified and provided with services.

The difference in the politics of old age policy noted in Part One of this volume has not been played out in the housing arena. Among the various interest groups concerned with elderly housing the message is almost interchangeable across our borders. Thus, an advocate piece published by One Voice—The Canadian Seniors Network—in 1989, looking at the future of seniors' housing in Canada, stresses a concern for holistic and participatory planning that includes the needs and views of minority and rural communities and "more effective working relationships among levels of government" (Canadian Seniors Network 1989). The document in all its substance and affect could have been written line by line by a comparable group in the United States—the Gray Panthers, for example.

Less concerned with participation and holistic solutions per se than One Voice, the American Association of Retired Persons (AARP) is a powerful, well-financed, and extremely sophisticated group lobbying on behalf of all elderly Americans, whose Legislation and Public Policy Agenda " . . . works to further the advocacy mission of the Association" (AARP 1991). Their Public Policy Agenda is revised each year and contains an up-to-date analysis of national legislation and the position of AARP on it.[3] In housing, the disparity between the two countries in political lobbying and interest groups was not a reality in the eighties. Presumably the same will hold true in the nineties, given ever-greater convergence between the two countries on the nature of elderly housing problems and remedies for them.

The Emerging Elderly Housing Paradigm

Today the housing policy paradigm for the elderly in both countries has shifted from a central concern for building quality and housing cost to a primary focus on finding ways of allowing people to age in place, i.e., to get either physical changes in their residences or supportive services to allow them to remain at home and out of special needs housing or nursing homes. Failing to find the means of living in their own residence, the individual should have access to sheltered or supportive housing.[4]

In both the United States and Canada, the uninitiated are consistently baffled (and even the housing expert sometimes confounded) by the number and diversity of housing programs, initiatives, and demonstrations aimed at providing more economic, appropriately retrofitted, and better serviced housing for the elderly. From "Granny Flats" to Reverse Annuity Mortgages, the journals are filled with experiments and demonstrations of innovative ways of solving in a humane way the housing dilemmas faced by those growing old. Nonetheless, the diversity of programs has at its core concern for four issues:

1. reducing the cost of housing to the elderly;
2. improving and transforming the physical condition, location, and servicing of that housing to meet the emerging needs of aging people;
3. providing greater choice for elderly households; and

4. finding ways of insuring that aging people are serviced by cost-effective programs.

Conceptualizing Elderly Shelter: Categories or Continuum

On both sides of the border, policymakers who think and write about elderly housing present two conceptual models for structuring the range of shelter options for the elderly. One model organizes those options into three categories. The other poses a continuum of options.[5] In its most pristine form the categorical approach sees elders as:

1. independent and needing to worry only about housing cost and the physical condition of their structures;
2. somewhat dependent and getting help either in their current dwellings or by moving into more sheltered environments; and
3. in the dependent living category which requires a "total package of services on site . . . delivered to the elderly with high levels of impairment" (Brink 1984, p. 16).

The alternative view presents the field as a continuum of shelter needs and therefore options, ranging from ordinary housing, i.e., no physical changes or services required (where physical condition and cost of housing could be issues), to totally dependent living which in its extreme form constitutes long-term care. The housing system thus inevitably blends into the long-term care system. The independent variable along the continuum of care is the character and intensity of services added to the basic provision of shelter with its "ordinary" concern for physical condition and cost. Services can be of two kinds: those which transform aspects of the physical character of the house (hand railings, ramps, etc.); and human services which provide support to the individual (meals on wheels, housekeeping, security, yard-work, shopping).

The continuum model, in my view, better captures the realities of the field. How one solution blends into another is important, and blending has implications for institutional relationships that are critical. What need emphasis are the links—the ways one solution connects to another—not the discrete character of the categories.

Whether interpreted as a continuum or a set of categories, the housing options and their institutional challenges in North America are remarkably similar. For all the bewildering array of intermediate options between owner-occupied houses and rented apartments and long-term nursing care or hospitals, a professional working in the elderly housing and service field from the United States would feel at home in Canada and conversely. The conceptual debates, the structure of the organizations dealing with those issues, and the problems of coordination among health, social service, and housing professionals are all cut from the same cloth. War stories about lack of coordination, conflict with the medical model, and problems with local zoning are familiar to a elderly housing veteran from either side of the border.

A central similarity is the image of gaps in the system—one which pervades the analyses of reflective practitioners in both countries. The following contention, while drawn from a handbook prepared by the AARP and the U.S. Conference of Mayors (U.S. Conference of Mayors 1986, p. 35), could as well have been written by CMHC:

> Clearly, there is a growing recognition of the need to develop effective alternative living arrangements to "fill the gap" between independent living and dependent living for those elderly who have need of some assistance but who do not require institutional care. Alternative housing offers a range of semi-independent living options for those elderly.

Note the similarities in the argument framed by Canadian experts (Schwenger 1988, p. i):

> We are experiencing large increases in the number of elderly, and the lack of housing alternatives reflects the perception that seniors are living either independently in their own homes or apartments, or dependent upon institutional care. In fact there is a continuum along which the elderly person should be able to move to receive shelter with support as necessary.
>
> Especially important is the semi-independent category of seniors who, with assistance and appropriate housing, could remain in the community. Housing alternatives for this group are grossly inadequate in Canada. . . .

The following tables provide three ways of ordering the array of alternative shelter options developed to fill gaps in the housing continuum.

Figure 13.1 sets out the continuum and highlights the relationship among intensity of service, cost, level of impairment, and type of housing facility. Table 13.1 describes the advantages and disadvantages the AARP associated with each approach in 1986. Table 13.2 connects specific types of housing alternatives to a continuum of impairment level (described now in terms of the three categories of independent, semi-independent, and dependent).

The policy paradigm represented by these various alternatives is the product of an elderly housing system which: (1) draws on public

Figure 13.1 CONTINUUM OF TYPES OF LIVING ARRANGEMENTS

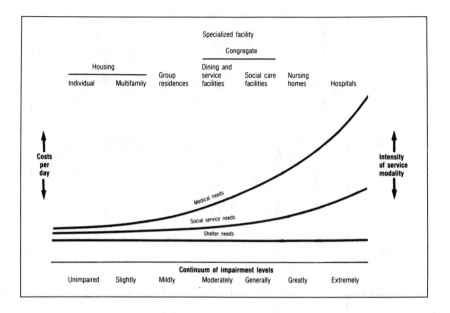

Source: Adapted from Freeland, Mark S., Carol E. Schendler, "Health Spending in the 80's: Integration of Clinical Practice Patterns with Management," *Health Care Financing*, Spring 1984, Volume 5, Number 3, p. 24.

and private resources; (2) coordinates housing, social service, and health domains; and (3) integrates the policies of local, regional (i.e., state or province), and federal government to put the right people in the right boxes. In an ideal policy world there would be an equilibrium state in which elderly users get exactly the support they need in the most cost-effective way.

Thus, there exists in both the United States and Canada clear recognition of the need for the continuum. Yet the small scale of most of the current alternative housing settings, the gaps in the continuum itself, and the profound separation between the housing and the long-term care systems, particularly in the United States, makes gap-filling a demanding challenge for the coming decades.

Implementing the Continuum

In Canada and the United States, the number of elderly who have actually experienced one or another of the options along the contin-

Table 13.1 ADVANTAGES AND DISADVANTAGES OF SELECTED ALTERNATIVE HOUSING ARRANGEMENTS

Type	Advantages	Disadvantages
Accessory Apartments	• provide additional income for elderly homeowners • companionship and security • increase supply of affordable rental housing • personal support services may be provided in lieu of rent	• initial construction cost to homeowners • neighborhood concern about lowered property values • zoning restraints • possible housing and building code violations
Board and Care Homes	• home-like environment • afford fragile, isolated elderly opportunity to interact with others • economical	• not licensed, concerned with standards and treatment of residents • owner/operators often lack training • little planned social activities
Congregate Housing	• provides basic support services that can extend independent living • reduces social isolation • provides physical and emotional security	• tendency to overserve the needs of tenants; promoting dependency • expensive to build and operate • those without kitchen facilities restrict tenants independence • expensive for most elderly without subsidy
ECHO, Granny Flats	• facilitates older persons receiving support support from younger family members; option to remain in individual home • smaller housing unit, less expensive to operate	• potential to lower property values • attitude and impact on neighborhood concerns about housing and building code violations

	Advantages	Disadvantages
Home Equity Conversion	• convert lifetime investment into usable income • allow elderly with marginal incomes to remain in familiar surroundings • can be used to finance housing expenses, ie: make necessary repairs, utilities, taxes	• risk that homeowner will live longer than term of loan • homes of lower value (often the type owned by elderly) may not provide monthly payments large enough to be worth cost of loan • inflation may erode the value of the loan over the years • reluctancy by homeowner to utilize due to lack of information, concern for lein on property and/or impact on estate for heirs.
Life Care Facilities	• offers pre-paid health care • security and protection against inflation and financially draining illnesses • wide range of social activities with health and support system	• too expensive for many elderly • no protection should the facility go out of business • older person receives no deed to property • no guarantees that monthly payments will not rise • location is usually rural, isolated from community services.
Shared Housing	• less expensive due to shared costs for household operators • companionship, security • promotes intergenerational cooperation and understanding • more extensive use of existing housing • program inexpensive to operate	• problems with selection of individual to share home • amount of privacy reduced • does not meet medical and personal problems • added income may mean owner is no longer eligible for public benefits • city zoning ordinances may prohibit

Source: Adapted from A Manual of Housing Alternatives for the Elderly, Vol. I, Rosalyn Katz, Ph.D. Health and Welfare Planning Association for the City of Pittsburgh and Housing Choices for Older Homeowners, American Association of Retired Persons.

Table 13.2 HOUSING ALTERNATIVES AND HOUSING LEVELS

Type of Housing Alternative	Level of Housing		
	Independent	Semi-Independent	Dependent
Single Family Dwelling	X		
Regular Apartment Rental	X		
Condominium	X		
Cooperative[a]	X		
Home Equity Conversion[b]	X		
Home Maintenance and Repair	X	X	
Shared Housing	X	X	
Accessory Apartment	X	X	X
ECHO Housing	X	X	X
Life Care Community	X	X	X
Congregate Housing		X	
Personal Care Boarding Home			X

Source: *A Manual of Housing Alternatives for the Elderly, Volume III*, Need and Demand Projections, September, 1984, pgs. 151, 152, 155.
a. Has potential as semi-independent level if congregate dining is offered within the structure.
b. Has potential as both semi-independent and dependent levels if converted equity is used to cover costs of in-home care services.

Independent
Living arrangements appropriate for individuals/couples capable of handling their own housekeeping, cooking and personal care. Included in this category are such dwellings as: single family homes, apts, condominiums, coops, etc.

Semi-independent
Living arrangements which provide assistance for those who are not totally self-sufficient but capable of tending to their own personal care such as bathing and grooming. Included in this category are such dwellings as: congregate housing, ECHO housing, life care communities.

Dependent
Living arrangements which provide 24-hour personal/custodial care for more severely impaired individuals who do not need daily nursing or medical care. Included in this category are such facilities as foster homes, personal care boarding homes.

uum is relatively small. Canadian analysts bewail the absence of real alternatives to the status quo and the extent to which " . . . supportive housing has been rare" (Blandford et al. 1989, p. 826). In their 1990 survey, AARP (1990, p. 8) found that only "five percent of the respondents live in a retirement community or building planned specifically for older adults."

While the matching of households with the appropriate resources appears cost effective, sensible, and user sensitive, there is in fact little experience in the United States with such fine tuning. As Struyk et al. (1988, p. 5) accurately note:

> ... [There is a] lack of coordination in the administration of programs dealing with housing problems and those providing support services. The joint provision of services is largely unexplored territory, except for the fledgling congregate housing program, some local efforts in which federal resources are effective coordinated, and certain pilot programs being conducted under Medicaid waivers.

There is more experience in Canada, but it too is limited. The Director for the Center on Aging at the University of Manitoba explains it thus (Chappell 1990, p. 5):

> Supportive housing is ... being recognized throughout the country as the option of choice. However, recognizing the need and providing adequate alternatives in order to meet the need are very different objectives. There are problems with implementing a range of supportive housing options. ... The fact that housing tends to be a separate administrative jurisdiction means that continuity of care and coordination of services between health, social service, and housing departments of government are difficult to implement.

The challenge to policymakers is how to provide a range of housing and service options that are cost effective (if not least cost) yet still meet the desires and needs of the elderly. It is critical to distinguish between desire and need. For what elderly individuals want—to stay in their neighborhoods—may simply be financially impossible given the requirement for supportive services that such a decision entails.

As the tables in this chapter make clear, opportunities and problems exist with each of the options along the continuum. While there are minor differences in the nature of those issues in the United States and Canada, the central theme is the similarity in each country. A set of policy challenges is embedded in this array of programs, challenges which—with two important exceptions—are consistent across the U.S.-Canadian border.

These exceptions, however, are critical to understanding how the *implementation* of the continuum may differ in the United States and Canada and why, given current political, institutional, and attitudinal realities, Canada has a better chance of actually establishing a cost-effective and equitable continuum of programs.

The first of these differences is programmatic: the fact that Canada has an articulated long-term care policy and the United States does not. The second is more subtle: the relationship of attitude to the challenge of program design.

HOUSING ASSISTANCE AND LONG-TERM CARE: THE MISSING LINK

The relationship between . . . housing and long-term institutional care is one that is seldom made by planning organizations and providers of health services to the elderly. . . . *A better balance is needed between resources that are available to the housing and health sectors.* This would require examination of inappropriate placement of the elderly in institutional care.

—Metropolitan Toronto District Health
Council (Schwenger 1988, pp. i–ii)

. . . a number of crucial interrelationships need to be stressed at the outset. In some cases, such as links between housing and long-term care needs, the relationship is a direct one: more appropriate housing for older disabled persons can enable them to live at home rather than move to an institutional setting. *Careful coordination of legislation may thus improve the long-term care picture through changes in housing policy.* [emphasis added]

—AARP (1991, p. 1)

As the above statements exemplify, reflective policymakers in North America are aware that the line between the housing and long-term care systems is an arbitrary one. They posit that if cost-effective, responsive service is to be provided to an increasingly frail elderly population, the barrier between the systems must be removed. The housing, social service, and health systems must find ways of working together cooperatively and of recognizing in practice what the policymakers realize in theory: namely, that there is a continuum from totally independent to totally dependent living.

The institutional and organizational challenges to establishing a true continuum are, however, profound. Coordination and comprehensiveness are expressions that have been used for years in the housing and human service fields. Veterans of the two arenas smile knowingly when the terms are applied to the health field and its relationship to the service and housing agenda.

As observers on both sides of the border make clear, there is little if any tradition of coordination between the health—i.e., long-term care—and the service sector, let alone the housing system. For such coordination to occur at the federal, provincial/state, and municipal levels requires a major shift in mind-set of the various practitioners involved in the different sectors. To implement that shift requires a reformulation of rules, regulations, incentives, understanding, and support at the local level.

Yet, given the complexities and difficulties in producing a continuum where there is currently a dual system, the comparative advantage of Canada over the United States seems clear. And it is here that differences between the two countries inform the comparative agenda. As Newman and Struyk (1988, p. 4) point out, "basically, the United States has no articulated long-term care policy." AARP (AARP 1991, pp. 37 and 39) is equally pointed: "Long-term care is an issue which concerns everyone in our society. Older people represent about two-thirds of those who require long-term care assistance. . . . The current delivery system suffers from fragmentation and large gaps in coverage." Kane and Kane (chapter 12 of this volume) point out that the U.S. system is fragmented by funding, but that in Canada all but two small provinces have opted to include LTC as a universally insured service, financed through federal block grant funds and additional provincial funds. Given current policy realities, Canada is better positioned to blend the housing and long-term care systems, if for no other reason than that there is in place a LTC system with which to blend.

It is, of course, conceivable that the fragmented LTC system in the United States could be transformed by a confluence of political will and policy initiatives. Because no such integrated system is now in place does not preclude one in the future. If, for example, the current debate about national health insurance resulted in a program which included LTC, the United States would—at least legally—be even with Canada. Even then there would be little experience with such a universal program and clearly much sorting out required before the process could run smoothly.

Program Design: The Challenge of Targeting

The challenge to policymakers, working in the various levels of government, is to produce a range of services and incentives for the elderly which represent a cost-effective combination of physical and social services. Matching the growing needs (and desires) of the elderly with the appropriately efficient level of service and spatial transformation becomes the great quest. The overall challenge is one of gap-filling, where programs do not exist along the housing service continuum and devising effective ways of moving services to people or people to services.

This matching of people to programs is not easy and raises the long-standing program design issue of targeting: how does one design programs and policies such that the right people get into the appropriate programs? Conceptually and operationally, the problem is to keep out the people who belong elsewhere and to insure that the eligible individuals get into the program. A simple diagram illustrates the goal: to maximize the number of eligible people occupying the "in" box while keeping ineligibles out.

	in	not in
eligible	X	0
ineligible	0	X

This dilemma of fit—of targeting—is one which Charles Murray in *Losing Ground* (1984) says is virtually impossible to achieve. The intellectual response to Murray is to argue that good design—the appropriate mixture of carrots and sticks—can go a long way towards meeting the problem.

Public Attitudes: Fair Play or Beat the System

Given the very real difficulties of creating a continuum that ensures "right fit," Canada appears in a better position than the United States to meet the challenge. The comparative advantage for Canada arises partly from the attitudinal difference between the two countries portrayed by the Kanes in chapter 12 of this volume. Baldly put, that difference is one in which U.S. providers of nursing home service are constantly trying to beat the system (see chapter 11 of this volume for further discussion).

There is at least some evidence that the U.S. entrepreneurial approach to seeking the most desirable part of the market exists among other providers and participants along the elder care continuum. Newman and Struyk (1988, p. 5), summarizing the findings about the cost effectiveness of community-based programs for the frail elderly, report that:

Community-based programs have found it difficult to prove that they are cost effective. The key stumbling block, as revealed by a series of experimental programs has been *an inability to define the target population correctly* [emphasis added].

The issue may be one of definition, i.e., a program design issue of not having found the appropriate way to determine which household is most at risk. Or it may be the attitudes in which entrepreneurship on the part of elderly households and their service providers result in queue jumping and overutilization of services by people who are not at risk.

There is some evidence that the "attitudinal factor" plays out in Canada to get the right elderly in more cost-effective settings. For example, in discussing several experimental programs in Manitoba, Neena Chappell (1990, p. 6) deals with targeting and reports results quite different from those Newman and Struyk describe in the United States.

> During the 80's concern arose in Manitoba that, despite the cost effi-ciencies of [multilevel care facilities] some of the disadvantages may not warrant their continued support. In particular there was concern that those entering the housing units to multilevel care facilities were becoming dependent earlier than necessary.... There was ... concern that these facilities tended to funnel their residents from lower to higher levels of care to the exclusion of applicants from other locations and that there was a "premature entry" to the facility's personal care home.

So far the discussion appears like one that could occur in the United States. But the findings of a province-wide study of a variety of elderly living situations in Manitoba are strikingly different. According to Chappell (1990), the study revealed no indication that mul-tilevel care facilities unduly funnel their residents from lower to higher levels of care, and no evidence of premature entry into the personal care home of the facility.

Granted, there are differences between the two experimental situ-ations, the absence of controls, and all the other reasons why the comparison is not "scientific." But as both countries strive to develop continua of care that are responsive and cost effective, it is worth noting that Manitoba Canadians did not work to beat the system but rather appear to have played by the rules. On the other hand, their neighbors to the south seem to have engaged in the kind of entrepre-neurial activity described by the Kanes.

The "public regarding" behavior of the Canadians—produced not by rules and regulations but by a sense of fair play—may lie at the heart of any viable cost-effective continua of care. If so, the challenge for the United States then, is how to develop such a sense of civic behavior.

Notes

1. Since "the elderly" are parsed into a number of categories it is worth getting out a definition of terms early in the paper. I take the following U.S. Bureau of the Census population categories as being in good currency: "older" = 55+; "elderly" = 65+; "aged" = 75+; and "very old" = 85+. Newman and Struyk (1988) define "frail elderly" as "persons in serious risk of institutionalization in the absence of receipt of support services."

2. The issue is in reality somewhat more complex than simply the desire to help out the locality's elderly. The local policymakers' wish for elderly units relates to the desire to free up single family homes in which the elderly are overhoused. Opening up opportunities for younger families to those homes means that new units do not have to be built, but rather that the existing stock of structures more appropriate for families with children is recycled. Elderly public housing units for low-income elderly become a means of free up those houses without displacing the elderly from the community they identify as home. The production of low-rent elderly housing becomes then a doubly useful policy.

3. The housing research and policy competence of the AARP is impressive. "Understanding Senior Housing for the 1990's," a survey of elder "preferences, concerns, and needs" while by definition an advocacy piece (AARP 1990), is a closely reasoned and detailed look at the cutting edge of issues confronting older people as they try to figure out how to deal with their ever-restricted capacities and the demands of the structures in which they live.

4. By focusing on a shifting paradigm I do not mean to ignore the significance of either of the traditional elderly housing concerns: the household cost of shelter or the physical condition of their shelter in which the elderly live. In both countries there are millions of elderly, particularly very old, single women who are living in physically deteriorated situations and/or paying an excessive amount of their dwindling income for rent or mortgage payment. These have been and will continue to be real issues of public policy concern in both countries. See Struyk (1988) and AARP (1991) on the U.S., and Brink (1994) on Canada.

5. While worrying about the distinction between the two organizing devices may seem excessively academic, the alternative framing does lead to somewhat different conclusions.

References

American Association of Retired Persons [AARP]. 1990. "Understanding Senior Housing for the 1990s." Washington, D.C.: AARP.

"Beyond Shelter: A Study of NHA Financed Housing for the Elderly Canadian." 1973. Ottawa: Canadian Council on Social Development.

Blandford, Audrey, Neena Chappell, and Susan Marshall. 1989. "Tenant Resource Coordinators: An Experiment in Supportive Housing." The Gerontologist 29 (6) 826–29.

Brink, Satya. 1984. "Housing Elderly People in Canada: Working Towards a Continuum of Housing Choices Appropriate to their Need." Working paper, Planning Division, Canadian Mortgage and Housing Corporation.

Canadian Seniors Network. 1989. "Habitat: Final Report and Recommendations." Ottawa: One Voice—Canadian Seniors Network.

Chappell, Neena L. 1990. "Housing for Canadian Elders: Current Directions and Future Innovations." Paper presented at conference, *Choices Today, Options Tomorrow, Senior Housing for the 90's.* Canadian Mortgage and Housing Corporation, Vancouver, British Columbia, June 1990.

Katz, Michael B. 1989. *The Undeserving Poor.* New York: Pantheon Books.

Murray, Charles A. 1984. *Losing Ground: American Social Policy: 1950–1980.* New York: Basic Books.

Newman, Sandra J., and Raymond J. Struyk. 1988. "Housing and Supportive Services: Federal Policy for the Frail Elderly and Chronically Mentally Ill." Cambridge, Mass.: MIT Housing Policy Project.

Schwenger, C. 1988. "Housing and the Health of the Elderly." Toronto: Metropolitan Toronto District Health Council (March).

Struyk, Raymond J., Margery A. Turner, and Makiko Veno. 1988. *Future U.S. Housing Policy.* Washington, D.C.: The Urban Institute Press.

"Towards a Just and Caring Society." 1991. Washington, D.C.: American Association of Retired Persons.

U.S. Conference of Mayors. 1986. "Assessing Elderly Housing." Washington, D.C.: U.S. Conference of Mayors.

ABOUT THE EDITORS

Vernon L. Greene is professor of public administration at Syracuse University's Maxwell School of Citizenship and Public Affairs. He serves as president of the National Academy on Aging, is a fellow of the Gerontological Society of America, and is a member of the editorial boards of *The Journal of Gerontology: Social Science* and *The Gerontologist*. His research is concerned mainly with issues of health and social services policy for frail older people.

Theodore R. Marmor is professor of public policy and political science at Yale's School of Management. Formerly editor of the *Journal of Health Politics, Policy and Law*, his research has concentrated on the politics and policy issues of the modern welfare state. He is coauthor, with Jerry Mashaw and Philip Harvey, of *America's Misunderstood Welfare State* (1992). His most recent book is a collection of essays entitled *Understanding Health Care Reform*, published in 1994 by Yale University Press.

Timothy M. Smeeding is professor of economics and public administration and director of the Center for Policy Research at Syracuse University's Maxwell School of Citizenship and Public Affairs. His research focuses on the economic status of the elderly and on cross-national issues in social policy. His previous books include *The Vulnerable*, with John Palmer and Barbara Boyle Torrey, and *Should Health Care be Rationed by Age?*

Morris L. Barer is director of the Centre for Health Services and Policy Research, and a professor in the department of Health Care and Epidemiology, at the University of British Columbia. He is also an associate of the Population Health Program of the Canadian Institute for Advanced Research. He served until recently as senior editor for health economics with *Social Science and Medicine* and as founding treasurer of the Canadian Health Economics Research Association. He has published widely in the areas of comparative health care financing, Canadian physician resource policy, and health care costs and utilization.

Margaret Pabst Battin is professor of philosophy and adjunct professor of internal medicine, Division of Medical Ethics, at the University of Utah. She has authored, edited, or co-edited nine books, and has won prizes for her short stories. In recent years, she has been engaged in research on active euthanasia and assisted suicide in Holland and Germany. Her most recent book, *The Least Worst Death*, is a collection of her essays on end-of-life issues written over the last fifteen years.

Robert H. Binstock is professor of aging, health, and society at Case Western Reserve University's School of Medicine, Department of Epidemiology and Biostatistics. A former president of the Gerontological Society of America, he has served as director of a White House task force on older Americans and as chair and member of a number of advisory panels to the U.S. government, state, and local governments, and foundations. He is author of some 150 articles on politics and policies affecting aging. His 17 books include *Too Old for Health Care?*, *Dementia and Aging: Ethics, Values, and Policy Choices*, five editions of *America's Political System*, and three editions of the *Handbook of Aging and the Social Sciences*.

Deborah A. Chassman is an adjunct professor at the George Mason University Law School, where she teaches welfare law and policy. A former senior executive service official at the federal Department of Health and Human Services, Ms. Chassman now assists federal, state, and local governments to develop, operate, and evaluate welfare reform programs.

Fay Lomax Cook is professor of education and social policy and associate director of the Center for Urban Affairs and Policy Research at Northwestern University. Her publications include *Who Should Be Helped? Public Support for Social Services, The Journalism of Outrage: Investigative Reporting and Agenda Building in America*, and *Support for the American Welfare State: The Views of Congress and the Public.*

Clyde Hertzman is on faculty in the department of Health Care and Epidemiology, and a faculty member with the Centre for Health Services and Policy Research, at the University of British Columbia. He is also a fellow of both the Population Health Program, which he coordinates, and the Program in Human Development, of the Canadian Institute for Advanced Research. He has written extensively and conducted research in a wide variety of areas, including the determinants of health, occupational and environmental health, and health policy.

Robert L. Kane is a graduate of Harvard Medical School. Formerly the dean at the School of Public Health at the University of Minnesota, he currently holds an endowed chair in Long-Term Care and Aging there. Prior to his arrival in Minnesota, he was a senior researcher at the RAND Corporation and a professor at the UCLA Schools of Medicine and Public Health. His writings have included international comparisons of long-term care and studies of innovative ways to improve care for older persons.

Rosalie A. Kane is a professor of public health at the University of Minnesota, where she is also on the faculty of the Center for Biomedical Ethics and the School of Social Work. Previously she was a social scientist at the RAND Corporation and a faculty member at UCLA. She is a former editor-in-chief of *The Gerontologist.*

Julie E. Kaufman is a research gerontologist at the Univeristy of Illinois at Chicago. Her general research field is the intersection of social policy and human development. Currently she is at work on a project focusing on minority use of long-term care among the elderly. Previous research includes caregiver adaptation to spouses with Alzheimer's, and educational outcomes of low-income urban African-American youth whose families moved to white middle-income suburbs.

Langley C. Keyes is a professor in the department of Urban Studies and Planning at MIT, where he has been teaching since 1967. Interspersed with his academic career have been several forays into the world of practice: HUD in 1967; Model Cities and The Community Builders in Boston in the early seventies, and three years at the Massachusetts Executive Office of Communities and Development in the eighties. His book, *Strategies and Saints: Fighting Drugs in Subsidized Housing*, was published by the Urban Institute Press in 1992.

Joanne Gard Marshall is associate professor in the faculty of Library and Information Science at the University of Toronto, where she teaches courses in online information retrieval and health science information resources. Professor Marshall also holds cross appointments in the Department of Health Administration, the Centre for Studies of Aging, and the Centre for Health Promotion at the University. Her research interests include the adoption and use of information technology.

Victor W. Marshall is director of the Centre for Studies of Aging and professor of behavioral science at the University of Toronto. He also serves as network director of CARNET: The Canadian Aging Research Network. His current research interests focus on work and aging, long-term care issues, health promotion, and theoretical developments in the sociology of aging.

Robert Miller is assistant professor of health economics in residence at the department of Social and Behavioral Sciences and the Institute for Health and Aging, University of California, San Francisco. He recently has published an article on the use and cost experience of Canadian publicly insured long-term care programs for the elderly, and has published articles on managed care plans, including their past performance and potential impact.

Marilyn Moon is a senior fellow with the Health Policy Center of the Urban Institute. Prior to this position, she served as director of the Public Policy Institute of the American Association of Retired Persons and as a senior analyst at the Congressional Budget Office. Dr. Moon has written extensively on health policy, policy for the elderly, and income distribution. Her current work focuses on health system reform and financing. She has recently published *Medicare Now and in the Future* (Urban Institute Press, 1993).

Brian B. Murphy is a senior research analyst at Statistics Canada. His research field is income distribution. He specializes in the study of government taxation and social spending and microsimulation. He has previously taught at Carleton University. His most recently published papers are (with Ross Finnie and Michael Wolfson) "A Profile of High Income Ontarians," and (with Michael Wolfson) "Pensions, Deficits and Ageing: Impacts for Ontario's Residents."

John Myles is professor of sociology and director of the Pepper Institute on Aging and Public Policy, Florida State University. He is presently engaged in research on the effects of changes in labor markets and welfare states on the structure of the economic life course. His most recent book, coauthored with Wallace Clement, is *Relations of Ruling: Class and Gender in Postindustrial Societies* (Montreal: McGill-Queens University Press, 1994).

Marina V. Pascali is a doctoral student in health services research and policy analysis at the University of California at Berkeley, where she is specializing in health economics. Her current research interest is the effects of alternative cost control mechanisms on the utilization of physician services in British Columbia.

Paul Pierson is associate professor of government at Harvard University. He has written extensively on comparative politics and public policy, and is the author of *Dismantling the Welfare State? Reagan, Thatcher, and the Politics of Retrenchment*.

Jill Quadagno holds the Mildred and Claude Pepper Eminent Scholars Chair in social gerontology at Florida State University. She is presently engaged in research on work, retirement, and long-term care policy.

Her most recent book is *Unfinished Democracy: Race, Rights and the War on Poverty* (Oxford, 1994).

Patricia Ruggles is a senior economist with the Joint Economic Committee of the U.S. Congress. She has written extensively on poverty, including a recent book, *Drawing the Line*, and a soon-to-be completed book entitled *Living on the Edge*. She has also published articles on the distribution of income and the impact of public income support programs. Before joining the JEC, she was a senior research associate at the Urban Institute, an ASA/NSA fellow at the Bureau of the Census, and an analyst at the Congressional Budget Office.

Miriam Smith is assistant professor of political science at Carleton University. She has written widely on Canadian politics and is the author of *Labour Without Allies: The Canadian Labour Congress in Politics.*

Carolyn L. Weaver is director of Social Security and Pension Studies at the American Enterprise Institute, where she has been a resident scholar since 1987. Prior to joining AEI, she held positions at the Hoover Institution, Tulane University, and Virginia Tech. She also served as chief professional staff member on social security and disability policy for the U.S. Senate Committee on Finance, and as senior advisor to the National Commission on Social Security Reform. Dr. Weaver is the editor of *Social Security's Looming Surpluses: Prospects and Implications.*

Michael C. Wolfson is the director general, Institutions and Social Statistics Branch, Statistics Canada. In addition to his federal public service activities, Dr. Wolfson is a fellow of the Canadian Institute for Advanced Research, Population Health Program and an Associate of the program on Technology and Economic Growth. His recent research interests include income distribution, tax/transfer and pension policy simulation analysis, corporate structure, demographic microsimulation, the design of health information systems, and analysis of the determinants of health.